A History of the

Permanent Professors

of the United States Air Force Academy

A History of the
PERMANENT PROFESSORS
of the United States Air Force Academy

JAMES H. HEAD AND ERLIND G. ROYER

Fulcrum Group
Golden, Colorado

Library of Congress Cataloging-in-Publication Data

Names: Head, James H. (James Howard), 1942- author. | Royer, Erlind G. (Lindy), 1939- author.
Title: A history of the permanent professors of the United States Air Force Academy / by James H. Head and Erlind G. Royer.
Description: Golden, CO : Fulcrum Group, [2018] | Includes index.
Identifiers: LCCN 2018041374 | ISBN 9781682752340
Subjects: LCSH: United States Air Force Academy--Faculty--Biography. | United
   States Air Force Academy--History.
Classification: LCC UG638.5.M1 H43 2018 | DDC 358.40092/273--dc23
LC record available at https://lccn.loc.gov/2018041374

Printed in the United States
0 9 8 7 6 5 4 3 2 1

Fulcrum Group
4690 Table Mountain Drive, Suite 100
Golden, CO 80403
800-992-2908 • 303-277-1623

CONTENTS

FOREWORD

Retired Brigadier Generals Lindy Royer and Jim Head have compiled a literal treasure trove of fascinating and relevant information that should become mandatory reading for anyone—faculty, military trainers, commanders, coaches, staff—being assigned to the United States Air Force Academy. I have known Lindy and Jim, Permanent Professors #44 and 52, respectively, for many years, during which time they each in their own way have left indelible marks on me. Perhaps most notable, beyond their distinguished military careers and service on the Academy faculty, they continue to serve their families, their communities, and their beloved Air Force Academy, even long after retirement.

Every mission element of the AF Academy has its own identity, and rightly so, but for any person assigned to teach, lead, coach, and mentor cadets to put a myopic focus on their own organization is shortsighted and detrimental to the mission of developing leaders of character for the Air Force and beyond. I cannot think of a better way to gain an appreciation for the founding, history, accomplishments, and heritage of the Air Force Academy than to learn about the evolution of academic programs and curriculum changes shaped by the faculty as presented in this comprehensive account of the first 100 Permanent Professors. One will also gain an appreciation for the involvement and influence of the Permanent Professors far beyond academics, reaching across mission areas to every facet of the Academy and well beyond.

From Permanent Professor #1, the highly admired "Gen McD," the first Dean, Robert McDermott, to the newest, #100, Dave Caswell, Permanent Professors have been instrumental in so much more than reading, writing, and arithmetic. Many will be surprised to learn that virtually every national accreditation review and most key internal studies have been led by Permanent Professors. As I became the 18th Superintendent, the professional work of Permanent Professors had resulted in top marks for USAFA. Permanent

Professor #71, Rich Fullerton, had just led the effort that won re-accreditation of the entire Academy program; #70, Neal Barlow, did the same for our specialized engineering degrees; and #83, Tom Yoder, had headed up the successful NCAA Certification. During my tenure, we established a new Permanent Professor position for the Academy's Center for Character and Leadership Development and appointed Joe Sanders (#89). Hans Mueh, #51, was our Athletics Director, and #74, Dana Born, was Dean of our Faculty. Furthermore, I constantly drew wisdom from the experience and insight of the Permanent Professors in our Academy Board deliberations.

The reader of this seminal work will learn about the processes by which Permanent Professors are selected, how they are nominated by the President and confirmed by the Senate, and how they may earn retirement as Brigadier Generals. Readers will also become aware of an Air Force policy implemented in the early 1990s that forever altered faculty composition by adding civilians and later, a statute that allows for the Dean of the Faculty to come from other than the Permanent Professor ranks as has, to date, always been the case. Perhaps most important and relevant, this book offers insights into many innovative initiatives that have dramatically enhanced cadet experiences and vaulted USAFA to the forefront of modern military and civilian higher education.

But more than anything, this is a book about people. The Permanent Professors as a group did more to shape the Air Force Academy than any other. These pages tell the story of these men and women—the first 100—starting with those who came early and laid the foundation, to those who came later and expanded the academic programs and cadet learning opportunities, to those most recently appointed Permanent Professors who are poised to carry the Academy to new heights.

I sincerely thank Generals Head and Royer for writing this book; I only wish I would have been able to read it as part of my preparation for the job of Superintendent.

Michael C. Gould
Lieutenant General, USAF (Ret)
USAF Academy Superintendent, 2009–2013
Colorado Springs

PREFACE

By The Friends of the Air Force Academy Library

One of the primary missions of The Friends of the Air Force Academy Library is the preservation of the heritage and history of the Academy. With that goal in mind, the Friends are proud to sponsor this book on the history of the Permanent Professors. Since the establishment of the position of Permanent Professor, no other body has been so important and significant in the evolution, operation, and accomplishments of the Academy. Aside from their primary mission of determining the focus of the curriculum and academic direction of the Academy, the Permanent Professors have been, and continue to be, both corporately and individually, intimately involved in nearly every aspect of the institution's mission, be it academic, military, athletic, or professional. Theirs is truly a history that all elements of the Academy need to understand. The Friends can think of no other singular project as important in documenting the history and heritage of the institution than the story of this small group of 100 officers. We are honored to be part of this effort.

The Board of Directors of
The Friends of the Air Force Academy Library

PREFACE

By the Authors

We decided to write this book to honor the individuals who have served as Permanent Professors at the Air Force Academy, especially as younger Permanent Professors might not know many of their predecessors. Permanent Professors at the Academy are credited with revolutionizing military education in America, setting an example that was emulated by both the United States Military Academy at West Point and the US Naval Academy at Annapolis. Our initial concept for this book was mostly biographical, to research and write a short biographical sketch of each of the Permanent Professors and include some comments on the responsibilities and accomplishments of the group. It seemed an appropriate occasion for a little history; when we began we could see that the 100th Permanent Professor would soon be appointed. With only 100 Permanent Professors in the 60 years since the Academy was established, it seemed a small enough group to manage.

We ourselves come from the middle of this group of 100, numbers 44 and 52 in the chronological sequence. We are old enough to have known personally most of those who came before us. We admire those early leaders, both for who they were and what they did. In researching this book, our respect for them continued to grow, and we are delighted to offer some commemoration of their service. We also know most of the Permanent Professors who came after us. We are proud of them for what they have already accomplished, and we are honored to add them to the list in expectation of much to come.

As we got further into the project we decided that the history of Permanent Professor leadership in developing innovative academic programs and enhancing cadet opportunities deserved considerable attention. It seemed to us that many of these topics are actually persistent challenges that will continue to regularly demand the attention of the Permanent Professors. We hope the background provided here will be of use as these issues continue to be addressed. We wish we had better understood them in our day.

We have chosen to focus on the achievements of these individuals rather than on their personalities and private lives. Most of our subjects were (are) married with families, and like other military officers, they drew (draw) strength and purpose from the support of spouses and children. The Academy is a place where an officer's family can contribute positively to cadets' lives and truly make a difference, and Permanent Professor spouses have definitely left their imprint. Nevertheless, we set those stories aside, but with a heartfelt acknowledgment for all that spouses provide. We especially wish to thank our wives, Lynda and Jan, for their tremendous support during the research and writing of this book. During the past two years, they have sacrificed a lot of time with us—time that could have been given to more enjoyable activities.

The book would not have been published without the encouragement and support of The Friends of the Air Force Academy Library, and especially the President, Brigadier General Phil Caine. The Friends is a non-profit group that works to enhance the quality of the McDermott Library and to acquire, preserve, and publish materials that capture the heritage and tradition of our Air Force and Air Force Academy. We are grateful for their sponsorship.

We owe a special debt of gratitude to Brigadier General Paul Pirog, who graciously agreed to proofread our drafts. Paul did much more than find our errors, he gave us so many insightful suggestions that he almost became a third co-author. The reader cannot know how much he improved our work, but we do. We also wish to thank Lieutenant General Mike Gould for his kindness in writing the Foreword, to Brigadier General Mark Wells for lending us his article on the history of the Permanent Professor badge, and to Brigadier General O Sampson for letting us reproduce his essay on the Military Oath of Office.

We also gratefully acknowledge the assistance of many others who helped in important ways. Dr. Mary Elizabeth Ruwell, Director of the Air Force Academy's McDermott Library Special Collections Branch, used her authoritative knowledge of the archives to help us find important material. Ms. Peggy Litwhiler and Ms. Melissa Robohn helped with photographs, and Ms. Jessica Maiberger-Horner with oral histories. Ms. Jody Owen, Secretary to the Dean, provided photos and documents and connected us with the right office when we had specific questions. Brigadier General Andy Armacost, Dean of the Faculty; Colonel Gary Packard, Vice Dean; and Dr. Steve Jones, Senior Associate Dean, gave us their time for many useful conversations. Dr. Tom Mabry, Associate Dean for Student Academic Affairs and Academy Registrar, used his profound knowledge of the curriculum to answer many questions. Dr. John Sherfesee, Director of Studies and Analysis and Civilian Faculty Programs, provided insight on faculty issues. Colonel Rolf Enger, Lieutenant Colonel Don Rhymer, Lieutenant Colonel Steve Simon, Lieutenant Colonel Mark Garney, Colonel Jeff Butler, Professor Barry Fagan, and Colonel Rex Kiziah participated in helpful discussions on many topics. And lastly our sincere thanks to Mr. Bob Baron, Ms. Patty Maher, and Ms. Alison Auch at the Fulcrum Group, who turned our concept into a beautiful book.

James H. Head	Erlind G. Royer
Monument, Colorado	Colorado Springs, Colorado

INTRODUCTION

The United States Air Force Academy is a large, complex, multifaceted institution. It is led by a Superintendent who directs a four-year regimen of cadet military training, academics, athletics, and character development leading to a Bachelor of Science degree and a commission as a second lieutenant. A cadre of Permanent Professors provides senior leadership, strategic direction, organizational stability, and long-term program continuity for academic, physical education, and character and leadership development programs. Thus, an understanding of the Permanent Professors, their challenges, and their accomplishments illuminates many of the most important themes of the institution. However, this history of the Permanent Professors is not a comprehensive history of the Air Force Academy, nor is it a complete history of the faculty. Rather it is a partial history of an important part of the Academy. We chose to relate this as a story (written by a physicist and an electrical engineer), not as an extensively footnoted and thoroughly documented historical account. For the latter, we refer you to the Fagan and Ringenbach volumes referenced below (both of those authors hold doctorates in history).

We make almost no specific mention of the Commandant of Cadets and the military training mission. That story is vital to understanding the Air Force Academy—it is the story of many outstanding military leaders and of a Cadet Wing striving for excellence. It is an important story, but we don't cover it here because that story is too important to be treated lightly, and because it is not our story to tell. We know many of the leaders in the Commandant's organization—Commandants, Vice Commandants, Group AOCs, Squadron AOCs—and their programs in basic cadet training, leadership development, honor education, flight training, soaring, parachuting, and survival training. This is heritage we all would benefit from understanding better, and we hope it will be told from the inside, by those with firsthand knowledge and insight.

Aside from physical education, importantly led by a Permanent Professor, we also make no significant mention of the Athletic Department. We fully subscribe to General Douglas MacArthur's belief that "Upon the fields of friendly strife are sown the seeds that, upon other fields, on other days, will bear the fruits of victory." However, as proud as we are of the accomplishments of our student-athletes, the history of Air Force Academy athletics is well beyond our ability to relate.

There is also little mention of the Superintendent's team at Headquarters USAFA, the Preparatory School, the Academy as an Air Force base, the magnificent physical facilities, the infrastructure, the expansive natural setting, or the people and organizations who make life in the Cadet Area possible. Neither is there specific mention of the Association of Graduates or the USAFA Endowment, each of which is a major contributor to the institution.

And especially, there is no attempt to chronicle the Cadet Wing or measure the accomplishments of the "long blue line" of graduates. So, what's left?

What is told here is the story of the Permanent Professors, those men and women who have received special Presidential appointments and Senate confirmation to lead the Academy's academic programs. The 100 individuals selected to date for this prestigious group, serving as Department Heads and as Deans, have initiated and developed much of what makes this magnificent Air Force Academy so great. We record here something of their story. We hope you enjoy learning about these individual Permanent Professors and their contributions. And if you are preparing to serve or are serving at the Academy, our desire is that you find this book both informative and inspiring.

REFERENCE BOOKS

The following books were useful to the authors in preparing this work:

Ambrose, Stephen A. *Duty, Honor, Country: A History of West Point*. Baltimore: The John Hopkins University Press, 1966.

Andrus, Burton C., Jr., ed. *25ᵗʰ Anniversary Pictorial Review of the United States Air Force Academy, 1954–1979*, USAFA Association of Graduates. United States Air Force Academy, Colorado: printed by Walsworth, Marceline, Missouri, 1979.

Fagan, George V. *The Air Force Academy: An Illustrated History*. Boulder, Colorado: Johnson Books, 1988.

Fagan, George V. *Air Force Academy Heritage: The Early Years*. Golden, Colorado: Fulcrum Publishing, 2006.

Lovell, John P. *Neither Athens Nor Sparta? The American Service Academies in Transition*. Bloomington and London, United Kingdom: Indiana University Press, 1979.

MacArthur, Douglas. *Reminiscences*. Annapolis, Maryland: Naval Institute Press, 1964.

Melinger, Phillip S. *Hubert R. Harmon: Airman, Officer, Father of the Air Force Academy*. Golden, Colorado: Fulcrum Group, 2009.

Ringenbach, Paul T. *Battling Tradition, Robert F. McDermott and Shaping the U.S. Air Force Academy*. Chicago: Imprint Publications, 2006.

The United States Air Force Academy's First Twenty-Five Years, Some Perceptions, Prepared for the Dean of the Faculty under the auspices of The 25ᵗʰ Anniversary Committee, United States Air Force Academy, Colorado, 1979.

The following two works are unpublished but available in the McDermott Library Special Collections Branch as are the official *USAFA Annual Historical Reports*, which contain a wealth of information:

Sherfesee, John. "The Professionalism of the USAFA Faculty, 1954–1997: A Policy-Driven Evolution of Roles and Responsibilities," Vols. 1 and 2, PhD dissertation, University of Denver, 1999.

Woodyard, William Truman. "A Historical Study of the Development of the Academic Curriculum of the United States Air Force Academy," PhD dissertation, University of Denver, 1965.

Finally, we list a pair of novels by a graduate and former faculty member that tell an Academy story with notable historical accuracy:

Beason, Doug. *The Cadet* (Wild Blue U, Foundation of Honor, Book 1), Monument, CO: WordFire Press, 2015.

Beason, Doug. *The Officer* (Wild Blue U, Foundation of Honor, Book 2), Monument, CO: WordFire Press, 2016.

ACRONYMS

We generally avoid acronyms and abbreviations, but following are a few you should be familiar with:

ABET—Accreditation Board for Engineering and Technology
AF—Air Force
AFB—Air Force Base
AOC—Air Officer Commanding
CIA—Central Intelligence Agency
CINC—Commander in Chief
DIA—Defense Intelligence Agency
DoD—Department of Defense
HQ—Headquarters
NASA—National Aeronautics and Space Administration
NATO—North Atlantic Treaty Organization
NCAA—National Collegiate Athletic Association
ROTC—Reserve Officer Training Corps (AFROTC—Air Force ROTC)
SAC—Strategic Air Command
SecAF—Secretary of the Air Force
STEM—Science, Technology, Engineering, and Mathematics
US—United States
USAF—US Air Force
USAFA—US Air Force Academy
USAFE—US Air Forces in Europe
USMA—US Military Academy
USNA—US Naval Academy

THE GENESIS OF THE UNITED STATES AIR FORCE ACADEMY

Not long after the first manned heavier-than-air aircraft flight, informed by the experience of World War I, early airmen recognized the unique training required for an air service comparable to the United States naval and ground forces. Since the air service was a part of the US Army, it was natural for the United States Military Academy at West Point, New York, to serve as a model. This chapter briefly traces the actions leading to the establishment of the United States Air Force Academy, the factors that so strongly influenced its founding principles, and the leadership that guided its early days.

THE LONG ROAD TO TODAY'S ACADEMY

With the first flight by the Wright brothers at Kitty Hawk, North Carolina, on December 17, 1903, it could be argued it was inevitable that there would someday be an Air Force Academy. However, the road to the opening of such an academy was long and arduous, contrasted with the rapid acceptance of the airplane as an instrument of war. Under the supervision of the Army's Signal Corps Aeronautical Division established in 1907, the Army accepted its first aircraft, the Wright brothers' "Flyer," on April 2, 1909, after fewer than eight months of testing. Only two years later came the first wartime use of aircraft for reconnaissance, artillery coordination, and bombing by Italy and Bulgaria, 1911–1913. Congress authorized an Aeronautical Section of the Signal Corps in 1914. The US Navy had commenced pilot training two years earlier. The first American use of heavier-than-air aircraft in military operations came on March 13, 1916, when the Signal Corps' 1st Aeronautical Squadron performed aerial reconnaissance along the US border with Mexico. Shortly thereafter 38 American pilots prepared for combat in World War I as volunteer members of the French Foreign Legion's Lafayette Escadrille Squadron formed by the French government in April 1916. (To join this squadron required a pledge of allegiance to the French Foreign Legion, not to a government, so it avoided the loss of citizenship that had deterred American volunteers from joining other nations' air forces already in the fight.) The squadron fought in the Battle of Verdun and the Somme Offensive during 1916, becoming known for daring and effectiveness. The United States entered World War I on April 6, 1917, but had no modern combat aircraft and only fledging training programs. Their first combat was not until October 1917. Although the Air Service did participate in the Second Battle of the Marne at Château-Thierry and Belleau Wood in early 1918, their first offensive action was not until the Battle of Saint-Mihiel in September 1918. Many of the American members of the Lafayette Squadron were absorbed into American units, providing valuable combat experience. At the beginning of the war, the Signal Corps' air arm numbered 1,200 personnel. When the armistice was signed on November 11, 1918, the US Army Air Service was 195,000 strong with 78,000 personnel in Europe. More than 10,000 pilots manned 42 air squadrons.

Just 15 days later, on November 26, 1918, there was the first formal call for a separate air academy. Lieutenant Colonel Hanlon, Chief of the Mechanical Instruction Branch, wrote in a letter to the Air Service Chief of Training: "As the Military and Naval Academies are the backbone of the Army and Navy, so must the Aeronautical Academy be the backbone of the Air Service." His letter went on to state goals and objectives for such an academy, urge Congressional action, and recommend the appointment of a board of officers to undertake site selection and detailed planning for establishing and operating a United States Aeronautical Academy. Within a month the President of the University of Texas made the first of what would become many offers of a site location, when he offered a site near Austin for an Air Service Academy, provided it had the same relationship to the Air Service as West Point did to the Army. The November 26, 1919, *Comments on Strength, Organization, and Training of the Air Service, Pamphlet No. 12,* published by the Office of the Director of the Air Service, stated the policy that the only way to train Air Service officers was in the Air Service itself and this could best be done with an Air Service Academy. During 1919, aircraft industry members and Air Service officers including Brigadier General William "Billy" Mitchell had proposed, as had a resolution introduced into the House of Representatives, the creation of an aeronautical academy. The bill died at the end of the session. This flurry of activity introduced the issues that would plague proposals for an air academy for the next 34 years: what should be the mission, goals, and objectives; should the curriculum emphasize overall academics or technical and scientific subjects only; what military studies should be included and should flying training be required for all; what would it cost; and finally, where would it be located? Air Service leaders attempted to have Military Aviation introduced into the West Point curriculum in 1919, but they were rebuked by the Superintendent because there was no time available in the curriculum. Brigadier General Douglas MacArthur, who then became Superintendent, continued to ignore proposals by Air Service officers.

In 1922 a Senate resolution called for the Secretary of War and the Secretary of the Navy to report to Congress if it was feasible and advisable to establish a school for aeronautics and if it was practical for such a school to exist at the Naval Academy and the Military Academy. The resolution contemplated appointments to these academies of young men who desired to be commissioned in the US Army Air Service. The official response by the Secretary of War came less than a month later. It stated that while it was feasible, it was neither practical nor advisable because the country's need for aviators was being met by existing training. Meanwhile perhaps the most vociferous of the advocates for military aviation was Brigadier General Billy Mitchell, Assistant Chief of the Air Service. His speeches and writings were supported by pilots of the Air Service, whose flights were setting new records in 1923–1924, demonstrating to the public the promise of military aviation. General Mitchell's outspoken efforts resulted in the loss of his job and return to his permanent rank of colonel. His inflammatory rhetoric following the Navy's *Shenandoah* dirigible disaster in 1925 and multiple airplane crashes led to his court-martial and resignation. This controversy diminished the calls for an air academy, but not the need for Air Service training.

By 1925 the Air Service had established training centers for officers and airmen at Brooks and Kelly Fields in Texas, at Scott and Chanute Fields in Illinois, McCook Field in Ohio, and an Air Tactical School at Langley Field in Virginia. In 1930 Randolph Field, Texas, was dedicated and soon became the center of Air Service training. In 1934 the Baker Board, chaired by former Secretary of War Newton D. Baker, recommended that West Point provide cadets with 20 hours of flying training. Reluctantly, West Point officials finally implemented 25 hours (14½ in the air) of training in the summer of 1936. These training centers; the doctrine developed at Langley and later at Maxwell Field, Alabama; and the West Point training comprised the resources available to the United States when it entered World War II in December 1941. Congressional action early in 1942 allowed the West Point training to expand so that by the summer of 1942 60 percent of the senior and junior classes had volunteered and were receiving flying training. By the end of September 1945, following the surrender of Germany and Japan that ended World War II, 657 West Point cadets had received flying training. To put this in perspective, between July 1939 and August 1945, the US Army Air Corps advanced flying training schools had commissioned 190,443 pilots. World War II had clearly demonstrated the critical importance of air power in the defense of the United States and the need for a substantial number of dedicated, well-trained officers to carry out this mission.

To further the concept of a separate Air Academy, Army Regulation 95-5 created the United States Army Air Forces (AAF) on June 20, 1941. Major General Henry H. "Hap" Arnold became Chief of the Army Air Forces and Acting Deputy Chief of Staff for Air with authority over both the Air Corps and Air Force Combat Command. By agreement between the Army Chief of Staff, General George C. Marshall, and Arnold, debate on separation of the Air Force into a service co-equal with the Army and Navy was postponed until after the war. In 1942, acting on an executive order from President Roosevelt, the War Department granted the AAF full autonomy, equal to and entirely separate from the Army Ground Forces and Services of Supply. The Air Force Combat Command and the Office of the Chief of Air Corps were abolished, and Arnold became AAF Commanding

General and an *ex officio* member of the Joint Chiefs of Staff. Further enhancing the AAF's status, in March 1943 Arnold was promoted (wartime) to full general, and in December 1944 he was appointed a five-star General of the Army, placing him fourth in Army rank seniority behind Marshall, MacArthur, and Eisenhower. In October 1944, anticipating the war's end, Lieutenant General Ira C. Eaker (co-author with Arnold of three books extolling the merits of air power [1936, 1941, 1942]) wrote Arnold urging him to propose legislation to establish an air academy.

Even before the end of World War II hostilities with Japan in August 1945, members of Congress began submitting proposals for an air academy. Some included specific locations, ranging from Texas to Colorado and Missouri to California, or leaving selection of the location to military leaders. None of the nine resolutions proposed between 1945 and 1950 made it out of committee as they were not supported by the War Department or, later, the Department of Defense. Indeed, it was the National Security Act of 1947 establishing the Department of Defense and a separate United States Air Force that started serious efforts by the Air Force to solve the problem of maintaining a well-trained officer corps. After much negotiation, the first Secretary of the Air Force, Stuart Symington, worked out an agreement with the Army and the Navy that 25 percent of the graduates from their academies could volunteer to be commissioned in the Air Force beginning with the Class of 1949. A condition was that at least half of the volunteers had to be medically qualified to be pilots. In exchange, the Air Force was to provide qualified officers to teach subjects in the curricula of Annapolis and West Point. This last point later proved to be valuable in establishing the Air Force Academy academic program because it forced the Air Force personnel system to identify officers with advanced degrees in the subjects taught at the academies. It also caused the establishment of a system for officer advanced academic education to provide an ongoing supply of qualified instructors. The activation of numerous reserve officers for the Korean War in the early 1950s provided a second opportunity to identify officers with wartime experience and advanced degrees. Many of these officers so identified had been teaching at civilian institutions.

Meanwhile Secretary Symington, senior Air Force leaders, and the Secretary of Defense initiated studies and convened several boards to study air academy options as well as the broader issue of the role of service academies in the defense of the nation. The most extensive of these efforts was the full-time Air Force Academy Planning Board, which had been established at Air University, Maxwell AFB, AL, after the Air Force Chief of Staff, General Hoyt S. Vandenberg, designated Air University as the agency responsible for air academy planning. This Board published its report in January 1949. The report reiterated many of the reasons for an air academy put forth in Air Service memoranda in 1919 and 1922. It was very detailed as to site selection criteria, goals, objectives, and curriculum content and was remarkable for its close resemblance to the other service academies, especially West Point. This multitude of studies and reports prompted Secretary of Defense James Forrestal to appoint a Service Academy Board in March 1949. This prestigious Board was co-chaired by retired General Dwight D. Eisenhower, President of Columbia University, and Dr. Robert E. Sterns, President of the University of Colorado. This Board was charged to look at all aspects of the service academies as well as reserve officer training at civilian institutions and make any necessary recommendations for improvement. Its final report in January 1950 strongly supported the service academies and the establishment of an Air Force academy equal in stature to the Army and Naval academies. Further, it emphasized the attributes that the academies should develop in their cadets including educational knowledge, practical experience, mental alertness, problem-solving abilities, motivation, morality, and a commitment to high morale and spirit as well as service to the nation. Now the task became to obtain legislative approval for the air academy.

In 1949 proposed legislation for an air academy was introduced in the House of Representatives, and a request was submitted by the Secretary of Defense. Opposition by the Bureau of the Budget effectively killed both initiatives. Next, a bill was produced by the Air Staff to meet Bureau of Budget objections and introduced by the Chairman of the House Armed Services Committee, Carl Vinson, in August 1949. However, the Air Staff immediately began working on an improved bill, and Chairman Vinson directed his staff to write a new bill to correct objections he had to the existing one. Soon Vinson announced that the site location should be included in the bill. In December 1949, General Vandenberg decided a dedicated staff at Headquarters USAF was required to handle matters pertaining to the air academy. Lieutenant General Hubert R. Harmon was put in charge. In mid-1951 a proposal fully coordinated within the Department of Defense and by the Bureau of the Budget was introduced by Chairman Vinson, but no hearings were conducted on the bill in 1951 or 1952. The elections of 1952 caused further delay as the Republican Party took control of the Congress and the White House. General Harmon and his staff worked diligently to inform the new executives and members of Congress of the need for an air academy. Finally, in January 1953, a bill fully coordinated within the Executive Branch and nearly identical to the previous one was introduced; however, hearings were postponed until a year later. Committee hearings were conducted by the House Armed Services Committee in January 1954 and the Senate Armed Forces Committee in February. The House approved the measure on January 21 and the Senate on March 8. A conference committee agreed on a compromise bill on March 29, and both chambers approved the bill later that day. On April 1, 1954, President Eisenhower signed Public Law 325, ending the 35-year quest for an Air Force Academy. The next challenge was to complete the search for a site for the Academy.

MEETING THE START-UP CHALLENGES

In late 1949 as legislative activity increased, Secretary Symington appointed an Air Force Academy Site Selection Board. This Board studied 354 sites in 22 states recommended by individuals, chambers of commerce, or governmental agencies. Using many of the criteria developed earlier by the Air Force Academy Planning Board, the sites under consideration were narrowed down to 29. These 29 were personally visited by the Board members, who then produced a list of eight sites: Camp Beale, CA; Colorado Springs, CO; Grapevine, Randolph AFB, and Grayson County, TX; Charlotte and Salisbury, NC; and

Madison, WI. The Board declined to make a selection but wrote a memorandum expressing their preference for the Colorado Springs site. This memo was placed in a sealed file in the Secretary of the Air Force's office by General Harmon, and the Board was dissolved in late 1952. The 1954 act that President Eisenhower signed into law authorized the Secretary of the Air Force to select the academy site upon the unanimous recommendation of a five-member site selection commission established by him. There were provisions for reaching a decision if a unanimous recommendation was not obtained.

Secretary Talbot appointed a Site Selection Commission composed of former Air Force Chief of Staff General Spaatz; Lieutenant General Harmon; Dr. Virgil Hancher, President of Iowa State University; Merrill C. Meigs, Vice President of the Hearst Corporation; and Reserve Brigadier General Charles Lindbergh. Secretary Talbot met with them one day before the announcement of their appointment on April 6, 1954. The announcement was accompanied by a solicitation for nominations of potential sites. By the cutoff date of April 21, proposals had been received from 580 sites in 45 states, including 57 in California and 51 in Texas. The commission developed site criteria that were added to and refined as their work progressed. Chief among the additions was one recommended when the Board visited West Point and Annapolis to gather their views on requirements for a suitable site. Both academies felt their effectiveness was hampered by a lack of space to expand. Therefore, the commission decided the site should contain at least 15,000 acres of land. The commission considered each site, taking advantage of the previous Site Selection Board's data and findings when appropriate. The commission visited 34 sites and viewed an additional 33 from the air. When the site visits concluded, the commission met in the Pentagon, and General Harmon read the previously sealed recommendation letter from the Site Selection Board. Three of the commissioners wanted Colorado Springs, but the two civilians were opposed or undecided. So General Lindbergh agreed to accompany these two to Colorado Springs, which also would allow him to confirm that the altitude would not hinder cadet flying training. (It was during this visit that the Pine Valley

Airport manager, much to his embarrassment, failed to recognize General Lindbergh when he tried to rent a plane.) After many phone calls and a final meeting in the Pentagon among the Air Force Chief of Staff, General Nathan F. Twining; General Spaatz; Mr. Meigs; and General Harmon, the commission decided to recommend three sites to Secretary Talbot. The sites recommended in their final report on June 3, 1954, were the site about 8 miles north of Colorado Springs, one roughly 10 miles from Alton, IL, and one on the south shore of Lake Geneva, WI.

The announcement of the three sites caused a varied reaction among the residents of the three areas. In Illinois and Wisconsin, more densely populated areas than the Colorado Springs venue, there were mixed reactions that included organized public protests. The few objections in Colorado Springs were overwhelmed by a very favorable response by a group organized by the Chamber of Commerce. This group had been working together diligently since 1949 to bring the Academy to Colorado Springs. The Governor of Colorado and the state legislature encouraged the selection of Colorado Springs, with the latter appropriating $1 million to purchase the required land. Remaining health concerns and water supply questions were dispelled by favorable results from medical studies and arrangements by Colorado Springs officials to purchase water and have it piped across the mountains to a treatment plant to be built on the south side of the proposed Academy site. Secretary Talbot announced his selection of the site north of Colorado Springs on June 24, 1954. At the same time, he announced a temporary site would be established in Denver while construction took place at the permanent site. The law establishing the Air Force Academy had authorized the expenditure of $1 million to provide a temporary site. General Harmon soon visited Denver and inspected the Army's deactivated Fort Logan and Lowry AFB. On July 19 he recommended Lowry AFB to Secretary Talbot, who announced that day that Lowry was to be the interim site. These announcements must have been satisfying to President Eisenhower who enjoyed visiting his mother-in-law in Denver and vacationing in Colorado until his heart attack in 1955. His "summer White House" had been the headquarters building on Lowry AFB.

To direct all this effort as well as the manning of the new academy, Secretary Talbot wrote to General Harmon on July 27, 1954, that "The United States Air Force Academy is established and will operate as a separate operating agency… under the direct control of the Chief of Staff, United States Air Force.…" He also said in the letter that the Academy would be attached to the Air Training Command for reporting, logistical support, and administration. On August 14, 1954, USAF Academy General Order Number 1 established the Academy at Lowry AFB effective July 27, and in the order General Harmon assumed command of the Academy effective August 14. His Pentagon office continued to provide support to the new academy, and its successor does so to this day. On that first day there were seven Academy personnel present for duty.

Lowry AFB was purchased by the Army in 1937 and a flying field was then built. Lowry provided technical training to more than 400,000 personnel during World War II but was being downsized following the armistice in Korea. Eventually the Academy rehabilitated 50 of the training center buildings. Some, such as the substantial brick buildings designed for training classrooms, transitioned quite easily into a U-shaped academic area. Twenty-four wooden two-story, open-bay barracks each were modified into 28 two-man dormitory rooms. The dining hall was named General Billy Mitchell Hall, and the social center for cadets was named General H.H. Arnold Hall. Both names would later adorn the buildings with the same functions at the permanent site. A cadet parade ground, six football fields, seven tennis courts, and five fields for softball were built.

With the work on facilities underway, the next priority was to bring to Lowry AFB the personnel who would welcome the first class that would report in less than one year. This work had been underway since 1948 when Air Force officers first began submitting applications for duty at an air force academy. The selection of the first members of the Academy faculty and staff was of utmost importance to the success of the Academy. Before examining this successful effort, it is useful to understand the foundational knowledge that had been gained from the operation of the United States Military Academy since its establishment in 1802.

USMA TRADITION: SHAPING THE UNITED STATES AIR FORCE ACADEMY

It is well known that non-British Europeans played a pivotal role in the United States winning the Revolutionary War. These Europeans, largely trained by war experience or in French and German military schools, directed the building of fortifications and the effective use of artillery fire. In the 1700s these schools had dropped their aristocratic traditions and had instead begun emphasizing mathematics, physics, chemistry, geography, tactics, and the use of artillery. After the war, American leaders agreed that the greatest danger to the new democracy was the rise of an aristocratic class that historically had been supported by armies in Europe. Reasoning therefore that armies were dangerous, our leaders conceived of an army led by officers trained at a military academy. Once trained, these officers would return to lead local citizen-soldier militias. This led to calls for establishing a military school to train engineers and artillerists for the defense of the new nation.

During the Revolutionary War, the largest fort in the American Colonies had been built at West Point to control river traffic at a narrow point in the Hudson River. A Polish military school dropout who then went to Paris to study drawing and military science before joining the American Revolution designed the fortifications at West Point. Congress authorized the purchase of the fortifications and surrounding land in 1790, increased the numbers of the Corps of Engineers and Artillerists stationed there, and established the rank of Cadet and the purchase of books in 1794. However, no books were bought and no classes held. In 1798 Congress authorized an increase in the Corps as well as the hiring of four teachers. But no qualified teachers could be found to fill the positions. Meanwhile in the 20 years following the end of the Revolutionary War, 19 colleges had been established in the United States, many of them by state legislatures who recognized they needed an educated populace to serve in local and state governments.

Finally, on March 16, 1802, Congress passed the Military Peace Establishment Act. Of the 29 sections in the act, 26 removed all military officer appointments, established a new method for appointing officers with detailed instructions on pay and rank, and authorized one regiment of artillerists and two regiments of infantry. Clearly, there was still a fear of a large standing army. The remaining three sections of the act authorized a Corps of Engineers to be stationed at West Point, which would constitute a military academy. The act authorized 7 officers and 10 cadets, while limiting the future total to 20 officers and cadets. The Chief Engineer was also to be the Superintendent of the academy. Classes began in April 1802 with the two authorized captains as instructors, one a graduate of Harvard, the other of Yale. Degrees were granted after one year of study by an Academic Board consisting of the Superintendent and the instructors. In spite of virtually no entrance requirements and what would now be considered little academic study, during the War of 1812, none of the fortifications built by West Pointers were lost to the enemy. Just prior to the war Congress had authorized an increase to 250 cadets, prescribed both age and mental prerequisites, and added three Permanent Professor positions in Natural and Experimental Philosophy (Physics), Mathematics, and Engineering. This set the general principles followed to this day. These Permanent Professors and the Superintendent made up the Academic Board. It is interesting to note that all cadets had to study the French language because the textbooks for their courses were all written in French. Still there was little discipline to the admissions, education and training, or graduation processes. It fell to the fifth Superintendent, Sylvanus Thayer, to create the system that would prevail until after the establishment of the United States Air Force Academy.

Before Major Thayer became Superintendent in 1817, he had graduated from Dartmouth College in 1807, but he did not attend the ceremonies because he was on his way to enroll in the Academy at West Point. He graduated in one year and became the Corps of Engineers' Inspector of Fortifications in New England. He was an Assistant Professor of Mathematics at West Point in 1810. During the War of 1812, Thayer observed the poor performance of the American army and attributed it to lack of preparation. He requested a furlough to go to Europe and study the methods of education and training afforded officers there. Instead of being granted a furlough, however, Thayer was sent on official duty with funds to buy books, maps, and equipment for the Academy. He returned after nearly a year in France with about a thousand books as well as maps and charts that formed the basis of the first American military library. During his stay in France, Thayer became convinced that the French prescriptive method of education was the proper one. This method was used both in French military schools and the University of France and prescribed the entire course of study. It differed from the more liberal German elective method that Harvard faculty studying the German system at the same time decided to adopt. The latter system subsequently became the model for the rest of American higher education; but not West Point.

The Superintendent prior to Thayer had a very poor relationship with the faculty because, among other things, he imposed on their rights, refused to hold examinations, and granted commissions against their advice. Finally, he was removed by President Madison and Thayer was appointed Superintendent. Thayer first asked the faculty to provide him all the details of the courses they taught. In August 1817, after studying these submissions, Thayer began to lay out his proposed four-year course of study. Meanwhile he was imposing a discipline that had not been seen before. All cadets were on an indefinite vacation when he arrived; he called them all back. He then examined them and dismissed 43 for not meeting standards. He forbade cadets to bring money and ended the issuance of pay vouchers, so all cadets were on the same financial footing. Some graduates were not serving in the Army after graduation, so he made all cadets sign a pledge to serve at least one year. He canceled the annual vacations and instituted summer encampments where they learned soldiering in the field. Thereafter, the only time away from West Point that cadets would have was as Third Classmen (sophomores) when they would receive a summer furlough. He required all new cadets to report not later than June 25, in time for the encampment. He abolished favoritism and based advancement on merit alone. Cadet performance was evaluated through daily recitations, weekly ranking, and in semi-annual examinations. A system of demerits was implemented so that a cadet whose academic performance was excellent, but whose behavior was poor, would be properly evaluated. One of Thayer's first acts had been to assign an army officer as Commandant of Cadets who was responsible for cadet tactical training, imposing discipline, and assigning demerits. A merit list was instituted so points awarded for good performance and deleted for bad behavior could be tallied in a non-personal, objective manner. A graduating cadet's standing on this class ranking then was used objectively by the Academic Board to assign them to a corps in the army. A similar system is used to this day at all US military academies.

Thayer had found one additional aspect of both German and French education that he wanted to bring to West Point: the principal of forming small class sections containing students of like ability. To facilitate better cadet evaluation, Thayer added daily, graded recitations to the model. This method of instruction required more teachers, and Thayer was supported in his desire to have recent academy graduates assigned back to the academy to teach. Thayer's goal was to free the Permanent Professors from teaching duties, so they could better guide execution of their programs. He also involved the Board of Visitors in the spring examinations. This Board, formed by the Secretary of War in 1816, was chartered to visit, evaluate, and provide reports to the Secretary. It was composed of outstanding men from every part of the country, including both critics and supporters of West Point. Thayer used this Board, continuous review of the curriculum and course content, and other means to significantly improve West Point's reputation. This system of outside reviewers and attention to continuous improvement of academic instruction prevails at all the military academies today. This in turn made a West Point education desirable to young men and caused issues with admission to the academy, which Thayer struggled with. One result was a *de facto* rule of Congressional appointments, which exist to this day.

By the time Thayer left West Point in 1833, thoroughly discouraged by President Andrew Jackson's nearly complete lack of support, all the serving Permanent Professors had been selected by him. This group was made up of 4 civilian Professors (Mathematics, Rhetoric and Moral and Political Science, Natural and Experimental Philosophy, and Engineering), 1 lieutenant Acting Professor of Chemistry and Mineralogy, 13 lieutenant assistant professors, and 12 teachers/instructors of tactics and foreign languages. Compare this academic staff of 30 with the 4 Professors and 8 other academicians that existed in 1818. As a group the Professors were outstanding in their fields and in several cases had written textbooks that were recognized as the best, or among the best, in the world. All the Permanent Professors had come from civilian life, but when on West Point they were considered Army lieutenant colonels and wore the uniform and had the privileges of that rank. Many of them served at West Point until their retirement or death. Their efforts, assisted by the lieutenant assistant professors and instructors/teachers, and the curriculum championed by Thayer graduated the engineers who would oversee most of the infrastructure construction that led to the settling of the United States. West Point was the only scientific and engineering school in the United States until Rensselaer Polytechnic Institute was founded more than two decades after West Point. Still, all courses aimed to support the engineering discipline. It was only in the senior Engineering course that Professor Dennis Mahan taught a few lessons about the tactics and strategies of warfare that guided both sides in the Civil War. For his sweeping changes, Thayer later became known as the "Father of the Military Academy."

During the Civil War the performance of West Point graduates confirmed the value of their training and education but also revealed a weakness that would not be corrected for over 55 years. Of the 60 major Civil War battles, West Pointers commanded both sides in 55 of them. In the other 5, a West Pointer commanded one side. However, their command was of an army of citizen-soldiers, and this fact revealed a significant weakness of the West Point experience. The close, fraternal relationship among West Point graduates did not sit well with the many more volunteer and Regular Army officers and enlisted men who were excluded from this inner circle. This, and lack of change to accommodate the lessons of the Civil War, observations from the Prussian War (1870–1871), as well as newer warfare technology, led to criticism of West Point between the end of the Civil War and World War I. What little change that did occur at West Point during this period was not initiated by the Permanent Professors comprising the majority of the Academic Board but rather by the Commandant of Cadets within his areas of tactical training and physical education. Again, in World War I, the Army leadership largely was made up of successful West Point graduates; however, the same issue of lack of empathy with the citizen-soldier arose. In addition, early graduations to support the war led to a chaotic situation in the Corps of Cadets. Colonel Douglas MacArthur, USMA Class of 1903, became Superintendent in 1919. Charged by the Army Chief of Staff to revitalize the institution, he strove to make sweeping changes.

MacArthur had observed the schism between West Point graduates and the citizen-soldiers, which became the vast majority of the Army as it mobilized quickly for World War I. He also observed the West Point graduates' lack of preparation for the new tactics and technology employed during the war. When he became Superintendent, he immediately had to address the length of the program, which had been promised to be one year long for the Class of 1919 but was then extended, and post-war was set by Congress at three years. Under pressure from MacArthur, the Academic Board, and graduates, Congress relented and reauthorized the four-year program. This was one of the few times MacArthur had the support of the Academic Board. When he tried to make changes to the curriculum, he encountered strong resistance from the Permanent Professors who, by law, were the majority of the Academic Board and controlled the curriculum. By 1919 there were eight colonels and three lieutenant colonels serving as Department Heads and thus Permanent Professor members of the Academic Board. MacArthur brought about a few changes by convincing individual Professors to change their methodologies. The only changes agreed to by the Board were that Professors would visit three civilian institutions to observe and learn, instructors would spend their first year of assignment to the Academy at civilian institutions studying the subject they were to teach, more general lectures by men of authority and reputation would be given to the entire Corps, and a new combined course in Economics and Political Science (reduced from his request for four courses that included Psychology and Sociology) was created under a new

Department of Economics, Government and History. The Professor in charge of the new department was directed to double the amount of time spent on his subjects and cover all social science subjects. These changes were designed to reduce the isolation that MacArthur saw as having the biggest impact on the ability of West Point graduates to command effectively. His observations and reading had led him to believe that adherence to old traditions at West Point had led to a huge disconnect between the cadets' knowledge when they graduated and the mores of the society that shaped the citizen-soldiers that they would command. To further reduce this gap, he introduced the "whole man" concept that led to physical education being required for all classes and mandatory intramural sports for all cadets. He relocated the on-site summer encampment, which had become more of a social event than the training Thayer had intended, to Camp Dix, New Jersey, where the cadets underwent basic training with Regular Army troops. He also began granting significant privileges to cadets, allowing them to leave West Point on passes. The latter two changes were intended to provide cadets with opportunities to interact with the outside world. Due to the single furlough during the sophomore year instituted by Thayer, this interaction was lacking in their four-year experience. MacArthur's intent was to produce graduates that would command respect and who understood the "mores and standards" of the men they would command (MacArthur, *Reminiscences*, 81).

MacArthur made three other significant changes. One was to implement a system to support the honor code instituted by Thayer. Second, he added evaluation of a cadet's leadership, character, and physical performance (the "whole man") to the order of merit. Third, he attempted to eliminate the practice of hazing the entering cadets by putting officers in charge rather than upperclassmen. This hazing, strongly supported by tradition, had reached such a level that it was blamed for a cadet suicide in 1919. The first two initiatives, modified by experience, continue in practice today at all military academies. Hazing, however, remains an issue to some degree for every Superintendent at every military academy to this day. Unfortunately, when MacArthur was reassigned in 1922 the next Superintendent restored the on-site summer encampment and cadet supervision of new cadet training. Subsequent superintendents embraced the MacArthur reforms and they were slowly implemented.

The years before and during World War II saw several changes that ultimately would have significant impact on the US Air Force Academy. The new Head of the Department of Economics, Government and History in 1930 was Colonel Herman Beukema, who would serve until 1954. His classmates in the USMA Class of 1915 included cadets Eisenhower, who would later become President, and Harmon, the first USAF Academy Superintendent. Beukema incorporated as much social science, taught in the context of war, into the curriculum as possible. The text he wrote on foreign governments also was adopted by numerous civilian institutions. Meanwhile in 1925 West Point was accredited as an "approved technological institution" by the Association of American Universities, and in 1933 Congress approved the granting of a Bachelor of Science degree to graduates. This made it easier for graduates to enter graduate schools to pursue advanced degrees. Also during this period, military "graduate" colleges such as the Army Command and Staff College (founded 1881), Army War College (1901), and the Army Industrial College (1924) taught the lessons learned in previous wars and expanded their curricula and improved their instruction. Thus, the stage was set for the United States' entry into World War II. Coincidently, the West Point graduates who would form the majority of the new Air Force Academy faculty leadership were being educated in this system.

During World War II West Point graduates again were very visible in the top positions of the Army and generally demonstrated initiative, flexibility, and understanding of political affairs. However, West Pointers did not dominate command positions as they had previously, largely due to the education and training provided Regular Army officers in the military graduate schools. Of the commanders at division-level or above, 57 percent were USMA graduates chosen from the 41 percent of the Regular Army officers who were grads. After the war, General Maxwell D. Taylor became the Superintendent and made many changes brought about by advances in technology and the lessons of the war. He was helped by an Act of Congress, dated June 26, 1946, that added nine Permanent Professors who would serve in each of the nine departments already authorized a Permanent Professor Department Head, established the position of Professor of Law and the Professor of Ordnance as Permanent Professors, and provided an additional Permanent Professor as Dean of the Academic Board. The Dean was to be appointed from among the Permanent Professors who had served as heads of departments, and the Dean of the Academic Board would have the rank, pay, allowances, retirement rights, and other benefits authorized for permanent brigadier generals. These Permanent Professor authorizations would still be in effect in 1954 and apply to the Air Force Academy when it was established. The new Permanent Professors proved to be ardent proponents of the principals MacArthur had introduced. One of these new Professors had become a brigadier general in the war, but he returned to West Point as a colonel to serve with Colonel Beukema. Fencing and Horsemanship were dropped; Nuclear Physics, Electronics, Communications, Russian and US History, International Economics, and Psychology were among the courses added. In 1948 the First Classmen were tested against 1,174 men from 41 liberal arts colleges using the General Education Test of the College Record Examination. The West Point men's average index score was 589 compared to the liberal arts seniors' 523. The cadets scored better in five subject areas, falling below the others only in fine arts and biological science, neither of which was taught at West Point. Clearly West Point had recaptured its position as one of America's better universities. Even though in 1964 the curriculum still was prescriptive with no electives, the practice of sectioning classes by ability allowed a formal Advanced Academic Program with more than 20 advanced courses for the more capable cadets.

The foregoing evolutionary history of the USMA sets the stage for understanding the new United States Air Force Academy, because the planning (1948–1954), the initial staffing (1954–1955), and the education and training of the first class to graduate (1955–1959) were led by officers who were predominately USMA graduates or who had taught there.

Early Leadership Sets the Tone

The early senior leaders of the Air Force Academy were nearly all graduates of the United States Military Academy. The Superintendent, Lieutenant General Herbert H. Harmon, graduated from the USMA in 1915 and returned as an instructor, 1929–1932. He commanded flight training units, 1940–1942, and was the Special Assistant for Air Academy Matters, from December 1948 until assuming command of the USAFA in August 1954. General Harmon recognized the importance of getting key personnel identified and assigned. He had asked for appointment of a Dean of the Faculty and Commandant of Cadets as early as October 1951 and repeated this request several times. When General Harmon assumed command of the USAFA, he did so from the single room available to the seven Academy personnel present for duty at Lowry AFB and with only one senior leader among them, the Dean of the Faculty, Brigadier General Don Z. Zimmerman, who had been appointed July 22, 1954.

General Zimmerman had an impressive record. He had earned Bachelor's and Master's degrees, and a commission as a second lieutenant in the US Army Reserve prior to graduating from West Point sixth in a class of 299 in 1929. After flying duty, he earned a Master's degree in Engineering (Meteorology) from the California Institute of Technology in 1936. He then instructed Air Corps Primary Flying for four years and wrote the *Weather Manual for Pilots* used throughout the Air Corps and US Army. He returned to West Point in 1940 and taught Mathematics for the fall semester. Due to the war in Europe, he spent nearly a year studying long-range weather forecasting, and in early 1942 he was appointed Director of Weather for the Army Air Forces and the US Army. During the Korean War, he served in staff positions in HQ Far East Air Forces and was promoted to brigadier general. While General Zimmerman's military credentials and academic achievements as a student were impressive, General Harmon had reservations about his lack of academic teaching and administrative experience.

At a 1954 White House dinner with his West Point Class of 1915 classmates (President Eisenhower, General Omar Bradley, and others),

General Harmon expressed his concerns. Retired Colonel Beukema recommended that Harmon consider Colonel Robert F. McDermott, currently teaching in the Social Sciences Department at West Point, to be the Professor of Economics and Vice Dean of the Faculty. Colonel Beukema as the Professor and Head of Social Sciences at West Point had been very impressed by McDermott. Within a few days, General Harmon was interviewing Colonel McDermott in the latter's office at West Point. General Harmon offered Colonel McDermott the two positions, but McDermott turned him down, saying that he wanted to return to flying. When Harmon became more persuasive, McDermott did not waiver and told Harmon that he couldn't be assigned to the Air Force Academy because he had orders to Japan with a port call in fewer than 30 days. (Air Force regulations at the time did not allow changes to orders under those circumstances.) The next day McDermott received orders canceling his Japan orders and assigning him to the Air Force Academy as Professor of Economics. This assignment, brought about by the traditional close bond among West Point classmates, would prove pivotal in the development of the Air Force Academy as McDermott would later be dubbed the "Father of Modern Military Education." Colonel McDermott arrived at Lowry AFB on October 18, 1954, as Professor of Economics and became Vice Dean as an additional duty on November 12, 1954. He had attended Norwich College for two years before entering the USMA, graduating in 1943. After flying combat in Europe during World War II, he served as a Personnel Staff Officer, 1945–1948. He earned a Master's degree in Business Administration from Harvard University in 1950. He then served as an Instructor in the Department of Social Studies at the USMA until his departure for Lowry.

To lead the Academy's military training General Harmon chose Colonel Robert M. Stillman, who was appointed Commandant of Cadets on September 1, 1954. Colonel Stillman attended Colorado College in Colorado Springs on a football scholarship for two years before entering the USMA and graduating in 1935. For the next three years, he returned to West Point each fall as a member of the football coaching staff. He participated in two low-level B-26 bombing missions over Europe, being shot down on his second one. Captured in Holland May 17, 1943, he remained a prisoner of war until April 29, 1945. While serving in the Pentagon as Chief of Officers' Assignments, he became involved in Academy planning, working with General Harmon. General Stillman chose all of his senior staff from the ranks of West Point graduates, and they set out to implement a training system closely modeled on the Military Academy's methods. The Commandant was responsible for military, flying, and physical training until the Department of Physical Education was transferred to the Director of Athletics in 1959. One of Colonel Stillman's first actions that has endured was to request a change in the military organization of the cadets. The planning had stipulated an air division with two wings, three groups per wing, with six squadrons in each group. Feeling this was administratively awkward and unnecessarily complicated, Stillman proposed a single cadet wing with squadrons of 100 men organized into 6 groups to form the wing. His proposal was approved and evolved to the current cadet wing organization of 4 groups and 40 squadrons.

The Athletic Director, Colonel Robert V. Whitlow, was appointed on June 29, 1954. He was an excellent golfer and, while stationed at HQ Air Defense Command in Colorado Springs, had played golf with local and Pentagon generals and other officials including soon-to-become Secretary of the Air Force Talbott, General Harmon, General O'Donnell (AF Deputy Chief of Staff, Personnel), and even President Eisenhower. Graduating from the USMA in 1943, he had won letters in football, basketball, and track. Before entering West Point he had played football for three years at UCLA. A very enthusiastic sportsman, he attacked every task with zeal and scheduled the Academy's first football game with the University of Denver for October 8, 1955, fewer than three months after the first cadets reported for duty on July 11, 1955. With strong support from Secretary Talbott and General O'Donnell, he continued to promote intercollegiate sports vigorously, especially football. This led to conflicts with academics, concerns about accreditation, and even conflicts with the USMA's recruiting of athletes. He brought in as his assistant Major Frank Merritt, who served as assistant football coach and would later become the Director of Athletics.

During site selection (April–June 1954), General Harmon's staff prepared lists of qualified individuals for his review. Emphasizing the importance of this task was the requirement by Secretary of the Air Force Talbott that he must approve General Harmon's selections. After Harmon, with the assistance of the AF Deputy Chief of Staff, Personnel, and the AF Chief of Staff, obtained approval for key faculty and staff positions, the Secretary removed this restriction in August 1954. General Harmon then decided that he would let his leaders (Dean, Commandant, Athletic Director) choose their own personnel using guidelines that had been established by the Air Force Academy Planning Board Report in 1949 and refined since. Selection criteria to guide Professors as they selected their faculty were formalized in October 1954 by the Dean of the Faculty.

By the end of October 1954, eight professors, the librarian, and the Assistant Dean of the Faculty/Director of Audio-Visual and Training Aids, Service Training, and Examination had reported for duty at Lowry. The latter, Colonel Arthur E. Boudreau, was a USMA graduate and had been recalled to active duty in 1948 from his position as Dean of the Inter-American College, Coral Gables, FL. He had chaired the Curriculum Committee of the Air Academy Planning Group at Maxwell AFB before becoming General Harmon's Executive Officer on his Pentagon staff; he also had played a key role in the selection of the final Academy site. These early selections were exceptionally well-qualified and are shown below, along with two lieutenant colonels who played early key roles developing the required freshman courses. Lieutenant Colonel Woodyard would become the Professor of Chemistry in August 1955, and Lieutenant Colonel Sullivan would develop a new Philosophy course before being replaced by Colonel Thomas L. Chrystal, Professor of Philosophy, in July 1955. Chrystal was a 1934 USMA graduate with a Master of Arts degree from Columbia University and had taught at the USMA for five years.

Of the men listed in the following table, five (Moody, Wilson, Higdon, McDermott, and Woodyard) would later be appointed Permanent Professors. It should be noted that since the appropriate provisions of the laws pertaining to West Point were to apply to the Air Force Academy (Section 5

Name	Date Reported (1954)	Position	Education	Years Teaching Experience
Col Arthur E. Boudreau	27 Sep	Assistant Dean of Faculty	MA	Administrator
Col Peter R. Moody	27 Sep	Prof of English	BA, Wofford College MA, Duke USMA 1942	5, USMA
Col James V.G. Wilson	30 Sep	Prof of Chemistry & Physics	USMA 1935 MS, Illinois	6, USMA
Lt Col Arthur J. Larsen	30 Sep	Director of Library	BS, MA, PhD, Minnesota	Historian
Col Allen W. Rigsby	11 Oct	Prof of Law/Staff Judge Advocate	BA, Law, Oklahoma	None
Col Archie Higdon	14 Oct	Prof of Mathematics	BS, South Dakota State MS, PhD, Iowa State	12, Iowa State 3, USMA
Col Josephus W. Bowman	14 Oct	Prof of Geography	USMA 1939 MPA, Harvard	3, USMA
Col Robert F. McDermott	18 Oct	Prof of Economics	USMA 1943 MBA, Harvard	4, USMA
Col John L. Frisbee	18 Oct	Prof of History	BA, Hartwich MA, Georgetown	3, USMA
Col James S. Barko	18 Oct	Prof of Engineering Drawing	USMA 1937 MS, Cornell	None
Lt Col William T. Woodyard	Oct	Assoc Prof of Chemistry	BS, MS, Missouri	3, USMA
Lt Col Cornelius D. Sullivan	20 Nov	Acting Prof of Philosophy	BA, MA, Toronto	(unknown)

of the April 1, 1954, law), 21 Permanent Professors were expected to be authorized. Hence, there was an implied tenure to the Professors' appointments, but no procedures were yet in place to nominate the appointment of Permanent Professors.

Using the selection criteria promulgated by General Zimmerman, the Professors, aided by a HQ USAF Selection Board, selected 55 instructors for assignment to the Academy by November 8, 1954. A similar process would be followed each year until the cadet wing reached its authorized strength and the faculty was fully staffed. The table below presents the military and educational characteristics of the initial cadre of officers, compared with the percentage goals that had evolved by 1955.

Characteristic	Actual Percent	1955 Goal-Percent
USMA Graduates	33	At least 25
Regular Officers	56	At least 50
Reserve Officers	42	
Rated Officers	53	At least 60
Non-Rated Officers	47	
B.S. Degrees	17	0
M.A./M.S. Degrees	67	
Ph.D. Degrees	16	

The faculty was now on board to prepare for the freshman classes and equip the laboratories for academics to begin in September 1955, only 10 months away. Lurking in the background was the second priority, to obtain accreditation prior to the graduation of the first class in 1959. Application of the laws governing the USMA again came into play. Since the USMA and the US Naval Academy were not authorized to grant degrees without accreditation, it was assumed a like condition would be imposed on the Air Force Academy. Further adding to the pressure was the Academy Catalog published in 1954, which stated that a Bachelor of Science degree would be awarded graduates.

The initial *de facto* organization of the faculty was aligned under the professors of the core curriculum disciplines. For the first year these disciplines (courses) were Chemistry, English, Graphics, History, Mathematics, Philosophy (logic), Geography, and Physical Training. Physical Training and its spring semester replacement, Airmanship, were taught under the Commandant of Cadets. On November 12, 1954, the Dean created a Faculty "Committee of the Whole" composed of the professors and assigned them the task of addressing the roles and responsibilities of the faculty. The Dean also established three sub-committees: the Scientific Studies Committee, the Social Sciences Committee, and the Humanities Committee. On September 1, 1954, the Special Assistant for Air Academy Affairs Curriculum Planning Group had published a report entitled *Air Force Academy Program of Instruction*, which contained detailed course syllabi for each course in the prescribed curriculum. But General Zimmerman told the Committee of the Whole that they were to consider three issues: the freshman curriculum, the four-year curriculum, and the freshman schedule, suggesting that the planned curriculum was subject to modification. To review items of general concern to the entire faculty, the Dean established three more committees to consider such items as grading, elimination of cadets for deficiencies, cadet academic awards, homework assignments, curricula and schedules for the three upper classes, classroom furniture, improving faculty education opportunities, and faculty and department organization, to name a few. To implement and guide this interim committee organization, General Zimmerman appointed Colonel McDermott to be the Vice Dean of the Faculty.

Meanwhile, the Dean continued to work with the individual professors as they refined the goals, objectives, and syllabi of the freshman courses. Work was also underway to determine textbooks that might be used and the long lead tasks of specifying and obtaining classroom and specialized laboratory equipment for Chemistry, Graphics, Physics, and Engineering. The Dean also directed the faculty through a series of policy letters, which among other things guided faculty behavior in staff meetings, assigned responsibilities to the different academic ranks, established procedures for extra instruction given to cadets outside of the classroom, and established expectations for faculty participation in professional meetings to maintain currency in their disciplines. In September 1955, the Dean established a Freshman Committee with responsibility for continuously reviewing the freshman curriculum in order to improve it both for the current and subsequent years. As all these committees and the professors brought their recommendations to the Dean for his approval, or to forward to the Superintendent as appropriate, the formation of the faculty, the curriculum, and the cadet schedule took place. During his many years working toward the Academy's establishment, General Harmon had formed a clear, detailed vision of what the Academy should be and how it should operate. Therefore, he was intimately involved in decisions regarding the curriculum, the cadet schedule, and the selection and education of faculty. As items for decision were debated before him, the Superintendent was increasingly impressed with the depth of knowledge and articulate arguments made by the professors, which generally overwhelmed those of the Commandant and Athletic Director.

During this formative period three professors became most influential in the decision-making process. Colonel Moody was an articulate advocate for the humanities and social sciences and Colonel Higdon had equally strong arguments in favor of the sciences; they debated their cases eloquently when conflicts for time in the curriculum arose. As the Vice Dean and Secretary of the Committee of the Whole, Colonel McDermott had the responsibility of submitting all recommendations, so he, within reason, could shape the arguments, try to sway recalcitrant professors, and determine the way items were presented to the Dean and Superintendent for decisions. Colonel McDermott welcomed informed debate but was strongly focused on developing a balanced curriculum producing "whole man" graduates capable of academic statesmanship and dynamic, inspired leadership. He was a formidable, well-prepared foe in arguments with those holding different views. This was demonstrated in late 1954 during the first meeting to consider admission criteria for the new class. As usual, McDermott had prepared well and presented a detailed list of desired attributes. Colonel Whitlow quickly recognized that many of the athletes he was trying to recruit could not meet McDermott's criteria, so he proposed a method of granting exceptions for special cases. The argument became so heated that the Dean ordered Colonel McDermott to remain in the Dean's office in the afternoon, so the admissions process could continue without him. Incensed, McDermott asked the Superintendent to overrule the Dean, but General Harmon declined to do so. Perhaps part of his reason for upholding the Dean may have been the openly stated view of the Secretary of the Air Force and the DCS for Personnel, General O'Donnell, that the best publicity the Air Force

Academy could obtain was to have a winning football team. This focus later became an issue when Colonel McDermott arranged a visit by Andrew M. Patillo, Jr., a consultant to the North Central Association of Colleges and Secondary Schools, which was the accrediting body for the Academy. Gaining accreditation in time for the Class of 1959 was to be a real challenge, as accreditation was not normally granted until at least a full four years of instruction had been demonstrated.

General Harmon's original misgivings about General Zimmerman's academic administrative experience had been borne out as the Dean tried to impose his own narrow view on the focus of the curriculum, became bogged down in detail and slow to make decisions, and failed to impress visitors from the North Central Association, which was to evaluate the Academy for accreditation. These factors led to his reassignment on December 1, 1955. General Harmon assumed the additional duty as Dean of the Faculty and McDermott, as Vice Dean and Secretary to the Committee of the Whole, became the Superintendent's conduit to the faculty. Fortuitously, Economics was to be a junior year course, so McDermott was not pressed to spend time developing it. A review of all critical faculty matters was quickly ordered by the Superintendent. The resulting report, largely reflecting Colonel McDermott's views, recommended establishing a faculty senate composed of the Dean and all professors. Implemented on December 15, 1955, as the Academic Policy Board, this body later became the Faculty Council with membership to include all Department Heads (who may not have been a Permanent Professor, due to sabbatical assignments or vacancies), which to this day considers all things faculty-related and makes recommendations to the Dean, or through the Dean, to the Superintendent or the Academy Board.

Another way that the professors influenced Academy decisions was through membership on the Academy Board. Early staff meetings held by General Harmon at Lowry AFB included the professors, Dean, Director of Athletics, Commandant, Director of Flying Instruction, Director of Physical Training, and the Director of Military Instruction. This body began calling themselves the "Academic Board" after the governing body at West Point. However, they soon realized the USAFA group had more non-academic members than did West Point's, so the name changed to the "Academy Board." This informal Board became an organizational reality in August 1955, when, after considering a proposal from Colonel McDermott, the Superintendent formed an Academy Board consisting of himself, the Dean, the Commandant, five Professors, and the three directors of instruction under the Commandant. This Board was to recommend men for appointment as cadets by the Secretary of the Air Force, consider cadet disenrollment actions, and perform other duties assigned by the Superintendent. However, it was not to consider academic matters or admission criteria. HQ USAF officially recognized the Air Force Academy Board in January 1956 to consist of the Superintendent, Dean, Commandant, and heads of academic and airmanship departments as appointed by the Superintendent, with the Registrar to be the non-voting Secretary. The Academy Board was reorganized in March 1956, when General Harmon was both the Superintendent and the Dean, by deleting the Superintendent and adding one professor. While patterned after the Academic Board at West Point, the USAFA Academy Board had a much broader scope, more non-academic representation, and less power over the curriculum. By default, the curriculum decisions reverted to the Faculty Council, sitting as a Curriculum Committee. In August 1956, when General Briggs became Superintendent, he revised the Board's role again; now the Board would be the decision authority for curriculum and related matters and the Faculty Council would make recommendations on these subjects.

Changes in Academy leadership continued after General Zimmerman's departure. Major General James E. Briggs had been identified by the AF Chief of Staff to replace General Harmon, who planned to retire in the summer of 1956. General Briggs graduated from the USMA in the Class of 1928, holding the highest cadet rank. He had returned to West Point as a member of the Mathematics faculty, 1940–1942. During World War II and the Korean War, he held numerous operational flying and staff positions. He gained invaluable insight into the Academy as Chairman of the USAF Academy Curriculum Review Board that convened in February 1956. The Board was established by the AF Chief of Staff at General Harmon's request to examine the current curriculum and either approve it or suggest changes. Feeling the cadet workload was too heavy, a view shared by the Commandant and Director of Athletics, Colonel McDermott had tried unsuccessfully to get the Faculty Council to reduce the workload. Each Professor was unwilling to give up any cadet time devoted to his discipline. McDermott was now in a position to push for changes he thought were required. The Curriculum Review Board recommended a reduction in workload, agreed with McDermott's proposed reorganization of the faculty into departments grouped into divisions according to academic disciplines, more faculty teacher training, and replacing the Academy Board with an Academic Board modeled after the USMA's. The Superintendent agreed with all recommendations except the last one, which he felt was unnecessary because the faculty already held a majority membership on the Board.

General Harmon's intense desire to get everything right about his new Academy presented a very heavy workload: making the unending decisions involved in developing processes and overseeing day-to-day operations, guiding the design for the permanent site, and ensuring favorable public affairs and relations with Congress to enhance the Academy's reputation and keep funding flowing. This workload had taken its toll. In May 1956 he was diagnosed with advanced cancer. General Brigg's arrival at the Academy was moved forward to June 1956, and he became the Assistant Superintendent to relieve Harmon's workload. In one of his first meetings after reporting to the Academy, General Briggs told Colonel McDermott that he was to become Superintendent on August 1 and intended to appoint McDermott as Dean of the Faculty. Soon McDermott sent a memorandum to Briggs recommending Permanent Professors be appointed to ensure stability, integration, continuity, and evolution of the instructional program. Briggs agreed and started his own search for the best qualified individuals, but he would not recommend anyone for another seven months. In a second memorandum, McDermott laid out his views on the functions, title, duties, and relationships of the Dean. He felt the Dean should have overarching control of the curriculum. Further, he argued the Dean should be able to nominate Permanent Professors, should write their effectiveness reports (being written by the Superintendent at that time), and should be the authority to select and relieve all faculty members. During this turbulent summer an attempt to have the Dean, Commandant, and Director of Athletics report to the Academy Chief of Staff rather than the Superintendent was successfully thwarted by General Briggs's rejection of the proposal after he became Superintendent.

A critical factor in the accreditation of an institute of higher learning is its library. In early 1956 it became clear that the Air Force would not extend Lieutenant Colonel Larsen, who had done an outstanding job establishing the library, beyond his mandatory retirement date. A curriculum change for Academic Year 1956–1957 had moved American History to the junior year, making the American History course chairman, Lieutenant Colonel George V. Fagan, available for other duties. A PhD in History with teaching experience at Temple University and the USNA, Fagan had been actively recommending books for the library's collections. General Harmon appointed Fagan the Acting Director of the Library effective June 1, 1956. Thus began his exemplary service in that post for the next 13 years, the last 6 as a Permanent Professor. The only Permanent Professor to never head a department, Fagan played a significant role in the design of the permanent site library and the early accreditation of the academic program.

In August 1956 the Academy Board approved McDermott's proposed faculty organization of equal numbers of related departments organized into divisions representing Humanities, Social Sciences, Basic Sciences, and Engineering Sciences (see following chapters). He then turned his attention to achieving accreditation and providing academic enrichment opportunities for deserving cadets. While a cadet at West Point, McDermott had very much disliked repeating courses that he had previously mastered during his prior two years at Norwich College. The appeal of attending the new Air Force Academy and learning to fly was bringing in many cadets with prior college experience who were suffering the same frustration with the prescribed, inflexible curriculum. Colonel Higdon had already experimented with a voluntary accelerated course in math during the first year. Over 100 cadets had participated with 35 completing three extra courses for five extra credit hours. In the fall semester of 1956, voluntary enrollments in accelerated courses in Math, Chemistry, English, and Graphics numbered 268 cadets. That December, McDermott proposed his enrichment program to the Professors: cadets would receive validation credit for courses they had previously taken at civilian colleges that were equivalent to those prescribed in the curriculum (these cadets could take elective courses instead), gifted cadets could take extra courses, and the social sciences/humanities course offerings would be expanded to broaden knowledge and extra science courses provided to deepen knowledge. This break with the tradition of a prescribed curriculum for all at West Point and Annapolis would lead in 1958 to the approval of majors in Basic Science, Engineering Sciences, English, Western Culture, and Public Affairs. Later that year even more flexibility was granted a cadet with a concentration of 17 semester hours or more in an area, allowing him to graduate with a major developed with a department or division and approved by the Faculty Council and the Dean. In the Class of 1959, over 10 percent of the class earned a major and over 29 percent of the Class of 1960 did so.

Accreditation was still an issue that had to be addressed. Through numerous visits to the North Central Association beginning in February 1955, McDermott and others learned the process and guidelines for accreditation and developed strategies to overcome the deficiencies they expected accreditors to uncover. Although the curriculum had been developed closely aligned with that of West Point, the original planners, and later the Professors, had invited numerous reviews of their work by outside civilian experts. These resulted in many refinements and a deeper understanding of the civilian education system and accreditation challenges. This was in sharp contrast to the isolationism that had prevailed at West Point prior to MacArthur and that still lingered there. In the summer of 1957 Colonel McDermott put Colonel Woodyard, his teaching colleague and next-door neighbor at West Point, in charge of the accreditation effort. Woodyard had proven himself as Professor and Head of the Chemistry Department. The Superintendent established the USAFA Accreditation Committee with Woodyard as chairman and included members of the Superintendent's and Commandant's staffs. Working full time, Woodyard identified concerns about faculty tenure, faculty academic qualifications, and faculty participation in academic decision-making, among others. The work of 20 committees culminated in June 1958 when the Self-Study Report was flown to Chicago in a T-33 aircraft by Woodyard. This preparation for accreditation, begun in the early planning for the Academy, ended successfully with the very unusual accreditation of the Academy in April 1959 before its first class had graduated.

One of the concerns raised in the accreditation review was that of faculty tenure. Applying the laws governing the USMA as directed in the 1954 act, the USAF Judge Advocate General had ruled that the provisions for Permanent Professor appointments were applicable to the Air Force Academy. In February 1957, General Briggs sent Colonel McDermott's nomination package to the Air Staff, recommending his appointment as Permanent Professor (but not Permanent Dean, which would carry with it promotion to brigadier general). Included were recommended policies for the selection of the Permanent Professors, retention on flying status, and adjustment in McDermott's date of rank as a colonel. Extensive delays ensued as the Air Staff wrestled with this landmark decision. Thinking the cost of retaining flying status was the issue, General Briggs wrote a long letter explaining his rationale for this request. Finally, on October 16, 1957, the Secretary of the Air Force approved Colonel McDermott as the first Permanent Professor and approved retaining him and future Professors on flying status. Using the rationale that McDermott was no longer on the Line of the Air Force promotion list, the change in his date of rank as a colonel to August 15, 1943, also was approved. This date, fewer than six months after he graduated from West Point, was sufficiently early to ensure he outranked the most senior colonel on the faculty. Colonel McDermott would be nominated for Dean by the Superintendent, Major General Briggs, on May 16, 1959, and the Secretary of the Air Force forwarded his nomination on August 27. The President approved, and the Senate confirmed his appointment as permanent Dean and promotion to brigadier general effective September 15, 1959.

The next three Permanent Professors, Colonels Woodyard, Moody, and Higdon, were appointed in 1958. This photograph, from that year,

shows these first four Permanent Professors (from left, Colonels McDermott, Woodyard, Moody, and Higdon). The scene is a familiar one, from the
Dean's office in Fairchild Hall overlooking the terrazzo to Harmon Hall and
the Rampart Range beyond.

These four members of the initial cadre, who had worked so hard
to make the new USAF Academy successful, saw their contributions and
potential for further progress recognized. They would be the first to admit
they had not accomplished this monumental task by themselves; the enthusiasm, hard work, and dedication of the other leaders and personnel assigned
to the faculty as well as other Academy organizations certainly had done
their share. As history would show, the innovative changes undertaken by
these early Academy leaders would soon cause a revolution in military education at the other US military academies.

THE PERMANENT PROFESSOR SYSTEM

Management of the Permanent Professors from appointment to retirement, is described in this chapter. The position of Permanent Professor at the United States Air Force Academy was established in 1957. Title 10, United States Code §9331, currently authorizes 23 Permanent Professors and a Dean of the Faculty. Other sections of 10 U.S.C. provide additional definition of the program. The treatment of the Air Force Academy in these provisions is generally identical to that of the United States Military Academy at West Point, much as the entire legal basis of the United States Air Force paralleled that of its parent service, the United States Army. (The Naval Academy authorized Permanent Professors beginning in 2008.)

The most salient feature of the program is the ability for each Permanent Professor to serve in their position, usually Department Head, at the Academy for many years, thus providing stability and continuity to the Academy's academic program while enhancing military professionalism to the entire institution. The continuation of active duty beyond a colonel's normal 30-year career raises unique challenges with regard to pay, professional development, evaluation, and retirement. Each of these issues is addressed in the policies that govern this unique program. The provisions for Permanent Professors in Public Law, as well as Department of Defense, Air Force, and Air Force Academy policies and procedures, have been gathered into a single Air Force Academy Instruction, 36-3532, which provides guidance for managing Permanent Professors to include nomination and appointment, continuation, and retirement.

The 23 authorized Permanent Professor positions at the Air Force Academy currently are allocated as follows:

The Department Heads of the 20 academic departments (one of whom serves as the Vice Dean of the Faculty)

The Vice Dean of the Faculty

The Vice Dean for Strategy and Curriculum

The Head of the Department of Physical Education (Department of Athletics)

The Director of the Center for Character and Leadership Development

In practice, the Vice Dean of the Faculty's position has been filled on a rotating basis by one of the Department Heads; therefore, that Permanent Professor authorization has been unused. However, in 2018 the Dean elected to establish a second Vice Dean position, the Vice Dean for Strategy and Curriculum, and use the Permanent Professor authorization for it. The Vice Dean of the Faculty position continued to be filled on a rotating basis. The Center for Character and Leadership Development, initially under the Commandant of Cadets, was reorganized during 2016–2018, emerging on July 1, 2018, as a new unit reporting directly to the Academy Superintendent with the Permanent Professor as Center Director and Department Head.

APPOINTING A PERMANENT PROFESSOR

The process of appointing a new Permanent Professor begins at the Air Force Academy, but it ends with the President of the United States and the Senate. Per 10 U.S.C. §9333(b), "The permanent professors of the Academy shall be appointed by the President, by and with the advice and consent of the Senate." The processes described below for selecting and nominating a Permanent Professor are those of the Dean's organization, where it is normal to fill two or more positions every year. For the positions outside the faculty, which may only be filled once a decade, similar procedures are followed, modified to fit their unique circumstances.

In the early days of the late 1950s and 1960s, when the academic structure of the Academy was rapidly changing, vacancies existed almost everywhere, and selection of individual Permanent Professors was done personally and privately by the Dean and the Superintendent. Since those beginnings, the Dean has established an orderly procedure for what often becomes a yearlong process. Permanent Professor vacancies due to the retirement of an incumbent in an academic department are usually known many months in advance, although openings have also occurred more suddenly. In either case the procedure to select a replacement is the same: first a careful Air Force-wide search, then interviews, and finally a nomination.

The Dean of the Faculty first determines that a vacancy exists or may exist in the near future. Next, a Search Committee is appointed by the Dean. The Committee normally consists of three Permanent Professors. The chair is the senior Permanent Professor in the academic division of the vacancy, supplemented by a Permanent Professor from a similar division, and a third from a division of the opposite academic hemisphere. For example, a committee searching to fill an Aeronautics Department Head vacancy would normally be led by an engineer, with a representative from Basic Sciences and another from either Humanities or Social Sciences. Most recent practice has allowed for the committee also to have a full professor civilian faculty member (typically from the discipline being competed) and an "external reviewer." The committee's duty is to conduct an Air Force-wide survey of potential nominees, solicit applications from qualified individuals, select and interview the leading candidates, and develop a rank-order recommendation for consideration by the Dean and the Superintendent. The nominees must be outstanding Air Force officers highly qualified in academic disciplines they would oversee and teach, as well as having demonstrated excellent military professionalism and leadership qualities.

The Search Committee requests the personnel system to identify all Air Force field grade officers who possess a doctorate or appropriate professional degree in a relevant academic field. From this list and associated personnel briefs, the Committee identifies a smaller group of best qualified individuals and invites each to formally apply for the open position. Applicants provide the committee with details of their military and leadership experience, professional academic experience (teaching, research, and scholarly publications), and two or three letters of recommendation. The

Academy provides travel support for the top candidates to come to the Academy for interviews, during which time the candidates have opportunities to meet and discuss issues with the Dean, the Search Committee, groups of Permanent Professors, the department members of the department in which the vacancy exists, and others. Following the interviews, the Search Committee develops its recommendation (rank order of top interviewees) and presents its top candidates to all the Permanent Professors for the group's review and its independent recommendation.

The Superintendent, who is the nominating official, receives the Dean's recommendation, along with one from the Search Committee and another from the body of Permanent Professors. These lists could be different, but in practice they are usually the same. Of course, the Superintendent may accept the Dean's recommendation, return it for reconsideration, or select someone else. Some Superintendents have preferred to only get the Dean's recommendation, but in this case the Dean has the other two recommendations to help reach a decision. Having made the selection, the Superintendent nominates the selected individual to the Chief of Staff of the Air Force and the Secretary of the Air Force. If approved at that level, the selection is forwarded through the Office of the Secretary of Defense to the President of the United States for formal nomination to the United States Senate for confirmation.

Upon confirmation by the Senate, the individual is appointed to a new statutory status, "Permanent Professor," separate and distinct from their previous status and service category. Unless especially junior, the Permanent Professor normally serves with the grade of colonel. There is a provision (10 U.S.C. §9336) that ensures that junior officers appointed as Permanent Professors would serve as lieutenant colonels until "after the date on which they would have been promoted had they been selected for promotion from among officers in the promotion zone." For this reason, although the statute was a little different during their service, Pete Carter, Phil Erdle, Cary Fisher, Joe Monroe, and Ron Thomas were majors when appointed Permanent Professors, but within days they were promoted early to lieutenant colonel. Mal Wakin was a captain when appointed

Permanent Professor the same day as Erdle and Thomas and became a lieutenant colonel with them 20 days later. Thus, each began their Permanent Professorships as lieutenant colonels. The appointment is as Permanent Professor, normally with duty as Head of an academic department, but there have been a few occasions where the Permanent Professor was first assigned to the Dean's Staff. Al Hurley, Phil Erdle, Cary Fisher, Joe Monroe, and Erv Rokke were Assistant Deans before being named Department Heads. All, including Thomas and Carter, became colonels when appointed Department Head in accordance with the statute at the time. One notable exception is George Fagan, who served with distinction as the Director of the Library for 13 years and did much to increase the academic reputation of the Academy. Regardless of the assigned duty, whether as a Department Head or other assignment at the Academy or elsewhere, the Permanent Professor's status is unchanged.

One peculiarity of the Permanent Professor position is related to command authority. According to 10 U.S.C. §9334, Permanent Professors "exercise command only in the academic department of the Academy." This has been interpreted by some to mean that the Permanent Professor cannot be a "commander" in the full Air Force meaning and cannot have command authority in the sense of the Uniform Code of Military Justice. This is an interesting artifact of our Army heritage. In much earlier times, the Military Academy occasionally needed to appoint a Permanent Professor directly from civilian academia. These men made fine professors but were unprepared for the command functions and so were denied the military command prerogatives of regular Army lieutenant colonels. This restriction, embodied in the law, was passed along to the Air Force. One can argue that the restriction is wholly unnecessary in the modern era, for the Air Force as well as for the Army, since Permanent Professors were career officers before selection for the special duty. Nevertheless, the restriction remains. In practice it is little more than a mild annoyance, and it has sometimes been interpreted differently or ignored completely.

A key feature of the Permanent Professor program is that the Permanent Professor may continue on active duty beyond 30 years of service, the limit for other colonels. The mandatory retirement age is specified in 10 U.S. Code §1252, which states that unless retired or separated earlier, each Permanent Professor of the United States Air Force Academy "shall be retired on the first day of the month following the month in which the officer becomes 64 years of age." This foresees the eventuality that a Permanent Professor's active duty may extend to 35 or 40 years or even more. It is presumed that they will continue beyond 30 years, and it is normally in the best interests of the Air Force and the Academy that they do. However, such an extended tenure calls for special provisions for pay, professional development, and retirement.

The pay of a Permanent Professor is that of any other officer of the same grade and longevity, except that there is a special provision for service beyond 36 years. A Permanent Professor who has completed 36 years of cumulative creditable service based on the date used to compute longevity pay receives an additional pay of $250 per month. (This additional pay is not used in computing retired pay.) This provision was established in 37 U.S.C. §203(b) in 1963, and it is the only longevity pay raise a Permanent Professor may receive after 30 years of service. There have been efforts over the years to secure earlier and more frequent pay raises for the Permanent Professors, but none has been successful.

In order to encourage their continued professional development, Permanent Professors are expected to take sabbatical assignments (normally every five years). The sabbaticals are (as defined in Academy Instruction) "in fields directly related to their Permanent Professor responsibilities to ensure they remain current in their discipline or serve in the operational AF for the purposes of refreshing their operational experience in their primary career field." The emphasis on taking sabbaticals, as well as their duration, frequency, and location, has varied through the years. While on sabbatical, the Permanent Professor remains on Academy manning documents, so the gaining unit (military or civilian) gets an extra person "for free." Moreover, even while on sabbatical, the Permanent Professor continues to be treated as a Permanent Professor for purposes of promotion or retirement (see next page).

A final provision for professional development of the Permanent Professor is that extensive performance reviews are conducted after completion of the 30th, 35th, and 40th years of commissioned service. These reviews are in addition to the annual performance reports prepared by the Dean for each Permanent Professor. These special reviews serve two purposes. First, they call for the Dean and the Superintendent formally to evaluate the merits of further continuance. But, just as importantly, they compel the Permanent Professor to formally review their own performance, contributions to their academic discipline, and involvement across the entire Academy, while providing a focus on the future. These reviews also serve as a basis to recommend Permanent Professors for promotion to the grade of brigadier general upon retirement.

RETIREMENT IN THE GRADE OF BRIGADIER GENERAL

Promotion of a Permanent Professor to the grade of brigadier general is described in the Academy Instruction:

> Upon retirement, any Permanent Professor whose grade is below brigadier general, and whose service as such a Professor has been long and distinguished, may, at the discretion of the President, be retired in the grade of brigadier general (10 U.S.C. §8962) without the pay of that grade. For this retirement promotion, the individual must have 30 or more years of total active federal commissioned service and 10 or more years of continuous service as a Permanent Professor or department head. In conformance with the desire of the President, Deputy Secretary of Defense memorandum, 21 July 1964, delegated approval authority for these promotions to the SecAF. The SecAF further delegated retirement promotion appointment authority to the SecAF Personnel Council (30 August 1967 memorandum).

The Secretary's 1967 Memorandum contained an alternative criterion for promotion, namely that the Permanent Professor would be eligible with 25 or more years Total Active Federal Commissioned Service, at least

13 years as a Department Head or higher, and a contemporary in the Line of the Air Force had been promoted to brigadier general. In reality, this additional criterion is no longer very useful. It was helpful to some of the early Permanent Professors who were appointed while still very junior in grade; however, no officer that junior has been appointed for over 40 years. Given the current rigid selection process, it is unlikely any person so junior would be appointed in the future.

These specific criteria for the promotion of Permanent Professors were developed at the Air Force Academy. In 1966 the Air Staff directed the Superintendent to develop a specific policy for this issue. The Dean (Brigadier General McDermott) drafted the new policy and the Superintendent (Lieutenant General Moorman) sent the proposed policy to the Air Force Deputy Chief of Staff for Personnel on August 23, 1967. In his letter the Superintendent stated the following:

> The law reserves this honor for those professors whose service as such has been long and distinguished. In developing a policy which could be applied in all such retirements I deemed it necessary to define what was long and to equate the criteria somewhat with the line of the Air Force experience with promotions to brigadier general. It is necessary also to consider the contributions made by the retiring professor, both to the military service and to the USAF Academy. I thought it particularly significant that the policy should not entice, in any way, a permanent professor to submit his request for retirement....

The policy statement attached to the letter (with the two criteria identified above) was approved promptly and appeared in the SecAF memo of August 30, 1967. It is worth noting that this is the only opportunity for promotion that Permanent Professors have (other than selection for Dean). Although chosen for their professional qualities, Permanent Professors never again meet a promotion board, as do all other colonels.

The first retirements were in the 1960s. Jim Wilson was the first Permanent Professor to retire, in 1965, and he was promoted to brigadier general at that time. Archie Higdon and Pete Moody retired in November 1967, and, based on the recommendation of the Superintendent, they were promoted at retirement. All three of these officers met the "new" criteria. Five other officers, including three who retired that year, one who retired in 1968, and another who retired in 1969, did not meet the criteria and were not promoted at the time (although they were all promoted later as noted below).

PROMOTIONS AFTER RETIREMENT—CORRECTIONS OF RECORDS. In the early 1990s five of the early retired Permanent Professors—Wes Posvar (retired in June 1967), Chris Munch (July 1967), Wil Ruenheck (November 1967), Al Miele (November 1968), and George Fagan (August 1969)—were promoted to brigadier general by the Air Force Board for Correction of Military Records. The action was based on the argument that they had retired or applied for retirement before the specific criteria were established. Apparently, the Superintendent at the time of their retirement (Lieutenant General Moorman) and the then Superintendent (Lieutenant General Hosmer) both concurred that these officers' service had been long and distinguished. Wes Posvar was promoted in 1991, George Fagan and Wil Ruenheck in early 1993, and Chris Munch and Al Miele somewhat later, all retroactive to their dates of retirement.

SUBSEQUENT PROMOTIONS—EXCEPTIONS TO POLICY. There are exceptions to every policy.

> Harvey Schiller retired in 1986 with 25 years of service and 6 years as Permanent Professor. He was promoted to brigadier general in 2004 based on his exceptional contributions as a Permanent Professor and his continued contributions to the nation in subsequent prominent positions.

> Ron Reed was promoted to brigadier general when he was retired for medical reasons in 2005. With nearly 28 years of service and nearly 11 years as Permanent Professor, Ron's promotion was justified on the basis that his distinguished service was cut short by cancer.

> Roger Bate retired in 1973 after 26 years of service and 11 years as Permanent Professor. Apparently, he had been recommended

for promotion at the time by the Dean (Brigadier General Woodyard), but the grade had not been awarded—no known reason. His long and distinguished contributions were recognized when he was promoted to brigadier general in 2008.

Rich Hughes retired in 1995 with 28 years of service and 8 years as a Permanent Professor. He was promoted in 2010 based on his continued service to the Academy, post-retirement.

In each of these four instances, the promotion was approved by the Air Force Personnel Council upon the recommendation of the Superintendent. The Air Force Personnel Council appears to rely heavily on the Superintendent's recommendations in such cases.

Permanent Professors continue to be considered for retirement promotion to brigadier general under the established policy, now virtually unchanged for more than 50 years. Altogether, of the Permanent Professors who retired, just under 80 percent were promoted to brigadier general through this provision.

The pay for retired Permanent Professors is that of other officers retired from active duty in the pay grade of colonel. The amount of pay is a percentage of the final basic pay or the High-36 basis, depending on individual circumstances. The percentage begins at 50 percent for 20 years of active service and grows by 2½ percent per year thereafter. Before 2007, the multiplier was capped at 75 percent. However, since 2007 the maximum multiplier is no longer capped; rather it continues to grow at the 2½ percent rate with every year served beyond 30 years to, say, 90 percent at 36 years, 100 percent at 40 years, and even beyond! Although this is not a special provision for Permanent Professors, they are especially well-placed to benefit from the change.

THE DEAN OF THE FACULTY

The initial Dean of the Faculty was Brigadier General Don Z. Zimmerman, who served from July 1954 until December 1955. When General Zimmerman was reassigned, the Superintendent, Lieutenant General Harmon, assumed additional duty as Dean until Colonel McDermott was appointed Acting Dean. Colonel McDermott was formally appointed Dean of the Faculty by Major General Briggs, when he became the second Superintendent on August 1, 1956 (McDermott was promoted to brigadier general in September 1959 and is regarded as the first permanent Dean). General Briggs had observed Colonel McDermott's grasp of the Academy's academic needs and his leadership when he led the Academy Curriculum Review Committee in February 1956. Upon his arrival at the Academy in June 1956 as Assistant Superintendent, General Briggs met with Colonel McDermott and told him that he was to be the Dean as soon as General Briggs became the Superintendent. It would appear this was General Briggs's decision, undoubtedly concurred in by the Chief of Staff and Secretary of the Air Force. Lieutenant General Moorman selected Colonel Woodyard, then Vice Dean, to be the second permanent Dean of the Faculty. The nomination was coordinated with the Air Staff, the Office of the Secretary of Defense, and sent to the Senate by the White House. The nomination was confirmed by the Senate on May 17 to become effective on August 1, 1968.

Permanent Deans of the Faculty			
Robert F. McDermott	1957–1968	Ruben A. Cubero	1991–1998
William T. Woodyard	1968–1978	David A. Wagie	1998–2004
William A. Orth	1978–1983	Dana H. Born	2004–2013
Ervin J. Rokke	1983–1986	Andrew P. Armacost	2013–Present
Erlind G. Royer	1987–1991		

In the original concept, the Dean of the Faculty was appointed Dean for an unspecified period. The first permanent Dean of the Faculty, Brigadier General McDermott, served in the position for 11 years until his voluntary retirement in 1968. His successor, Brigadier General Woodyard, served for 10 years and was involuntarily retired in 1978. General Woodyard was ending his ninth year as Dean when Lieutenant General Tallman was appointed Superintendent in June 1977. Soon after his arrival, General Tallman announced his desire to replace the Dean with an officer of his own choosing. Perhaps the reason was to build a more cohesive leadership team, or perhaps it was simply to reduce the power and influence that had accrued to the office of the Dean. However, the Dean did not accept the invitation to retire.

The authority to retire a Permanent Professor is vested in the Secretary of the Air Force, and in April 1978 General Tallman requested the Secretary appoint a new Dean to replace General Woodyard. The Secretary, John C. Stetson, appointed a committee to review the matter. There followed an open and pointed exchange of views, much of which was played out in the newspapers. Ultimately, the Secretary elected to approve the Superintendent's recommendation to appoint a new Dean. General Woodyard's opinion of the matter was published in an open letter to the faculty, where he noted that his firing was not based on cause, nor was it based on any displeasure with the academic performance of cadets. He stated that he resisted the demand to retire voluntarily in order to preserve academic freedom; that the academic program was placed in jeopardy by the power of a military commander to replace subordinates at will. General Woodyard was offered the option to retire or continue at the Academy as a Permanent Professor in the grade of colonel. He retired without ceremony in August 1978 with 37 years of active service, the longest continuous service of any general officer in the Air Force, and the last remaining member of the original contingent of officers who established the Academy at Lowry AFB in 1954.

In concurring with the Superintendent's recommendation, the Secretary expressed full support for the concept of tenure for the Academy's Permanent Professors. He acknowledged the Permanent Professor status as specified in law and justified by the need for stability, continuity, and academic excellence in the development of the Academy's academic program. However, he also noted that administrative and managerial positions such as the Dean or Department Head, even if held by Permanent Professors, were not protected by law or custom but rather were subject to the decisions of management. The Secretary further recommended that the Dean be appointed for a fixed term.

Following the Secretary's decision to replace General Woodyard as Dean, the Superintendent formed a search committee to help him identify three Dean of the Faculty candidates from among the Permanent Professors who had served as heads of academic departments. The Search Committee consisted of General John Roberts, Commander of Air Training Command; retired USAF Lieutenant General Brent Scowcroft; Professor Sheila Widnall, MIT; and Dr. Chester Alter, Chancellor Emeritus, University of Denver. General Tallman forwarded the names of the three candidates to Secretary Stetson, who selected Colonel William A. Orth for nomination by the President and confirmation by the Senate. Colonel Orth was made Acting Dean on August 1 and then promoted to brigadier general and appointed Dean of the Faculty on September 1, 1978. Much the same procedure was followed for the selection and appointment of the next three Deans. The search committees were composed of two or three Air Force general officers, often with PhDs and/or experience at the Academy, one or two well-respected civilian educators, and someone from HQ USAF. Notably, one Superintendent chose to chair the committee as a non-voting member and a major general member of the same committee became the Academy's Superintendent shortly after the selected Dean took office. Also, one of the distinguished educators served two terms on the Academy Board of Visitors, served on at least two search committees, and later became Secretary of the Air Force. It is clear the committees were carefully chosen to comprise a group well qualified to make these important recommendations.

Brigadier General Orth was given a five-year term as Dean. His term could have been extended by the Secretary for another five years, but General Orth chose to retire after five years in 1983. His successor, Brigadier General Erv Rokke, served three years, 1983–1986, before returning to the Line of the Air Force as a colonel and the Air Attaché designate to the Soviet Union (later Erv would earn the rank of lieutenant general and serve as President of the National Defense University); the fifth, Brigadier General Lindy Royer, served four years, 1987–1991, and retired. Since the five-year term policy was formulated, three Deans have been extended beyond the initial five-year tour. The sixth permanent Dean, Brigadier General Randy Cubero, served for seven years, 1991–1998; the seventh, Brigadier General Dave Wagie, served for six years; and the eighth, Brigadier General Dana Born, served for nine years.

In 1994 the Superintendent, Lieutenant General Hosmer, published a memorandum with the subject "Tour of Duty for Deans of the Faculty at the Air Force Academy." In it he referred to the "unwritten policy" that the Dean would have a fixed tenure of five years, renewable by the Secretary of the Air Force for up to another five years. The memorandum put on record the undocumented policy and made a specific recommendation. General Hosmer stated the policy as follows:

> The policy for the tenure of the Dean of the Faculty at the Air Force Academy should be that a Dean will, in normal circumstances, serve 5 years. The Dean always has the option to retire as a brigadier general, or revert to tenured permanent professor status as a colonel, before his normal tour is concluded. If the Superintendent believes it to be in the best interest of the Academy for the Dean to continue beyond 5 years, and if the Dean is willing, the Superintendent may extend the Dean's tour of duty for additional periods not to exceed a total of 4 years. Such an extension is subject to the agreement of the Secretary of the Air Force.

General Hosmer recommended that this policy be provided in writing to each candidate for the position and that the selected Dean should acknowledge understanding of it.

Beginning with General McDermott, the permanent Dean of the Faculty has been a Permanent Professor who was promoted to the grade of brigadier general as the Dean. The concept started to change in 1992 when 10 U.S.C. §9335 was revised to delete the grade provisions (though not the requirement for selection from the Permanent Professors). But then the law was revised again in 1999 to add those grade provisions back in along with plain language that the brigadier general authorization would count against the service's authorized number of general officers. In 2003, however, Section 9335 was revised to state: "If a person appointed as the Dean is not an officer on active duty, the person shall be appointed as a member of the Senior Executive Service." This change occurred during heightened scrutiny at the Academy for sexual assault reporting and prosecution and perhaps aimed to alter the nature of the faculty and increase the civilian influence there. The 2003 revision also included changing 10 U.S.C. §9331(b)(2) from authorizing a "Dean of the Faculty, who is a permanent professor" to just a "Dean of the Faculty." It is not clear whether a civilian Dean, if one were selected, would be subject to the five-year term limitation.

The policy change to allow for a civilian Dean of the Faculty brought changes to the selection procedure. For the 1998 selection, the possibility of a civilian Dean had been acknowledged, but the law still required the candidates be selected from the Permanent Professors. Rather than accept a list of the top candidates, the Secretary at the time, F. Witten Peters, decided to personally interview the finalists. The Superintendent after convening a selection committee sent three officers to interview with the Vice Chief of Staff and the Secretary. They selected Colonel Dave Wagie, who then served as Dean from 1998 to 2004.

For both of the next selections in 2004 and 2013, the position of the Dean of the Faculty was advertised nationally, and applications were received from civilian as well as military candidates. In 2004 the selection committee identified the most qualified candidates, all of whom were Permanent Professors. After interviews with the Air Force Chief of Staff and the Secretary, the Secretary made the selection. In 2013, 85 applicants responded to the national solicitation for candidates. Of the 10 selected to interview with the selection committee, 2 or 3 were civilians. Colonel Andy Armacost was selected after interviewing with the AF Chief of Staff and Secretary. To date, each of the Deans selected under the new policy, Generals Born and Armacost, came from the ranks of the Permanent Professors.

In 2003, when 10 U.S.C. §9331(b)(2) was amended to explicitly state that the Air Force Academy Dean was not a Permanent Professor, the Army section of Title 10 continued to state the opposite: that the Dean at West Point is a Permanent Professor. Title 10 U.S.C. §4331(b)(2) establishes for the Military Academy "A Dean of the Academic Board, who is a permanent professor," and §4335(a) specifies "The Dean of the Academic Board shall be appointed as an additional permanent professor from the permanent professors who have served as heads of departments of instruction at the Academy." Therefore, while Air Force Chief of Staff General John P. Jumper and Secretary James G. Roche accepted the civilian Dean, the Army leadership rejected the measure, preferring to continue to guarantee in law that the faculty leadership of their Military Academy remain military.

PERMANENT PROFESSOR LEADERSHIP CHALLENGES

Within the first few years of the Academy's founding, the framework for the academic program was created. This included defining the curriculum, building supporting facilities at the interim and permanent sites, finding academic leaders, establishing the academic structure, and hiring the faculty. The construction of the facilities at the temporary site at Lowry Air Force Base, as well as the permanent facilities near Colorado Springs, has been described elsewhere in great detail. Here we take up a discussion of some "persistent challenges"—issues that were never really "solved" but rather required continued attention and refinement over the past 60 years and will likely continue to do so into the future.

The persistent challenges we have identified are the general categories listed here:

- The Leadership Team
  The Permanent Professors
  Faculty Organization
- Faculty Composition and Development
  Military/Civilian Mix
  Faculty Development
  Visiting Faculty
- Accreditation
  Institutional
  Of Specific Disciplines
- Curriculum
  Core Curriculum
  Modernization
  Maintaining a Balance

- Enhancing Cadet Performance
    - Within the Curriculum
    - Ensuring Up-to-Date Technology
    - Summer Programs
    - Graduate School Programs
- Research and Support of the Air Force
    - Organizing for Research
    - Research Centers

We begin the present story with a discussion of how the Air Force Academy faculty was organized at the top level to conduct its mission.

THE LEADERSHIP TEAM

THE PERMANENT PROFESSORS

In September 1959 when the Dean of the Faculty and the first Permanent Professor, Robert McDermott, was promoted to brigadier general as the first permanent Dean, the basic components of the Permanent Professor system were essentially in place. Three other Permanent Professors had been appointed in 1958 and were leading their departments: Bill Woodyard (Chemistry), Pete Moody (English), and Archie Higdon (Mechanics). Jim Wilson (Electrical Engineering) and Chris Munch (Law) would soon follow. The processes for selecting, nominating, and appointing Permanent Professors had been established: nominations from the Academy through the Air Staff and Department of Defense to the President and the Senate. And some of the finer points of the Permanent Professor system had been decided. For instance, the Academy's request to grant sabbatical assignments for Permanent Professors had been approved by HQ USAF in May 1959.

The Academy's seventh Permanent Professor was appointed in the Spring of 1960, Wes Posvar (Political Science), at which time there were six Permanent Professors in place and serving as Department Heads. Except for Woodyard and Higdon, all were graduates of West Point. With only 6 Permanent Professors on hand to lead 15 academic departments, General McDermott moved steadily to fill the vacancies. His goal was to identify the most promising, academically qualified officers for their long-term leadership potential, which often meant selecting younger men rather than the traditional appointment of the most senior officer in the unit. General McDermott moved deliberately, and in the following year three new Permanent Professors were appointed: Wil Ruenheck (History), Al Miele (Foreign Languages), and Wayne Yeoman (Economics).

The photograph here shows the three new appointees, Ruenheck, Miele, and Yeoman, taking the oath of office from General McDermott, on October 24, 1961, while the Academy Superintendent, Major General William S. Stone, looks on.

In 1962 two more Permanent Professors were appointed, George Fagan (Cadet Library) and Roger Bate (Astronautics). Then in 1964, three more officers were appointed as Permanent Professors: Phil Erdle (Mechanics), Ron Thomas (Electrical Engineering), and Mal Wakin (Philosophy). However, these three officers were quite junior in rank; they were Permanent Professors as lieutenant colonels, but they did not assume positions as Department Heads for another year or more. Mal Wakin was the most junior; he was Captain Wakin when appointed and Lieutenant

Colonel Wakin the next day! The goal was to fill all 22 of the authorized Permanent Professor positions as soon as practical. In 1966 another four officers were appointed Permanent Professors: Gil Taylor (Geography), Jesse Gatlin (English), John Mione (Physics), and Al Hurley (History). And in 1967 another four: Em Fluhr (Civil Engineering), Mark Kinevan (Law), Pete Carter (Life Sciences), and Dan Daley (Aeronautics).

At the same time, Permanent Professors were beginning to retire. The first to retire was Jim Wilson, who retired in 1965 (as a brigadier general). Pete Moody and Archie Higdon followed in 1967. Thus, the Permanent Professor dynamic had run its full cycle, from appointment to service to retirement. By the late 1960s, the Permanent Professor program had approached a steady-state condition, namely that searches were mostly for the successors to the original appointees. Of course, that is the situation to this day, where most academic departments have seen four, five, or six Permanent Professors. Actually, the 84 Permanent Professors presently on the retired roster have a cumulative 983 years of service in the positions, for an average of about 12 years each.

A pair of interesting developments almost came to pass in 1966. HQ USAF invited the Academy to consider whether the number of Permanent Professors should be increased, especially in light of the increase in the strength of the Cadet Wing from 2,800 to 4,417. The Dean and Superintendent argued that an increase from 22 to 40 Permanent Professors would be appropriate (the target of 40 authorizations was later reduced to 30). The reasoning for the increase was, in part, that some departments (viz., English and Mathematics) had grown large enough to warrant dividing, many Permanent Professors were away for extended periods (on sabbaticals), and highly important staff positions should be filled full-time by Permanent Professors (e.g., Assistant Dean for Graduate Programs, Assistant Dean for Research, etc.). At the same time, the Academy prepared a proposal to increase the pay of Permanent Professors, based on comparisons with pay of senior professors at universities. Although there already was a modest additional pay of $250 per month for Permanent Professors with more than 36 years of service, it was argued a pay increase was needed as an incentive for Permanent

Professors to stay until age 64. Both of these actions, increase in number and increase in pay, would have required a change to Public Law. Despite some support from the Academy's Board of Visitors, neither action was endorsed by the Air Staff and both issues were dropped; neither has been seriously raised again. With these initiatives set aside, the Permanent Professor system reached its maturity by 1967. All the elements were in place upon which to build for the generations to come.

FACULTY ORGANIZATION

ACADEMIC DEPARTMENTS AND DIVISIONS. During the first year at the interim Academy site, the Dean of the Faculty organized the academic body into seven academic departments: English and Foreign Languages; History; Human Relations (Law, Geography, Philosophy, Psychology); Economics and Government; Mathematics; Chemistry, Physics and Electrical Engineering; and Applied Sciences (Mechanics and Materials, Graphics, Thermodynamics, Aerodynamics). A year later, in August 1956, as the faculty and curriculum were filling out to meet the need for sophomore courses, some new departments were created and then further organized into Academic Divisions.

The four academic divisions were Humanities, Social Sciences, Basic Sciences, and Applied Sciences. A Division Chairman was named for each division. The academic divisions gathered departments of similar academic disciplines to provide mutual support as well as to better coordinate curriculum planning in addition to course integration and development. The Division Chair is a coordinator, not a director, and the sole role is one of leadership in academic matters; the Chair has no supervisory or administrative authority over other departments or courses.

At this time, the leader of each department was officially appointed as a Department Head, where the title was changed from "Chair" to "Head" to emphasize the distinction between the duties of the Chair of a civilian academic department and those of the leader of a military unit. The Department Head encompassed not only the academic duties of the Chair but also the responsibilities associated with military command. Appendix B includes a breakdown of the duties of the Department Heads and Division Chairs.

VICE DEAN OF THE FACULTY. In addition to the academic departments and divisions, the first Dean of the Faculty organized a staff function, which included a Vice Dean, a Deputy Dean, and several support directorates. Colonel Robert F. McDermott was appointed Vice Dean in 1954 and continued as Vice Dean until appointed the Acting Dean in 1956. Subsequently, the position of Vice Dean was abolished for 10 years. Before 1965, some of these duties were handled by an Associate Dean for Academic Affairs, Colonel Jim Wilson. When Jim Wilson retired in 1965 the duties were generally divided between an Associate Dean for Humanities and Social Sciences (Colonel Pete Moody), an Associate Dean for Engineering and Basic Sciences (Colonel Archie Higdon), and an Associate Dean for Educational Services (Colonel Winston Fowler). The reorganization in 1966 established a single position of Vice Dean of the Faculty; Colonel Pete Moody was the first to occupy the position. Since then, the Vice Dean of the Faculty has always been one of the Permanent Professors, who was detailed into the position from their department. A list of the Vice Deans is in Appendix B.

The duties of the Vice Dean of the Faculty are essentially those of a Chief of Staff: to lead the faculty organization in the absence of the Dean, to provide advice to the Dean on all Academy matters, and to supervise the faculty staff agencies. The principal staff agencies supporting the academic mission are Research, Registrar and Student Academic Affairs, Educational Innovation, Cadet Library, and International Programs. These are briefly described in Appendix B.

In 2018 the Dean, Brigadier General Armacost, elected to use the unfilled 23rd Permanent Professor authorization to establish a new staff office, "Vice Dean for Strategy and Curriculum." This became a second Vice Dean, for the traditional Vice Dean of the Faculty position was retained. Effective in the summer of 2018, Colonel Gary Packard was appointed Vice Dean for Strategy and Curriculum and Colonel Troy Harting the Vice Dean of the Faculty. Gary Packard's position was permanent in the sense he would not return to the Department of Behavioral Sciences and Leadership (a new Permanent Professor is to be appointed there).

DEAN OF THE FACULTY. The Dean of the Faculty has the ultimate responsibility for properly administering the academic program. But the Dean shares the authority over academics with the Department Heads, the Faculty Council, the Curriculum Committee, and the Academy Board. The Dean, within policies prescribed by the Superintendent and in consultation with the Permanent Professors, establishes academic policies on organization, curriculum development, scheduling, instructional workloads and standards, and personnel. The Dean is responsible for monitoring the instructional activities of the departments and is the first-line supervisor of each Department Head to whom are delegated virtually all authority for the day-to-day operations of the academic program. In consultation with the Superintendent, the Dean appoints Division Chairs, Department Heads, and chairs of *ad hoc* committees. The Dean frequently interacts with the Commandant of Cadets, the Director of Athletics, and the Superintendent to identify and coordinate the resolution of issues or the pursuit of opportunities that may arise. The Dean is often the face of the faculty to the Board of Visitors, the charitable organizations supporting the Academy, and distinguished visitors to the Academy. The Dean frequently travels to speak to Academy alumni chapters or parents' clubs across the country and is the Executive Agent for the Academy Board.

THE ACADEMY BOARD. The first Academy Board was formed by General Harmon in September 1955 with 6 of the 11 members being faculty. HQ USAF formally established the Air Force Academy Board on January 20, 1956, to consist of the Superintendent, Dean, Commandant, and heads of academic and airmanship departments as appointed by the Superintendent. The Board is the Academy's senior advisory body, chaired by the Superintendent. In its current configuration, the 12 voting members of the Academy Board are the Superintendent, Vice Superintendent, Commandant of Cadets,

Dean of the Faculty, Director of Athletics, the four academic division chairs, Director of Athletic Programs/Physical Education, Vice Commandant, and a Member-at-Large (appointed by the Superintendent). The Board provides advice regarding virtually all aspects of the cadet program. It advises on the selection of each entering cadet and the disposition of deficient cadets (retention or disenrollment). The Board also advises on the academic, military, and physical requirements for graduation and the standards by which cadets are measured, as well as recommending those who meet the requirements for graduation and commissioning. In particular, the Academy Board establishes the academic curriculum (the Curriculum Committee is a standing committee of the Academy Board) for approval by the Superintendent.

FACULTY COMPOSITION AND DEVELOPMENT

MILITARY/CIVILIAN MIX

Discussions of the faculty composition—whether all military or a military/ civilian mix—took place from the beginning of planning for the Academy. There was agreement that faculty in the sciences and engineering disciplines should be military, where the service had a strong base. However, the Air Academy Planning Group and the first Dean, General Zimmerman, preferred to have civilians in the humanities and social sciences. Colonel McDermott, as the Vice Dean, argued persuasively for an all-military faculty and convinced both General Zimmerman and General Harmon to follow that model.

In the summer of 1957 HQ USAF raised the issue again and requested the Academy consider adding civilians to the faculty, but the Superintendent and Dean decided to maintain the all-military position. General McDermott enumerated five reasons why the Air Force Academy should have an all-military faculty (*The Composition of the AFA Faculty*, September 1957):

1. The Air Force can provide a quality faculty from its own ranks. Air Force officers represent a cross-section of all professions with many

thousands of academic degrees and experience in research, management, politico-economics, and teaching.

2. The feasibility of obtaining a qualified civilian faculty is questionable. Due to the remoteness of the Academy and its limited programs, first-rate faculty would gravitate toward bigger universities where they would receive more recognition.

3. High teaching standards are better maintained with a military faculty. Contrary to practices in civilian institutions, military supervisors would visit classrooms, evaluate teaching, and enforce standards of performance.

4. A military faculty motivates a cadet to an Air Force career. The only tangible device to achieve this is to place the best possible officer before the cadets for all four years.

5. A military faculty provides a long-term gain for the Air Force. The knowledge gained by young officers in graduate school and teaching at the Academy would provide better service when they returned to their career field.

These arguments were powerful at the time, and they effectively settled the question in favor of preserving the all-military faculty, at least temporarily.

It is interesting to note whether these arguments retain their strength after the passage of 60 years and from a position of already having added a significant civilian component to the faculty. The first point remains sound—there is a wealth of talent across the Air Force. However, in recent years certain academic fields, the humanities in particular, have struggled to find qualified officer-instructors. Other factors affecting the argument are that AF manning priorities have changed and that the current high operations tempo restricts who can be released for faculty assignments.

The second argument, that it was questionable whether the Academy could attract quality civilians, may have been the case in the 1950s, but the Academy is now adjacent to a large community with much to attract an educated populous. Moreover, the actual experience in hiring quality civilians for the faculty has been very positive. To the third point, the majority of civilians brought on board have readily adapted to the Academy way of mentoring. Both civilians and military go through the same new instructor training, welcome classroom visits by department leadership, and buy into the Air Force team approach.

The fourth argument, about officers being the best role models for cadets, continued to be made years later. Here is how General Woodyard reiterated the point (Faculty Operating Instruction No. 30-4, Faculty Selection, February 1, 1969):

> One key to Academy mission accomplishment is the quality of instructors on the all-military faculty. In his four years at the Academy a cadet spends more hours under closer supervision receiving instruction as a student in a small academic section than he does in any other supervised activity. In this learning situation the instructor teaches not only by what he says but also by who he is. His job is not merely to transmit knowledge but also to impart the qualities of leadership required of an officer in the United States Air Force. The hallmarks of leadership in the military profession are the highest standards of personal integrity, devotion to duty, and dedication to the service of the nation. These ideals are not self-generated; they must be imparted. They can be imparted only by those in frequent contact with the cadets and only to the extent that the instructor is a living example of these ideals. This explains not only why we have an all-military faculty but also why only the finest officers should be privileged to serve on it.

Few would disagree that cadets must be exposed to many officer role models. However, civilians can be good role models, too—role models of citizenship and role models of excellence in many areas.

The final argument from General McDermott's list continues to be reiterated by present-day Permanent Professors when they speak of the Academy's second graduating class—the large group of officers who each year complete their faculty tours and return to the "big Air Force." They take with them valuable experiences and additional insights from their Academy exposure.

The issue of adding civilians to the Academy faculty resurfaced in 1975–1976 and again in 1992, as described more fully in Appendix C. The 1975 economic analysis by the General Accounting Office and a study on educational excellence by the Department of Defense (by the "Clements Committee"), urged adding civilians at the 5 to 10 percent level. However, the issue was effectively set aside again, in part because the Academy had begun a new Distinguished Visiting Professor Program. Finally, in 1992 a Congressional initiative demanded an aggressive civilianization program, and the Secretary of the Air Force responded that the Academy would move toward a goal of 50 percent civilian faculty as quickly as possible.

The Dean formed a working group to develop a program to implement the civilianization effort. The effort was led by Colonel Jim Head, Permanent Professor of Physics. Despite much initial resistance from some, the Permanent Professors outlined the main features of what they believed were essential elements of a successful civilian faculty program. A key issue was no lifetime tenure, as was common in universities and colleges. Rather, the civilians should have term appointments, renewable, much as the military faculty. Next, the faculty wanted great flexibility with position descriptions, review and selection of candidates, and appropriate control over hiring and salary decisions—in short, not the standard Federal government civil servant General Schedule classification and pay system. Colonel Head's team developed the policies and procedures to permit hiring and paying civilian faculty members under an excepted civil service authority similar to that at Air University and the Air Force Institute of Technology. In December 1992, the Superintendent submitted the Academy's plan to go to about 25 percent civilians by 2000 and pause there to evaluate the next phase. The AF Chief of Staff approved the plan, which was provided to Congress in March 1993.

The Civilian Faculty Plan went forward aggressively, with 14 positions advertised for Academic Year 1993–1994, expanded across all academic departments by the fall of 1994, and built steadily to about 25 percent by 2000 (numbers include visiting faculty, normally about 5 percent of total). The program spread across all academic departments, bringing additional disciplinary expertise as well as a more diverse hiring pool. Moreover, the option of hiring civilians brought relief from some of the persistent challenges of military faculty staffing. On many occasions, a temporary military shortfall could be overcome by the availability of a short-term temporary civilian hired for a semester or a year. On other occasions, constant military shortfalls (either in hard-to-fill academic areas or highly stressed military fields) were overcome by permanent military-to-civilian conversions. The overall assessment at the time of the pause in 2000 was that civilians had been a net enhancement for the Academy.

After the target of 25 percent civilians was reached, the civilian faculty numbers continued to grow slowly. The main impetus for the growth of the civilian faculty was the difficulty in filling military faculty positions, especially for rated officers. At the start of the 2017–2018 academic year, the civilian faculty proportion of the total authorized teaching faculty had grown to about 36 percent. Another round of 46 military-to-civilian faculty conversions in 2018 brought the civilian component to 40 percent of the teaching faculty..

Initially the goal was to have 60 percent rated personnel on the Academy faculty; this was later reduced to 50 percent. From the inception the rated officer target was challenging, but rated officers were available for assignment to non-flying duties. By the late 1960s, when the Air Force was at war in Southeast Asia, the Academy experienced increased difficulty in attaining its goal. For rated officers, more than non-rated, a faculty assignment can be regarded as an interruption to their career progression. This is especially true if it has to be preceded by graduate school. Add in the staffing shortages and operational demands in flying fields, and the Academy frequently has had rated faculty positions vacant. Consequently, most of the 46 military-to-civilian conversions for 2018 involved the elimination of a (vacant) rated position in favor of a civilian position that can be filled.

FACULTY DEVELOPMENT

NEW FACULTY ORIENTATION AND INSTRUCTOR TRAINING. The salient feature of the Academy faculty is rapid turnover of the junior military instructors who come for three or four years and return to the Air Force. During the years of the all-military faculty, this group might have amounted to 100–150 new instructors every year. At present, with a sizable civilian faculty, the number of new military faculty members is reduced, but there is a steady stream of newly hired civilians, some of whom also have little teaching experience. Regardless of their teaching experience, both officers and civilians who are "new" to the Academy face the challenge of understanding the institution in which they are going to work. Recognizing these needs, the Dean organized a New Faculty Orientation, and departments conducted New Instructor Training programs.

From at least 1960 to the present, it has been expected that all newly assigned (and returning) faculty attend a New Faculty Orientation program. The purpose is to ensure all personnel understand the mission of the Academy and to explain the facets of the Academy that are unique. Typically, the orientation includes briefings by the Dean and representatives from the Superintendent, Commandant, and Athletic Director. It features presentations on the Cadet Wing, the Honor System, curriculum, scheduling, the library, as well as classroom standards, best teaching practices, and student services.

In addition, each academic department has a training program for new instructors. It is a major team-building activity as well as the best opportunity to impart the key responsibilities, department policies, procedures, standards, and expectations to the new and returning faculty. Experienced faculty can demonstrate lesson planning and appropriate educational pedagogy. New faculty give practice lessons, under supervision, in regular classroom conditions. This is an extremely valuable investment made by each department involving the direct participation of the Permanent Professor/Department Head and many of the department's other senior faculty. Two prominent features of the Academy system, core courses and small class sizes, make this training especially vital.

TENURE. The turnover of military faculty has a downside in that much of the valuable experience they take with them is lost from the Academy. Therefore, a program was instituted in 1964 to ensure some military officers besides the Permanent Professors would be available for extended faculty duty to help sustain continuity in the academic programs. This was the Tenure Associate Professor Program. A limited number of officers, majors and lieutenant colonels, would be authorized to remain on the faculty beyond their initial assignment on renewable four-year tours. The target was for 10 percent of the faculty to be "tenured" (in addition to the Permanent Professors). The increased stability helped sustain the goal of at least 25 percent doctoral degrees on the faculty and enhance accreditation efforts. Tenure associate professors and tenure professors were later called sequential tour officers to more precisely describe the limited nature of their appointments. In 2009 the program was redefined as the Senior Military Faculty (SMF) Program. Officers selected for SMF status, lieutenant colonels and senior majors (by exception), are expected to remain current in their operational discipline by taking yearlong "re-bluing" assignments every five years or so. The combination of Permanent Professors and SMF positions is currently limited to 15 percent of authorized USAFA faculty strength.

SABBATICALS. The sabbatical program at the Academy developed as the number of senior faculty increased. In higher education the term "sabbatical" has come to mean any extended absence in the career of a professor for a specific purpose, say writing a book or traveling for research. At the Air Force Academy, the term also can mean increasing or updating professional military experience. Sabbaticals were authorized for Permanent Professors beginning in 1959, for tenure professors and tenure associate professors in 1966, and, since 1993, for civilian professors and associate professors.

By the early 1960s many of the Academy military faculty members were encouraged to plan for sabbatical assignments. The normal expectation was that one might have a sabbatical after four years of continuous faculty service, and that additional sabbaticals might be authorized every five to seven years thereafter. Some tension developed over the desire for Permanent Professors to take an assignment for "military reorientation" versus the traditional sabbatical assignment. The 1968 Board of Visitors expressed the opinion that reassignment to military duties should not be considered a sabbatical in the accepted academic sense. The distinction between the two types of assignments was clear, but both came to be known as sabbaticals. In sum, Permanent Professors, along with other senior faculty members, were permitted and encouraged to take sabbatical assignments, and almost anything they could imagine would fit under one category or the other.

For the most part, Permanent Professors took few purely academic sabbaticals, but there were some. Pete Moody took a sabbatical to Cambridge University, 1961–1963, where he earned his Doctorate. Wes Posvar was at Harvard, 1962–1964, also earning his PhD. However, there were many who took sabbaticals to military units with a strong academic component. As an example, Bill Woodyard left the Chemistry Department to attend the Industrial College of the Armed Forces in 1961. He later had a tour in Brussels with the European Office of Aerospace Research, 1965–1967, which set up a series of sabbaticals to that office for Permanent Professors in the sciences and engineering, including John Mione, Bob Lamb, Cary Fisher, and Ron Reed.

On the side of a military sabbatical with an academic flavor, Al Hurley initiated and participated in a program to engage Academy officers in supporting the war in Southeast Asia, known throughout the Air Force as Project CHECO (Contemporary Historical Evaluation of Combat Operations). From 1968 to 1972 many Academy officers went to Vietnam and produced over 100 classified studies of the war, researched and written on the scene and drawing on their training to gather information, analyze data, and write clearly. Several Permanent Professors from the humanities participated in Project CHECO, including Carl Reddel and Jesse Gatlin. Dick Rosser was on sabbatical in London, 1969–1971, doing research at the International Institute of Strategic Studies and attending the British Imperial Defence College. General McDermott, while Dean, took a year, 1964–1965, to be on the faculty at Air University. Mike DeLorenzo was Vice Commander, Air Force Research Laboratory, 2001–2003. Bob Giffen was the US Air Attaché to Germany, 1986–1987.

There later developed the concept of an "internal sabbatical," which was an assignment at the Academy, but outside one's department. Prime examples are the many Permanent Professors who left their departments for a year or two while serving as Vice Deans of the Faculty. Another is Jim

Woody who was the Vice Commandant of Cadets for two years. Yet another example is Randy Cubero, who took an internal sabbatical to explore the concept of public-private partnership in developing videodiscs for foreign language learning, sharing technology and profits through a Cooperative Research and Development Agreement. Another is Greg Seely, who for 18 months led the Academy's Installations Directorate.

Visiting Faculty

Distinguished Visiting Professors (DVPs). A program to bring a few prominent civilian professors to the Academy for yearlong visits was initiated for Academic Year 1975–1976 in response to the issues raised by the Clements Committee (see above). The DVP Program grew slowly; by 1985–1986, there were six DVPs on board. Over time, the emphasis and character of the program changed, due largely to budgetary restrictions and partly to the difficulty of attracting the kind of high-level visitors the program initially intended. The Visiting Faculty Program, as it is now called, includes 20 or so visitors each year, nominally one per academic department.

Endowed Chairs. Brigadier General Philip J. Erdle, Permanent Professor, retired, formed the Academy Research and Development Institute (ARDI) in 1984 with the goal of establishing an endowed chair in each USAFA academic department; to date ARDI has endowed eight chairs. Beginning in 2007, the USAFA Endowment has endowed chairs for the Center for Character and Leadership Development. Some details of these endowed chairs are in Appendix C.

Military Officer Exchange Program. Colonel Al Miele, Permanent Professor and Head of Foreign Languages, is credited with initiating the foreign officer exchange program, which brought allied officers as language instructors and provided authenticity and cultural value to enhance the Academy's courses. The exchanges began in the 1960–1961 academic year, with an officer from Peru and one from West Germany, and rapidly expanded in the years that followed. By the time of Colonel Miele's retirement in 1968, the program had included officers from Argentina, Belgium, Bolivia, Chile, France, Germany, Mexico, Peru, Republic of China, and Spain. There were also exchanges of officers from English-speaking countries—Australia, Canada, and the United Kingdom—who taught military training, navigation, and Political Science. The exchange program has ebbed and flowed over the years, subject to manpower policies and funding. For 2017–2018, the list includes Brazil, Germany, Spain, France (in Aeronautics), Korea (in Engineering Mechanics), and Japan (in Military and Strategic Studies).

ACCREDITATION

INSTITUTIONAL ACCREDITATION

Beginning with the first detailed planning for the Air Force Academy in 1948, accreditation always had been an important requirement. Legislative law required West Point and Annapolis to have accreditation in order to grant degrees. It was assumed this provision of the law would be applied to the AF Academy as well. In 1957 Colonel Woodyard, Professor and Head of Chemistry, was appointed by the Superintendent to chair an Accreditation Steering Committee to prepare a self-study required for use by the regional accrediting agency, the North Central Association of Colleges and Schools (NCA). (The group's work to deliver the report by July of 1958 is detailed in Chapter 1.) The accreditation evaluators' report recommending the unusual accreditation of the Academy in April 1959 before its first class had graduated stated: "[M]ission is clear, well understood and supported by all" and "… *esprit de corps* developed in less than four years is… a great tribute to the military and educational leadership of the Academy." The evaluators were "…surprised and gratified that the Air Force Academy places great emphasis on a broad program of general education." They praised the evenly divided attention given to basic and applied sciences and humanities and social science. They saw the need for better accounting practices, for a field house and on-base flying facility, and increased faculty competence as measured by a higher percentage of faculty PhDs who were more evenly distributed among disciplines. However, the latter concern was mitigated in their view by the many officers in the pipeline pursuing PhDs, new faculty orientation and enthusiasm, detailed lesson plans, close senior faculty oversight, and finally by the "…high caliber of the faculty as human beings and military officers." The Academy was granted the maximum accreditation. Although there would be concerns raised in subsequent accreditation evaluations about cadet and faculty workloads, cadet and faculty diversity, faculty research, and available funding, the Academy has always been granted the maximum accreditation term. Each of the five subsequent successful Accreditation Steering Committees has been chaired by a Permanent Professor, as is the current self-study, led by Colonel Dan Uribe, Head of the Department of Foreign Languages. It should be noted that while the bulk of the preparation involves the faculty, there are significant portions of the self-study data that must be obtained from virtually all Academy organizations. More information on these self-study and accreditation reports can be found in Appendix D. A good example of the continuing commitment of Permanent Professors to higher education is retired Permanent Professor Cary Fisher, who was recently elected as a Public Member of the Higher Learning Commission Board of Trustees, the NCA's successor organization.

ACCREDITATION OF SPECIFIC DISCIPLINES

Most academic disciplines have national societies or associations formed for the mutual benefit of educators in those subjects. Some of these have seen the need to provide accreditation of specific degree programs to identify those institutions who meet applicable quality standards. It is desirable for the Academy to seek and achieve accreditation in disciplines where it is available. The Air Force requires accredited degrees for graduates to work in some engineering disciplines.

ENGINEERING PROGRAMS. As soon as the Engineering Sciences major was approved by the Academy Board in 1958, the Permanent Professors in the Engineering Division actively sought accreditation by the Engineering Council for Professional Development (ECPD). The ECPD was founded in 1932 by seven engineering societies and began accrediting engineering programs in 1936. In 1980 the ECPD was renamed the Accreditation Board for Engineering and Technology (ABET) to more accurately describe their emphasis on accreditation. Currently, ABET is supported by 35 professional societies who set standards and provide experts to serve as evaluators. Under the vigorous leadership of Permanent Professor #4, Archie Higdon, the Academy prepared a self-study report and then hosted an evaluation visit. In October 1962 the Engineering Sciences major was accredited. In October 1967 the newly established degree programs in Aeronautical Engineering, Civil Engineering, Electrical Engineering, and Engineering Mechanics were granted initial accreditation, and the Engineering Sciences major was reaccredited. All were for the maximum term. Astronautical Engineering was added to the list of accredited engineering programs when the others were reaccredited in 1973. In 1979 the General Engineering (Divisional) major was accredited, which allowed cadets having problems in a disciplinary engineering major or seeking a broader engineering education to earn an accredited engineering degree. In the following years additional programs were accredited: Mechanical Engineering (1991), Environment Engineering (1997), Computer Engineering (2003), and Systems Engineering (2009). In the nine evaluations following the one in 1962, ABET has accredited all programs for the maximum term, many for several years retroactively. A steering committee of the engineering Permanent Professors, headed up by the Chair of the Engineering Division, has managed the preparation of the self-studies and the evaluation visits. The next ABET evaluation visit will be in 2021. Additional detail on the evaluation findings for each evaluation visit and the leadership provided by the Permanent Professors can be found in Appendix D.

It is interesting to note that several engineering Permanent Professors as well as many other engineering faculty members have devoted much volunteer time over many years to assist, literally worldwide, in the accreditation process. Permanent Professor Cary Fisher has evaluated over 40 Engineering programs.

The example provided by Ron Thomas, Permanent Professor and Head, Department of Electrical Engineering, led two former Air Force Academy Electrical Engineering faculty members who retired as USAF lieutenant colonels to work full-time for ABET. Dr. George Peterson served as the Executive Director of ABET for 15 years. George was succeeded in 2009 by Dr. Michael Milligan, who is currently Chief Executive Officer and Executive Director of ABET. Ron also performed numerous evaluation visits and was honored in 1992 as an ABET Fellow for his accreditation leadership.

COMPUTER SCIENCE PROGRAMS. In response to the anticipated boom in computer science education, ABET helped establish the Computing Sciences Accreditation Board (CSAB) in 1985. That year the Academy's Computer Science program was the first in the nation to be visited for evaluation and was granted accreditation. CSAB merged with ABET in October 2001, and the Computing Accreditation Commission of ABET now accredits Computer Science and related programs. The Academy's Department of Computer Science was renamed Computer and Cyber Sciences in 2017 to reflect the increasing emphasis on cyber operations, and it was administratively moved to the Engineering Division. Consequently, the accreditation cycle for the programs in Computer Science and Computer and Network Security (accredited in 2016) has been synchronized with that of the Academy's engineering programs.

As Department Head for Computer Science, Permanent Professor Bill Richardson worked vigorously to modernize and formalize the discipline at the Academy and across the nation. He was ultimately named Chairman of the Computer Science Accreditation Board. He was honored as a CSAB Fellow for his leadership in the early years of Computer Science as it grew into a widely recognized academic discipline. Retired Permanent Professor David Gibson currently serves on the Executive Committee of ABET's Computing Accreditation Commission, and retired Lieutenant Colonel Larry Jones, inspired by Bill Richardson, served as ABET President, 2014–2015.

CHEMISTRY. The American Chemical Society (ACS) accredits the Academy's Chemistry, Biochemistry, and Materials Chemistry options taught by the Department of Chemistry. The first accreditation for Chemistry in November 1967 was due to the efforts of Permanent Professor and Head, Department of Chemistry, Bill Woodyard. The Department of Chemistry has maintained accreditation (now called approval for certification) ever since by submitting an annual report with a periodic report due every six years to the ACS Committee on Professional Training. A site visit may be requested by the Committee.

MANAGEMENT. Permanent Professor Rita Jordan led the effort that in 2001 gained the initial accreditation for the Management major by the Association to Advance Collegiate Schools of Business (AACSB). Air Force was the first service academy to gain this accreditation. The Management Department has maintained this accreditation by completing a continuous improvement review process that includes a self-study and evaluation visit every five years.

NATIONAL COLLEGIATE ATHLETIC ASSOCIATION CERTIFICATION

The NCAA certifies higher education athletic programs to ensure integrity in the institution's athletics program and compliance with NCAA rules and regulations as well as to help athletic departments improve. NCAA legislation mandating athletics certification was adopted by members in 1993. The certification process required a self-study by the institution that covered governance and commitment to rules compliance, academic integrity, gender/diversity issues, and student athlete well-being. After reviewing the self-study, the NCAA performed a site visit with the results of study review and visit reported to the NCAA Committee on Athletics Certification. The first Academy Self-Study Steering Committee was chaired by Permanent Professor Bob Giffen in 1989; the second study was led by Permanent Professor Hans Mueh in 1999. Permanent Professor Tom Yoder chaired the third one in 2009 with certification received in March 2011. The current NCAA process requires an annual report that the Athletics Department's Compliance Office provides. No other reports or visits are required as long as an institution remains in compliance.

CURRICULUM AND CURRICULUM CHANGES

Chapter 1 describes the development of the curriculum up through the approval of academic majors for the Classes of 1959 and 1960. This section provides a short recap and goes on to describe major curricular changes in the ensuing years. The next section describes some other initiatives intended to enhance the cadets' opportunities to excel.

The Permanent Professors bear the major burden of maintaining an academic curriculum to meet the needs of the Air Force and maintain accreditation. In addition, the overall academic workload must be managed within the total demands on a cadet's time, which also include military training, physical education, sports, and military leadership roles within the Cadet Wing. The core curriculum is designed to prepare all cadets for a lifetime of dedicated service to the nation. The Professors also must design, deliver, and maintain relevant major courses of study that meet the Air Force's needs and are meaningful to the cadets. Balancing the academic demands of a specialized field of study with the broad educational objectives of the core is a persistent challenge. While this section only describes major changes in the curriculum, it is of interest that the Curriculum Committee, whose membership is more than 80 percent Permanent Professors, considers well over 100 proposed changes to the curriculum every year. Each is carefully analyzed to ensure that the potential impact on the core, individual majors, and cadet workload is acceptable.

CORE CURRICULUM

> The core curriculum "is rooted in the best traditions of the past, taught in the context of the present, and continually reexamined in the light of the future needs of the Air Force."
>
> —Maj Gen James E. Briggs, USAFA 2nd Superintendent

The prescribed curriculum approved on April 29, 1954, for the first class of cadets had nearly equal semester hours of social sciences and humanities when compared to those for basic sciences and engineering. This balance has been a key feature in the core curriculum since early planning began in 1948 and still remains so. This principle has been reaffirmed and validated by each of the many external reviews conducted since 1949. The first cadets that entered in the summer of 1955 faced a completely prescribed curriculum, but as explained in this section, much flexibility has been introduced to interest and challenge the cadets while still ensuring that all graduates meet common core educational learning objectives, now called learning outcomes.

The rigidity of this first curriculum is illustrated in the photo to the right showing the Dean of the Faculty, Brigadier General McDermott, before a permanent display of the curriculum. This initial lack of flexibility soon changed, but the balance in the core has remained. One measure of the maturation of the curriculum is that the USAFA Catalog completely describing the application, appointment, and entrance testing as well as the curriculum for Academic Year 1955–1956 was 51 pages, whereas the 2017–2018 *Curriculum Handbook* describing only the curriculum and associated procedures is now 386 pages.

There was an almost overwhelming emphasis on refining the curriculum in the early years. For example, there were three major changes to the curriculum during the first year of classes, Academic Year 1955–1956. The external Academy Curriculum Review Board comprising general officers and chaired by Major General Briggs that met in February 1956 recommended one of these changes. After reviewing the Board's recommendations, the faculty changed the semester hours for eleven courses and added two courses, a 2-semester-hour course in Aircraft Design Appreciation and 10 semester hours of foreign language (French or Spanish).

However, in 1957 General Briggs, now the Superintendent, cautioned the members of the Academy Board that it was time to stop listening to outside reviewers and let the curriculum stabilize. Changes still occurred, though, with the elimination of the core navigation program with the Class of 1961 and the May term that had been devoted to military training. At the same time navigation training was moved to the Dean of the Faculty as was the Commandant's classroom leadership training, which resolved one of the concerns raised by the accreditation report in 1959.

MODERNIZATION

ENRICHMENT PROGRAM. Although the Academy's initial curriculum was modeled after that of West Point, the faculty was quick to recognize the need to allow cadets to enrich and accelerate their education. The West Point faculty had provided a formal Advanced Academic Program for qualified cadets for several years, but their curriculum was still fully prescribed with no other enrichment opportunities. Colonel Higdon had successfully experimented with advanced mathematics courses during the first semester in Fall 1954. This led to advanced courses in mathematics, chemistry, English, and graphics in the fall of 1956 and the Enrichment Program proposed by Colonel McDermott and approved in the spring of 1957. The Enrichment Program provided four basic ways to enrich the cadets' academic program: (1) transfer credit, (2) validation credit, (3) substitution of an advanced course for a prescribed course, and (4) overload, by voluntarily taking one or more courses beyond the normal semester requirement.

Many consider this USAFA Enrichment Program the trigger for the most significant academic achievement in the history of the Academy. Its significance can be understood because it led to the introduction of academic majors, and increased graduate school opportunities, as well as to adoption of majors at the other military academies.

OPTIONAL MAJORS. All cadets were expected to carry equal six-course loads each semester, so cadets with validation or transfer credits could concentrate on a discipline by filling vacancies with selected courses and/or overloading. Thus, the Enrichment Program led in 1958 to the approval of three defined majors. Other majors could be constructed by a cadet working with a Department Head who then obtained approval by the Faculty Council and the Dean. Other majors were added and approved. When the first class graduated in 1959, over 11 percent of the class had earned a major in Basic Science, Engineering Sciences, English, or Public Affairs. The success of these programs prompted General McDermott in October 1959 to propose that the Academy provide graduate training and grant Master's degrees. Although the proposal was supported by the faculty, the Academy Board, the Superintendent, and the Air Staff, it ultimately failed because it was strongly opposed by the other academies and the Air Force Institute of Technology. For the Class of 1960, majors in Aeronautical Engineering and Humanities were added, and nearly 30 percent of the class earned a major. By the time the Class of 1965 graduated, the Academy had made available additional majors in History, Management, and Astronautical Engineering (the latter was the first undergraduate degree in that discipline in the country). It is a testament to cadet academic ambition that nearly 86 percent of the Class of 1965 took 18 to 22 semester hours beyond the core to earn a major, and more than 8 percent of the class had earned two majors.

MAJORS FOR ALL. The next innovation, in 1964, was the "majors for all" program wherein all cadets beginning with the Class of 1966 would earn an academic major. Additional core options had been added increasing the total to four, to be chosen from a limited list. Graduates in 1966 earned degrees in nine academic disciplines, and nearly12 percent of the graduates earned two majors. However, it soon became clear that it was unrealistic for every cadet to complete all requirements for a disciplinary major within the allotted four years. In order to allow otherwise worthy cadets to graduate, the Academy Board created divisional majors for the Class of 1967 and subsequent. This provided a path to graduation for a cadet who failed a required course in a disciplinary major but still had sufficient credits to graduate. Further flexibility was provided in 1975 when, effective with the Class of 1979, the Academy Board was able to graduate a cadet without an academic major under unusual circumstances. The "majors for all" requirement was discontinued in 1981, when the Basic Academic Program was introduced and majors became optional.

However, almost all cadets graduate with a disciplinary major. In the Class of 2014 only 3 out of 1,073 had no major while 25 had double majors. More than 30 majors are now offered, including 6 interdisciplinary majors. The table in Appendix E identifies majors by the year they were introduced. The current majors are listed with their sponsoring department(s) in Chapter 4.

MAINTAINING A BALANCE

Major curriculum changes normally occurred because of significant program reviews, which are described briefly below. A table with additional details is in Appendix E. From the very beginning the Air Force Academy has welcomed the advice of civilian educators as consultants. These include committees or boards convened by Congress, the Department of Defense, or the Air Force; the Academy's Board of Visitors; and the numerous accreditation evaluations. All have had a varying degree of influence on the curriculum. Virtually all external input has strongly supported the basic principle of a core curriculum balanced between humanities and social sciences on the one hand and basic sciences and engineering on the other.

During 1969–1970, an *ad hoc* committee of the Curriculum Committee completed a comprehensive review of the core curriculum. One driver was the desire for all flight-qualified cadets to be able to complete the Pilot Indoctrination Program using the T-41 aircraft without having to overload. The Curriculum Committee recommended, and the Academy Board approved, a core course reduction from 38 to 36 courses (105 to 99 semester hours) effective with the Class of 1974. This also entailed changes to practically all majors' programs, specifying fewer hard requirements and allowing more cadet choice of major course options.

In 1973–1975 the internal *20th Anniversary Study*, under the leadership of Permanent Professor Phil Erdle, was a complete introspective examination of every program affecting the cadet way of life. The study's Curriculum Review Committee was six Permanent Professors and two additional officers representing military training and physical education.

The study reaffirmed the principle of the core, the balance within the core, and the majors' programs. After considering nearly 200 proposals, the Curriculum Committee approved changes that became fully effective with the Class of 1980. At this time, to provide the cadets more flexibility and choice, four divisional majors (Humanities, Social Sciences, Engineering, Basic Science) were created. A new Aviation Science major was also introduced for classes from 1978 to 1985 with the same reduced major's requirements as the divisional majors. To address cadet workload the academic graduation requirement was reduced from 145½ semester hours (53 courses) to 138 or 144 semester hours (46 to 48 courses), depending upon the major chosen. This reduction was obtained by reducing majors' requirements to 27 semester hours for the divisional majors or 33 for the interdisciplinary and disciplinary majors. However, based on AF requirements five courses were added to the core: Modern Physics, Material Engineering, Engineering Design, English, and Management, which increased the core from 99 to 111 semester hours. An additional change in the attempt to increase science and engineering graduates was to move core engineering courses so cadets encountered them in earlier semesters. Changes also included adoption of equal-length semesters beginning in Fall 1976 (previously 15 weeks fall and 18 weeks spring), reduction of the daily schedule from seven 50-minute periods to six 60-minute periods, and establishment of a flight core requirement for all cadets (T-41 or Aviation Fundamentals for non-rated). To facilitate the latter and allow more time for cadets in high leadership positions, cadets became eligible to take a course in the summer prior to their final year to reduce their course load. The implementation of equal 42-lesson semesters had far-reaching consequences as it increased scheduling flexibility and reduced course preparation and printing costs. Fall semester examinations prior to the Christmas break were retained.

The next significant internal review was the *25th Anniversary Review Committee* in 1979. Using results of this study, the "majors for all" requirement was relaxed and cadets were then able to choose, or be directed to, the Basic Academic Program, or BAP. The BAP had the fewest number of courses and semester hours required for graduation. Its purpose was to "provide another form of academic self-determination for cadets." Among other things it allowed for special concentrations to make an individual more competitive for medical school or a specific graduate scholarship opportunity. It also offered a graduation alternative for cadets unable to complete a major in four years.

In 1985–1986 a major curriculum review that focused on the relevancy of each core course produced changes that provided greater flexibility for the cadets and departments to structure their majors. A reduction in the core from 37 to 30 courses (111 to 90 semester hours) was conditioned on the departments providing more elective courses within their majors' requirements and giving every cadet at least one completely unspecified optional course. Thus, elective courses increased to 15 (45 semester hours) in the divisional majors and 16–18 (48–54 semester hours) in the disciplinary majors. In some cases, the former core courses had to be added to the major's course requirements. For example, two mathematics courses deleted from the core were still required in several engineering, interdisciplinary, and basic sciences majors. The principle of a "tracked core" was also introduced, which provided different versions of core courses depending on the cadet's major. These were generally tailored with one version for humanities and social sciences majors and the other for basic sciences and engineering, although which version was required for a major was left to the departments (with Curriculum Committee approval.)

The decade 1990–2000 saw no major reviews of the curriculum other than those by accrediting organizations. However, there was a series of changes to the core. In 1991 a graduation requirement for a grade point average of at least a 2.00 (C) in the core courses was established to ensure basic competency in the core subject matter. Also notable was increased emphasis on foreign languages. In 1994 the introductory courses increased from 4½ to 6 semester hours with contact time increased to daily meetings. In 1997 the requirement for two semesters of language regardless of major was restored for all cadets unless they passed a proficiency test.

The Dean, Brigadier General Randy Cubero, started identification of learning outcomes at the Academy in the mid-1990s. Measuring achievement of self-identified outcomes became the method used by the accrediting agencies ABET and HLC/NCA during the 2000s. The Academy developed outcomes for all facets of the cadet experience. Now each course or activity was expected to state their learning goals and objectives in terms of outcomes. In turn, core courses were required to show how their outcomes contributed to the Academy outcomes that defined what all cadets should have learned by graduation. This activity was led Academy-wide by Permanent Professor Tom Yoder. Of course, within each department a review of every course was led by the Permanent Professor/Department Head, assisted by the department's curriculum committee and each course director. These outcome-based analyses drove curriculum changes beginning in the mid-2000s.

A major curriculum change was accomplished during 2002–2004 for the Classes of 2006 and subsequent. The Air Force stated a need for more basic science and engineering graduates, and it was hoped that a "leveling of the playing field" would encourage more cadets to enroll in majors in those fields. Total semester hour requirements were reduced to 141 for divisional majors and 147 for disciplinary and interdisciplinary majors. This change maintained a reasonably balanced core curriculum, while reducing the total core requirements, and provided more choice and flexibility in the majors' programs. Previously constrained majors created more options, and all disciplinary and interdisciplinary majors now required the same number of courses. The change added a core leadership course but still reduced the core academic curriculum from 94 to 91 semester hours and accommodated the new Academy Flight Screening Program. The new core curriculum required 48 semester hours in basic sciences/engineering and 43 semester hours in humanities/social sciences. To recognize the global Air Force mission, the foreign language exposure increased for many cadets by requiring four semesters of language for all humanities and social science majors regardless of skill level. With the increased emphasis on outcomes, the goal of producing leaders of character was affirmed by requiring successful participation in each of the character development programs that were tailored by the Commandant for each class.

The Basic Academic Program was discontinued with the Class of 2000 and "majors for all" returned. However, it soon became evident that an alternative to the BAP was needed, and the Bachelor of Science Program (BSP) was adopted. The BSP is an alternate path to graduation below the divisional majors' requirements with 132 semester hours required. The BSP has entry restrictions and results in a Bachelor of Science degree with no major, again ending the "majors for all" requirement with the Class of 2007.

During 2006–2008 a "transformed" curriculum was approved and implemented for the Class of 2011 and subsequent. Two years of curriculum transformation efforts at the Academy developed the following significant changes: added Portuguese as the eighth foreign language taught at the Academy, added a 1-semester-hour First Year Experience course designed to develop cadet skills and knowledge to successfully and responsibly engage in the learning process, and replaced two engineering core courses with a *Science and Technology Energy/Systems Core Option* and the other with a first-year course, Introduction to Air Force Engineering, to better attract engineering majors through an experience earlier in the curriculum. As part of this transformation, the Academy Board also approved the institutional USAFA Outcomes content, which included all seven Educational Outcomes, and the outcomes development and assessment processes. These processes included breaking down the high-level outcomes into four supporting tiers of ever-increasing specificity and detail. In turn, this created many minor curriculum changes as lower level USAFA Outcomes were incorporated into core course descriptions in the *Curriculum Handbook*. The outcomes process has led to increasing integration among the core courses and greater assurance that each course builds on previous courses and cadets can be held accountable for their prior learning experiences.

During the Academic Year 2008–2009 the Academy revised the USAFA Outcomes content, revised the outcomes development and assessment processes, and established the unmanned aerial systems (UAS) course sequence composed of a summer airmanship course and two UAS upgrade courses. The next academic year divisional core equivalent courses were established to provide flexibility in awarding credit for coursework completed by USAFA cadets during Study Abroad, International Exchange, and Service Academy Exchange programs. In 2011 a new major in Philosophy was established, and the next year saw a new major in Applied Mathematics. Also in 2012 a major change was developed by the Division Chairs to closely align the core courses with the Academy Outcomes. The Curriculum Committee concluded more work was needed and the proposal was not supported. This alignment would become a major feature of the next major revision. The requirement for all cadets to complete two semesters of foreign languages was reinstated in 2015, and the four divisional majors were replaced by a General Studies major in which a cadet chooses a coherent course of study in engineering, basic sciences, humanities, or social sciences.

External forces drove the next major curriculum change. The Congress imposed budget sequestration constraints that led to elimination of 35 faculty manpower positions. In turn, the core curriculum was reduced by three courses. While realigning the core curriculum with the Academy Outcomes, some courses were increased in credit from 3.0 semester hours to 3.5, 4.0, or 4.5 semester hours. The net change was from 32 academic courses (96 semester hours) to 29 courses (93 semester hours). The changes approved in 2017 became fully effective with the Class of 2021. Adjustments were needed for the Classes of 2019 and 2020 during the transition to the new curriculum. Much effort was expended to ensure that each course in the new core curriculum supports the nine Academy Outcomes:

- Critical Thinking
- Application of Engineering Methods
- Scientific Reasoning and the Principles of Science
- The Human Condition, Culture, and Societies
- Leadership, Teamwork, and Organizational Management
- Clear Communication
- Ethics and Respect for Human Dignity
- National Security of the American Republic
- Warrior Ethos as Airmen and Citizens

The new core curriculum consists of 29 Dean of Faculty academic courses (93 semester hours), 10 Athletic Department physical education courses (5 semester hours), 1 course each year administered by the Center for Character and Leadership Development, a significant number of Commandant of Cadets military training and leadership courses and programs, and airmanship courses that require satisfactory completion. In addition to the academic core, all cadets take an academic major (42–51 semester hours beyond the core) or the Bachelor of Science Program (30 semester hours beyond the core).

The new core consists of courses at the foundational, intermediate, and advanced levels, all carefully designed to support one or more of the above outcomes while providing a closely knit, coherent core course of study. It includes carefully constructed options for cadets to select courses at the two upper levels. Foundational courses are prescribed. At the intermediate level the cadet must choose one of three mathematics courses or a behavioral sciences two-course sequence to learn statistical reasoning in support of the "Critical Thinking Outcome." The second intermediate level option is a choice of two out of three basic science courses that support the outcome "Scientific Reasoning and the Principles of Science." The advanced level options are three choices within two "baskets" of upper division offerings. Each course among these choices is aligned with educational outcomes as described below. Basket Choice #1 is the *Advanced Science, Technology, Engineering, and Math (STEM) Option*, where cadets pick one course from a list of courses that support "Application of Engineering Methods" or "Scientific Reasoning and the Principles of Science." Basket Choice #2 is the *Advanced Sociocultural Option*, where cadets pick one course from a list of courses that support "The Human Condition, Cultures, and Societies," "Leadership, Teamwork, and Organizational Management," "Ethics and Respect for Human Dignity," "National Security of the American Republic," or "Warrior Ethos as Airmen and Citizens." Choice #3 is the *Advanced Open Option* where cadets choose any course from either Basket #1 or #2. In terms of relative balance, the new core curriculum requires 13 basic sciences and engineering courses (43 semester hours) and 14 humanities and social sciences courses (44 semester hours), including Basket Choices #1 and #2.

Enhancing Cadet Performance

The principal enhancements in the curriculum relating directly to the core and majors were described above. The present section describes some curriculum enhancements of a more general nature as well as many other opportunities created by the Permanent Professors for cadets to excel.

Enhancements within the Curriculum

Independent Study Courses. Every cadet with a schedule that allows an open elective course and adequate academic standing may pursue independent study of a subject approved by a faculty mentor and the Department Head. The independent study elective for credit became available through a curriculum change effective for the Class of 1966. These studies can be set up for 1, 2, or 3 semester hours of credit. The courses range from individual study and tutorial on a specific topic, to intensive reading and analysis, to creative writing, or even to independent laboratory research. Each independent study normally culminates in a written report. Over the past several academic years, independent study courses averaged about 425 enrollments per year, usually for 3 semester hours of credit, and mostly by senior cadets in the spring semester. This is in addition to the capstone courses described below.

Capstone Courses. Capstone design courses have been an integral part of each engineering major, as well as majors such as Behavioral Sciences and Operations Research, because of the widely recognized need by industry and the armed services for such experience. Engineering (Engr) 400 was introduced in 1976 as a design course required for all cadets. Design challenges were presented to each cadet section, who worked as a team to thoroughly research the design problem, possible solutions, and methods for implementing their chosen solution. Engr 400 was often cited by graduates after several years of service as one of the most, if not the most valuable course they had taken. Regardless, pressure to achieve other learning outcomes led to the demise of Engr 400 (later Engr 410) as a core requirement in 2005. However, since then capstone courses have been added to many majors to provide cadets the opportunity to integrate and apply their knowledge by solving realistic problems. Most Academy majors now have a capstone course requirement, known variously as *Capstone Design, Capstone Seminar, Capstone Research, Capstone Practicum,* or even *Capstone Thesis.* Following the process used by their discipline, cadets as individuals or often in teams perform research to fulfill the requirement presented to them. An individual or team of faculty will mentor the cadets as they progress through the one- or two-semester course. Most teams are now interdisciplinary, so valuable lessons on leadership, followership, and team dynamics are also learned.

AUDITING.   Another way for cadets to enrich themselves is by auditing courses. Upper-class cadets may audit a non-core course with permission of the appropriate Department Head. Obviously, the cadet may not later take for credit any course they audited (or even began to audit). The expectation is that the auditor will do some preparation for the course but will not participate in graded assignments or take examinations.

SPACE, UAV, AND RPA OPERATIONS.   With the sophistication of Academy research in space, unmanned aerial vehicles (UAVs), and remotely piloted aircraft (RPA) cadets are afforded many opportunities to develop valuable operational skills. A Basic Space Operations course allows cadets to staff the Academy ground station, leading to certification as space operators for the FalconSat program and awarding of basic space operations wings. Cadets in other courses can do ground school and pilot training with small UAVs and RPAs, leading to Flight Test Operator status. Over 300 cadets per year are participating in these programs.

ACADEMIC HONORS PROGRAM.   A new academic Honors Program was added to the Academy's curriculum in Fall 1980. It was not an honors major but instead offered the participating cadets special honors versions of existing core courses. The program was voluntary and offered the benefit of having an enhanced classroom environment and the opportunity to graduate "with Honors." The Honors Program was discontinued with the Class of 1993, but some departments continued offering honors sections of core courses for another decade. The opportunity of gathering the best students into special sections of courses resurfaced with the Academy Scholars Program.

ACADEMY SCHOLARS PROGRAM. Beginning with the Class of 2007, each cadet who completes the requirements of the Academy Scholars Program graduates as an Academy Scholar. The Scholars Program was instituted by the Dean, Brigadier General Born, to better develop a pool of intellectually inspired and well-rounded scholarship candidates who would be comfortable in scholarship competitions. The program aims to help selected volunteer cadets reach their full potential by offering a challenging path through the core curriculum starting in their second semester. The Scholars curriculum initially consists of special core course sections (core substitutes) that deepen the scholars' intellectual development, primarily in the liberal arts. Cadets who wish to take Academy Scholars courses, but who are not formally in the program, may do so on a space-available basis with the approval of the program director. The pedagogical principle of this enrichment program involves forming small learning communities (a cohort of cadets enrolled in the same sections) to provide close interaction among the same students over a four-year period, in courses pursuing a coherent theme—the development of the Western intellectual tradition. The Permanent Professors play a key role by early identification of cadets for the program. At present about 50 cadets per year graduate with the Academy Scholar distinction. Most of the cadets who win nationally competitive scholarships come from the Scholars group.

FOREIGN EXCHANGE PROGRAMS. A significant element of enhancing cadet experiences is the Foreign Exchange Program, which has enabled thousands of cadets to travel and study abroad and to interact with foreign cadets at the Air Force Academy. It all started with the cadet exchange program with *l'École de l'Air*, the French Air Force Academy, initiated by Permanent Professor Al Miele as a way to strengthen the bonds of friendship and understanding between the two Air Forces at a time when France was distancing itself from NATO. In 1969 nine USAFA cadets from the Class of 1970 were sent to Salon-de-Provence for the fall semester and six French cadets came to USAFA. This successful exchange has continued for nearly 50 years, with up to eight cadets exchanged each way, each year.

That insightful beginning demonstrated the benefits of offering cadets opportunities to study a foreign language in a foreign culture, and its success encouraged other efforts. The Academy has now substantially expanded exchange opportunities and includes opportunities for a semester of study at foreign universities as well as military academies. For the semester abroad programs, each candidate must demonstrate how the specific courses in the semester abroad fit into the requirements of their academic major. For the Academic Year 2017–2018, 36 Academy cadets went for a semester to foreign academies in Brazil, Canada, Chile, Colombia, France, Germany, Japan, Singapore, and Spain; and USAFA welcomed a similar number of semester exchange cadets from these countries. Another 22 cadets studied for a semester at civilian universities in Brazil, China, Georgia, Japan, Mexico, and Morocco.

ENSURING UP-TO-DATE TECHNOLOGY

When the academic building, Fairchild Hall, was constructed at the permanent site, it was equipped with a closed-circuit television system that distributed to each classroom and lecture hall. This provided the faculty a unique capability that they exploited to enhance cadet learning.

The first classes of cadets were issued slide rules to assist them in making calculations in technical courses. The Department of Mathematics was responsible for teaching cadets how to use the slide rules and had large, 6-foot-long demonstration models in the classrooms as seen in the photo.

When the Frank J. Seiler Research Laboratory was established at the Academy in 1962, it installed a mainframe computer partly justified to support the Academy. Soon, terminals were being used to teach computer programming, to access the library's card catalog, for research, and for other academic and administrative tasks. By 1988 the Directorate of Academic Computing Services under the Dean of the Faculty operated 14 minicomputers, which had replaced the large mainframe, as well as several microcomputer and terminal laboratories. In addition, there were several analog computers for certain calculations in engineering and physics.

After the invention of the handheld electronic calculator, the faculty turned away from slide rules and issued scientific calculators to cadets entering in 1976. Calculator capabilities evolved very rapidly due to their commercial success. To stay abreast of the rapid changes, the faculty convened a committee each year to select the calculator for the incoming cadet class. The introduction of calculators presented challenges for both cadets and faculty. As calculators expanded cadets' computational ability, the faculty revised approaches to both homework and testing as well as grading standards. Calculators remain the cadets' personal computational devices today, with every cadet being issued a scientific calculator sufficient for all core courses. More advanced calculators are required for some majors and are purchased individually by cadets majoring in those disciplines.

Personal computers began to be available around 1980. As personal computers became widely used, local area networks (LANs) were developed to allow transfer of documents and data among network users. Permanent Professor John May led a faculty committee in 1983 that developed the concept of a campus-wide LAN connecting faculty and cadet personal computers (now called microcomputers). Once approved, the Academy's Communications Squadron became responsible for implementing this "Microcomputers in the Dormitories" project. Their design called for one mainframe computer, one printer, and one government microcomputer in each cadet dormitory room, all connected by a LAN with two connections to the mainframe. Permanent Professor Lindy Royer, with his Air Force systems development background, questioned this design, and the responsibility for the system soon moved to the faculty under Colonel Royer's leadership. An *ad hoc* team, which included future Permanent Professor Lieutenant Colonel Bill Richardson and others in the Department of Computer Science, conducted a comprehensive require‑ ments analysis and developed performance‑based system requirements. A key feature was that each cadet would be issued a microcomputer as their personal property, which they would take with them when they graduated. This ensured that each entering class would have current microcomputer technology. With considerable assistance from the Air Force Communications Command, which provided several million dollars of funding, a contract was awarded for the LAN in September 1985 and construction started.

Concurrently, an Academy faculty member was advising an Air Force Systems Command procurement action to furnish microcomputers for the entire DoD. This contract was awarded to the Zenith Corporation in early 1986. The Academy team negotiated for the cadet systems, one shown at the right, the additional capability to receive and dis‑ play television. This enabled the faculty to distribute video materials directly to cadet dormitory rooms. This campus‑wide fac‑ ulty‑to‑student communication capability was the first of its kind in the world. With West Point and Annapolis following the Air Force lead and providing microcom‑ puters to their cadets and midshipmen, most of the first microcomputers pro‑ duced by Zenith in early 1986 went to the academies for their classes of 1990.

The Academy moved carefully and deliberately as it adopted tech‑ nology to enrich each cadet's academic experiences. The first LAN was constructed of coaxial cable to avoid technical risk. Permanent Professor Bill Richardson led an upgrade of the LAN in 1992 that used fiberoptic cable. Wireless routers were added later and now provide cadets access to the LAN and internet everywhere on campus. Likewise, there has always been readily available technical support for cadets, with loner slide rules, calculators, and computers to issue if the cadet's item cannot be repaired on the spot. Network access and software support was and is provided by easily accessible, walk-in service desks. Currently, a software image is prepared by the faculty and loaded on each cadet and faculty computer that provides a common office software suite as well as other software required by the curriculum. A faculty committee solicits bids and chooses microcomputers for each class just as they do for the calculators. The cadet computer purchases have kept up with the technology, so recent classes have been issued a tablet, notebook, or "two-in-one" tablet/notebook. Now cadets bring their computers to class, clearly not possible originally, as illustrated by the photos.

SUMMER PROGRAMS

FIELD ENGINEERING AND READINESS LABORATORY (FERL). The FERL was established in 1994 by Colonel Dave Swint, Permanent Professor and Head, Department of Civil Engineering. He envisioned exposing students to hands-on experiences with heavy equipment, surveying, construction methods, and construction materials, thereby providing motivation and a solid foundation for learning scientific theory and engineering design principles in more advanced courses. With support from the Air Force Civil Engineering community, he acquired funds to build and equip the laboratory, and he implemented a summer program for Civil Engineering majors. FERL is now a nationally unique 50-acre facility, demonstrating a systems approach to learning that bridges the gap between theory and practice—a concept that has evolved into the "construct first, design later" methodology for engineering education. The lab's design and construction activities produce housing for Native Americans and integrate cadet education with readiness training and community service. It also provides facilities to support cadet and faculty research. Mentoring is provided by department faculty, augmented with civil engineering craftsmen from the Air Force Reserve Command.

CADET SUMMER RESEARCH PROGRAM (CSRP). The CSRP permits a limited number of First Class cadets to spend part of their last Academy summer working on research projects at various military and governmental research facilities. It started informally in the summer of 1964, when eight cadets accompanied officers on summer consultations to Air Force agencies. Based on the good reports, the formal CSRP program was launched in 1966 with 43 cadets participating (26 to Air Force agencies, 15 to aerospace industries, and 5 to NASA). The costs of these programs were paid by the host organization. By giving up some or all of their summer leave, the participating cadets can extend for four to six weeks of research time. Often, the summer projects for officers and cadets would continue at a lower level upon return to the Academy. For the past few years about 240 cadets have traveled for CSRP each summer. Top cadet researchers from the summer program are nominated for the Thomas D. Moore Award, and the winner is recognized by a senior Air Force researcher during a ceremony each fall. Named for Major Thomas D. Moore, a former Professor of Physics and Electrical Engineering at the Academy, this award celebrates the outstanding work of cadets during the Cadet Summer Research Program.

LANGUAGE IMMERSION. In 2017, 140 cadets participated in summer foreign language immersion programs in the eight languages taught at the Academy. Selected cadets spent the first summer period studying in Brazil, Chile, China, France, Germany, Japan, Latvia, Mexico, Morocco, Panama, Portugal, Senegal, Spain, and Ukraine.

GRADUATE PROGRAMS

SCHOLARSHIPS. Cadet Bradley C. Hosmer, the top graduate in the Academy's first class, 1959, won a Rhodes Scholarship (later as a lieutenant general, he returned to the Academy as its 12th Superintendent and first graduate to command his alma mater, 1991–1994). Every year since, Air Force Academy cadets have competed for and won prestigious national scholarships. The Academy's most recent Rhodes Scholar, its 39th, is Jaspreet Singh from the class of 2018. Winning prestigious national scholarships, like the Rhodes, draws much positive attention to the Academy and validates to a certain extent the quality of the institution.

Of course, the mission of the Academy is to produce officers for active duty assignments, not to produce graduate students. However, the prospects of attending graduate school, either immediately upon graduation or soon thereafter, has proven to be motivating for many cadets. The Academy has always encouraged academic excellence, and providing opportunities for graduate work is part of the incentive. In addition to the incentive for cadets, selection of graduates for advanced study helps the Air Force fill requirements for advanced degrees in certain fields such as science, engineering, and cybernetics. It also prepares graduates identified for teaching potential to return as faculty members. To coordinate the Academy's efforts, General McDermott established an Associate Dean for Graduate Programs; Permanent Professor Mal Wakin held that post for more than 30 years, 1963–1995. It is now the Graduate Studies Office under the Associate Dean for Student Academic Affairs, which assists cadets in discovering which scholarships are open to them, determines their eligibility to compete, and provides assistance as appropriate. The mentoring program, initiated by Colonel Wakin, draws on the experience of Permanent Professors and other senior faculty to mentor scholarship candidates and to conduct mock interviews to hone their skills in that special environment.

The various graduate programs are described below, but we'll start with the results for the Class of 2018, the most recent for which complete data is available. Descriptions of each program follow the list. A total of 121 graduates from 2018 went directly to graduate school. This is the breakdown:

33 national competitive scholarships
37 Graduate School Program
33 Air Force graduate school assignments (2 to law school)
18 Health Profession Scholarship Program (13 to medical school)

NATIONAL COMPETITIVE SCHOLARSHIPS. Academy cadets may compete with students from other universities for scholarships and fellowships to study for advanced degrees in the United States and overseas. Among the major scholarships available to cadets are the Rhodes, Marshall, Gates, Fulbright, John F. Kennedy School of Government at Harvard, as well as fellowships from the Hertz Foundation, National Science Foundation, Draper Laboratory, and many more. Scholarship/Fellowship recipients will incur an additional active-duty service commitment.

COOPERATIVE GRADUATE PROGRAM (COOP). The COOP Program was proposed by the Permanent Professors and started in 1963 as a means of offering top cadets an opportunity to earn a Master's degree in seven to nine months after graduation. The program allowed cadets to complete some of the course requirements at USAFA and, following their graduation, attend summer term and fall semester at a civilian university. For pilot-qualified graduates, the program would be completed in time for the officer to enter a winter pilot-training class. On the faculty side, the program was popular because it allowed participating departments to provide a few graduate-level courses, which were both exciting for instructors to teach and rewarding for their professional academic development. The program flourished—departments worked with selected universities to develop the programs, enough cadets willingly took on the extra course workload, and many graduates earned advanced degrees right at the start of their Air Force careers.

By 1970, a typical year at the height of the program, Permanent Professors had established COOP programs for over a dozen academic disciplines: Aeronautics (Purdue), Applied Mathematics (North Carolina State), Astronautics (Purdue), Civil Engineering (Illinois), Electrical Engineering (Stanford), Engineering Mechanics (Stanford, Georgia Tech, and Michigan State), Geography (Oklahoma), History (Indiana), International Affairs (Georgetown and Tufts), Economics (UCLA), Management (UCLA), Psychology (Purdue), and Physics (Ohio State). In the class of 1970, 87 graduates pursued degrees under the COOP Program, which was over 10 percent of the class of 787. This was in addition to 16 graduates who attended medical school, 8 to law school, 9 to the Air Force Institute of Technology, and 20 recipients of national competitive scholarships. Altogether, nearly 18 percent of the class of 1970 had graduate school as their first assignment.

Despite its popularity, the COOP Program had its problems. The main issue was low retention of COOP graduates. The Air Force developed statistical data revealing higher-than-normal attrition among officers who participated in the COOP. This discovery was disappointing to advocates of the program. It was made more disappointing when accompanied by anecdotes of participation in anti-Vietnam War protest activities on campus by some COOP participants. There was a second problem. In some fields, especially science and engineering, Master's degrees earned by COOP participants were thought to have been somewhat out of date five to six years later when these graduates completed their flying commitments and needed to use their graduate training in non-flying assignments. In 1972 the Air Force decided to discontinue the COOP Program. Accordingly, the program was phased out beginning with the class of 1972, terminated with the class of 1975, and not available effective with the class of 1976.

HONOR GRADUATE PROGRAM. This became known as the "Blue Chip Program." As an alternative to COOP, the Honor Graduate Program was established beginning with the class of 1973. The proposal came from the Permanent Professors as a way to continue to provide incentives to encourage the cadets to live up to their potential. In securing the approval of HQ USAF, the Superintendent, Lieutenant General A.P. Clark, described the program with these words:

> That the top 15 percent of the cadets in Graduation Order of Merit (includes academic and military performance) of each graduating class be given an assurance by the Air Force which in effect guarantees that they have been selected for graduate education at some time in the future. In the case of those graduates who go on to UFT [Undergraduate Flying Training], the time to exercise this option could be five to eight years following completion of flying training. For those not going to UFT the time could be three to eight years following graduation from the Academy. Assuming satisfactory performance in the Air Force, the graduates who possess these guarantees of graduate education could elect to attend any graduate school to which they could gain admission and at which the Air Force has a contract and in any discipline for which the Air Force has a stated requirement. (Ltr, SUPT to Lt Gen Robert J. Dixon, DCS/P, HQ USAF, February 16, 1972)

This program ran successfully for more than a dozen years. Its principal problem, from the Academy's viewpoint, was that it did little to help the rated staff shortages on the faculty. This issue was an important driver for establishing the "Graduate School Program."

GRADUATE SCHOOL PROGRAM (GSP). In 1986–1987 the Academy conducted a comprehensive study of the benefits and pitfalls of reinstituting a COOP program of immediate graduate education. The objective was to give graduates more time to complete an advanced degree and enable the departments to nominate cadets for the program who had been identified as excellent potential faculty members. The GSP increases the pool of officers with graduate degrees to help ensure that graduates are available and prepared to return to the Academy as faculty members in the future. In 1988 after the Dean, Brigadier General Royer, advocated for the program with HQ USAF staff and briefed the Air Force Council, the Secretary of the Air Force approved the program to send approximately 50 additional graduates directly to graduate school in one-year programs leading to a Master's degree, beginning with the class of 1990. At present, the GSP is some 30 years mature and has proven itself successful as a faculty preparation program. Candidates for this program must be willing to return to the Academy as academic instructors after gaining Air Force experience. Many departments allocate the GSP slots to cadets entering flying training because they represent the demographic hardest to obtain otherwise. The main issue with the GSP is that the number of slots available is determined annually by the Air Force Educational Resources Board; therefore, quotas can fluctuate from year to year.

MEDICAL SCHOOL. Academy graduates from as far back as the Classes of 1963 and 1964 have attended medical school and gone on to serve the Air Force as physicians. In 1961–1962 Colonel Bill Woodyard, Permanent Professor of the Department of Chemistry and Physiology, added Organic Chemistry and Biology courses that helped cadets qualify for medical school. However, before 1966, the only path was in an "excess leave status" (the officers receive no pay or allowances while in this status and they pay for school themselves or accept scholarships or other financial assistance). On July 1, 1966, the Air Force Surgeon General drastically revised the program from an excess leave to a fully sponsored active duty program with full pay and allowances. At this time, Colonel (Dr.) Pete Carter was brought to the faculty and began to build what might be described as the Academy's pre-med program for cadets. Pete was appointed Permanent Professor in 1967; he was the first (and so far, the only) medical doctor to be appointed a Permanent Professor. First, he built the small minor in Life Sciences into a full major. HQ USAF then authorized 2 percent of each graduating class to attend medical school under Air Force auspices. These cadets were selected from those who majored in Life Sciences. In 1968, 12 graduates were selected (by the Office of the Surgeon General) for medical school.

Despite some hiccups over the years (temporary cancellations by Congress in 1974 and by SecAF Roche in 2003), the program continues and has expanded in scope to the broader health professions arena. A major step forward was initiated by Colonel Ron Reed. While Ron was Permanent Professor and Head of the Department of Biology, 1993–2005, he advocated for allowing cadets to also go to dental and nursing schools; both those routes opened in 2006. At present, the Academy can send up to 3 percent of graduates per year to health professions degree and training programs. Most attend medical school, but cadets may compete for scholarships in dental, nursing, physician's assistant, clinical psychology, or physical therapy schools. The Class of 2018 had 18 graduates who entered medical training.

LAW SCHOOL. There are basically two routes for an Academy graduate to go to law school. In 1963 one graduate entered law school in the "excess leave status" (described earlier). The Excess Leave Program (ELP) became more popular, and by the late 1960s five to six graduates per year were taking this route, subject to a cap of 1 percent of the graduating class. In 1973 Congress directed the services to discontinue sending academy graduates directly to law school. Rather, Congress authorized a fully funded program, the Funded Legal Education Program (FLEP), by which officers with between two and six years of service may be selected for law school. At present, both the ELP and the FLEP are available to graduates. Both routes lead to service in the Judge Advocate General Corps, and quotas for each are determined by The Judge Advocate General who manages the career field. In addition, Colonel Paul Pirog, Permanent Professor and Head of the Law Department, 2004–2014, was able to establish a USAFA-ELP program in 2012 solely for Academy graduates who were Legal Studies majors to go directly into law school. Over the past few years one or two cadets per year have applied for and been selected for the USAFA-ELP program.

RESEARCH AND SUPPORT OF THE AIR FORCE

An academy is a center of learning, and the learning applies both to the students and the faculty. The students (mostly) learn from the faculty, and the faculty learns from research. Naturally, education is the primary purpose of the Air Force Academy, but it was recognized from the onset that research was a necessary supplementary function. The Academy, therefore, encouraged and supported research in most fields of professional interest to its faculty. The Academy's policy was based on certain fundamental principles enunciated by the Dean, Brigadier General McDermott—namely that effective teachers at the university level must sustain an active interest in new ideas; that effective research is reflected in improved, more relevant instruction; and that research and writing create an atmosphere of inquiry in which learning can best take place. The Permanent Professors strongly supported the value of scholarship and committed to make time available for faculty research.

ORGANIZING FOR RESEARCH

The Academy itself was not organized for research; it was organized for teaching. Aside from the small Seiler Laboratory and the Office of Faculty Research (mentioned below), the personnel for research were assigned to academic departments, where everyone's primary duty was teaching cadets.

Each faculty member in every department understood that cadets were the mission—the entire purpose of the department was education of cadets. As a matter of practice, faculty members always did more than teach classes. Some engaged in development of new courses or improved pedagogy, and others committed a lot of time to the cadet flight programs, cadet clubs, athletics teams, or various other activities outside the department. Still others reached out to the greater Air Force to contribute their expertise in researching essential problems. Department Heads were challenged to manage the department's workload while supporting this broad array of expectations. As military faculty members arrived annually from graduate school or from their Air Force units, they brought a fresh stream of research proposals. The challenge faced by Permanent Professors and Department Heads was selecting which projects to support with limited resources. The criteria for accepting research projects became: (1) is the project important to the Air Force, and (2) how can cadets participate? Faculty members and cadets were able to apply their knowledge firsthand to current research questions. The success of these research projects confirmed the importance of research in cadet education and faculty professional development.

FRANK J. SEILER RESEARCH LABORATORY. The Frank J. Seiler Research Laboratory (FJSRL) was established by HQ USAF at the Academy in 1963 to further opportunities for faculty and cadet research. It began in 1962 in response to a proposal from General McDermott. At first it was called the Colorado Astronautical Research Laboratory; a year later it was renamed for Colonel Seiler, an Air Force research pioneer who envisioned that if Air Force Academy cadets could be involved in real-world research efforts, they would be better prepared for their future assignments. The Laboratory was part of the Air Force Office of Aerospace Research, later administered by the Air Force Office of Scientific Research (AFOSR). FJSRL was a tenant unit at the Academy, with offices and laboratory space in Fairchild Hall. FJSRL had a particularly important role in promoting an awareness of, and interest in, the importance of scientific research to the Air Force within the faculty and the Cadet Wing. Initially FJSRL focused on basic research in chemistry, aerospace mechanics, and applied mathematics (computers and numerical analysis of trajectories and reentry aerodynamics). It had a low-density shock tube, two chemistry labs, and the Burroughs B5500 mainframe computer, which was also used to teach computer programming to cadets. Later, the Laboratory also developed laser physics research as a major concentration. FJSRL was instrumental in supporting research in science and engineering, and many faculty members were able to join research teams with Seiler scientists. Even when the FJSRL was disestablished in 1994, it played a crucial role in advancing Academy research, as described below. The legacy is recognized in the naming of an annual faculty research award: The Frank J. Seiler Award for Research Excellence.

In the spring of 1962, General McDermott established the Office of the Assistant Dean for Research, later renamed the Director of Faculty Research, and now an Associate Dean for Research (see Appendix B). The Office was to do full-time research as well as help coordinate the research efforts in the departments. At least part of the motivation for establishing this dedicated in-house research organization was to support the Academy's bid to obtain authorization to award Master's degrees. The Office began with five full-time researchers: three officers on research projects in the physical sciences, one on research in the social sciences, and one on research in the humanities. The number of full-time researchers grew to 14 by 1967.

In 1969 Academy officials began to discuss with HQ USAF a program to increase research productivity and to address directly the needs of the Air Force. Both the Dean, Brigadier General Woodyard, and the Superintendent, Lieutenant General Moorman, understood that the Academy faculty was very capable of addressing and resolving the kind of problems for which commanders were requesting help. However, without additional personnel the Academy would be unable to accept the work. The Academy proposed to reorient the Academy's research away from discipline-oriented research to research aimed at addressing select Air Force problems. The Board of Visitors also argued for increased research activity. The proposal that took shape was for a Sponsored Research Program, organized under the Director of Faculty Research, drawing on faculty and cadet researchers and augmented by additional manpower authorizations. The number of additional spaces needed varied from one proposal to another, but numbers from 30 to 60 were requested. In the end, cost and manpower became the overriding factors and the concept of a centrally managed Sponsored Research Program was set aside in 1971. At that point, the Dean determined that the faculty research program could best be managed solely by the individual academic departments, and the role of the Director of Faculty Research was reoriented to providing support for departmental research and coordination of the Academy efforts with external agencies.

The standard adopted for research was that 10 percent of the overall faculty workload should be devoted to research and writing. The Permanent Professor or Department Head allocated research time during the academic year along with teaching assignments. During the summer period when the teaching load was greatly diminished, faculty not needed for course preparation or to support cadet summer programs were encouraged to spend their time in writing and research.

Two summer programs provided officers and cadets the opportunity to dedicate time for research. These were the Cadet Summer Research Program, which has been covered above, and a Faculty Summer Consultant Program begun in 1963. The Academy encouraged its officers to work with Air Force commands on projects where the officer's expertise could contribute. One of the Permanent Professor's responsibilities was to identify appropriate summer research positions that were most useful to the Air Force and the officer's professional development.

A strength of research at the Academy was the steady influx of new faculty members with fresh ideas and experience in current Air Force research topics. Since most faculty members were on three-to-four-year tours of duty, the turnover produced instability. Officers would arrive, small research teams would coalesce, projects would develop and flourish for a few years, but research on that topic would rapidly diminish when the key faculty members moved on. One advantage was that research areas were generally current, but the downside was that research projects were often short-lived. The singular exception was aeronautics. The Aeronautics Laboratory with jet engine test stands and a low speed wind tunnel was built as part of the original construction at the permanent site. Under the leadership of Permanent Professor Dan Daley and his skilled faculty, the Aero Lab attracted a sustaining flow of money for research to improve performance of existing aircraft and perform feasibility studies and experiments of advanced aircraft concepts. A tri-sonic wind tunnel was added, a major expansion of the building in the late 1980s added another wind tunnel, and a Mach 6 tunnel was added in 2016. The facility was made available for outside researchers, including NASA, Air Force, Navy, and Army, subject to the principal stipulation that each project allow for cadet participation.

Faculty research overall did make progress in the 1960s through the 1990s. A particular boost was the 1968 expansion of Fairchild Hall, which provided vital new laboratory space (Astronautics, Engineering Mechanics, and Physics Departments) as well as much needed expansion of other faculty areas.

Two events coincided in 1994 that led to an extraordinary boost for faculty research. The first was the military construction project leading to the Fairchild Hall Annex (originally and still often called the Consolidated Education and Training Facility, or CETF). The second was the closing of the Frank J. Seiler Research Laboratory. The first was expected, and its benefits had been planned and programmed. The second was unanticipated; it took awhile for its benefits to be understood. The major planned benefit of opening the Fairchild Hall Annex was of course the additional floor space for offices, classrooms, and laboratories—both the new laboratories in Chemistry, Biology, Civil Engineering, and Astronautics Departments in CETF and the additional space in the renovated Fairchild Hall.

Research Centers

The surprise deactivation of the Seiler Laboratory dealt a significant blow to the ongoing research programs in chemistry, aeronautics, and laser physics. This was a major problem for the three affected departments and their Permanent Professors, Colonel Hans Mueh, Colonel Mike Smith, and Colonel Jim Head. Even though they were closing the Seiler Laboratory, Air Force leaders respected their commitment to encouraging cadet and faculty research by transferring three research staff positions to the Academy. Even so, the closing of the Laboratory threatened to disrupt or terminate important collaborative efforts involving the work of dozens of officers. However, adversity was indeed the mother of invention, and a new organizational concept emerged: distributed Research Centers. Working with the Dean, Brigadier General Cubero, an innovative partnership was devised between the Academy, the Air Force Office of Scientific Research, and the Air Force Research Laboratory (AFRL), which established three new Research Centers. The new Centers were the Chemistry Research Center, the Aeronautics Research Center, and the Laser and Optics Research Center. Although the work was to some extent interdisciplinary, each Center was administered by an academic department. The key agreement between the three partners was steady funding from AFOSR; manpower, facilities, and administrative support from USAFA; and manpower and project support from AFRL. These Centers inherited most of the desirable equipment from the Seiler Laboratory, but they were much more focused and more closely connected to cadets and departmental interests. The Seiler Laboratory's legacy is richly celebrated in the accomplishments of these three research centers.

The three new Research Centers were built on a common model: the Dean of the Faculty used one of the manpower positions from the Seiler Laboratory for each Center's full-time director, the AFRL provided a manpower position for a research scientist/engineer for each Center, and AFOSR provided three-year funding for each Center for equipment and to hire two additional researchers. Each of the three departments assigned a lab technician to their Center and assumed the administrative and logistics support. A vital catalyst in pulling this concept together was the availability of the new civilian faculty program, which provided the flexibility to hire researchers as faculty "overhires" who were paid with outside research money.

Since being established, these three Research Centers have become premier centers of Air Force expertise. Observing their demonstrable success, other departments organized research groups along similar lines. This has led to the virtual explosion of Research Centers across the faculty. The Academy is now home to 19 Research Centers and two Institutes, representing focus in

areas of basic science, engineering, warfighter effectiveness, and high-performance computing. There is a complete list of the current centers in Appendix
F, along with a brief description of each Center's core competencies. Those
associated with an academic department are also highlighted in Chapter 4.

One example is the Center for Aircraft Structural Life Extension
(CAStLE). CAStLE was formed in 1995 in the Department of Engineering
Mechanics under Permanent Professor Cary Fisher's leadership. Its goal was
to bring research to bear on the vexing problems of materials degradation
and structural testing and analysis. Building on facilities in Fairchild Hall,
and providing many opportunities for cadet involvement, CAStLE received
sustaining funding from AFRL. During the past decade, under Permanent
Professor Tom Yoder, the CAStLE dramatically expanded to become the
DoD's premier agency for science and technology of aging aircraft, including
advisory and contracting responsibilities.

The newest venture is Air Force CyberWorx, a public-private design
center focused on cyber capability that brings together a variety of problem
solvers—cadets, industry leaders, academics, and Air Force leaders—to design
effective solutions to operational problems identified from the Air Force. AF
CyberWorx stood-up in the fall of 2016 and in the first year tackled several AF
problems using a methodology of "design thinking," an approach that focuses
on rapid prototyping and a willingness to take risks. USAFA cadets work with
commercial partners to develop, expand on, and test any and all ideas offered.
Plans to build a $50 million, 33,000-square-foot facility in the Cadet Area are
being finalized, with construction to begin as early as Fiscal Year 2019. Fittingly
the building itself is a public-private partnership, using appropriated funds for
Military Construction and donated funds from the USAFA Endowment.

CHAPTER 4
LEADERS AND THEIR DEPARTMENTS

In this chapter, we trace the development over time of the academic departments. We do not attempt to write the history of each department. Rather, we paint a brief sketch of the department's origins, pay tribute to the Permanent Professors and others who served as Department Heads, and briefly describe the departments as they present themselves today.

The early structure of the academic departments, organized into four academic divisions, has remained essentially intact to this day. (See chart on next page.)

THE PERMANENT PROFESSORS AND OTHER DEPARTMENT HEADS

In almost every instance, a Permanent Professor was selected and appointed to lead a particular academic department. (In this context, we treat the Center for Character and Leadership Development as a department.) It is fair to say that the fundamental building blocks of any college or university are its academic departments. The departments are the basic units because the departments offer the courses, the departments structure the majors' programs, and the departments hire and guide the faculty who interact directly with students. As the long-term leaders of their departments, each Permanent Professor's influence is firmly stamped on their department. Each department is different, in part because their disciplines demand different approaches to education and offer different opportunities for students. Each department is also unique because each grew and developed under different, distinctive leaders.

The idea behind appointing Permanent Professors was to stabilize the academic program through appointment of "permanent" Department Heads

THE FOUR ACADEMIC DIVISIONS	
1956 DIVISIONS	**2018 DIVISIONS**
HUMANITIES English Foreign Languages Law	**HUMANITIES** English and Fine Arts Foreign Languages History Philosophy
SOCIAL SCIENCES Economics History Military History Political Science Psychology	**SOCIAL SCIENCES** Behavioral Sciences and Leadership Economics and Geosciences Law Management Military and Strategic Studies Political Science
BASIC SCIENCES Chemistry Graphics Mathematics Physics	**BASIC SCIENCES** Biology Chemistry Mathematical Sciences Physics
APPLIED SCIENCES Aerodynamics Electrical Engineering Mechanics Thermodynamics	**ENGINEERING** Aeronautics Astronautics Civil and Environmental Engineering Computer and Cyber Sciences Electrical and Computer Engineering Engineering Mechanics

who would provide long-term continuity, free of the frequent reassignment process normal in the officer corps. Of course, the Permanent Professors were not actually "permanent." Some moved to different positions, others left for a year or two for career-broadening assignments (sabbaticals), and some retired. In the absence of their Permanent Professor, department leadership fell to another individual appointed Department Head, sometimes specified as Acting Department Head. These appointments ran from a few months to several years' duration. Whether permanent or not, the duties and responsibilities of the Department Head were the same: stability and continuity of curriculum, quality of instruction, and organizational management. Therefore, in the lists that follow for each department, the names of the Department Heads are shown year by year. Each of these individuals is due some measure of credit for the success of the institution.

In the pages that follow, we include a brief description of each department under the caption "The Department Today." This simple snapshot is intended only to identify the department's main focus, the expanse of its curriculum, and some noteworthy features. This section is drawn mainly from statements the department makes about itself; for instance, on the Academy's website.

When referencing the core courses, these requirements are for the new Core Curriculum, which was adopted in 2017 for the classes of 2021 and subsequent, as discussed earlier in Chapter 3.

We conclude each department page by identifying some of the interests, facilities, and programs that make the department unique. Although each department's main mission is to teach cadets, each also offers special opportunities and emphasis for enriching cadet experiences and faculty professional development that enhance that goal.

DEPARTMENT OF AERONAUTICS
ANTECEDENT DEPARTMENTS
Aerodynamics (1955–1960)

Thermodynamics (1955–1960)

Aeronautics (1960–Present)

DEPARTMENT HEADS

1956–60	Lt Col Gerhardt C. Clementson (Aero)	1984–85	Lt Col Richard C. Oliver
	Col Paul H. Dane (Thermo)	1985–94	*Col Michael L. Smith*
1960–61	Col Clementson	1994–95	Col Randall J. Stiles
1961–62	Col Bernard W. Marschner	1995–00	*Col Smith*
1962–65	Lt Col Gage H. Crocker	2000–04	*Col Douglas N. Barlow*
1965–66	Lt Col Orlando J. Manci Jr.	2004–05	Col Steven C. Pluntze
1966–67	Lt Col Blaine R. Butler Jr.	2005–08	Dr Aaron R. Byerley
1967–73	*Col Daniel H. Daley*	2008–13	*Col Barlow*
1973–74	Col John P. Thomas	2013–14	Dr Russell M. Cummings
1974–80	*Col Daley*	2014–15	*Col Barlow*
1980–81	Col Richard F. Felton	2015–16	Col Angela W. Suplisson
1981–84	*Col Daley*	2016–18	*Col John D. Cinnamon*
		2018–	Lt Col Barrett T. McCann

PERMANENT PROFESSORS

Daniel H. Daley   Michael L. Smith   Douglas N. Barlow   John D. Cinnamon

THE DEPARTMENT TODAY: The Department of Aeronautics supports cadets, the Air Force, and the world through a variety of studies in aerodynamics, flight mechanics, propulsion, aircraft structures, and experimental methods. Every cadet receives an introduction to aircraft design, fluid mechanics, airfoil and wing aerodynamics, aircraft performance, and stability and control. Cadets majoring in Aeronautical Engineering have two course design sequences to choose from—aircraft design or aircraft engine design.

CURRICULUM: The department offers 23 courses in Aeronautical Engineering.

CORE COURSE: Aero Engr 315. Fundamentals of Aeronautics

MAJORS: Aeronautical Engineering
Systems Engineering (Interdisciplinary)

NOTEWORTHY: Since its inception, the department has been a major contributor to technological developments and the security of the United States through aerospace studies. This is enabled through the Aeronautics Research Center and the High-Performance Computing Research Center. The department's Aeronautics Laboratory is demonstrably the best-equipped such facility in all of academia, with wind tunnels ranging from low-speed to Mach-6 hypersonic, operational turbojet engines, and a rocket test cell. These centers provide very meaningful research experiences for cadets and faculty through projects supporting customers in the Air Force, Department of Defense, other government agencies, and commercial partners.

DEPARTMENT OF ASTRONAUTICS

ANTECEDENT DEPARTMENTS

Astronautics (1958–1967)

Astronautics and Computer Science (1967–1982)

Astronautics (1982–Present)

DEPARTMENT HEADS

1958–60	Col Benjamin P. Blasingame	1982–86	*Col Robert B. Giffen*
1960–62	Col Richard C. Gibson	1986–89	Lt Col Douglas H. Kirkpatrick
1962–63	Col Francis J. Hale	1989–94	*Col Giffen*
1963–64	*Col Roger R. Bate*	1994–00	*Col Michael L. DeLorenzo*
1964–65	Lt Col Richard G. Korthals	2000–02	Lt Col Thomas L. Yoder
1965–66	*Col Roland E. Thomas*	2002–05	*Col DeLorenzo*
1966–67	*Col Bate*	2005–08	*Col Martin E.B. France*
1967	Lt Col Jacob C. Baird	Fall 2008	Lt Col Lynnane E. George
1968–70	*Col Bate*	Spr 2009	Lt Col William L. Cochran
1970–72	Lt Col Bradford W. Parkinson	2009–14	*Col France*
1972–78	*Col John P. Wittry*	Fall 2014	Lt Col David B. French
1978–79	Lt Col Edward J. Bauman	2015–18	*Col France*
1979–81	Lt Col Thomas J. Eller	2018–	Lt Col Luke M. Sauter
Spr 1982	Lt Col John A. Zingg		

PERMANENT PROFESSORS

Roger R. Bate   Roland E. Thomas   John P. Wittry   Robert B. Giffen

Michael L. DeLorenzo   Martin E.B. France

THE DEPARTMENT TODAY: In 1958, the very year NASA was formed, the department was established. Astronautics focuses on cadet space education: orbits, spacecraft systems, launch vehicles, re-entry, operations, and mission management. The major in Astronautical Engineering is the broad application of science and engineering to aerospace operations. Our majors actually are rocket scientists, and our motto is "Learning Space by Doing Space." Cadets have designed, built, and launched rockets to the edge of space and have designed, built, and operated satellites that are currently in Earth orbit.

CURRICULUM: The department teaches 14 courses in
               Astronautical Engineering, 5 courses in Space Operations,
               and supports other courses in the Engineering Division.
CORE COURSE: Astro Engr 310. Introduction to Astronautics
MAJORS: Astronautical Engineering
               Systems Engineering (Interdisciplinary)
               Space Operations (Interdisciplinary)

NOTEWORTHY: The department's Space Systems Research Center designs, builds, tests, and flies cadet-built satellites funded by the Department of Defense and various Air Force agencies in order to achieve real Department of Defense space objectives. In addition, our cadets, from fourth year to first year and all majors, operate our ground station, controlling satellites that contribute to our national security and our understanding of the space environment. The astronautics laboratories contain other items unique to an undergraduate school, including facilities for rocket design and build-up and high-fidelity orbital analysis software to support research and classroom activities. The department sponsors the Summer Space Program, a one-week introduction to Air Force space systems, taught by cadets to more than 200 cadets per year.

DEPARTMENT OF BEHAVIORAL SCIENCES AND LEADERSHIP

ANTECEDENT DEPARTMENTS

Psychology (1956–1958)

Leadership Studies, under Commandant (1958–1961)

Psychology (1961–1962)

Behavioral Sciences (1962–1965)

Psychology and Leadership (1965–1971)

Life and Behavioral Sciences (1971–1975)

Behavioral Sciences and Leadership (1975–Present)

DEPARTMENT HEADS

1956–58	Lt Col Fred E. Holdrege Jr.	1992–93	Col David B. Porter
1958–61	Lt Col Gabriel D. Ofiesh	1993–95	*Col Hughes*
1961–64	Col Herman F. Smith	1995–01	*Col Porter*
1964–68	Col Henry E. Wojdyla	2001–02	Lt Col Robert J. Jackson
1968–70	Col Joseph M. Madden	2002–04	*Col Dana H. Born*
1970–71	Col Robert E. Stackhouse	2004–10	*Col Gary A. Packard Jr.*
1971–75	*Col Peter B. Carter*	Spr 2011	Col Randall W. Gibb
1975–85	*Col John L. Williams Jr.*	2011–16	*Col Packard*
1985–92	*Col Richard L. Hughes*	2016–	Col Joseph D. Looney

PERMANENT PROFESSORS

Peter B. Carter   John L. Williams, Jr.   Richard L. Hughes   David B. Porter

Dana H. Born   Gary A. Packard, Jr.

THE DEPARTMENT TODAY: The study of Behavioral Sciences lays the scientific foundation for understanding of self and one's ability to work with others. This understanding is conveyed to cadets through study of behavior and mental processes across diverse levels of analyses, emphasized through topics such as perception, cognition, learning, memory, social interactions, mental health issues, and the biological basis of behavior. Majors choose concentration in one of several areas: Clinical/Counseling Psychology, Experimental Psychology, Leadership, Sociocultural, Human Factors, or Health Professions.

CURRICULUM: The department offers 25 courses in Behavioral Sciences and supports courses in Social Sciences.

CORE COURSES: Officership 100-400. Leadership

Beh Sci 110. Introduction to Behavioral Science

Beh Sci 231. Basic Research Methods and Statistical Tools (core option)

Beh Sci 360. Sociology (Advanced Sociocultural Choice)

MAJORS: Behavioral Sciences

Systems Engineering (Interdisciplinary)

NOTEWORTHY: The department is a national leader in the areas of respect for human dignity, diversity, inclusion, gender equity, and race relations. They have contributed to the national dialogue in multiple social justice arenas such as religious respect, sexual assault prevention, racial equality, Don't Ask, Don't Tell repeal, and transgender military service. The Warfighter Effectiveness Research Center, the research arm of the department, is dedicated to facilitating faculty and cadet research in the behavioral sciences that enhance warfighter effectiveness. Collaborators include government laboratories, academia, industry, and military operators. The department is a leader in the Air Officer Commanding Master's Degree Program (through partnership with the University of Colorado, Colorado Springs) and the Cadet Commander's Leadership Enrichment Seminar (partnered with the Center for Character and Leadership Development).

DEPARTMENT OF BIOLOGY

ANTECEDENT DEPARTMENTS

Life Sciences (1968–1971)

Life and Behavioral Sciences (1971–1975)

Chemistry and Biological Sciences (1975–1980)

Biology (1980–Present)

DEPARTMENT HEADS

1968–75	*Col Peter B. Carter*	2002–05	*Col Reed*
1975–79	*Col Robert W. Lamb*	2005–06	Col Paul W. Fisher
1979–80	Lt Col David W. Seegmiller	2006–12	*Col John L. Putnam*
1980–92	*Col Orwyn Sampson*	2012–13	Dr David Westmoreland
1992–93	Col William J. Carney	2013–16	*Col Putnam*
1993–00	*Col Ronald D. Reed*	2016–	*Col Steven C.M. Hasstedt*
2000–02	Col James S. Kent		

PERMANENT PROFESSORS

Peter B. Carter   Robert W. Lamb   Orwyn Sampson   Ronald D. Reed

John L. Putnam   Steven C.M. Hasstedt

THE DEPARTMENT TODAY: The Department of Biology promotes the development of the cadet's scientific talents through a carefully planned program of academic instruction, practical laboratory experience, and individual research projects. The Biology major provides a multidisciplinary approach to the study of human performance in air and space, evolution, exercise, biomechanics, ecology, environmental science, and cutting-edge cell and genetic engineering. Some cadets pursue specialized areas of interest such as aviation and flight, human factors in aviation and space, athletics/sports performance, ecology, cell and molecular biology, or professional or advanced degree preparation for careers in the health professions or the Biomedical Science Corps.

CURRICULUM: The department offers 20 courses in Biology.

CORE COURSES: Biology 215. Introductory Biology with Laboratory
(Basic Science Option)
Biology 345. Aerospace Physiology
(Advanced STEM Choice)
Biology 370. Human Nutrition
(Advanced STEM Choice)

MAJOR: Biology

NOTEWORTHY: The department boasts numerous facilities and learning resources including a molecular biology lab, aerospace physiology lab, genetics lab, cadaver lab, and greenhouse. The Life Sciences Research Center supports cadet and faculty research in a broad range of biological sciences topics. Funded by the Air Force Office of Scientific Research and the Air Force Surgeon General, the center's three main research thrusts are biomedical, biosystems, and human health and performance.

DEPARTMENT OF CHEMISTRY

ANTECEDENT DEPARTMENTS

Chemistry, Physics and Electrical Engineering (1954–1955)

Chemistry (1955–1960)

Chemistry and Physiology (1960–1967)

Chemistry (1968–1975)

Chemistry and Biological Sciences (1975–1980)

Chemistry (1980–Present)

DEPARTMENT HEADS

1954–55	Col James V.G. Wilson	1980–86	*Col Harvey W. Schiller*
1955–61	*Col William T. Woodyard*	1986–02	*Col Hans J. Mueh*
1961–62	Lt Col Harrison E. Kee Jr.	2002–03	Col Clifford M. Uttermoehlen
1962–65	*Col Woodyard*	2004–05	Col Timothy J. Brotherton
1965–66	Col Robert H. Brundin	2005–10	*Col Michael E. Van Valkenburg*
1966–68	Lt Col Charles K. Arpke	2010–11	Dr Donald M. Bird
1968–69	Lt Col Alfred D. Norton	2011–15	*Col Van Valkenburg*
1969–70	Lt Col John R. Comerford	2015–16	Col John M. Garver
1970–79	*Col Robert W. Lamb*	2016–18	*Col Van Valkenburg*
1979–80	Lt Col David W. Seegmiller	2018–	Col Tasha L. Pravecek

PERMANENT PROFESSORS

William T. Woodyard   Robert W. Lamb   Harvey W. Schiller

Hans J. Mueh   M.E. VanValkenburg

THE DEPARTMENT TODAY: The department provides all cadets with a fundamental education in chemistry. From developing the materials that extend the life of our aircraft fleet, to understanding space sensor and satellite technology, to analyzing chemical and biological warfare data, to improving personal body armor, chemistry is critical to Air Force operational mission success and is at the forefront of research programs. The department also provides a comprehensive curriculum for cadets interested in chemistry, biochemistry, or materials chemistry.

CURRICULUM:	The department offers 29 courses in Chemistry.
CORE COURSES:	Chem 100. General Chemistry I Lecture and Lab
	Chem 200. General Chemistry II Lecture and Lab (Basic Science Option)
	Chem 222. Analytical Chemistry (Advanced STEM Choice)
	Chem 350. Chemistry of Weapons (Advanced STEM Choice)
MAJORS:	Chemistry
	Biochemistry
	Materials Chemistry

NOTEWORTHY: The Chemistry Research Center focuses on next-generation, high-performance materials to meet operational Air Force and DoD mission partner needs. Major projects include material for new solar/green technologies, stimuli-responsive coatings for chemical warfare nerve agent detection, and high-temperature resins and high-strength fibers for next-generation solid rocket motor casings.

DEPARTMENT OF CIVIL AND ENVIRONMENTAL ENGINEERING

ANTECEDENT DEPARTMENTS

Civil Engineering (1966–1973)

[prior CE courses taught by Mechanics]

Civil Engineering, Engineering Mechanics and Materials (1973–1979)

Civil Engineering (1979–1997)

Civil and Environmental Engineering (1997–Present)

DEPARTMENT HEADS

1966–68	Col Winston C. Fowler	2005–06	Lt Col Steven T. Kuennen
1968–81	*Col Wallace E. Fluhr*	2006–10	*Col Seely*
1981–82	Lt Col Edward A. Osborne Jr.	2010–11	Lt Col Jeffery L. Heiderscheidt
1982–91	*Col David O. Swint Sr.*	2012–15	*Col Seely*
1991–92	Lt Col James L. Brickell	2015–18	*Col John A. Christ*
1992–00	*Col Swint*	2018–	Lt Col Joel A. Sloan
2000–05	*Col Gregory E. Seely*		

PERMANENT PROFESSORS

Wallace E. Fluhr   David O. Swint Sr.   Gregory E. Seely   John A. Christ

THE DEPARTMENT TODAY: The Department of Civil and Environmental Engineering implemented a systems approach to learning that bridges the gap between theory and practice—a concept that has evolved from the "construct first, design later" methodology for engineering education. Its majors are equipped to meet the challenges of environmental degradation, infrastructure design, construction and sustainment, energy needs, natural disaster responses, installation resiliency, sustainable development, and community planning.

CURRICULUM: The department offers 26 courses in Civil Engineering.
CORE COURSE: Civ Engr 356. Sustainability in the Built Environment
(Advanced STEM Choice)
MAJOR: Civil Engineering

NOTEWORTHY: The department operates a large field site to construct and test experimental earth structures, a fully functional soils laboratory, two fully capable wet labs, a static structural testing capability via a 25-foot-long reaction floor with multiple hydraulic actuators, and a high-bay laboratory space with a five-ton crane and multiple universal testing machines. The department also has extensive experience with multiphase flow simulation techniques executed via a research-funded computer network. Most notably, the department pioneered an intensive approach to civil engineering education through its Field Engineering and Readiness Laboratory (FERL), a 50-acre site in Jacks Valley at which they hold a three-week summer program that exposes cadets to hands-on experiences in surveying, construction methods, construction materials, environmental and geotechnical design, and fundamental structural engineering concepts. This experience provides a solid foundation for learning scientific theory and engineering design principles in more advanced courses. A featured project at FERL is construction of two 900-square-foot, one-bedroom, one-bath Navajo hogans in partnership with the Southwest Indian Foundation. These hogans are then donated to families on the Navajo Reservation near Gallup, NM.

DEPARTMENT OF COMPUTER AND CYBER SCIENCES
ANTECEDENT DEPARTMENTS
Astronautics and Computer Science (1967–1982)
Computer Science (1982–2017)
Computer and Cyber Sciences (2017–Present)

DEPARTMENT HEADS

1967	Lt Col Jacob C. Baird	1992–95	Lt Col Dennis L. Schweitzer
1968–70	*Col Roger R. Bate*	1995–98	*Col Samuel L. Grier*
1970–72	Lt Col Bradford W. Parkinson	1998–01	Lt Col William C. Hobart
1972–78	*Col John P. Wittry*	2001–08	*Col David S. Gibson*
1978–79	Lt Col Edward J. Bauman	2008–09	Dr Martin C. Carlisle
1979–81	Lt Col Thomas J. Eller	2009–14	*Col Gibson*
1982–87	*Col Joseph Monroe*	2014–15	Dr Martin C. Carlisle
1987–92	*Col William E. Richardson*	2015–17	*Col Gibson*
1992	Lt Col Lawrence G. Jones	2017–	*Col David J. Caswell*

PERMANENT PROFESSORS

Roger R. Bate   John P. Wittry   Joseph Monroe   William E. Richardson

Samuel L. Grier   David S. Gibson   David J. Caswell

THE DEPARTMENT TODAY: The department helps cadets understand the principles, capabilities, applications, limitations, and vulnerabilities of computer-based systems. The Computer Science major focuses on computer programming, software engineering, and computing theory. The major in Computer and Network Security focuses on computer programming, embedded systems, networks, telecommunications, computer systems, computer investigations, and cyber operations.

> CURRICULUM: The department offers 29 Computer Science and 4 Cyber courses.
>
> CORE COURSE: Comp Sci 110. Introduction to Computing and Cyber Operations
> Comp Sci 210. Introduction to Programming (Advanced STEM Choice)
>
> MAJORS: Computer Science
> Computer and Network Security
> Operations Research (Interdisciplinary)
> Systems Engineering (Interdisciplinary)

NOTEWORTHY: The department is home to the Academy Center for Cyberspace Research, which conducts research in cyber warfare, information assurance, unmanned aerial systems, and cyberspace education. The department is a National Security Agency National Center of Academic Excellence in cyber operations and cyber defense education. Department members coach the USAFA Cyber Competition Team, which competes very well at the national level against other schools and teams from professional cyber organizations.

DEPARTMENT OF ECONOMICS AND GEOSCIENCES

ANTECEDENT DEPARTMENTS

Economics and Government (1954–1956); Economics (1956–1960)

Military History and Geography (1956–1958); Geography (1958–1960)

Economics and Geography (1960–1966)

Economics and Management (1966–1973); Geography (1966–1973)

Economics, Geog. and Management (1973–1981); Economics (1981–1986)

Economics and Geography (1986–2005)

Economics and Geosciences (2005–Present)

DEPARTMENT HEADS

1954–59	*Col Robert F. McDermott*	1974–77	Lt Col Edward L. Claiborn
1956–57	Col Josephus A. Bowman (MH&G)	1977–80	*Col Lee D. Badgett*
		1980–81	Lt Col Robert L. Taylor
1957–58	Col Wilfred W. Smith (MH&G)	1981	Lt Col William J. Weida
		1982–86	*Col Kenneth H. Fleming*
1958–60	Lt Col Wiley L. Baxter (Geog)	1986–89	Lt Col Michael S. Anselmi
1959–64	*Col Wayne A. Yeoman* (Econ)	1989–94	*Col F Raymond E. Franck*
1964–66	Col Robert G. Taylor (Econ & Geog)	1994–96	Lt Col Laurence C. Vliet
		1996–00	*Col Franck*
1966–73	*Col Taylor* (Geog)	2000–01	Lt Col Steven Slate
1966–72	*Col Yeoman* (Econ & Mgt)	2001–08	*Col Richard L. Fullerton*
Fall 1972	Lt Col Wade R. Kilbride	2008–11	Col Neal J. Rappaport
Spr 1973	Lt Col Edward B. Oppermann	2011–14	*Col Fullerton*
1973–74	*Col Marcos E. Kinevan*	2014–	*Col Jennifer C. Alexander*

PERMANENT PROFESSORS

Robert F. McDermott   Wayne A. Yeoman   Col Robert G. Taylor   Marcos E. Kinevan   Lee D. Badgett

Kenneth H. Fleming   Raymond E. Franck   Richard L. Fullerton   Jennifer C. Alexander

THE DEPARTMENT TODAY: The department addresses complex systems, from economics to weather forecasting and physical, human, and regional geography. The Economics major allows cadets to focus on business, finance, international economics, public policy, or quantitative economics. The Meteorology major uniquely focuses on the impact of weather on military operations. The Geospatial Science major provides international insight and cultural and physical understanding of the battle space.

CURRICULUM: The department offers 23 Economics, 17 Geospatial Science, and 6 Meteorology courses, and supports courses in Operations Research, Foreign Area Studies, and Social Sciences.

CORE COURSES: Econ 201. Introduction to Economics
Geo 351. Introduction to Physical Geography
(Advanced STEM Choice)
Geo 412. World Cultural Geography
(Advanced Sociocultural Choice)

MAJORS: Economics
Geospatial Science
Foreign Area Studies (Interdisciplinary)
Meteorology (joint with Physics)
Operations Research (Interdisciplinary)

NOTEWORTHY: Department resources provide access to state-of-the-art geographic information processing methods such as digital image processing and geographic information systems. A modern, fully equipped Meteorology Laboratory provides access to online data and weather-forecasting tools.

DEPARTMENT OF ELECTRICAL AND COMPUTER ENGINEERING
ANTECEDENT DEPARTMENTS
Chemistry, Physics and Electrical Engineering (1954–1956)
Electrical Engineering (1956–2006)
Electrical and Computer Engineering (2006–Present)

DEPARTMENT HEADS

1954–62	*Col James V.G. Wilson*	1988–00	*Col Alan R. Klayton*
1962–66	Col Harold J. Bestervelt	2000–02	Col Parris C. Neal
1966–79	*Col Roland E. Thomas*	2002–08	*Col Klayton*
1979–81	Col David R. Carroll	2008–13	*Col Jeffrey T. Butler*
1981–82	*Col Joseph Monroe*	2013–14	Col Anne L. Clark
1982–83	Lt Col Albert J. Rosa	2014–18	*Col Butler*
1983–87	*Col Erlind G. Royer*	2018–	Lt Col Brian J. Neff
1987–88	Lt Col Michael F. Guyote		

PERMANENT PROFESSORS

James V.G. Wilson   Roland E. Thomas   Joseph Monroe   Erlind G. Royer

Alan R. Klayton   Jeffrey T. Butler

THE DEPARTMENT TODAY: The department provides all cadets with an introduction to the principles of Air Force electronic and cyber systems through analysis and evaluation of analog, digital, and radio-frequency systems. The impact of electrical and computer engineering in the 21st-century battlefield is more vital than ever before. The Air Force's increasing reliance on electronic surveillance, electronic warfare, cyber warfare, advanced communication systems, and modern computers has created a high demand for Electrical and Computer Engineers. The Electrical and Computer Engineering majors prepare students with a deep understanding of the basic principles of modern electronic and cyber systems such as "smart" computer-guided munitions, advanced "fly-by-wire" aircraft, radio systems capable of communicating through hostile electronic jamming environments, terrain-following radar, electronic attack, cyber security, and much more.

CURRICULUM: The department offers 29 courses in Electrical and Computer Engineering as well as supporting several courses in General Engineering.

CORE COURSE: ECE 315. Principles of Air Force Electronic and Cyber Systems

MAJORS: Electrical Engineering
Computer Engineering
Systems Engineering (Interdisciplinary)

NOTEWORTHY: The department's Academy Center for Unmanned Aircraft Systems (UAS) Research focuses on adding autonomy to UAS, allowing one operator to control multiple unmanned aerial vehicles that can autonomously search, find, identify, and track various targets. UAS serve as an excellent platform for cadets across various disciplines to conduct meaningful research supporting the warfighter. The department also supports research in radio-frequency communications and sensors as well as embedded cyber-physical systems.

DEPARTMENT OF ENGINEERING MECHANICS
ANTECEDENT DEPARTMENTS
Mechanics (1956–1966)
Engineering Mechanics (1966–1972)
Engineering Science, Mechanics & Materials (1972–1973)
Civil Engineering, Engineering Mechanics and Materials (1973–1979)
Engineering Mechanics (1979–Present)

DEPARTMENT HEADS

1956–63	*Col Archie Higdon*	1984–05	*Col Fisher*
1963–64	Col Charles W. Sampson	Spr 2006	Lt Col Terry T. Thompson
1964–65	*Col Higdon*	2006–12	*Col Thomas L. Yoder*
1965–73	*Col Philip J. Erdle*	2012–13	Col Andrew G. Szmerekovsky
1973–79	*Col Wallace E. Fluhr*	2013–15	Lt Col Donald W. Rhymer
1979–82	*Col Cary A. Fisher*	2015–18	*Col Yoder*
1982–84	Lt Col Thomas A. Kullgren	2018–	Lt Col Cory A. Cooper

PERMANENT PROFESSORS

Archie Higdon   Philip J. Erdle   Wallace E. Fluhr

Cary A. Fisher   Thomas L. Yoder

THE DEPARTMENT TODAY: Mechanical Engineering is a broad discipline of design and analysis of mechanics and motion, thermodynamics and fluids, materials and structures, and control. Beginning with an introduction to the fundamental principles of statics and mechanics of materials applied to aerospace systems, the curriculum spans incredible mechanical engineering systems in aerospace, automotive hardware, power generation facilities, and manufacturing.

> CURRICULUM: The department offers 14 courses in Engineering Mechanics and 14 in Mechanical Engineering.
>
> CORE COURSE: Engr Mech 220. Fundamentals of Mechanics
>
> MAJORS: Mechanical Engineering
> Systems Engineering (Interdisciplinary)

NOTEWORTHY: In the Applied Mechanics Laboratory, cadets are encouraged to use a variety of wood- and metal-working equipment such as lathes, computer-controlled mills, welding equipment, material testing systems, composite material fabrication tools, and additive manufacturing devices (3D printing). Among many other projects, cadets design and fabricate various off-road vehicles and a formula car for national intercollegiate design competitions. A separate garage facility, complete with a full-scale chassis dynamometer, provides a unique opportunity for cadets to apply skills learned in their courses. The department's Center for Aircraft Structural Life Extension is the Academy's largest research facility, specializing in aircraft structural integrity and technology required to maintain aging aircraft and national infrastructure. This Center functions as a *de facto* government laboratory providing science and technology support, delivering commercial products and services directly to the Offices of the Secretary of Defense, the Air Force, and the greater aerospace and aircraft structural community.

DEPARTMENT OF ENGLISH AND FINE ARTS

ANTECEDENT DEPARTMENTS

English and Foreign Languages (1954–1956)

English (1956–1973)

English and Fine Arts (1973–1977)

English (1977–1999)

English and Fine Arts (1999–Present)

DEPARTMENT HEADS

1954–61	*Col Peter R. Moody*	1999–02	*Col Thomas G. Bowie Jr.*
1961–63	Lt Col Cortland P. Auser	2002–03	Lt Col Howard Swartz
1963–65	*Col Moody*	Spr 2004	Dr Richard W. Lemp
1965–77	*Col Jesse C. Gatlin Jr.*	2004–09	*Col Kathleen Harrington*
1977–82	*Col Jack M. Shuttleworth*	2009–10	Lt Col Thomas G. McGuire
1982–84	Lt Col James C. Gaston	2010–14	*Col Harrington*
1984–94	*Col Shuttleworth*	2014–16	Lt Col Candice L. Pipes
1994–95	Lt Col Richard W. Lemp	2016–	*Col Harrington*
1995–99	*Col Shuttleworth*		

PERMANENT PROFESSORS

Peter R. Moody   Jesse C. Gatlin Jr.   Jack M. Shuttleworth

Thomas G. Bowie   Kathleen Harrington

THE DEPARTMENT TODAY: The department believes that critical and imaginative thinking and clear, effective communication are the foundations of outstanding leadership, both inside and outside the Air Force. Through studying literary texts spanning three millennia and numerous cultural traditions, cadets grapple with some of the most perplexing questions of the human condition: What does it mean to be human? What are the sources of human greatness and human depravity? Why do we yearn, through literature and art, to share our stories with others? Why is it vital to listen to these stories in a complex and interconnected world? Ultimately, the aim is to develop warrior-scholars whose conceptions of leadership are buttressed by wisdom—a wisdom captured and communicated by literature and art.

CURRICULUM: The department offers 22 English courses and 8 Fine Arts courses.

CORE COURSES: English 111. Introductory Composition and Research
English 211. Literature and Intermediate Composition
English 411. Language, Literature, and Leadership
(Advanced Sociocultural Choice)

MAJORS: English
Humanities (Interdisciplinary)

NOTEWORTHY: The department enriches the intellectual experiences of cadets through a variety of opportunities, including sponsoring and coaching an internationally ranked cadet Forensics Team and providing studio opportunities to explore the visual, musical, and dramatic arts. Additionally, faculty and cadets participate in the Air Force Humanities Institute, a forum for exploring a broad range of intellectual traditions and paradigms that enrich one's understanding of the human condition. The department publishes the journal *War, Literature, and the Arts*, which is a cornerstone of the new Digital Humanities Center.

DEPARTMENT OF FOREIGN LANGUAGES

ANTECEDENT DEPARTMENTS

English and Foreign Languages (1954–1956)

Foreign Languages (1956–Present)

DEPARTMENT HEADS

1954–58	*Col Peter R. Moody*	1990–98	*Col Gunther A. Mueller*
1958–60	Col George L. Holcomb	1998–00	Col Jill M. Crotty
1960–68	*Col Alfonse R. Miele*	2000–06	*Col Mueller*
1968–71	Col Francis W. McInerney Jr.	2006–07	Lt Col Daniel Uribe
1971–78	*Col William Geffen*	2007–08	*Col Mueller*
1978–81	Lt Col Ruben A. Cubero	2008–13	*Col Uribe*
1981–83	Lt Col Daniel G.M. Hannaway	2013–15	Lt Col Jean-Philippe N. Peltier
1983–90	*Col Cubero*	2015–	*Col Uribe*

PERMANENT PROFESSORS

Peter R. Moody   Alfonse R. Miele   William Geffen   Ruben A. Cubero

Gunther A. Mueller   Daniel Uribe

THE DEPARTMENT TODAY: The department provides future officers with broad-based, foreign area-related skills to master strategies for global engagement, partnership, and mutual security responsibilities. This entails courses in Arabic, Chinese, French, German, Japanese, Portuguese, Russian, and Spanish—eight of the most important languages in the world. Within each language there is a broad spectrum of courses, from primarily skills development to a broader appreciation of a particular culture, history, and literature. These skills are further developed through the department's international programs and through academic programs in Foreign Area Studies.

CURRICULUM: The department offers a wide spectrum of courses in eight languages and supports the several courses in Foreign Area Studies.

CORE COURSES: Foreign Lang 131 & 132. Basic sequence in one of eight languages

MAJORS: Foreign Area Studies (Interdisciplinary)
Humanities (Interdisciplinary)

MINORS: Arabic, Chinese, French, German, Japanese, Portuguese, Russian, and Spanish

NOTEWORTHY: The department's Foreign Language Learning Center utilizes the latest language learning technology, which allows multiple languages to be taught simultaneously while providing the capability for individual learning and group or teacher-led activities using any type of multimedia. The department manages the Academy's Office of International Programs, which includes:

- Cadet Summer Language Immersion Program (at a foreign university or language school)
- Cadet Semester Exchange Abroad Program (at a foreign military academy)
- Cadet Semester Study Abroad Program (at civilian universities)
- Foreign Academy Visit Program (during International Week)
- Cultural Immersion Program (spring break or summer)
- Four-Year International Cadet Program (foreign cadets at the Academy)
- Military Personnel Exchange Program (foreign officers on Academy faculty or staff)

DEPARTMENT OF HISTORY

ANTECEDENT DEPARTMENTS

History (1954–1957)

History and Philosophy (1957–1958)

History (1958–Present)

DEPARTMENT HEADS

1955–57	Col John L. Frisbee	1988–94	*Col Reddel*
1957–60	Col John R. Sala	1994–95	Lt Col William J. Williams
1960–66	*Col Wilbert H. Ruenheck*	1995–99	*Col Reddel*
1966–70	*Col Alfred F. Hurley*	1999–05	*Col Mark K. Wells*
1970–71	Lt Col Elliott L. Johnson	2005–07	Lt Col Vance R. Skarstedt
1971–76	*Col Hurley*	2007–13	*Col Wells*
1976–77	Col Philip D. Caine	Fall 2013	Lt Col Edward A. Kaplan
1977–80	*Col Hurley*	2014–15	*Col Wells*
1980–81	Col John F. Shiner	Spr 2016	Col Kaplan
1981–87	*Col Carl W. Reddel*	2016–	*Col Margaret C. Martin*
Fall 1987	Lt Col Harry R. Borowski		

PERMANENT PROFESSORS

Wilbert H. Ruenheck   George V. Fagan*   Alfred F. Hurley   Carl W. Reddel

Mark K. Wells   Margaret C. Martin

Note: Colonel Fagan was Director of the Academy Library, 1956–1969. He was appointed a Permanent Professor of History in 1962 but did not serve as History Department Head.

THE DEPARTMENT TODAY: The department teaches history for the profession of arms. For more than 2,000 years, history has been a warrior's constant companion, a guide for leading, deciding, and acting wisely in challenging and uncertain times. The department provides all cadets instruction on the evolving ideas and methods of waging war throughout modern history and a comprehensive global survey of human civilization and its significant changes over time. History is a unique discipline because it instills powerfully logical, but not rigid, habits of mind; it recognizes that humans, individually and collectively, primarily shaped the past and will shape the future; and it is based on the fundamental belief that no event or decision is exactly the same as any other, although discernable patterns exist. Cadets in the History major seek a deep, nuanced, and balanced understanding of the past as an essential foundation for effectively confronting complex and ambiguous situations.

CURRICULUM: The department offers 45 courses in History as well as a number of courses listed under Humanities and Social Science disciplinary labels.

CORE COURSES: History 100. Introduction to Military History
History 300. World History
History 394. The American Way of War
(Advanced Sociocultural Choice)

MAJORS: History
Foreign Area Studies (Interdisciplinary)
Humanities (Interdisciplinary)

NOTEWORTHY: The department sponsors the annual Harmon Memorial Lecture in Military History. The lecture provides cadets, faculty, and staff the opportunity to interact with a leading scholar on a significant contemporary topic of interest to future military leaders. The department has published a compendium of all Harmon lectures through 1987 and is presently at work on a companion volume through 2017.

DEPARTMENT OF LAW

ESTABLISHED IN 1956

DEPARTMENT HEADS

1956–58	Col Allen W. Rigsby	2001–02	Col Chester H. Morgan II
1958–66	*Col Christopher H. Munch*	2002–07	*Col Paul E. Pirog*
1966–67	Lt Col William C. Hamilton Jr.	2007–08	Col Charles W. Hasskamp
1967–88	*Col Marcos E. Kinevan*	2008–14	*Col Pirog*
1988–97	*Col Richard R. Lee*	2014–15	Lt Col Daniel A. Olson
1997–01	*Col Michael R. Emerson*	2015–	*Col Linell A. Letendre*

PERMANENT PROFESSORS

Christopher Munch   Marcos E. Kinevan   Richard R. Lee   Michael R. Emerson

Paul E. Pirog   Linell A. Letendre

THE DEPARTMENT TODAY: The Department of Law helps cadets develop the analytical skills that will permit them to identify, understand, and resolve the legal issues they will likely encounter after graduation. Increasingly, complex legal considerations permeate every aspect of modern life in both civilian and military environments. The Legal Studies major is not a "pre-law" program. Rather, the Legal Studies major provides students with enhanced knowledge of the law as part of a broadly focused education. Cadets will build expertise in the study of law and its role and function in both American society and the international community.

CURRICULUM: The department offers 18 Law courses and supports courses in Social Sciences.

CORE COURSES: Law 220.   Law for Air Force Officers

Soc Sci 483. Principles of Negotiation
(Advanced Sociocultural Choice)

MAJOR: Legal Studies

NOTEWORTHY: The department sponsors and coaches a cadet Moot Court Team and a cadet Mock Trial Team, which offer cadets opportunities to improve their oral communication, critical thinking, teamwork, and leadership skills, while simultaneously providing an education about the American legal system in competition against other colleges and universities. Additionally, cadets compete in the Cyber 9/12 annual competition regarding international cyber policy. The department's cadets also compete against international military academies on the Law of Armed Conflict and International Humanitarian Law. The department manages two programs that serve cadets, faculty, and the Air Force: The Law, Technology, and Warfare Research Cell serves as the department's intersection between technology and the law; and the Legal Alternative Dispute Resolution Program teaches negotiation and mediation strategies. The department's military faculty serve as Board Legal Advisors to Cadet Honor Boards. Finally, the department conducts training for graduating cadets in the Uniform Code of Military Justice.

DEPARTMENT OF MANAGEMENT

ANTECEDENT DEPARTMENTS

Economics and Management (1966–1973)

Economics, Geography and Management (1973–1981)

Management (1981–Present)

DEPARTMENT HEADS

1966–70	*Col Robert G. Taylor*	1990–97	*Col Woody*
1970–74	*Col Wayne A. Yeoman*	1997–01	*Col Rita A. Jordan*
1974–77	Lt Col Edward L. Claiborn	2001–02	Col Kevin J. Davis
1977–80	*Col Lee D. Badgett*	2002–08	*Col Jordan*
1980–81	Lt Col Robert L. Taylor	2008–13	*Col Andrew P. Armacost*
1981–82	*Col James R. Woody*	2013–14	Dr Steve G. Green
1983–84	Maj Charles J. Yoos II	2014–18	*Col Troy R. Harting*
1984–88	*Col Woody*	2018–	Col Scott G. Heyler
1988–90	Col Robert E. Pizzi		

PERMANENT PROFESSORS

Robert .G. Taylor   Wayne A. Yeoman   Lee D. Badgett   James R. Woody

Rita A. Jordan   Andrew P. Armacost   Troy R. Harting

THE DEPARTMENT TODAY: The department aims to produce critical thinkers who are able to adapt quickly in today's dynamic, technologically complex, global environment. Management majors study traditional managerial and business topics such as organizational perspectives and theories, global organizations, complex human systems, financial and managerial accounting, managerial finance, human resource management, marketing, production and operations management, information systems, and strategic management. The department is heavily engaged in the Systems Engineering and Operations Research majors, disciplines that address the development and modeling of large, complex systems.

CURRICULUM: The department offers 26 courses in Management, 3 in Operations Research, and 4 in Systems Engineering.

CORE COURSES: Mgt 400. Management and Command
(Advanced Sociocultural Choice)
Ops Rsch 310. Systems Analysis (Advanced STEM Choice)

MAJORS: Management
Systems Engineering (Interdisciplinary)
Operations Research (Interdisciplinary)

NOTEWORTHY: Accredited by the Association to Advance Collegiate Schools of Business, the department is arguably the top undergraduate-only business program in the nation. Cadets participate in a wide variety of competitions in entrepreneurship, business venture planning, and operations research modeling. The department conducts Financial Literacy Seminars for cadets.

DEPARTMENT OF MATHEMATICAL SCIENCES

ANTECEDENT DEPARTMENTS

Mathematics (1954–1973)

Mathematical Sciences (1973–Present)

DEPARTMENT HEADS

1954–56	Col Archie Higdon	1986–91	*Col Daniel W Litwhiler*
1956–65	Col John W. Ault	1991–93	Lt Col Steven C. Gordon
1965–66	Lt Col John B. MacWherter	1993–94	Lt Col Ronald J. Berdine
1966–67	*Col Higdon*	1994–00	*Col Litwhiler*
Fall 1967	*Col Roger R. Bate*	2000–01	Lt Col Gerald Diaz
1967–70	Lt Col Monty D. Coffin	2001–05	*Col Litwhiler*
1970–78	*Col Robert R. Lochry*	2005–08	*Col John M. Andrew*
1978–80	Lt Col Tony M. Johnson	2008–10	Dr Bradley A. Warner
1980–85	*Col Lochry*	2010–16	*Col Andrew*
Fall 1985	Lt Col Nelson S. Pacheco	2016–	*Col Scott E. Williams*

PERMANENT PROFESSORS

Archie Higdon   Roger R. Bate   Robert R. Lochry   Daniel W Litwhiler

John M. Andrew   Scott E. Williams

THE DEPARTMENT TODAY: The department offers a broad yet focused education in problem solving, analytical reasoning, and technical communication—skills that prepare cadets to tackle the complex operational, managerial, and technical problems that routinely challenge Air Force officers. The Operations Research major entails development and application of new quantitative modeling methods to solve real management and economics problems.

CURRICULUM:	The department offers 33 Mathematics and 5 Ops Research courses.
CORE COURSES:	Math 141 & 142. Calculus I & II
	Math 300. Introduction to Statistics
	Math 243. Calculus III (Advanced STEM Choice)
	Math 245. Differential Equations
	(Advanced STEM Choice)
MAJORS:	Mathematics
	Applied Mathematics
	Operations Research (Interdisciplinary)

NOTEWORTHY: The Mathematics degree focuses on classical and modern mathematics while leaving flexibility for cadets to tailor a program that meets individual interests. The Applied Mathematics degree features a focused four-course interdisciplinary concentration coordinated with other departments. The Math Department chairs the Operations Research Steering Group, which coordinates the interdisciplinary Operations Research major (jointly administered by the Departments of Computer Science, Economics and Geosciences, Management, and Mathematical Sciences).

DEPARTMENT OF MILITARY AND STRATEGIC STUDIES
ANTECEDENT DEPARTMENTS
Commandant of Cadets:
Professional Military Studies (1981–1992)
Military Arts and Science (1992–1994)
34th Training Group (1994–2005)

Dean of Faculty:
Military and Strategic Studies (2005–Present)

DEPARTMENT HEADS

1981–86	*Col Philip D. Caine*	1998–99	Col Larry A. Smith
1987	Lt Col James R.W. Titus	1999–03	*Col Thomas A. Drohan*
1988–92	*Col Caine*	2003–05	Col Steven F. Baker
1992–94	*Col David A. Wagie*	2005–17	*Col Drohan*
1994–98	Lt Col Jerome V. Martin	2017–	Col Thomas T. Swaim

PERMANENT PROFESSORS

Philip D. Caine   David A. Wagie   Thomas A. Drohan

THE DEPARTMENT TODAY: The department provides cadets the professional military educational background for development as Airmen. Cadets use strategic thinking and operational planning concepts to evaluate and apply air, space, cyber, and joint capabilities to contemporary strategic problems and operational simulations. Cadets in the major pursue courses related to the uniquely demanding context of the military profession by framing the battle space, and evaluating theories, models, and perspectives for future applications of military and strategic power.

CURRICULUM: The department offers 24 courses in Military and Strategic Studies.

CORE COURSES: MSS 251. Airpower and Joint Operations Strategy
MSS 444. Space and Cyber Strategy for National Security (Advanced Sociocultural Choice)

MAJOR: Military and Strategic Studies

NOTEWORTHY: The department's Center for Airpower Studies aims to produce cognitively agile, action-oriented thinkers to meet the challenges of translating strategic guidance into operational and tactical successes to achieve national security policy goals with the military instrument of national power. The Center features the Cadet Battle Laboratory to provide an environment for presenting and solving strategic and operational challenges and the Air Warfare Laboratory to provide an environment for translating strategic guidance into kinetic and non-kinetic tactical action.

DEPARTMENT OF PHILOSOPHY

ANTECEDENT DEPARTMENTS

History and Philosophy (1957–1958)

[Philosophy courses in English (1958–1967)]

Philosophy and Fine Arts (1967–1973)

Philosophy (1973)

Political Science and Philosophy (1974–1977)

Philosophy and Fine Arts (1977–1999)

Philosophy (1999–Present)

DEPARTMENT HEADS

1957–58	Col John R. Sala	Fall 2009	Dr J. Carl Ficarrotta
1967–94	*Col Malham M. Wakin*	2010–15	*Col Cook*
1995–00	*Col Charles R. Myers*	2015–16	Dr Carl E. Bertha
2000–02	Lt Col William H. Rhodes	2016–	*Col Cook*
2002–09	*Col James L. Cook*		

PERMANENT PROFESSORS

Malham M. Wakin   Charles R. Myers   James L. Cook

THE DEPARTMENT TODAY: The department guides cadets to undertake their study of philosophy and religion as part of a life of energetic inquiry aimed at developing the virtues appropriate to a leader of character. It introduces cadets to a critical study of several major moral theories and their application to contemporary moral problems with special emphasis on the moral problems of the profession of arms. Highlighted are the officer's responsibilities to reason and act ethically; develop critical thinking skills; and to know civic, cultural, and international contexts in which the US military operates. Cadets learn influential normative theories about ethics and the foundations of character. The department offers special expertise in the sub-disciplines of ethics, logic, philosophy of religion, political philosophy, metaphysics, epistemology, aesthetics, philosophy of science, and philosophy of law.

CURRICULUM: The department offers 19 Philosophy courses.

CORE COURSES: Philos 310. Ethics

Philos 401. Comparative Religion
(Advanced Sociocultural Choice)

MAJORS: Philosophy

Humanities (Interdisciplinary)

MINORS: Philosophy

Religion Studies (Interdisciplinary)

NOTEWORTHY: The Department of Philosophy takes great pride in being the only stand-alone Philosophy Department among the US service academies, as well as the only one to develop a minor in Religion Studies. The department sponsors the annual Reich Lecture on War, Morality, and the Military Profession and the Alice McDermott Memorial Lecture in Applied Ethics. Faculty members frequently publish and provide editorial assistance in major disciplinary publications such as the international *Journal of Military Ethics*.

DEPARTMENT OF PHYSICS

ANTECEDENT DEPARTMENTS

Chemistry, Physics and Electrical Engineering (1954–1955)

Physics (1955–Present)

DEPARTMENT HEADS

1954–56	Col James V.G. Wilson	1974–78	*Col William A. Orth*
1956–57	Col Edwin W. Brown	1978–80	Lt Col Winston K. Pendleton
1957–59	Lt Col Bennett E. Robertson	1980–84	*Col John T. May*
1959–61	*Col Archie Higdon*	1984–87	Lt Col David J. Evans
1961–63	Col Gustav E. Lundquist	1987–94	*Col James H. Head*
1963–65	Lt Col Paul Baker Jr.	1994–96	Col Rolf C. Enger
1965–66	Lt Col George W. Brock	1996–04	*Col Head*
1966–69	*Col Anthony J. Mione*	2004–06	Lt Col Ryan K. Haaland
1969–70	Col William T. Haidler	2006–11	*Col Rex R. Kiziah*
1970–71	Lt Col Jack T. Humphries	2011–13	Lt Col Brian D. Griffith
1971–74	*Col Mione*	2013–	*Col Kiziah*

PERMANENT PROFESSORS

Archie Higdon   Anthony J. Mione   William A. Orth   John T. May

James H. Head   Rex R. Kiziah

THE DEPARTMENT TODAY: The department provides calculus-based physics courses for all cadets with emphasis on Newtonian mechanics, conservation principles, rotational motion, gravitation, orbital mechanics, wave motion, electrostatics, magnetism, electromagnetic induction, electromagnetic waves, and physical optics. Physics majors choose a concentration; common choices include Astronomy, Laser Physics/Optics, Nuclear Physics, Nuclear Weapons and Strategy, and Space Physics. The department offers meteorology courses in compliance with the World Meteorology Organization requirements for a Bachelor of Science degree in Meteorology or Atmospheric Sciences.

CURRICULUM: The department offers 27 Physics and 4 Meteorology courses.

CORE COURSES: Physics 110. General Physics I with Laboratory
Physics 215. General Physics II with Laboratory
(Basic Science Option)
Physics 264. Modern Physics (Advanced STEM Choice)
Physics 371. Astronomy (Advanced STEM Choice)
Meteor 320. Intro. to Meteorology and Aviation Weather
(Advanced STEM Choice)

MAJORS: Physics
Meteorology (joint with Economics and Geosciences)

MINOR: Nuclear Weapons and Strategy (Interdisciplinary)

NOTEWORTHY: The department is home to major research centers that support faculty and cadets in developing real-world solutions to enhance the capabilities of the Air Force and Department of Defense. These are the Laser and Optics Research Center, the Space Physics and Atmospheric Research Center, and the Center for Space Situational Awareness Research. Additionally, the Astronomical Research Group and Observatory conducts near-Earth and deep-space research including space object tracking. The Center for Physics Education Research engages in pedagogical innovation and the application of technology to the learning experience.

DEPARTMENT OF POLITICAL SCIENCE

ANTECEDENT DEPARTMENTS

Political Science (1956–1974)

Political Science and Philosophy (1974–1977)

Political Science (1977–Present)

DEPARTMENT HEADS

1956–57	Col John L. Frisbee	1983–84	Lt Col Robert P. Haffa
1957–62	*Col Wesley W. Posvar*	1984–90	*Col Douglas J. Murray*
1962–63	Col William G. McDonald	1990–92	Col Paul R. Viotti
1963–64	Maj Brent Scowcroft	1992–94	*Col Murray*
1964–67	*Col Posvar*	1994–96	Col William E. Berry Jr.
1967–69	*Col Richard F. Rosser*	1996–07	*Col Murray*
1969–71	Lt Col Charles R. Coble Jr.	Fall 2007	Dr Paul J. Bolt
1971–74	*Col Rosser*	2007–11	*Col Cheryl A. Kearney*
1974–77	*Col Malham M. Wakin*	2011–12	Dr Bolt
1977–80	*Col Ervin J. Rokke*	2012–16	*Col Kearney*
1980–82	Lt Col Curtis Cook	2016–17	Lt Col Joseph Foster
1982–83	*Col Rokke*	2017–	*Col Kearney*

PERMANENT PROFESSORS

Wesley W. Posvar   Richard F. Rosser   Malham M. Wakin   Ervin J. Rokke

Douglas J. Murray   Cheryl A. Kearney

THE DEPARTMENT TODAY: The department prepares cadets to comprehend domestic and international political events by examining political theories and ideologies, international relations, American politics, international security, defense decision-making, the politics of foreign governments, and political economy. The Political Science major allows cadets to study areas in-depth or to examine a variety of political topics, both domestic and international, that will shape their careers.

CURRICULUM: The department offers 33 Political Science courses and supports those in Foreign Area Studies.

CORE COURSES: Pol Sci 211. Politics, American Government and National Security

Pol Sci 302. American Foreign and National Security Policy (Advanced Sociocultural Choice)

Soc Sci 311. International Security Studies

MAJORS: Political Science

Foreign Area Studies (Interdisciplinary)

NOTEWORTHY: The Eisenhower Center for Space and Defense Studies provides cadets and faculty with unique opportunities to participate in research and policy discussions with senior leaders and experts in the military, civilian government, and private sector from the United States and major space-faring nations. In addition to its founding interest in space policy, the Center examines other frontiers of technology development to include cyber. Its journal, *Space and Defense*, promotes an ongoing discussion of space and security policy issues. The Academy Assembly and Model UN conferences provide opportunities for cadets to engage with cohorts from around the world. The department sponsors the annual Harry S. Truman lecture series and the Ira C. Eaker Lecture on national defense policy. The department has edited eight editions of the book *American Defense Policy* and is working on the next edition.

DEPARTMENT OF PHYSICAL EDUCATION

ANTECEDENTS

Physical Education has been a required part of the Academy program from inception. Initially organized under the Commandant of Cadets, it moved to the Athletic Department in 1959. The authorization in 2000 of a position for a Permanent Professor for Physical Education further solidified the program.

DEPARTMENT HEADS

1954–57	Lt Col W.C. McGlothin Jr.	1984–87	Col Michael P. Blaisdell
1957–60	Lt Col Casimir J. Myslinski	1988–93	Col Richard A. Wolf
1960–62	Lt Col James F. Frakes	1993–96	Col Gerald V. Boesche
1962–67	Lt Col John S. Sparks Jr.	1996–97	Mr Jeffery N. Heidmous
1967–70	Col Charles W. Oliver	1997–01	Col Laurence A Fariss
1970–71	Lt Col Anthony R. Cillo	2001–10	*Col William P. Walker*
1971–74	Col Charles W. Oliver	2010–14	Mr George Nelson
1975–77	Col Robert K. Strickland	2014–15	Lt Col Brandon K. Doan
1977–80	Col Don L. Peterson	2015–17	Lt Col Sean Tiernan
1981–83	Col Richelieu N. Johnson	2017–	*Col Maiya D. Anderson*
1983–84	Col Edwin R. Cliatt		

PERMANENT PROFESSORS

William P. Walker   Maiya D. Anderson

THE DEPARTMENT TODAY: Physical Education (PE) is an integral part of the Academy's curriculum and critical to cadets developing the Academy Institutional Outcomes. The department offers required and elective PE courses in a program designed to expose cadets to a wide variety of physical skills. Additionally, the department oversees programs in cadet fitness, intramural sports, and intercollegiate boxing. Cadets take physical fitness tests each semester to measure overall strength and conditioning. Proficiency is required in both the Physical Fitness Test (PFT) and the Aerobic Fitness Test (AFT). Scores on the PFT, AFT, and PE class grades go into calculating a cadet's Physical Education Average (PEA). Every member of the Cadet Wing participates in intramural, club, or intercollegiate sports; more than 3,000 cadets participate in 10 different intramural programs, which include team sports such as basketball, soccer, and ultimate frisbee.

> CURRICULUM: The department offers 24 Physical Education courses composed of 6 core courses and 18 elective courses.
>
> CORE COURSES: Cadets are required to take a total of 10 PE Courses, including 6 core courses and 4 electives. The core courses include fitness principles, boxing, swimming, water survival, and combative arts. The electives include both individual and team sports.

NOTEWORTHY: Historically, the Physical Education Department managed all gym facilities, weight rooms, and the Human Performance Laboratory. Although no longer strictly part of the Department, the Lab applies sports science principles to improve Academy athletic teams and individual cadet performance. Coaches, cadet athletes, and cadets receive specific physiological information by way of testing, research, training, and education. The Lab also provides subject-matter expertise on the Air Force fitness program and other aspects of human performance, offering scientific data through research and exercise science principles. As a result, the Lab offers a venue for cadet researchers and qualified interns to complete independent study research in the fields of exercise physiology, psychology, nutrition, biology, biochemistry, and biomechanics. The intercollegiate boxing program falls under the purview of the Physical Education Department. The USAFA Boxing Team competes very successfully in the annual regional and national tournaments hosted by the National Collegiate Boxing Association. The boxing coaching staff is instrumental in the development and delivery of the core PE boxing curriculum, which became a gender-neutral course in 2016.

CENTER FOR CHARACTER AND LEADERSHIP DEVELOPMENT
ANTECEDENT ORGANIZATIONS
Commandant of Cadets:
Center for Character Development (1993–2009)
Center for Character and Leadership Development (2009–2018)
Superintendent:
Center for Character and Leadership Development (2018–Present)

CENTER DIRECTORS

1993–94	Col Marian F. Alexander	2006–10	Col John B. Norton Jr
1994–96	*Col David A. Wagie*	2010–15	*Col Joseph E. Sanders III*
1996–02	Col Mark A. Hyatt	2015–16	Col John C. McCurdy
2002–04	Col John Herd	2016–	*Col Mark C. Anarumo*
2004–06	Col Joseph W. Mazzola		

PERMANENT PROFESSORS

David A. Wagie   Joseph E. Sanders III   Mark C. Anarumo

THE CENTER TODAY: The Academy's Center for Character and Leadership Development (CCLD) helps align academic, athletic, and military efforts to develop leaders of character. The goal is to advance understanding and implementation of effective character and leadership development practices across military, academic, and athletic settings—for cadets, faculty, and staff. The Center's Development Division focuses on cadet programs and faculty and staff development. The Integration Division works with all USAFA leaders to ensure effective character education and with other service academies, civilian institutions with character centers, Air University, and other agencies with whom we should maintain relationships. The Scholarship Division includes our senior scholars who perform research to advance understanding of the profession of arms and implementation of effective character and leadership development practices. The Operations Division supports the Center by scheduling, planning, and overseeing the numerous seminars, Air Force leadership meetings, international conferences, and other uses of the Center's facilities.

CURRICULUM: The Center oversees Character and Leadership programs across all four classes of cadets as well as for the Academy's faculty and staff. A cadet must successfully complete a CCLD core course or program each year to graduate.

NOTEWORTHY: The Center organizes and hosts the National Character and Leadership Symposium, one of the Academy's most visible leadership and development events. Attended by 4,000 cadets and over 300 guests, students, and faculty from military academies and universities across the nation and around the world, this nationally recognized forum brings together distinguished scholars, military leaders, and corporate executives with a popular student consortium to explore character and leadership issues. The Symposium provides cadets and permanent party the opportunity to enhance their understanding of character-based leadership. The Center also hosts the Falcon Heritage Forum, which is designed for cadets to connect with our nation's distinguished veterans/mentors in order to strengthen appreciation for Air Force heritage and to enhance their perspective as developing leaders of character in the profession of arms.

CHAPTER 5

BIOGRAPHICAL SKETCHES OF THE PERMANENT PROFESSORS

The following pages present a biographical sketch of each Permanent Professor, arranged by order of appointment, beginning with the appointment of Robert F. McDermott in 1956 and concluding with those just appointed as of this writing. Each of these short biographies attempts to illustrate the individual's military and educational background that was the basis for their selection, identify their special contributions to the institution during their tenure, and (where appropriate) describe some of their interests and activities after retirement from active duty.

As much as possible, the biographical information was drawn from materials prepared by the individuals themselves and made public as the kind of "official" biography common across the Air Force. Many old official biographies and similar records have been archived in the McDermott Library Special Collections Branch, which is also a rich source of photographs. Unfortunately, the Library's holdings are far from complete. Where feasible, the biographical sketches included here have been reviewed for accuracy by the subjects themselves. In other cases, close associates and some family members have provided the review. The authors of this book have made no attempt to verify the specific statements about career history, duties, degrees, awards, or the like made in each of these biographical sketches. Those facts are taken directly or indirectly from materials provided by the subject individual; we assume them to be accurate, but we do not assume responsibility for their accuracy. When we found conflicts about significant facts, we made every effort to resolve the discrepancies. In many cases we had more material than we included. We are totally responsible for decisions on what to include and what to omit.

PERMANENT PROFESSORS OF THE
UNITED STATES AIR FORCE ACADEMY

CHRONOLOGICAL ORDER BY APPOINTMENT DATE

1	McDermott, Robert F.	1957–1968
2	Woodyard, William T.	1958–1978
3	Moody, Peter R.	1958–1967
4	Higdon, Archie	1958–1967
5	Wilson, James V.G.	1959–1965
6	Munch, Christopher H.	1959–1967
7	Posvar, Wesley W.	1960–1967
8	Ruenheck, Wilbert H.	1961–1967
9	Miele, Alfonse R.	1961–1968
10	Yeoman, Wayne A.	1961–1972
11	Fagan, George V.	1962–1969
12	Bate, Roger R.	1962–1973
13	Erdle, Philip J.	1964–1979
14	Thomas, Roland E.	1964–1979
15	Wakin, Malham M	1964–1995
16	Taylor, Robert G.	1966–1975
17	Gatlin, Jesse C., Jr.	1966–1977
18	Mione, Anthony J.	1966–1974
19	Hurley, Alfred F.	1966–1980
20	Fluhr, Wallace E.	1966–1981
21	Kinevan, Marcos E.	1967–1988
22	Carter, Peter B.	1967–1975
23	Daley, Daniel H.	1967–1984
24	Rosser, Richard F.	1968–1973
25	Lamb, Robert W.	1970–1979
26	Lochry, Robert R.	1970–1985
27	Geffen, William	1971–1982
28	Wittry, John P.	1973–1984
29	Orth, William A.	1974–1983
30	Williams, John W., Jr.	1976–1986
31	Badgett, Lee D.	1976–1981
32	Rokke, Ervin J.	1976–1986
33	Shuttleworth, Jack M.	1977–1999
34	Fisher, Cary A.	1977–2005
35	Monroe, Joseph	1979–1987
36	May, John T.	1980–1987
37	Sampson, Orwyn	1980–1992
38	Schiller, Harvey W.	1980–1986
39	Caine, Philip D.	1981–1992
40	Swint, David O., Sr.	1982–2000
41	Reddel, Carl W.	1982–1999
42	Fleming, Kenneth H.	1981–1988
43	Woody, James R.	1982–1997
44	Royer, Erlind G.	1983–1991
45	Murray, Douglas J.	1984–2007
46	Giffen, Robert B.	1984–1995
47	Cubero, Ruben A.	1984–1998
48	Smith, Michael L.	1985–2000
49	Litwhiler, Daniel W	1986–2006
50	Hughes, Richard L.	1987–1995
51	Mueh, Hans J.	1987–2004
52	Head, James H.	1987–2006
53	Klayton, Alan R.	1988–2008
54	Lee, Richard R.	1988–1997
55	Richardson, William E.	1988–1994
56	Franck, Raymond E., Jr.	1989–2000

Permanent Professors of the
United States Air Force Academy

Alphabetical Index
(with order of appointment)

BRIGADIER GENERAL
ROBERT F. MCDERMOTT

Permanent Professor 1957–1968
Vice Dean of the Faculty 1954–1956
Dean of the Faculty 1956–1968

B.S., United States Military Academy
M.B.A., Harvard University

Bob McDermott, "McD," the Academy's 1st Permanent Professor, was born in Boston, Massachusetts, in 1920. He attended Norwich University from 1937 to 1939 and received a Bachelor of Science degree from the United States Military Academy in January 1943. He initially served as a fighter pilot and Assistant Group Operations Officer in the United States. From February 1944 until September 1945, McD flew 61 combat missions in the European Theater and served as Operations Officer for the 47th Fighter-Bomber Group. From 1945 to 1947 he served as a Personnel Staff Officer in HQ US Forces, European Theater. In 1947 he was assigned as a Personnel Staff Officer, Schools Branch, HQ USAF, Washington, DC. In 1948 he entered Harvard University and earned a Master's degree in Business Administration in 1950. He then was assigned as an Instructor in the Department of Social Studies at the US Military Academy. As an Assistant Professor McD wrote several handbooks for service personnel on insurance and personal finance that were revised by the West Point Department of Social Sciences in editions published as late as 1965. His department head, a West Point classmate of General Harmon, the first USAF Academy Superintendent, recommended McD to General Harmon for his faculty. Joining the Academy at its inception in 1954, McD served as Professor and Head of the Department of Economics with additional duty as the Vice Dean of the Faculty. In 1956 he was appointed the Dean of the Faculty, retaining his Department of Economics position as an additional duty. McD became the first USAF Academy Permanent Professor in September 1957 and the first permanent Dean of the Faculty in September 1959, which included promotion to brigadier general. He was Dean of the Faculty for the first 10 graduating classes of the Academy. For his numerous innovations at the Academy, many of which also were adopted by its sister service academies, McD has been called the "Father of Modern Military Education." Most notable of these innovations was the 1957 introduction and development of a curriculum enrichment program that broke from the military education mold set by Thayer at West Point nearly 150 years earlier. This new curriculum introduced elective courses that motivated, qualified cadets could take in addition to the prescribed curriculum previously followed by every cadet. This enabled the initial offering of majors in International Studies, Military Management, Basic Science, and Engineering Sciences. In the graduating Class of 1962, one cadet earned three majors, 35 percent earned two majors, and 35 percent earned one major. Later, while maintaining a balanced core program that ensured a well-rounded academic core foundation, McD introduced the concept of all cadets pursuing a major in an area of interest to them. By 1966 all cadets graduated with a Bachelor of Science degree and at least one major. Other innovations that McD introduced were a Tenure Associate Professor program that aimed to be comparable with civilian institutions by providing tenure for 10 percent of the faculty with PhDs, a sabbatical leave program so tenured faculty could stay current by rejoining the rest of the Air Force for a year, a summer research program for both cadets and faculty so they could help solve current Air Force problems, a successful program to assist cadets in pursuing nationally recognized graduate scholarships, and a faculty research program so faculty could remain at the cutting edge of their disciplines while engaging cadets in current AF research endeavors. McD's efforts also led to two notable Academy "firsts." The North Central Accreditation Board accredited the Academy before its first graduating class in 1959. And the Academy's then five undergraduate engineering degrees were the first service academy degrees accredited by the Engineers' Council for Professional Development (now the Accreditation Board for Engineering and

Technology). McD retired in 1968 to join the United Services Automobile Association (USAA) and become its Chief Executive Officer.

McD headed USAA, now an insurance and diversified financial services company, for 25 years. As Chairman and CEO, McD guided USAA to become a nationally recognized leader in the services sector. Under his leadership, USAA grew from the 16th to the 5th largest insurer of private automobiles in the nation. It also grew to be the nation's 4th largest homeowner insurer. During his tenure, USAA's owned and managed assets rose from $206 million to over $30 billion. In 1993 he retired and was appointed Chairman Emeritus. McD remained active in civic leadership roles. Among the honors he received are five honorary doctorate degrees, academic chairs endowed in his name at the US Military Academy and US Air Force Academy, an elementary school and university health science center building named after him, and a section of I-10 running through San Antonio, TX, named the McDermott Freeway. The Academy Research and Development Institute supports The Robert F. McDermott Endowed Chair in Academic Excellence at USAFA. Robert F. McDermott died in 2006 and is buried in San Antonio.

BRIGADIER GENERAL
WILLIAM T. WOODYARD

Permanent Professor 1958–1978
Vice Dean of the Faculty 1967–1968
Dean of the Faculty 1968–1978

A.S., St. Joseph Junior College
B.S., University of Missouri
M.S., University of Missouri
Ph.D., University of Denver

Bill Woodyard, the Academy's 2nd Permanent Professor, was born in 1919 in St. Joseph, Missouri. He earned an Associate's degree in Chemistry from St. Joseph Junior College in 1939. He became an Aviation Cadet in 1940 and was commissioned a second lieutenant in the US Army Air Corps in 1941. After completing training at Randolph Field, TX, he served as an Instructor Pilot at Craig AFB, AL, before being reassigned as a Training Squadron Commander at Napier Field, AL, 1941–1944. During this period, he also attended the Army Command and General Staff School at Fort Leavenworth, KS. After serving as Post Air Inspector at Napier Field in 1944, he was trained in the B-17 and B-29 bombers. In 1945 he was a B-29 Instructor Pilot at Maxwell Field, AL. Bill became a Squadron Commander in the 448th Bombardment Group in August 1945 at McCook Army Air Field, NE, and was en route to 20th AF HQ in Guam with a flight of B-29s when World War II ended. He returned to Carswell Field, TX, and served as a Squadron Commander with the 19th Bombardment Group until 1946. From February to June 1946 he was a pilot in "Project Sunset," ferrying B-29s back to the United States from the Pacific. As Commander of the 715th Air Materiel Squadron, Tempelhof Air Base, Berlin, Germany, from July 1946 to May 1947, Bill was charged with supplying the city of Berlin and the Allied Forces therein during the reconstruction. After commanding the 4700th Air Base Group at Lawson Field, Fort Benning, GA, for the remainder of 1947, he entered the University of Missouri in 1948. Bill earned his Bachelor's and Master's degrees in Chemistry in 1950 and 1951, respectively. From 1951 to 1954 he was a Chemistry Instructor, progressing to Associate Professor, at the US Military Academy, West Point, NY. In 1954 he became an Associate Professor of Chemistry as an original member of the Air Force Academy faculty at its interim site at Lowry AFB in Denver. Promoted to Professor of Chemistry in 1955, Bill then was appointed Professor and Head, Department of Chemistry in 1956. As Chairman of the Academy Accreditation Steering Committee, he was instrumental in achieving the Academy's academic program accreditation before the first class graduated in 1959. He was appointed a Permanent Professor in 1958, continuing as Professor and Head of the Department of Chemistry. He entered the Industrial College of the Armed Forces, Washington, DC, in 1961. After graduating in 1962 he returned to his former position at the Academy. He received a PhD in Higher Education from the University of Denver in 1965. While on sabbatical from the Academy faculty, he served as the Chief Scientist for the European Office of Aerospace Research at Brussels, Belgium, 1965–1967. Upon his return to the Academy he was appointed the Vice Dean of the Faculty. Bill was named Dean of the Faculty and promoted to the grade of brigadier general in 1968. During his tenure as Dean, he oversaw the *20th Anniversary Study* and implementation of its recommendations, which included adjusting graduation, core, and major course requirements as well as adding a flight requirement for all cadets. He instituted the Honor Graduate Program, the Cadet Exchange Program with the French *l'École de l'Air*, and the Distinguished Visiting Professor Program. The latter brought outstanding civilian Professors on sabbatical leave from their institutions to the Academy for an academic year. Bill Woodyard retired from the USAF in 1978.

After he retired Bill moved to Sun City West in Arizona. He immediately became the General Manager of the Recreation Centers in Sun City West for the Del Webb Corporation and continued in that role for 12 years. He served on the Boswell Memorial Hospital Corporate Board from 1980 to 1986 and the Del E. Webb Memorial Operating Board from 1986 to 2002. Bill died in 2018 and is buried in the Air Force Academy Cemetery.

BRIGADIER GENERAL
PETER R. MOODY

Permanent Professor 1958–1967
Vice Dean of the Faculty 1966–1967

A.B., Wofford College
B.S., United States Military Academy
M.A., Duke University
Ph.D., Cambridge University

Pete Moody, the Academy's 3rd Permanent Professor, was born in 1917 in Dillon, South Carolina. He graduated from Wofford College, Spartanburg, SC, in 1937 and was pursuing a Master's degree at Duke when prospects of war caused him to choose a military career. He entered the United States Military Academy in 1938 and graduated in 1942. During his first class year at West Point he taught English literature in place of faculty members who had left for combat. In 1944 he arrived in the European Theater as a fighter pilot with the 393rd Squadron. During the war he flew the P-38 and P-47 in 69 combat missions and earned a Distinguished Flying Cross and the French *Croix de Guerre* while rising to the rank of lieutenant colonel and becoming a Squadron Commander and Group Operations Officer. Operationally, he flew the first and last World War II missions for the 393rd Squadron. After the war he returned to West Point and taught English from 1946 to 1950. During this period, he completed his master's thesis and the degree was awarded by Duke in 1947. Following a semester at the Army Language School, Monterey, CA, and another at Air War College, Maxwell AFB, AL, Pete was assigned to the Military Assistance Advisory Group in Paris, France, as the Deputy Chief of the Air Force Section, 1951–1954. In this assignment, he worked actively with the French Air Force and was awarded the wings of a brevet pilot, French Air Force. It was from this position that he received orders to become the Base Commander of Stewart

AFB, NY. However, before he took command he was recruited to join the initial faculty cadre at the new Air Force Academy, where he became Professor of English in August 1954. In 1956 he was appointed Professor and Head of the Department of English with additional duties as Professor and Head of the Department of Foreign Languages and Chair of the Humanities Division. He was appointed a Permanent Professor in 1958. From 1961 to 1963, he was a student at Cambridge University in England, where he earned his PhD in English Literature in 1963. Returning to the Academy, he resumed his positions as Department Head and Division Chair. From 1966 to 1967 he was the Vice Dean of the Faculty. One of the towering figures of the initial academic leadership, Pete Moody was a driving factor in creation of academic majors in the Humanities and Military Arts and Sciences, as well as a central figure in nurturing the Graduate Scholarship Program. He retired in the grade of brigadier general in 1967.

Following his military service, Pete was the Vice President of Academic Affairs and later Provost at Eastern Illinois University, Charleston, IL, from 1967 to 1978. During his 11 years there he led the university's growth from an enrollment of 5,000 to more than 10,000. In 1994 he was named to the university's "Centennial 100," an elite list of individuals who significantly contributed to the university in its nearly 100 years of existence. He died in 2008 at his home in Fayetteville, NC, at age 91, and is buried in Arlington National Cemetery.

Brigadier General
Archie Higdon

Permanent Professor 1958–1967

B.S., South Dakota State College
M.S., Iowa State University
Ph.D., Iowa State University

Archie Higdon, the Academy's 4th Permanent Professor, was born in a log cabin in Saline, Missouri, in 1905. He received his Bachelor's degree in Mathematics and Speech in 1928 from South Dakota State College (now University), Brookings. He entered graduate school at Iowa State University, Ames, where he earned his Master's degree in 1930 and his PhD in 1936. His major was Applied Mathematics and his minor was Theoretical Physics. Archie taught at North Dakota State University, Fargo, for 4 years and Iowa State for 15 years, with an interruption from 1942 to 1946 when he served in the US Army Air Corps. He was recalled to active duty in 1951 during the Korean War and taught at the United States Military Academy for two years. (When he arrived at West Point his name was already well known in the Mechanics Department—they were using his textbook!) In 1954 Archie was recruited to come to the United States Air Force Academy as Professor and Head of the Department of Mathematics. However, Mechanics was the field of his national reputation, so when the Department of Mechanics was formed in 1956, Archie was made the Professor and Head of that new department. He was appointed Permanent Professor in 1958. In the Academy's formative years, Archie had a powerful influence on the curriculum and the facilities to support it. He served as Chair of the Basic Sciences Division and later Chair of the Engineering Sciences Division. As an additional duty, he was Acting Head, Department of Physics, from 1959 to 1961.

While the Academy was still in Denver, he was given the lead to design the science and engineering laboratories for the new permanent site. He drew from colleagues across the nation and worked with the architects to ensure these top-rate facilities were built and ready for the Cadet Wing's move in 1959. Over his distinguished career, Archie authored numerous articles on engineering education published in professional journals. His best-selling definitive textbooks include the co-authored *Engineering Mechanics* (1949) and *Mechanics of Materials* (1960), both of which were republished many times. From 1963 to 1964 he was on sabbatical as Assistant Director of Undergraduate Study Goals of Engineering Education for the American Society for Engineering Education (ASEE). In 1965 Archie returned to his position as Head of the Department of Mechanics, but that same year he moved to the Dean's office as Associate Dean for Basic and Engineering Sciences. When that position was merged into the new position of Vice Dean in 1966, Archie was once again made Head of the Department of Mathematics, coming full circle back to the position he had founded a dozen years earlier. He was promoted to brigadier general and retired from active duty in 1967.

Following his retirement, Archie Higdon became Dean of the School of Engineering and Technology at California State Polytechnic College, San Luis Obispo, where he served until 1972. In his second retirement, he continued a varied career as an engineering and technical education consultant, working with the state-level commissions in Colorado, Florida, Arkansas, Utah, and California. He has received several awards from ASEE. In 1974 he became an Honorary Member. In 1977 the Mechanics Division of ASEE established the Archie Higdon Distinguished Educator Award and Archie became the first recipient. He received their Distinguished Service Citation in 1979. He died in 1989 and is buried in the Air Force Academy Cemetery.

BRIGADIER GENERAL
JAMES V.G. WILSON

Permanent Professor 1959–1965
Acting Dean of the Faculty
1964–1965

B.S., *United States Military Academy*
M.S., *University of Illinois*

Jim Wilson, the Academy's 5th Permanent Professor, was born in Ellwood City, Pennsylvania, in 1913. He attended Geneva College before entering the United States Military Academy from which he graduated in 1935 with a Bachelor's degree. He earned his Army Air Corps wings at Randolph and Kelly Fields, TX, in 1936. He was then assigned to the 15th Observation Squadron, Scott Field, IL. During this tour he attended and then instructed the Autogiro Operation and Maintenance Course, Patterson Field, OH. In 1938 he was assigned to the 16th Observation Squadron at Fort Benning, GA, responsible for testing the autogiro. In 1939 he spent six months with the 9th Bombardment Group (Heavy) at Mitchell Field, NY. From 1940 to 1943, Jim was an Instructor of Mechanics in the Physics Department at the USMA. During 1943 Jim served with the 48th Bombardment Group (Dive) at Key Army Air Field (AAF), MI, and commanded the 404th Fighter Bomber Group at Orlando AAF, FL, moving with it to Congaree, SC; Burns AAF, OR; and Myrtle AAF, SC. In January 1944 he reported to the 337th Fighter Group at Sarasota, FL, before assuming command of the 59th Fighter Group, Thomasville AAF, GA. He then was sent in December to England with the 8th Air Force where he was assigned as the Deputy Commander of the 359th Fighter Group at East Wretham. He flew fighter escort until March 11, 1945, when his P-51 sustained a coolant leak and he was forced to bail out over northwestern Germany. Jim was interned as a Prisoner of

War in Barth, Germany, until repatriated in May 1945. Returning to the US, he served as Director of Operations and Training, 74th Reconnaissance Group, Stuttgart AAF, AK. Jim then earned a Master's degree in Electrical Engineering from the University of Illinois, Urbana–Champaign, in 1947. He was assigned to the USMA as an Instructor, Assistant Professor, and Associate Professor of Electrical Engineering from 1947 to 1950. In 1950 he joined HQ Air Research and Development Command, Wright-Patterson AFB, OH, and served as Director of Administration, Electronics Subdivision and Director of Electronics. After graduating from the Industrial College of the Armed Forces, his 14-month assignment before coming to the Air Force Academy was Deputy Chief of Staff (DCS), Operations, Japan Air Defense Force, Far East Air Forces, during the Korean War. Jim joined the Academy faculty at its interim location at Lowry AFB, CO. From October 1954 to July 1955, as Professor of Chemistry and Physics, he organized and staffed the Chemistry Department. For the next 10 months, he did the same for the Physics Department and was the Acting Head of the department. From 1956 to 1963 he organized, staffed, and ran the Department of Electrical Engineering as Professor and Head. He was appointed Permanent Professor in 1959 and remained Head of Electrical Engineering until a sabbatical, 1962–1963, as Assistant to the Director of Communications and Electronics, DCS, Operations, HQ Air Defense Command, Peterson AFB, CO. Jim returned to the Academy as Associate Dean for Academic Affairs and was Acting Dean of the Faculty during Brigadier General McDermott's sabbatical leave for the Academic Year 1964–1965. He was promoted to brigadier general upon his retirement from the USAF in 1965, the first USAFA Permanent Professor to retire.

After several months of retirement, Jim suffered a heart attack. However, he recovered and became Administrator of Academic Affairs at the University of Colorado, Colorado Springs, in 1966, retiring again in 1978. Jim Wilson died in 1983 and is buried in the Air Force Academy Cemetery.

BRIGADIER GENERAL
CHRISTOPHER H. MUNCH

Permanent Professor 1959–1967

B.S., United States Military Academy
J.D., University of Illinois

Chris Munch, the Academy's 6th Permanent Professor, was born in Charleroi, Pennsylvania, in 1921. He attended Washington and Jefferson College in Washington, PA, for a year prior to entering the United States Military Academy, from which he graduated in 1943. He earned his pilot wings, but was soon grounded for medical reasons. In 1945 he was sent to Columbia University for a graduate course in English preparatory to going back to West Point as an Instructor of English, 1946–1947. Moving to the Air Force in 1947, Chris was selected for Law School but was sent first to work in the legal office at Chanute AFB, IL. He entered the University of Illinois Law School in 1948. He earned his Juris Doctor in 1951 and was assigned to Headquarters Fifth Air Force, Korea, as Staff Judge Advocate. A year later he was sent to the Philippines as the Staff Judge Advocate for HQ 13th Air Force. In 1955 Chris Munch was assigned in the initial faculty cadre of the Air Force Academy as Assistant Professor of Law, with the additional duty as the Academy Staff Judge Advocate. However, he was recalled to the Philippines for a year to assist in preparations for base rights negotiations. He returned to the Academy in 1957 as Professor and Head of the new Department of Law, still with the additional duty as Academy Staff Judge Advocate. At that time, the curriculum had only a single law course, Elementary Law and Criminal Evidence. Chris oversaw the development of the course and wrote much of the text himself. In 1959 he was made a Permanent Professor. He continued to lead the Law Department for seven years until 1966, when he was sent on sabbatical as a Visiting Professor to the University of Denver Law Center. He retired from the Air Force in 1967. He was one of the retired Permanent Professors promoted to brigadier general, retroactively, in the early 1990s.

Following retirement Chris took the position as the University of Denver Law Center's Associate Dean for Academic Affairs, an office he held until 1980. After leaving his administrative position in the Dean's office, he continued to teach in the DU College of Law until 1995, when he retired as Professor Emeritus. Chris came out of retirement to help establish the School of Law at Chapman University, Orange, CA. He specialized in contracts, patents, trademarks, and copyrights. In 2001 DU established the Chris Munch Summer Institute on Intellectual Property for students to explore this rapidly expanding field of the law. He died in Denver in 2008.

BRIGADIER GENERAL
WESLEY W. POSVAR

Permanent Professor 1960–1967

B.S., *United States Military Academy*
B.A., *Oxford University*
M.A., *Oxford University*
Ph.D., *Harvard University*

Wes Posvar, the Academy's 7th Permanent Professor, was born in Topeka, Kansas, in 1925. He graduated first in his class from the United States Military Academy with a Bachelor of Science degree and his commission as a second lieutenant in the US Army Air Forces in 1946. His first assignment after pilot training was as Aircraft Project Officer and Fighter Test Pilot in the 3200th Fighter Test Squadron, Air Proving Ground Command, Eglin Field, FL. Wes was the first Air Force officer awarded a Rhodes Scholarship, earning both Bachelor and Master of Arts degrees in Philosophy, Politics, and Economics while at Oxford University, England, from 1948 to 1951. While at Oxford in 1949, he served with the forces supporting the Berlin Airlift. Wes next became an Instructor and Assistant Professor in the Department of Social Sciences at the US Military Academy from 1951 to 1954. From 1954 to 1957 he served in the Long-Range Objectives and Programs Group, Directorate of Plans, Deputy Chief of Staff for Operations, HQ USAF, Washington, DC. In 1957 he was named Head of the Department of Political Science of the Air Force Academy at its interim facility, Lowry AFB, CO. In 1960 Wes was appointed a Permanent Professor, continued as Department Head, and was the Chairman of the Social Sciences Division as an additional duty. In 1962 he began sabbatical graduate studies at Harvard University as a Littauer Fellow, graduating with a PhD in International Relations in 1964. From 1963 to 1964 he was also a Research

Fellow at the Massachusetts Institute of Technology. He was editor of the 1st edition of *American Defense Policy* (1964) and a contributor to numerous journals including *Orbus*, *Worldview*, and *Public Policy*. Wes served in the Southeast-Asia Theater in 1965. Returning to his previous posts at the Academy in 1966, he retired in 1967. He was promoted to brigadier general in 1991.

After his retirement, Wes immediately became the 15th Chancellor of the University of Pittsburgh, inheriting a university significantly in debt. He retired this debt by 1976. While at Pittsburgh, he was the founding Chairman in 1988 of the Federal Emergency Management Advisory Board and the National Advisory Council on Environmental Policy and Technology. During 1988 and 1989 Wes chaired a special commission on the West Point Honor Code. When he retired as Chancellor in 1991, he was credited with increasing the university's operating budget by sevenfold, its endowment by threefold, and significantly improving the university's programs and prestige. The Wesley W. Posvar Hall at the University of Pittsburgh was renamed in his honor in 2000. The Academy Research and Development Institute supports The Wesley W. Posvar Chair in Political Science at USAFA. Wes Posvar died in 2001 and is buried in the United States Military Academy Cemetery.

BRIGADIER GENERAL
WILBERT H. RUENHECK

Permanent Professor 1961–1967

B.S., *Washington University, St. Louis*
M.A., *New York University*
Ph.D., *New York University*

Wil Ruenheck, the Academy's 8th Permanent Professor, was born in St. Louis, Missouri, in 1917. He graduated from Kemper Military School, Boonville, MO, in 1936 and from Washington University, St. Louis, in 1938, at which time he received his commission from the Army ROTC program. As a young man, he was a talented first baseman playing in the minor leagues for the St. Louis Cardinals. He entered active duty in 1941 and served throughout World War II in supply depots in Oklahoma City, Kansas City, and New York City. After separating in 1946, he studied History at New York University, earning his Master's degree in 1949 and PhD in History and Economics in 1951. He was recalled to active duty in 1951, in the Air Force, and served in Japan during the Korean War, first as a staff officer in HQ Far Eastern Air Forces, Tokyo, Japan, then for two years in the Joint HQ, Far East Command. Afterward he was assigned for three years as Assistant Professor of Air Science at Washington State University, Pullman. He joined the faculty of the Air Force Academy Department of History in 1957 and in 1960 was appointed Head of the department; a year later, he was appointed a Permanent Professor. He guided the History Department through the establishment of the History major. From 1966 to 1967 he was on sabbatical to the Academy's Command Historian's office, where he wrote a history of the first 25 years of the United States Air Force, which paved the way for more comprehensive tomes by subsequent authors. He retired in 1967 and was promoted to brigadier general in 1993.

Upon retirement, Wil was a sought-after motivational speaker for over two decades for many civic clubs, state, and national organizations. In later years, he was a founding member of the non-profit Academy Research and Development Institute, dedicated to the endowment of civilian professorship chairs at the Academy. Wil Ruenheck died in 2008 and is buried in the Air Force Academy Cemetery.

BRIGADIER GENERAL
ALFONSE R. MIELE

Permanent Professor 1961–1968

B.A., *Fordham University*
M.A., *Columbia University*
Ph.D., *Columbia University*

Al Miele, the Academy's 9th Permanent Professor, was born in New York City in 1922. He graduated from Fordham University in 1942 with a Bachelor's degree in Romance Languages and a commission in the US Army from ROTC. From 1942 to 1945 he served in five battle campaigns in the European Theater with the Fourth Infantry Division, including the Normandy invasion, where he was awarded the Bronze Star, and the liberation of Paris. Following the war, Al was a language student at the University of Nancy, France, 1945, and at Columbia, where he earned his Master's degree in 1947. When the Air Force was established, he cross-commissioned to the new service. He was an Intelligence Officer with Air Training Command, then in 1948–1949 a student of Russian at the Army Language School. From 1949 to 1952 he taught French and Russian language and literature at the US Naval Academy. He returned to Europe in 1953 with duty at Allied Air Forces Central Europe, Fontainebleau, France; then for two years he was the Senior Aide-de-Camp to the Supreme Allied Commander Europe in Fontainebleau and Paris. In 1956 Al began his doctoral work in languages at Columbia, where he was awarded the PhD degree in 1958. With this exceptional preparation, Al arrived at the Air Force Academy in 1958 and became Acting Head of the nascent Department of Foreign Languages. In 1960 he was made Professor and Department Head and the following year appointed Permanent Professor. Al Miele was responsible for many groundbreaking contributions to the Academy's foreign language program. He introduced and fostered the audio-lingual form of instruction, putting oral communication first. He developed a state-of-the-art language laboratory. He increased the coverage in strategic languages by adding Chinese to the curriculum. He instituted and then enlarged the foreign officer exchange program with allied nations to provide authenticity and cultural value to language instruction. In 1967 the Republic of France awarded him the *Chevalier dans l'Ordre des Palmes Académiques* for significant contributions to the understanding of French culture and civilization as teacher and professor. He left the department after the Spring 1968 semester and served as Associate Dean and Chair of the Humanities Division until he retired from the Air Force later that year. He was promoted to brigadier general in the 1990s.

Following his active duty service, Al Miele continued to serve the nation in academic and foreign relations roles. He was President of The College of Saint Rose in Albany, New York, 1970–1972, the first male and first layperson to serve in that role. Later in the 1970s he was an administrator in the International Aviation Affairs Office of the Federal Aviation Administration and served as chief negotiator for an Aviation Technology Agreement with the Soviet Union. He also served in the Public Affairs Office of the Department of the Interior. He died in 2007 and is buried in the Air Force Academy Cemetery.

BRIGADIER GENERAL
WAYNE A. YEOMAN

Permanent Professor 1961–1972
Vice Dean of the Faculty 1968–1970

B.S., United States Military Academy
M.B.A., Harvard University
D.B.A., Harvard University

Wayne "Whitey" Yeoman, the Academy's 10th Permanent Professor, was born in Sandborn, Indiana, in 1923. He graduated from the United States Military Academy at West Point with the Class of 1946. He took pilot training in Chickasha, OK, then Stewart Field, NY. His primary training culminated at Williams Field (later Williams AFB, AZ). He flew the P-51 for a short time, but most of his flying career was in the Douglas B-26 *Invader* light bomber and ground attack aircraft (originally designated the A-26, later renamed B-26, but not to be confused with the Martin B-26 *Marauder*). He served at Langley AFB, VA, before being transferred to Japan. He was in Japan when the Korean War broke out in June 1950 and moved with his B-26 squadron to the west coast of Japan from where he flew sorties against targets in Korea. He flew low-level combat missions against North Korean columns and convoys, photo reconnaissance missions, and night interdiction missions against targets in North Korea (which he described as "pretty exciting"). He returned stateside in 1951, first to Langley, then to Shaw AFB, SC. He was sent to the Harvard Business School twice. He was first there from 1955 to 1957, earning his Master of Business Administration in preparation for duty on the Air Force Academy faculty. In 1964, he returned to Harvard for two years to continue his doctoral work; his Doctor of Business Administration degree was awarded in 1968. In 1957 he joined the Academy faculty as an Instructor of Economics, and in 1959 as a lieutenant colonel, he was made the Head, Department of Economics and Geography. He was appointed a Permanent Professor in 1961. He led the department through an interesting period of curriculum realignment. In 1966 the importance of the economics discipline was fully recognized, and the department was renamed the Department of Economics, while Geography became a distinct department. As Department Head, Whitey oversaw the establishment of academic majors in Economics and in Management, while supporting courses in International Affairs. He also established cooperative Master's degree programs in these disciplines (Economics at Georgetown University and Management at UCLA). Among his many contributions, Whitey is credited with developing the financial rationale for building an airfield at the Academy. His team tied pilot retention rates to training costs and proved it would be beneficial to move the Academy's T-41 flying training program from Peterson AFB to the Academy proper. His work secured the funding to build the Academy airfield, and as a result the Academy's airmanship programs gained their own base of operations. Throughout his faculty years, he was an active aviator, flying the T-29 aircraft in support of the cadet navigation program. He served as Vice Dean, 1968–1970, then returned to the department until his retirement in 1972.

After his retirement, Whitey joined Eastern Airlines and worked in several business economics roles, including Senior Vice President for Finance and later Chief Financial Officer. In these positions, he guided Eastern through the very turbulent period of airline deregulation and beyond. He retired from Eastern Airlines in 1987.

BRIGADIER GENERAL
GEORGE V. FAGAN

Permanent Professor 1962–1969

B.S., *Temple University*
M.A., *Temple University*
M.A., *University of Denver*
Ph.D., *University of Pennsylvania*

George Fagan, the Academy's 11th Permanent Professor, was born in Phil-adelphia, Pennsylvania, in 1917. He attended Temple University and was awarded his Bachelor's degree in Education in 1940 and Master's in History in 1941. That summer George enlisted in the Army Air Corps, was soon selected for officer training, and was commissioned in 1942. During World War II, he served in England in the quartermaster and supply field. After his active service he returned to Temple University and taught there until 1951, when he was recalled to active duty during the Korean War. From 1951 to 1954 George was assigned to the faculty of the United States Naval Academy. In 1954 he received his PhD in History from Penn, and was assigned to Maxwell AFB, AL, as Associate Editor of the Air University Press. Then in January 1955 he was sent to the Air Force Academy as an Associate Professor of History—one of the first members of the new faculty. George was appointed Director of the Academy Library in 1956, a position he held until his retirement in 1969. He played a significant role in securing the Academy's academic accreditation for the first graduating class in 1959. While the Academy was still located in Denver, George earned his Master's degree in Library Science from the University of Denver in 1957. In 1962 he was appointed Permanent Professor of History. Although he was a Permanent Professor, George was never a department head; rather he maintained his position as Director of the Academy Library. His unique appointment reflected the importance of the library to the early faculty leadership. During his administration, George oversaw the library's holdings increase from 20,000 to over 350,000 volumes, while establishing specialized, professional libraries for every academic department. Among his innovations was creation of the Special Collections, housing the archival documents and photographs of the Academy's development. He played a key role in the Academy's acquisition of the Richard Gimbel aviation collection, one of the most comprehensive aviation archives in the world. He retired in 1969 and was promoted to brigadier general in 1993.

After his retirement in 1969, George Fagan became the Librarian of the Colorado College, a position he held until 1984. During this 15-year tenure at CC, he helped push the library into the computer age, establishing one of the first digital library networks in the state. Even after his second retirement, George continued his strong advocacy for libraries as centers of historical research. In 1987 he became the first treasurer of the non-profit group The Friends of the Air Force Academy Library and for many years helped provide financial and material support to the Academy Library, including supporting the acquisition of the Stalag Luft III collection of prisoner of war memorabilia. His book, *An Illustrated History of the Air Force Academy* (1988), remains the definitive work on the institution's early days. George Fagan, one of the master builders of the Air Force Academy as an academic institution, passed away in 2012 and is buried in the Air Force Academy Cemetery.

BRIGADIER GENERAL
ROGER R. BATE

Permanent Professor 1962–1973
Vice Dean of the Faculty 1971–1973

B.S., United States Military Academy
M.A., Oxford University
Ph.D., Stanford University

Roger Bate, the Academy's 12th Permanent Professor, was born in 1923 in Denver, Colorado. He started college at the California Institute of Technology, Pasadena, in 1941 but then enlisted in the Army. In 1944 he entered the United States Military Academy at West Point, where he graduated in 1947. He spent the following three years as a Rhodes Scholar at Oxford University in England where he received a Master's degree in Nuclear Physics. He served in Korea with the US Army Corps of Engineers during the Korean War and was awarded the Bronze Star. From 1953 to 1956 he was loaned to the Oak Ridge National Laboratory, TN, where he worked on design of the military's first nuclear power reactor; after a year he was appointed Chief of the Reactor Theory Group in the laboratory director's office. In 1959 Roger was assigned to the US Air Force Academy. In 1962 he was recommissioned in the Air Force and was selected for Permanent Professor, and in 1963 he was appointed the first permanent head of the Department of Astronautics. He took a year's leave of absence, 1965–1966, to Stanford where he earned his PhD in Control Systems. Upon his return to the Academy he expanded the department's scope to include the study of the emerging field of computer science, as the department members had the greatest need for mathematical computing power. The department was renamed the Department of Astronautics and Computer Science in 1967. It was during this period that he co-authored what has become a classic text, *Fundamentals of Astrodynamics*, which is still in print 45 years later. Roger served as Head of the Department of Mathematics for the fall semester 1967, and was Vice Dean of the Faculty from 1971 until his retirement in 1973. He was promoted to brigadier general at a Department of Astronautics dining-in in 2008.

After his retirement from the Air Force in 1973, Roger joined Texas Instruments Corporation where he eventually became Chief Computer Scientist and Head of the Advanced Software Development Department. After retiring in 1991, he continued his interest in integrated systems development by joining the Software Engineering Institute (SEI) at Carnegie Mellon University in Pittsburgh, PA. While at SEI, he was the Chief Architect of the Capability Maturity Model Integration suite of products for use by the US defense community. Roger passed away in 2009 at his home in McKinney, TX.

Brigadier General
Philip J. Erdle

Permanent Professor 1964–1979
Vice Dean of the Faculty 1973–1978

B.S., *United States Military Academy*
M.S., *University of Michigan*
Ph.D., *University of Colorado*

Phil Erdle, the Academy's 13th Permanent Professor, was born in Bethlehem, Pennsylvania, in 1930. He graduated with a Bachelor's degree from the United States Military Academy, West Point, NY, in 1952 and was commissioned into the USAF. Phil entered primary pilot training at Bartow Air Base, FL, and continued at Bryan AFB, TX, where he received his pilot's wings in 1953. Phil received advanced flying instruction at Langley AFB, VA, and was assigned to the 5th Fighter Weapons Squadron, where he advanced to Flight Commander and Assistant Operations Officer. In 1956 he became the Aide-de-Camp to the 36th Fighter Bomber Wing Commander. Phil entered graduate school at the University of Michigan in 1958, graduating in 1960 with a Master's degree in Engineering Mechanics. He then was assigned as an Instructor in the Academy's Department of Mechanics. In 1963 he became Assistant Dean for Research in addition to his teaching duties. During these years, Phil completed the work for a PhD in Engineering Science and was awarded the degree by the University of Colorado, Boulder, in 1964. Phil was appointed Permanent Professor in 1964 and promoted to lieutenant colonel. He served as Professor of Mechanics and Assistant Dean, Basic and Engineering Sciences from 1964 to 1965, when he became the Head of the newly designated Department of Engineering Mechanics. Phil co-authored *Engineering Mechanics: Statics and Dynamics* with Archie Higdon, Arthur W. Davis, William B. Stiles, and John A. Weese, published in 1968. He was an advisor to the Vietnamese National Military Academy, publishing a curriculum evaluation report in 1968 (with R.E. Thomas). In 1971 the department was renamed the Department of Engineering Science, Mechanics and Materials with Phil remaining as Department Head. From 1970 to 1978 he was the Academy's Faculty Representative to the NCAA. He served as the Vice Dean of the Faculty from 1973 to 1978. Phil Erdle was promoted to brigadier general and retired from the USAF in early 1979.

Following his retirement, Phil worked for the Bechtel Corporation in Jubail, Saudi Arabia, where he managed numerous educational projects that helped transform the educational system of the Kingdom. Upon returning to Colorado, he founded the International Education Foundation, mentoring small minority-owned businesses in a first-of-its-kind business incubator in Colorado Springs. Subsequently Phil started several small minority-owned businesses in Colorado Springs. In 1984 Phil co-founded and served as President of the Academy Research and Development Institute (ARDI), establishing and managing endowed professorial chairs for the Academy. ARDI remains a major supporter of the Dean of Faculty and Academy missions. In recognition of his contributions, Phil was named an Honorary Member of the USAFA Association of Graduates and received the Superintendent's Award for Distinguished Service to the USAF and the USAFA. In 2002 The Philip J. Erdle Chair in Engineering Science was established in his honor by ARDI. Phil died in 2013 and is buried in the Air Force Academy Cemetery.

BRIGADIER GENERAL
ROLAND E. THOMAS

Permanent Professor 1964–1979

B.S., New Mexico State University
M.S., Stanford University
Ph.D., University of Illinois

Ron Thomas, the Academy's 14th Permanent Professor, was born in Austin, Texas, in 1930. He graduated from New Mexico State University, Las Cruces, in 1951 with a Bachelor's degree in Agricultural Engineering and again in 1952 with a Bachelor's in Electrical Engineering as well as an AFROTC commission. He was first assigned to Stanford University, earning his Master's degree in Electrical Engineering in 1953. He next was assigned to Wright-Patterson AFB, OH, as a Project Engineer working on design, test, and analysis of aircraft electrical power systems and flight simulators. In 1957 Ron was sent as a student to the University of Illinois, Urbana–Champaign, where he earned his PhD in Electrical Engineering in 1959. He then joined the Academy as an Assistant Professor in the Department of Astronautics. In 1964 he was appointed a Permanent Professor. In 1965 Ron was appointed the Acting Head of the Department of Astronautics, and he co-authored the department's textbook, *Introduction to Elementary Astronautics*. In 1966 Ron became the Head of the Department of Electrical Engineering. Over the next few years, he was instrumental in the Academy becoming the first service academy to have its five engineering degrees accredited by the Engineers' Council for Professional Development (ECPD, now the ABET). Beginning in 1972 he served many years as a Program Evaluator and Team Lead for the ECPD and ABET. In 1970 Ron co-authored a two-volume textbook *Signals and Systems: An Introduction to*

Electrical Engineering, which became the foundation for many subsequent editions. He also published numerous peer-reviewed journal papers. Ron was a curriculum innovator, establishing courses with comprehensive laboratory exercises that provided learning opportunities well beyond those found at most universities. He was an advisor to the Vietnamese National Military Academy, publishing a curriculum evaluation report in 1968 (with P.J. Erdle). Ron led a vigorous department research program supporting the Air Force Weapons Laboratory and the Rome Air Development Center. In 1970, during the Vietnam War, he personally led an investigation of the fire control system for the AC-130A Gunship in Thailand. Using field test results, he made on-the-spot modifications that created extraordinary increases in mission lethality. Ron was promoted to brigadier general upon his retirement in 1979.

After retirement, Ron worked for Motorola's Government Electronics Division, Mission Research Corporation, and Kaman Sciences. In 1985 he founded an independent engineering consulting company. Ron continued his scholarly pursuits by writing the textbook *Circuits and Signals: An Introduction to Linear and Interface Circuits* with Albert Rosa in 1984. He continued as an ABET Program Evaluator and served on the Engineering Accreditation Commission of ABET, 1980–1985; in 1992 he was honored as an ABET Fellow. In 1994 he co-authored with Rosa and G. Toussaint the popular text *The Analysis and Design of Linear Circuits*, now in its 8th edition. Ron's leadership in improving the cadet educational process is honored each year when the USAFA Department of Electrical and Computer Engineering awards the Brigadier General Roland E. Thomas Award to a faculty member for outstanding contributions to cadet education.

BRIGADIER GENERAL
MALHAM M. WAKIN

Permanent Professor 1964–1995

A.B., *University of Notre Dame*
A.M., *State University of New York,*
*   Albany*
Ph.D., *University of Southern*
*   California*

Mal Wakin, the Academy's 15th Permanent Professor, was born in 1931 in Oneonta, New York. He enrolled at the University of Notre Dame in 1948 and received his Bachelor's degree in Mathematics in 1952. A year later he earned his Master's degree in Secondary Education from the State University of New York at Albany. In 1953 Mal began his military career as an Aviation Cadet in the navigator training program. Commissioned in 1954, he completed his navigator training in 1955 at Ellington AFB, TX, and was assigned to an air rescue squadron at Norton AFB, CA, 1955–1957. After flying regularly for two years, he was sent to the University of Southern California in preparation for a faculty assignment at the Air Force Academy. Completing his PhD in Philosophy in 1959, Mal reported to the Academy and began an assignment that would span 36 years of faculty service. In 1964 while still a captain, he was appointed Permanent Professor of Philosophy and promoted to lieutenant colonel. In 1967 he was promoted to colonel and made Head of the newly formed Department of Philosophy and Fine Arts. He guided that department, in its various forms, for nearly 30 years, until his retirement in 1995. Mal emerged as one of the most esteemed military ethicists in the United States. He authored numerous works on ethics, leadership, and the military profession, including several books, among which are *War, Morality, and the Military Profession* (1979; rev. 1986) and *The Teaching of Ethics in the Military* (1982). He was featured as one of "12 great professors" in *People Magazine* in 1975, and the subject of a feature article in *Newsweek* in 1984. For 16 years he was Chair of the Joint Services Conference on Professional Ethics. Perhaps more significant than his articles and books, Mal carried his compelling message directly to people in influential addresses to faculty orientations, cadet character development events, symposia, and military and civilian audiences around the country and Canada, averaging 40 to 50 lectures annually.

Upon his promotion to brigadier general and retirement in 1995, Mal returned to the Academy for a year as The William Lyon Endowed Chair in Professional Ethics. His article "Professional Integrity" was published in *Airpower Journal* in 1996. From 1997 to 2016 Mal assisted the Center for Character and Leadership Development by helping teach the required seven-hour seminar on ethics and leadership to every senior cadet in the Wing. Each year a cadet or staff member is honored with the Malham M. Wakin Character and Leadership Development Award. His latest book, *Integrity First: Reflections of a Military Philosopher*, appeared in 2010. Mal Wakin is both the youngest Permanent Professor appointed and the longest serving. His enormous, enduring impact on the Permanent Professoriate and on the entire institution cannot be overstated.

COLONEL
ROBERT G. TAYLOR

Permanent Professor 1966–1975

B.A., University of California,
    Los Angeles
M.A., Indiana University
Ph.D., Indiana University

Robert Guilford "Gil" Taylor, the Academy's 16th Permanent Professor, was born in Lincoln, Nebraska, in 1921. He joined the Army Air Corps as an aviation cadet in 1942, after completing his Bachelor's degree at UCLA with majors in Economics and History. He earned his pilot's wings and was commissioned in 1944; following B-17 training he was assigned to the 303rd Bomb Group (Heavy), Molesworth, England. After flying a series of deep penetration bombardment missions, he was shot down in July 1944 and spent more than nine months as a prisoner of war in Stalag Luft I, Sagan, Silesia. He returned to the US after VE Day and assumed duties as a cadre faculty member of the newly formed Strategic Intelligence School, Pentagon, Washington, DC. From 1949 to 1953 he was assigned to the Air Force Reserve Officer Training Corps detachment at Indiana University, where in his off-duty time he completed his Master's degree in Geography. He then flew B-26s in the Korean War, and at the cessation of that conflict was assigned to Barksdale AFB, LA, as a B-29 Aircraft Commander and Director of Intelligence for the 376th Bomb Wing. In 1954 he rotated to Kadena Air Base, Okinawa, Japan, as Director of Intelligence, 307th Bomb Wing. Later that year he was assigned to HQ Strategic Air Command, Offutt AFB, NE, where he served in several intelligence positions, including Soviet Union area research, aircrew escape and evasion planning, collections, and intelligence inspections. In 1957 he joined the faculty of the Academy's

Department of Military History and Geography. During that tour, he also taught in the Department of Economics. From 1960 to 1962 he went back to Indiana and earned his PhD in Geography. He returned to the Academy in 1962 as an Associate Professor in the then joint Department of Economics and Geography, serving as Acting Department Head for two academic years, 1964–1966. In 1966 when the departments were divided again, he was appointed Permanent Professor and Head, Department of Geography. (Geography was re-merged with Economics in 1973, and for a while there was a Department of Economics, Geography and Management, until Management itself became a department in 1982.) During his time as Department Head, he helped the Academy acquire a major mineral collection, which was prominently displayed for cadets. His abiding interest in the formation of the Earth's crust and rock formations led to his book *Cripple Creek* (1966), later expanded to *Cripple Creek Mining District* (1973). In 1973 he took a sabbatical to do field and archival research in Britain, and upon return in 1974 became the Dean's Executive Officer until his retirement in 1975. He died in 1997 and is buried in the Air Force Academy Cemetery.

BRIGADIER GENERAL
JESSE C. GATLIN JR.

Permanent Professor 1966–1977

B.S., *United States Military Academy*
M.A., *University of North Carolina*
Ph.D., *University of Denver*

Jesse Gatlin, the Academy's 17th Permanent Professor, was born in Creswell, North Carolina, in 1923. He attended Oak Ridge Military Institute, NC, 1941–1942, preparatory to entering the United States Military Academy. He completed pilot training while a cadet at West Point, which was a requirement at that time for those aiming for the Air Corps. He graduated from USMA in 1945 and began his career flying the B-25 and B-17. Later he was stationed in Austria and Germany as a P-47 Thunderbolt pilot. During his flying career, Jesse also flew the B-26 and C-47. His experiences include duty as a Radiological Survey Officer during three atomic bomb tests at the Nevada Test Site, 1950–1953. From 1954 to 1955 Jesse was an exchange officer with the Royal Canadian Air Force in Ottawa, where he flew his only jet, the T-33. Following his exchange assignment, Jesse was sent to the University of North Carolina, Chapel Hill, in preparation for a teaching assignment at the Air Force Academy. He earned his Master's degree in English in 1957 and joined the Academy's Department of English. From 1959 to 1961 Jesse worked on his doctorate at the University of Denver, completing the PhD degree in two years before returning to the Academy. He was made Tenure Associate Professor in 1964, then Permanent Professor and Department Head in 1966. For a two-month period in 1968, he was on temporary duty in Vietnam and Thailand supporting the Air Force's Contemporary Historical Evaluation of Combat Operations (CHECO) project.

Jesse's literary publications include discussions of honor and the treatment of the US military and Air Force in fiction. In his article "The Role of the Humanities in Educating the Professional Officer," published in *Air University Review* in 1968, he makes a compelling case that the humanities are an indispensable part of an Academy education, concluding with the belief that "[it] is this sort of attitude—this widened perspective on past, present, and future—that the humanities can do much to promote." This belief is enduring, and it still guides the Academy's curriculum design. Jesse retired as a brigadier general in 1977.

After Jesse retired, he taught at the University of Colorado at Colorado Springs for eight years and for 27 years led a weekly literature class at the Colorado Springs Senior Center. He died in Colorado Springs in 2016 and is buried in the Air Force Academy Cemetery. Jesse's creativity was present at almost every Permanent Professor retirement dinner as well as Past Permanent Professors dinners for nearly four decades, usually composing on the spot and reading a clever poem (doggerel) to commemorate the event.

COLONEL
ANTHONY J. MIONE

Permanent Professor 1966–1974

B.S., *United States Military Academy*
M.S., *North Carolina State University*
Ph.D., *North Carolina State University*

John Mione, the Academy's 18th Permanent Professor, was born in 1927 in Brooklyn, New York. He graduated from the United States Military Academy in 1949, was commissioned in the Air Force, and was sent to Air Training Command for flight training. He graduated as a pilot in 1950 and was assigned to Tinker AFB, OK, flying the C-47. At that time, the concept of nuclear-powered aircraft was still thought viable, and the Air Force sponsored graduate work for several dozen pilots in order to develop a cadre of aircrew educated in nuclear technology; John Mione was one of those. In 1951 he was sent to North Carolina State College (now University) in Raleigh, where he earned his Master's degree in Nuclear Engineering in 1953. He then went to the Air Force Materials Laboratory, Wright-Patterson AFB, OH, where he eventually was responsible for all nuclear support activities in the Laboratory. In 1958 John was assigned to HQ Air Research and Development Command, Andrews AFB, MD, to continue work on the Aircraft Nuclear Propulsion Program. In 1960 and 1961 he was a student at Air Command and Staff College, where he was recognized as a Distinguished Graduate. He returned to North Carolina State in 1961 to pursue his PhD degree in Nuclear Engineering, which was awarded in 1964. John was assigned to the Department of Physics at the United States Air Force Academy in 1963 and was selected as Permanent Professor and Head in 1966. In 1969 John took a sabbatical assignment to the European Office of

Aerospace Research, Brussels, Belgium, supporting basic research programs from Europe to India. In 1970 he moved to London when the organization relocated to England. He returned to the Academy in 1971 as Department Head and Chair of the Basic Sciences Division. He led the Physics Department during its dynamic expansion, building a fledging department with no major into a broad-spectrum department with a robust curriculum and research laboratories for lasers, nuclear radiation, and space physics. Throughout his career he maintained active flying status; he was a Command Pilot with time in the C-46, C-47, B-25, and T-29 aircraft. He retired from the Air Force in 1974.

Following retirement, John was named Director of Energy Resources for the General Electric Company. He retired from GE in 1988 as Manager of their Neutron Devices Division Laboratory in Largo, Florida. In retirement, he endowed the A.J. Mione Award, given annually to a cadet for outstanding accomplishment in physics research. He died in 2009 and is buried in the Air Force Academy Cemetery.

BRIGADIER GENERAL
ALFRED F. HURLEY

Permanent Professor 1966–1980

B.A., *St. John's University*
M.A., *Princeton University*
Ph.D., *Princeton University*

Al Hurley, the Academy's 19th Permanent Professor, was born in Brooklyn, New York, in 1928. He graduated *summa cum laude* from St. John's University, Jamaica, NY, in 1950, with a major in English and a minor in Philosophy. That year he enlisted in the Air Force and was assigned to Reese AFB, TX. His talents were soon recognized, for he was sent to Officer Candidate School, Lackland AFB, TX, where he was commissioned in 1952 as a Distinguished Graduate. He earned his navigator wings at Ellington AFB, TX, in 1954 and then served on the staff of the Aircraft Observer Instructor Course at James Connally AFB, TX. In 1956 Al entered Princeton in preparation for an assignment to the Air Force Academy faculty. In 1958 he earned his Master's degree in History while completing course requirements for his doctorate, and he began teaching in the Department of History at the Academy. During this five-year tour he completed his dissertation and was awarded Princeton's PhD degree (1961). His book, *Billy Mitchell: Crusader for Air Power* (1964; 2006), is considered the definitive scholarly work on the subject. In 1963 Al was assigned as a C-97 Navigator, Wiesbaden Air Base, Germany, where he flew more than 70 reconnaissance missions during the height of the Cold War. A year later, he was assigned to the War Plans Division, HQ US Air Forces, Europe, Ramstein Air Base, Germany. Returning to the Department of History in 1966, Al was appointed Permanent Professor and Acting Department Head, then in 1967 he was promoted to colonel and Head. Al Hurley built a nationally regarded History Department, including establishing in 1968 a core course in World History, one of the first in the United States. He initiated and participated in a program to engage Academy officers in supporting the war in Southeast Asia, known Air Force-wide as CHECO (Contemporary Historical Evaluation of Combat Operations). From 1968 to 1972 the program produced over 100 classified studies of the war, researched and written on the scene. He directed development of the Military History Symposium, a biennial Academy event, which became the leading military history event in the Western world during the Cold War. The Symposium is widely recognized for its contributions to the military profession and the profession of Military History. He was a Guggenheim Fellow, 1971, and, during a sabbatical in 1976–1977, a Fellow of the Eisenhower Institute of the Smithsonian Institution, Washington, DC. Al was promoted to brigadier general and retired in 1980.

Following retirement from the Air Force, Al became the President of the University of North Texas. From 1982 to 2002 he was the Chancellor of the entire UNT System. As President and Chancellor, he spurred tremendous growth in enrollment, endowment, facilities, and academic stature. As a tribute to his accomplishments, the Board of Regents named the administration building, which stands at the center of the campus in Denton, the Alfred F. and Johanna H. Hurley Administration Building, in honor of this "unsung hero of higher education." After retiring from leadership, he continued to teach as a Professor of History until 2008. He died in 2013 and is buried in the Air Force Academy Cemetery.

BRIGADIER GENERAL
WALLACE E. FLUHR

Permanent Professor 1966–1981

B.S., *University of Kentucky*
M.S., *University of Illinois*
Ph.D., *University of Illinois*

Wallace Emory "Em" Fluhr, the Academy's 20th Permanent Professor, was born in 1932 and raised on a farm in Jefferson County, Kentucky. He graduated with a Bachelor's degree in Civil Engineering in 1954 from the University of Kentucky, Lexington, as a Distinguished Graduate of AFROTC. He was called to active duty immediately by the Air Force and served as Base Engineer until 1957 at Gunter AFB, AL. He then entered graduate school at the University of Illinois, Urbana–Champaign, where he earned both his Master's degree in Civil Engineering and Doctor of Philosophy degree in Structural Dynamics in 33 months. In 1960 Em was assigned as the Chief, Design Criteria and Research Division, AF Ballistic Missile Division, Los Angeles Air Force Station, to design protective shelters for the Titan II and Minuteman ballistic missile weapon systems. He received the Air Force Systems Command Annual Award for Scientific Achievement in 1961 for his work on this program. Although only a captain, he also was awarded the Legion of Merit for his efforts. In 1963 Em came to the Air Force Academy as an Instructor in the Department of Mechanics. He progressed through the academic ranks to Associate Professor and started the Civil Engineering program. He was selected as Permanent Professor in 1966 and named Professor of Civil Engineering. Em worked on the Dean of Faculty staff for two years before he was named Head of the Department of Civil Engineering in 1968. In the summer of 1973 he was appointed Head of the combined

Department of Civil Engineering, Engineering Mechanics and Materials and served in that capacity for six years. As a member of the Curriculum Committee of the 20th *Anniversary Study*, he contributed significantly to the concept of the expanded core curriculum and the overall reshaping of the total Academy program. In 1978 he led the successful effort to achieve maximum accreditation of the Academy's six engineering programs. In 1979 he was appointed Head of the Department of Civil Engineering and the Air Force Academy's Faculty Representative to the NCAA. An active participant in the American Society of Civil Engineers, he has been honored with the rank of Fellow. Em was promoted to brigadier general and retired from the USAF in 1981.

After retiring, Em Fluhr worked five years as Director of Operations of an international joint venture that developed the curriculum, trained Saudi instructors and administrators, and operated a more-than-1,000 student educational/training institution in Saudi Arabia. He then spent three years as a partner in a joint venture of American firms to restructure and improve operation of the electrical distribution system in Pakistan. Returning to the US, he spent the next five years designing and building homes in Arizona that had the flexibility to satisfy the needs of a family from newly married to retirement. Next, he became Vice President of Risk Control for Home Buyers Warranty Corporation in Denver, CO, turning the bankrupt insurance company into a healthy, prosperous corporation. After four years, he was promoted to Chief Executive Officer and Chairman of the Board of Directors of the corporation. Over the next 16 years, he grew the company to become the largest structural warranty company in the US. Em retired again in 2012.

BRIGADIER GENERAL
MARCOS E. KINEVAN

Permanent Professor 1967–1988

B.S., *United States Military Academy*
J.D., *University of California*

Mark Kinevan, the Academy's 21st Permanent Professor, was born in Los Angeles in 1924. He enlisted in the Army in 1943, but was soon selected for the United States Military Academy. After a preparatory year at Amherst College, he joined the West Point Class of 1947. Upon graduation, he transferred to the new US Air Force and served a year as Assistant Legal Officer at March AFB, CA, before enrolling in the University of California Law School (Berkeley), where he graduated in 1951. His first duty as a lawyer was at Hamilton AFB, CA, as Assistant Legal Claims Officer. In 1952 he was sent to Korea, where he became the Wing Legal Officer, 17th Bomb Wing. In 1953, he became the Base Staff Judge Advocate at McChord AFB, WA. Then in 1956 he was assigned to HQ US Air Force, the Pentagon, as Appellate Defense Counsel and later Judge, US Air Force Court of Military Review, where he published several significant legal opinions. He came to the Academy in 1960, both on the Department of Law faculty and as Assistant Staff Judge Advocate. In 1965 he was reassigned to HQ Pacific Air Forces, Hickam AFB, HI, as Deputy Staff Judge Advocate. He was admitted to practice before a number of prestigious courts, including the US Supreme Court. In 1967 he was recalled to the Academy and appointed Permanent Professor. He served as Professor and Head, Department of Law, for 21 years, until his promotion to brigadier general and retirement in 1988. During that extended period, he also saw added duties as the Command Staff Judge

Advocate and as Head of the Department of Economics, Geography and Management. Mark Kinevan made an enormous impact on the Law Department, growing the curriculum from an elementary business law concept to a mature curriculum relevant to problems future Air Force officers might face. He developed faculty expertise in laws of air and space employment, problems of command, and armed conflict. He established a vigorous research program to produce suitable texts and classroom materials. He personally wrote the text *Personal Estate Planning* and was co-author of the two-volume *An Introduction to Law*. Moreover, he provided faculty expertise to advise major commands on these subjects and conduct Personal Estate Planning workshops at Air Force bases throughout the country. Mark Kinevan was an ardent supporter of Falcon athletics; he served as the Officer Representative for the Falcon football team for 21 years.

A lifelong student of western history, Mark pursued his passion following his retirement. His book, *Frontier Cavalryman: Lt. John Bigelow with the Buffalo Soldiers in Texas* (1997), detailed Army life on the western frontier. Mark Kinevan died in 2008 and is buried in the Air Force Academy Cemetery.

COLONEL
PETER B. CARTER

Permanent Professor 1967–1975

B.S., Oregon State University
M.D., University of Oregon

Colonel (Dr.) Peter B. Carter, the Academy's 22nd Permanent Professor, was born in Portland, Oregon, in 1932. He received his pre-medical training at Oregon State University, Corvallis, graduating in 1954. He earned his medical degree from the University of Oregon School of Medicine, Portland, in 1958. Pete joined the Air Force while still a medical student and began his active duty as a Flight Surgeon at McChord AFB, WA. In 1964 he was transferred to the Air Force Academy Hospital where he was Chief of Internal Medicine and later Chief of Medical Services. Selected as a Permanent Professor in 1967, he was the first (and as of this date, the only) medical doctor to serve as a Permanent Professor. Since he was then a major, he was promoted to lieutenant colonel and assigned for one year in the Department of Chemistry and Physiology. In this period, he also served for five months as Medical Advisor to the Air Force Advisory Group Commander and Surgeon, Vietnamese Air Force, Tan Son Nhut Air Base, Vietnam. In July 1968 he was promoted to colonel and appointed Head of the new Department of Life Sciences. In this capacity, he was the driving force behind establishing the Academy's pre-medical program. In 1971 he oversaw the merger of two separate departments to form the Department of Life and Behavioral Sciences. Pete Carter resigned from the Air Force in the Spring of 1975, following which his department was divided, with the Biology portion returning to Chemistry and the Psychology portion reemerging as the Department of Behavioral Sciences and Leadership.

After the Air Force, Dr. Pete Carter built a long career as an internal medicine physician in Aberdeen, South Dakota. He was semi-retired but still actively working with the staff at Avera United Clinic at the time of his death. He died while a patient in the crash of Aberdeen's flight for life helicopter in 2002.

**BRIGADIER GENERAL
DANIEL H. DALEY**

Permanent Professor 1967–1984

B.S., *Purdue University*
M.S., *Massachusetts Institute of
Technology*

Dan Daley, the Academy's 23rd Permanent Professor, was born in Elmira, New York, in 1920. Following his graduation from Purdue University, West Lafayette, IN, in 1942 with a Bachelor's degree in Mechanical Engineering, he was assigned as an Engineering Project Officer in the Power Plant Laboratory at Wright Field, OH. He entered pilot training in 1943 at Brooks Field, TX. After earning his pilot wings, Dan saw duty as a Flight Instructor from 1943 until 1945 at Ellington Field and Randolph Field in TX. He attended Test Pilot School and served as a Test Pilot at Wright Field, OH, in 1945. Later in 1945 Dan began graduate studies at the Massachusetts Institute of Technology, Cambridge, in Aeronautical Engineering and earned his Master's degree in Aeronautical Engineering in 1946. The flight test methods and data reduction procedures developed in his thesis research form the basis of the static longitudinal stability test techniques used today in airplane flight testing. Dan was next assigned to the Army Air Forces Institute of Technology at Wright Field as an Assistant Professor, Department of Aerodynamics. He was a member of the nucleus of men who started the Institute in 1946 and developed and taught several of the first courses offered in aeronautical engineering at what is now the Air Force Institute of Technology. He was appointed Acting Head, Department of Mechanical Engineering in 1949, a position he held until 1955. During this time, the department was accredited by the Engineers' Council for Professional Development (now ABET).

While at AFIT, he authored several texts for use in various courses. In 1955 Dan was assigned as a Pilot with the 4930th Support Group, Eniwetok Atoll, in the Pacific Ocean and in 1956 as Pilot and Wing Flying Safety Officer, 483rd Troop Carrier Wing in Japan. From 1958 to 1961 he served as Chief of the Aerodynamics Section in the B-70 Weapons System Project Office, Wright-Patterson AFB. He became a member of the Department of Aeronautics at the Academy in 1961 as an Associate Professor. Dan was active in strengthening the courses offered by the department during his tenure as Associate Professor, Course Director, Chairman of two major departmental curriculum committees, and finally as Professor and Head of the department. One committee's work led to a curriculum proposal for an Aeronautical Engineering major with options in Aerospace Propulsion, Aerospace Structures, Flight Mechanics, and Aerodynamics. The Aeronautical Engineering major was approved for the Class of 1966. In 1965 Dan was selected by the Pakistan Air Force to assist them in establishing a College of Aeronautical Engineering at Karangi Creek, PAF Station, Karachi, Pakistan. He led the development of the laboratories, curricula, and staff of this first college in Pakistan to teach aeronautical engineers and served as the first Head of the current Department of Aerospace Engineering. Dan was appointed a Permanent Professor in 1967 and returned to lead the Department of Aeronautics. From 1972 to 1974 he served as the Chief Scientist, European Office of Research and Development, Air Force Systems Command, London, England. Dan returned to lead the Aeronautics Department until he was promoted to brigadier general and retired from the USAF in 1984.

Dan co-authored the book *Aircraft Engine Design* with William H. Heiser and Jack D. Mattingly, which was published in 1987 by the American Institute of Aeronautical and Astronautics, Inc. Dan also has contributed to several other books published by AIAA. Dan was honored as a Distinguished Alumnus of AFIT in 2002. He died in 2018 and is buried in the Air Force Academy Cemetery.

COLONEL
RICHARD F. ROSSER

Permanent Professor 1968–1973

B.A., Ohio Wesleyan University
M.P.A., Syracuse University
Ph.D., Syracuse University

Dick Rosser, the Academy's 24th Permanent Professor, was born in 1929 in Arcanum, Ohio. He graduated from Ohio Wesleyan University, Delaware, OH, with a Bachelor's degree in Economics in 1951. He completed two years of AFROTC his senior year at Ohio Wesleyan, his third-year ROTC studies during the summer of 1951, and his final year while earning a Master's degree in Public Administration in 1952 at Syracuse University, NY. His first assignment was Russian language training at Syracuse University, graduating in 1953. After attending the AF Security Service Communications Intelligence School at Kelly AFB, TX, he was assigned in 1954 to the National Security Agency in Arlington Hall, VA, as a Communications Intelligence Officer. Dick returned to Syracuse University in 1958 to pursue his doctorate in Political Science on a university scholarship and with USAFA's Department of Political Science sponsorship. On his way to Syracuse, he attended Squadron Officer School, Maxwell AFB, AL, and was a Distinguished Graduate. Dick was assigned to the Political Science faculty at the AF Academy as an Instructor in 1959 without completing his dissertation. The Academy assigned him to AFIT for academic year 1960–1961 to complete his dissertation, and he received his PhD in Political Science in 1961. He returned to the Academy as an Assistant Professor and progressed to Associate and then Tenure Associate Professor—among the first appointed. Dick chaired the committee whose recommendations resulted in the introduction of Area Studies into the curriculum. He was appointed Tenure Professor and Head, Department of Political Science in 1967. His book, *Introduction to Soviet Foreign Policy*, was published in 1968. That same year, Dick was appointed a Permanent Professor. From 1969 to 1971 he took sabbatical leave in London doing research at the International Institute of Strategic Studies and attending the British Imperial Defence College. Dick retired from the USAF in 1973.

Dick then became Dean of the Faculty and Professor of Political Science at Albion College in Albion, MI. In 1977 DePauw University, Greencastle, IN, appointed him their 17th President. Under Dick's leadership, DePauw restored historic East College, renovated Asbury Hall and Roy O. West Library, and built the Lilly Physical Education and Recreation Center. The University's endowment grew fourfold from $19.4 million to $83.2 million. From 1986 to 1993, he served as President and Chief Executive Officer of the National Association of Independent Colleges and Universities, an organization that lobbied on behalf of such institutions in Washington, DC. Until shortly before his death, he headed The Presidents Group, a consulting group of retired college and university presidents. Dick Rosser died in 2007 and is buried in the Air Force Academy Cemetery.

BRIGADIER GENERAL
ROBERT W. LAMB

Permanent Professor 1970–1979

B.S., *Arizona State University*
M.S., *New Mexico Highlands*
   University
Ph.D., University of Colorado

Bob Lamb, the Academy's 25th Permanent Professor, was born in 1929 in Lone Tree, Indiana. He began his higher education at Phoenix College, receiving an Associate in Arts degree in 1948, then at Arizona State University, earning a Bachelor's degree in Chemistry in 1950. A year later, Bob earned his Master's degree from Highlands University, Las Vegas, NM, and continued his graduate work in chemistry at Purdue University, where he was given a direct commission in the Air Force. After completing three months of basic training at Lackland AFB, TX, in 1953, he was sent to the Army Chemical Warfare Center at Englewood, MD, conducting research on the detection of toxic gases. In 1954 he was assigned to the Air Force Materials Laboratory at Wright-Patterson AFB, OH, as Research Chemist and Project Engineer. In 1956 Bob was assigned to the newly formed Air Force Academy, still at the temporary site in Denver, as Instructor of Chemistry, and two years later became the first officer sponsored by the department for a PhD. He spent two years at the University of Colorado, Boulder, and returned to the Academy in 1960, where he finished his dissertation and received his PhD in 1961. In 1963 Bob was reassigned for one year to the new Frank J. Seiler Research Laboratory, which was being established at the Academy to conduct basic research of potential use to the Air Force. His responsibility was to design, plan, and equip the chemistry laboratory, while advancing his own research interests in organic chemistry. In 1965 he was assigned to the

European Office of Aerospace Research in Brussels, Belgium, charged with developing insight into research and exploratory development programs across Europe, Africa, India, and the Middle East. Returning to the Academy in 1968, Bob became the Director of Advanced Courses, then Deputy Head of the Department of Chemistry. He was selected a Permanent Professor in 1970. During his tenure as Department Head, the Department of Life and Behavioral Sciences was divided, with the Life Sciences staff merging with Chemistry faculty to form the Department of Chemical and Biological Sciences. Bob admirably led this combined department for four years, building the programs to a level that permitted the establishment of the Department of Biology in 1980. Bob retired as a brigadier general in 1979.

In retirement, Bob spent more than two years as the Manager of Training and Education for the Bechtel Corporation in Jubail, Saudi Arabia. For the next 14 years Bob was Vice President of Boston University, first for three years as Vice President of External Programs, then as Head of Boston University's Overseas Graduate Program, which he ran from offices in Heidelberg, Germany, and later London, England. In 1996 he returned to the States and retired in Santa Fe, New Mexico.

BRIGADIER GENERAL
ROBERT R. LOCHRY

Permanent Professor 1970–1985

B.S., *United States Military Academy*
M.S., *Rensselaer Polytechnic Institute*
Ph.D., *University of California,*
  Los Angeles

Bob Lochry, the Academy's 26th Permanent Professor, was born in 1922 in Salt Lake City, Utah. He earned his commercial pilot license while attending Modesto Junior College, CA, and at the start of WWII he entered the United States Military Academy, graduating in 1945. He soon became a fighter pilot flying P-47s and P-51s in the Philippines. In 1947 he transferred to fly the P-80 in the first jet unit in the Pacific; his first jet flight was solo because there were no two-seat jet trainers at that time. Returning from overseas in 1948, Bob was a Test Pilot at Wright-Patterson AFB, OH, where he "flew 'really weird' airplanes under almost every combination of emergency situations." He was then selected for the West Point faculty and sent to Rensselaer Polytechnic Institute, Troy, NY, where he earned his Master's degree in Mechanical Engineering in 1950. He taught at West Point for three years after which he was again assigned to Wright-Patterson AFB for five years, 1953–1958, as a Project Director and Weapons System Program Manager for new fighter aircraft, including the tri-sonic XF-103, the YF-107, and the F-108. After a year at Air Command and Staff College, Maxwell AFB, AL, he was assigned in 1959 to the Air Force Space and Missile Systems Office in Los Angeles working on orbital intercept technologies and, later, classified satellite systems. He attended UCLA from 1962 to 1965, earning his PhD with three majors: Astrodynamics, Computer Science, and Research Management. In 1965 he joined the Academy's Department of Engineering

Mechanics and moved the next year to the Department of Astronautics and Computer Science. From 1967 to 1969, Bob was assigned to the 14th Aerospace Force (the forerunner of Air Force Space Command), serving for a year in Colorado Springs as Assistant Deputy Chief of Staff for Operations, then as Commander of the Space Surveillance Squadron at Shemya, AK. He next moved to the Office of the Secretary of Defense, the Pentagon, Washington, DC, with duty as Director of Space Technology. He was selected in 1970 as Permanent Professor and appointed Head of the Department of Mathematical Sciences. In that position, he led the largest academic department to many insightful accomplishments, including early development of computer-aided instruction and individual mastery learning. Perhaps Bob's chief contribution was the cadet major in Operations Research; his research established the need for the new interdisciplinary major, and his efforts led to its implementation as a joint venture between three departments. He spent 1978–1980 on military sabbatical at the Supreme Headquarters Allied Powers Europe Technical Center, The Hague, Netherlands. Bob Lochry was a leader across the institution's full spectrum. He was promoted and retired in 1985, after serving in uniform for 44 years. He died in 2015 and is buried in the United States Military Academy Cemetery.

COLONEL
WILLIAM GEFFEN

Permanent Professor 1971–1982

B.A., *University of California, Berkeley*
M.A., *Stanford University*
Ph.D., *University of Denver*

William Geffen, the Academy's 27th Permanent Professor, was born in Konigsberg, Germany, in 1925 and came to the United States in 1941. After finishing high school in New York City in 1943, he enlisted in the US Army and served in the infantry in France, Germany, and Austria. He was awarded the Combat Infantryman Badge, signifying participation in active ground combat, and he received the Bronze Star and Purple Heart medals. After the war, he took advantage of the GI Bill to obtain a Bachelor's degree in Political Science from Cal–Berkeley in 1947 and a Master's degree in Political Science from Stanford in 1948. From 1949 to 1951 he pursued doctoral work at Berkeley. In 1951 he accepted a direct commission in the Air Force and was recalled to active duty in 1952, with an assignment as Intelligence Officer for a fighter squadron in Portland, OR. In 1953 he was transferred to Germany and served as Intelligence Liaison between HQ US Air Forces Europe (USAFE) and the US Command of Berlin. In 1956 he was assigned to the office of the Assistant Chief of Staff, Intelligence, HQ USAF, the Pentagon, Washington, DC, where he developed specialized intelligence-collection training programs for intelligence field units and the air attaché system. In 1960 he was assigned to the Air Force Academy's Department of Foreign Languages as Instructor of German; he also taught courses in Political Science. In 1964 he went back to USAFE, where he was assigned to the War Plans Division. He returned to the Academy in 1967, this time to the Department of History as Chair of Western European Area Studies, where he also directed the 1969 Military History Symposium and edited its proceedings published as *Command and Commanders in Modern Warfare*. From 1969 to 1971 William Geffen spent 18 months in Vietnam, responsible for planning all US administrative and logistical support to the seven free world nations with forces operating there. His service was recognized with the first Oak Leaf Cluster to his Bronze Star as well as receiving a decoration personally from the President of Vietnam. Returning from Vietnam he completed his PhD degree in National Security Policy at the University of Denver in 1971. That summer he was appointed Permanent Professor and Head, Department of Foreign Languages. From 1979 to 1980 he went on a sabbatical assignment to the Defense Language Institute, Monterey, CA. Upon return, he worked on the Dean's staff until he retired in 1982. He died in Colorado Springs in 2009.

BRIGADIER GENERAL
JOHN P. WITTRY

Permanent Professor 1973–1984
Vice Dean of the Faculty 1978–1984

B.S., *Saint Louis University*
M.S., *Air Force Institute of Technology*
Professional Degree, University of Michigan

Jack Wittry, the Academy's 28th Permanent Professor, was born in 1929 in Aurora, Illinois. He received his Bachelor's degree in Aeronautical Engineering from St. Louis University, Missouri, in 1951 and was a Distinguished Graduate of their AFROTC program. He worked for McDonnel Aircraft Corporation until he was called to active duty later in 1951. He was assigned as an Aircraft Project Engineer and Assistant Chief of the Liaison Aircraft Section, Weapons Systems Division, Wright Air Development Center, Wright-Patterson AFB, OH. In 1955 he entered the Air Force Institute of Technology, WPAFB, and graduated with a Master's degree in Aeronautical Engineering in 1956. Jack was then assigned as an Aircraft Project Engineer, Weapons Systems Nuclear Powered Aircraft Project Office, Air Research and Development Command, still at WPAFB. From 1958 to 1960 he was an Advanced Propulsion Technologist, Research and Analysis Branch, Aircraft Nuclear Propulsion Office, Atomic Energy Commission, Washington, DC, responsible for developing advanced technology for space satellite nuclear power. During this assignment, he authored two chapters in the book *Nuclear Flight*. He then entered graduate school at the University of Michigan and earned a Professional Degree in Aeronautical and Astronautical Engineering in 1962. From 1962 to 1963, Jack was an Instructor in the Department of Mechanics at the Air Force Academy. In 1962 he transferred to the Department of Astronautics and progressed from Assistant Professor to Tenure Associate Professor while developing what is now the Astronau-tics Laboratory. From 1969 to mid-1970, he was the Deputy Head of the newly named Department of Astronautics and Computer Science. The following year he spent as the Chief of the Surveillance Systems Branch, Deputy for Operations, HQ Seventh AF, Tan Son Nhut Air Base, Vietnam. Returning to the Academy, Jack was appointed Department Head in 1972 and Permanent Professor in 1973. He developed the first computer science course for the core curriculum, chaired the Second Class Academic Review Committee, chaired the Cadet Summer Research Program, and chaired an ad hoc committee that developed specifications for academy-wide computer resources. From 1978 to 1984 he was Chairman of the Engineering Division and Vice Dean of the Faculty. During this time, he took a sabbatical leave of absence to the Naval Postgraduate School, Monterrey, CA, to develop courses in astronautics and space operations as well as teach courses in aero-nautics. He also attended the Wharton School Effective Executive Program at the University of Pennsylvania, University Park. As Vice Dean, Jack led the formation of the Department of Computer Science and the successful re-accreditation effort for all six engineering majors. In 1984 Jack was pro-moted to brigadier general and retired from the USAF.

Upon retirement, Jack became the Academic Dean at the California State University Maritime Academy in Vallejo, serving until 1992. From 1993 to 1996 he was President of the Board of Directors and General Man-ager at the Oakmont Golf Club, Santa Rosa, CA.

BRIGADIER GENERAL
WILLIAM A. ORTH

Permanent Professor 1974–1983
Dean of the Faculty 1978–1983

B.S., *United States Military Academy*
M.S., *Purdue University*
Ph.D., *Brown University*

Bill Orth, the Academy's 29th Permanent Professor, was born in 1931 in Coatesville, Pennsylvania. He was commissioned in the United States Air Force after graduation from the United States Military Academy in 1954. He then attended undergraduate pilot training at Bartow AFB, FL, and Laredo AFB, TX. In 1955 he graduated from combat crew training at Perrin AFB, TX, as an F-86D fighter pilot. He flew with the 324th Fighter Interceptor Squadron at Westover AFB, MA, until 1957, when he was assigned to the 512th Fighter Interceptor Squadron at Royal Air Force Station, Bentwaters, England, where he had the additional duty as Squadron Intelligence Officer. The 512th FIS moved to Sembach Air Base, Germany, in 1958. In 1959 he was transferred to Ramstein Air Base, Germany, where he served as an Intelligence Officer in the Intelligence Training Branch, HQ US Air Forces Europe, for five months. He entered graduate school in 1960 and earned his Master's degree in Mechanical Engineering from Purdue University, Lafayette, IN, in 1961. Bill was then assigned to the Air Force Academy's Department of Mechanics as an Instructor. In 1963 he returned to flying as a T-33 and T-37 Instructor Pilot with the 3575th Pilot Training Wing at Vance AFB, OK, and in 1964 became Chief of Wing Safety. In 1965 he left Vance to study for his PhD in Applied Mathematics at Brown University, Providence, RI. In 1968 Bill was again assigned to the Academy, this time as an Assistant Professor in the Department of Mathematics. He completed his doctoral dissertation while at the Academy and his PhD degree was awarded in 1970. In that year he again returned to flying, first as an A-37 pilot at England AFB, LA, then as Chief of Wing Safety for the 3rd Tactical Fighter Wing, and, later in 1970, as Commander of the 8th Special Operations Squadron (Fighter) at Bien Hoa Air Base, Vietnam. Bill flew 258 combat sorties in the A-37. Following his Vietnam tour, in 1971 he became Assistant Director of Accounting and Finance for the Deputy Chief of Staff, Comptroller, HQ Strategic Air Command, Offutt AFB, NE. Then Bill was assigned in 1972 as Director of Engineering and Construction under the Deputy Chief of Staff, Civil Engineering, HQ SAC. He was a registered Professional Engineer in Nebraska. He became Assistant Deputy Chief of Staff for Civil Engineering, HQ SAC, in 1973. In 1974 Bill returned to the Academy when he was appointed Permanent Professor and Head, Department of Physics. Bill was promoted to brigadier general and appointed the Dean of the Faculty in 1978 and served as the Academy's third Permanent Dean until he retired in 1983. During his tenure as Dean, the Academy adopted the Academic Honors Program, discontinued "majors for all" and instituted the Basic Academic Program, and initiated the Microcomputers in the Dormitories project.

After retiring from the Air Force, Bill Orth served as President of Trident Technical College, Charleston, SC, from 1983 to 1985. He then served as President of the National Education Center, Spartan School of Aeronautics, Tulsa, OK, from 1985 to 1987. From 1987 to 1993, he was President of Atlantic Community College, Mays Landing, NJ.

BRIGADIER GENERAL
JOHN W. WILLIAMS JR.

Permanent Professor 1976–1986

B.S., *Appalachian State University*
M.A., *Appalachian State University*
Ph.D., *Mississippi State University*

John Williams, the Academy's 30th Permanent Professor, was born in Charlotte, North Carolina, in 1929. Prior to entering the Air Force, he completed a Bachelor's degree in Music in 1951 and a Master's degree in Education in 1952 at Appalachian State University, NC. John entered Air Force pilot training at Greenville AFB, MS, in 1953. He earned his wings and was commissioned a second lieutenant in 1954. His first assignment was as a Pilot and then Aircraft Commander with the 11th Aeromedical Transport Squadron, Military Air Transport Service, at Scott AFB, IL. In 1957 John was transferred to Nouasseur Air Base, near Casablanca, Morocco, where he was Chief of the MATS Control Team. He transferred to Torrejon Air Base, Spain, in 1958 and served as Operations and Training Officer for the 1620th MATS Transport Control Center. He moved to McGuire AFB, NJ, in 1959 as a Pilot, Instructor Pilot, and Flight Examiner with the 12th Aeromedical Transport Squadron. In 1962 John became an AFROTC Instructor at Mississippi State University in Starkville. While at MSU, he completed almost all requirements for a PhD in Sociology. From 1966 to 1968 he was the Operations and Training Officer, US Mission to the Democratic Republic of the Congo, with additional duty as one of three pilots for the country's President. In 1968 John was assigned to the Air Force Academy as an Instructor in the Department of Psychology and Leadership. While teaching and flying in the cadet flying training program, he completed the requirements for his

PhD in Sociology, which was awarded by Mississippi State in 1971. In 1972 John volunteered for a tour in Vietnam and was selected as Aide and Executive Officer for the Director of Operations, 7th Air Force, Tan Son Nhut Air Base, Vietnam. When 7th AF moved to Bangkok, Thailand, in early 1973, he became the Secretary of the Joint Staff, US Assistance and Advisory Group. Returning to the Academy in 1973, he was assigned as Deputy Head, Department of Life and Behavioral Sciences. He completed a post-doctorate in Psychobiology at the University of California, Irvine, during this time. In 1974 John was appointed Department Head as the life scientists were being merged into the Department of Chemistry, and the Department of Behavioral Sciences and Leadership emerged as a separate department. He was appointed Head of this new department in July 1975. In 1976 John was selected as a Permanent Professor and remained as Head, Department of Behavioral Sciences and Leadership, until late 1985. John was promoted to brigadier general and retired from the USAF early in 1986.

John then went to Embry Riddle Aeronautical University, Daytona Beach, FL, as Vice President for Academics. After serving in this role for seven years, he became Chair of the Human Factors and Systems Department. Following retirement from Embry Riddle, John went back to flight school and received Flight Instructor and Instrument ratings. He then flew as a Pilot for four years for Sunrise Aviation at Ormond Beach, FL. He is now fully retired and living in Daytona Beach.

COLONEL
LEE D. BADGETT

Permanent Professor 1976–1981

B.S., *Virginia Military Institute*
M.A., *Oxford University*
Ph.D., *Yale University*

Lee Badgett, the Academy's 31ˢᵗ Permanent Professor, was born in St. Louis, Missouri, in 1939. He attended the Virginia Military Institute, graduating with Honors in 1961 with a major in Mathematics and a regular commission in the US Air Force. At VMI he was co-captain of a championship football team, two-time Academic All-American, Regimental Commander, and recipient of VMI's highest award for character and leadership. He was awarded a Rhodes Scholarship, and attended Oxford from 1961 to 1964, earning a Master's degree in Politics, Philosophy, and Economics while developing a lifelong interest in international economics. Following Oxford, Lee began his first of four assignments to the Air Force Academy, teaching the basic economics course as well as a senior-level course in European economic problems. After two years on the faculty, Lee was sent to Yale, where he worked on his doctorate, 1966–1969. He then returned to the Academy for another two years, completed his dissertation, and received his PhD in Economics in 1971. He next was assigned to Saigon, 1971–1972, on the staff of the Deputy Chief of Staff for Economic Affairs, Headquarters Military Assistance Command, Vietnam, where his work focused on economic development and international trade. He returned again to the Academy's Department of Economics, Geography and Management in 1972 and developed several advanced courses in international military-economics. In 1974 Lee was reassigned to the Office of the Secretary of Defense, the Pentagon,

Washington, DC, as Military Assistant to the Director of Net Assessment, dealing with the military-economic aspects of long-term competition between the US and the USSR. In 1976 he was appointed a Permanent Professor and served as Head of the Department of Economics, Geography and Management. In 1980 Lee left the Academy on a military sabbatical assignment to become the Head of the Defense Intelligence Agency's Liaison with British Military Intelligence in London. In 1981 he was reassigned as the Commandant, US Defense Intelligence College (now the National Intelligence University), Bolling AFB, Washington, DC. He retired from the Air Force in 1985.

Following retirement, Lee continued in higher education as Professor of Economics and Dean of the College of Business and Technology, Humboldt State University, Arcata, CA, 1985–1990. In 1990 he returned to his alma mater as Provost and Dean of the Faculty, Virginia Military Institute, holding the rank of brigadier general in the Virginia Militia. He retired from VMI in 1996 and took the position of Provost and Vice President of Academic Affairs at St. Thomas Aquinas College, Orangeburg, NY. He returned once more to VMI as a Visiting Professor in the Economics and Business Department, 2003–2006.

LIEUTENANT GENERAL
ERVIN J. ROKKE

Permanent Professor 1976–1986
Dean of the Faculty 1983–1986

B.S., *United States Air Force Academy*
M.A., *Harvard University*
Ph.D., *Harvard University*

Erv Rokke, the Academy's 32nd Permanent Professor, was born in Warren, Minnesota, in 1939. He received his commission as a second lieutenant upon graduation from the United States Air Force Academy with a Bachelor of Science degree in Political Science in 1962. His first assignment was to Harvard University where he completed a Master's degree in International Relations in 1964. In 1965 he completed the Air Intelligence Officer Course at Lowry AFB, CO. Assigned to the 67th Reconnaissance Technical Squadron, Yokota Air Base, Japan, in 1965, Erv successively served as the officer in charge of the plans and evaluation, production management, photogrammetric development, and production and quality control sections. Moving to Hickam AFB, HI, in 1967, he was a Photo-Radar Intelligence Officer in the 548th Reconnaissance Technical Group, Pacific Air Forces. In 1968 Erv became an Instructor in the Department of Political Science at the Air Force Academy. In 1969 he again entered graduate school at Harvard University, graduating with a PhD in International Relations in 1970. Returning to the Academy's Department of Political Science, he was an Instructor and, later, the Chairman of Instruction and an Associate Professor. He was co-editor of *American Defense Policy*, 3rd edition, 1973, which enjoyed several printings and was a basic text for Air Force Academy and ROTC courses. In 1973 Erv became a Plans Officer in the Office of the Defense Adviser in the US Mission to NATO, Brussels, Belgium. In 1976 Erv was appointed a Permanent Professor and served as an Assistant Dean of the Faculty. In 1977 he became the Head of the Department of Political Science, and in 1980 his sabbatical assignment was as the Air Attaché to the United Kingdom assigned to the American Embassy in London. Returning to lead the Department of Political Science in 1982, Erv was selected as the Dean of the Faculty and promoted to brigadier general in 1983. During his tenure as Dean, the Academy completed its first 25-year curriculum review. In 1986 Erv became the first, and to date the only, USAFA Permanent Professor to return to the Line of the AF. Again a colonel, Erv attended defense attaché training at the Foreign Service Institute in Arlington, VA, before becoming the Defense and Air Attaché to the Union of Soviet Socialist Republics, American Embassy, Moscow, in 1987, where he witnessed the last days of the Soviet Union. He was promoted to brigadier general again in 1988. Next, in 1989 he became the Associate Deputy Director of Operations for Military Support, National Security Agency, Fort George G. Meade, MD. After promotion to major general in 1991, Erv moved back to Europe as the Director of Intelligence for HQ US European Command at Stuttgart-Vaihingen, Germany. In 1993 he became the Assistant Chief of Staff, Intelligence, HQ USAF, Washington, DC. He began his last active duty assignment in 1994 when he was promoted to lieutenant general and appointed President of the National Defense University, also in Washington, DC. Erv retired from the USAF in 1997.

During his tenure at NDU and since, Erv has focused on advanced analysis relating to non-linear problem sets in the national security arena and worked with a private sector company that teaches related courses to American and friendly foreign intelligence services. Upon his retirement, Erv became the President of Moravian College in Bethlehem, PA. When he left Moravian College nine years later he was honored as an Honorary Alumnus for his outstanding improvements to the quality and quantity of the student body, curricula, programs offered, and college infrastructure. From 2007 to 2009, he occupied the Superintendent's Chair for Character and Leadership Development at the Academy. During this time Erv provided the vision and energy that culminated in the dedication in 2016 of the building that is the new home for the Center for Character and Leadership Development. He also served as the President of the USAFA Endowment from 2009 to 2011 and is a member of the Endowment's Board of Directors. Erv is currently the Senior Scholar in Residence at the Center for Character and Leadership Development. He and several colleagues have published a series of three articles on Combined Effects Power in the *Joint Force Quarterly*, most recently in *JFQ* 85, 2nd Quarter 2017. In recent years he has spent time as a Fellow at the Australian National Defense University and made substantial presentations at international conferences in Romania, Serbia-Montenegro, Germany, and the US.

Erv is a member of the Defense Intelligence Agency Attaché Hall of Fame, a recipient of the Jan Masaryk Medal of Achievement from the Czech Republic in 2006, and holds honorary degrees from Muhlenberg and Moravian Colleges in Pennsylvania and the Defense Intelligence College in Washington, DC. He is a member of the Advisory Council for the Education and Training Center of the US Institute of Peace, the Council on Foreign Relations, and the Board of Visitors for the Defense Language Institute.

Permanent Professor 1977–1999

B.A., Ohio Wesleyan University
M.A., Stanford University
Ph.D., University of Denver

Jack Shuttleworth, the Academy's 33rd Permanent Professor, was born in Covington, Ohio, in 1935. He graduated from Ohio Wesleyan University, Delaware, OH, in 1957 with a Bachelor's degree in English. As Cadet Wing Commander of the AFROTC program there, he was also named a Distinguished Graduate. After completing weapons controller school at Tyndall AFB, FL, Jack was assigned to an Aircraft Control and Warning Squadron in Freising, Germany, 1958–1961. Returning to the States, as a Master Weapons Controller he was assigned to a Radar Squadron at Bellevue Air Force Station, IL, 1961–1963, an assignment interrupted by an emergency deployment to Key West, FL, during the Cuban Missile Crisis. He was next sent to Stanford where he earned his Masters' degree in English and American Literature in 1964, prior to a teaching assignment at the Air Force Academy Preparatory School, 1964–1965. Jack was then selected by the Academy's Department of English for the doctoral program at the University of Denver, where he won a Woodrow Wilson Research Fellowship for study in Europe. His dissertation was published by the Oxford University Press. Jack returned to the Academy in the Department of English in 1967; his PhD in English Literature was awarded by DU in 1968. He co-authored a textbook *Satire: Aesop to Buchwald* (published in 1971), which was widely adopted. From 1971 to 1972 he went to Southeast Asia as Chief of Third Country Training for Military Assistance Command, Vietnam, responsible for the training of

Cambodian National Armed Forces. During this tour, Jack's work on sensitive, high-level projects was far from academic: he earned recognition by three countries, and especially noteworthy, he was made an honorary member of the US Army Special Forces. After returning to the Academy, he filled middle- and senior-level positions in the Department of English. He was the key figure in establishing the USAFA Executive Writing Course, which he took to dozens of bases and hundreds of senior military and civilian leaders, a valuable service rendered by his department to the greater Air Force for many years. Jack was appointed Permanent Professor in 1977. Among many areas of interest, Jack earned his Commercial Balloon Pilot rating and served the Academy for several years as Officer in Charge of the Cadet Balloon Club (1st Aero Balloon Squadron). From 1982 to 1984 he took a sabbatical assignment at the Royal United Services Institute for Defense Studies in London. During his tenure as Department Head, the fine arts staff and curriculum were transferred into the expanded Department of English and Fine Arts. Among his scholarly works are *The Life of Edward, First Lord Herbert Cherbury* (ed., 1976), *The Practical Writer, Paragraph to Theme* (1982), and *Writing Research Papers* (1984), as well as peer-reviewed essays and presentations at national and international forums. Jack was promoted to brigadier general and retired in 1999 after 42 years of service.

In retirement, Jack has traveled extensively and read widely. He taught a few sections of Humanities 200 and 400 at the Academy and finished editing *Hamlet*, a contribution to the Shakespeare authorship question and the Shakespeare Oxford Fellowship. He volunteered in the Penrose Hospital emergency room for eight years and is an active member of the Pen Collectors of America.

BRIGADIER GENERAL
CARY A. FISHER

Permanent Professor 1977–2005

B.S., United States Military Academy
M.S., California Institute of Technology
M.A., University of New Mexico
Ph.D., University of Oklahoma

Cary Fisher, the Academy's 34th Permanent Professor, was born in 1941 in Manhattan Beach, California. He graduated from the United States Military Academy with a Bachelor's degree in 1963 and entered the US Air Force upon graduation. Cary's first assignment was to the California Institute of Technology, Pasadena, from which he graduated with a Master's degree in Aeronautics in 1964. He then became the Project Director, Rocket Sled Blast Simulation Program at the AF Weapons Laboratory, Kirtland AFB, NM. While at Kirtland, Cary earned a Master's degree in Government and Political Science from the University of New Mexico. He attended Squadron Officer School at Maxwell AFB, AL, in early 1968, graduating as a Distinguished Graduate. Cary was assigned as an Instructor in the Department of Engineering Mechanics at the USAF Academy in 1968. In 1970 he became a graduate student at the University of Oklahoma, Norman, earning a PhD in Mechanical Engineering in 1972. Cary then was assigned as a Weapons Controller and Senior Director, 621st Tactical Control Squadron, Ubon Royal Thai AFB, Thailand. In 1973 Cary returned to the Academy as an Associate Professor and Assistant to the Dean, Faculty Secretariat. In 1977 he was appointed a Permanent Professor; he continued with his duties on the Dean's staff until appointed Head of the Department of Engineering Mechanics in 1979. In 1982 he took a sabbatical as the Chief Scientist, European Office of Aerospace Research and Development, Air Force Office of

Scientific Research, London. In 1983 Cary moved to the American Embassy in London as the Science Attaché. In 1984 he returned to the Academy as Head of the Department of Engineering Mechanics and assumed the additional duty of Engineering Division Chair in 1987. He served as President of the American Society for Engineering Education in 1994–1995, and in various capacities within the American Society of Mechanical Engineers, including Chair of the Mechanical Engineering Department Heads Committee. In 2002 Cary and his engineering colleagues developed the ABET-accredited Systems Engineering major. In 2003 he spent four months as Senior Military Liaison Officer to HQ Kosovo Force, United Nations Mission, Pristina. He has authored more than 50 published reports and journal articles on engineering topics, curriculum development, and engineering education. He is a registered Professional Engineer in the State of Colorado. Cary was promoted to brigadier general and retired from the USAF in 2005.

Cary has continued his involvement in engineering education, both as an ABET Program Evaluator and as an ABET Foundation Consultant. To date he has evaluated 40 undergraduate engineering programs, including programs at 10 overseas campuses. Cary was recently elected as a Public Member of the Higher Learning Commission Board of Trustees. The Higher Learning Commission has the regional accreditation responsibility for all post-secondary educational institutions in the central United States.

COLONEL
JOSEPH MONROE

Permanent Professor 1979–1987

B.S., North Carolina A&T State
    University
M.S., Texas A&M University
Ph.D., Texas A&M University

Joe Monroe, the Academy's 35th Permanent Professor, was born in Rowland, North Carolina, in 1936. Following high school, he enlisted in the Air Force in 1954 and served in Africa and Turkey for three years. His performance as an airman earned him an Air Force ROTC scholarship at North Carolina A&T State University, Greensboro, where he earned his Baccalaureate degree in Mathematics, English, and French in 1962. During his senior year he was the AFROTC Cadet Commander. As a second lieutenant, Joe was assigned to Sheppard AFB, TX, and began his career-long work in data automation. From 1964 to 1966 at Lowry AFB, CO, he provided computer programming support to the Air Intelligence Training Center and was selected for AF-sponsored graduate work at Texas A&M University. He earned his Master's degree in Computer Science from Texas A&M in 1967 and came to the Academy as an Instructor in the Department of Astronautics and Computer Science. He had a one-year deployment, 1969–1970, as Director of Data Automation at Nakhon Phanom Royal Thai Air Base, Thailand, before returning to Texas A&M for his PhD, which he was awarded in 1972. Joe Monroe was the first African-American to earn a PhD in Computer Science in the United States. Upon graduation, he rejoined the Academy faculty. In 1979 he was appointed Permanent Professor, as a lieutenant colonel, serving as Assistant to the Dean of the Faculty. In 1981 Joe was promoted to colonel and made Head of the Department of Electrical Engineering. A year later in 1982 he was named Head of the newly formed Department of Computer Science. He made important contributions to computer software systems for Air Force personnel, logistics, and intelligence data systems. Joe Monroe retired in 1987.

In 1988 Joe accepted a faculty position at Fayetteville State University, North Carolina. In 1991 he returned to North Carolina A&T State University, where he was later named the Ronald E. McNair Endowed Professor and Chair of Computer Science. He was appointed Dean of the College of Engineering at North Carolina A&T in 2000 and retired from this position in 2009.

COLONEL
JOHN T. MAY

Permanent Professor 1980–1987
Vice Dean of the Faculty 1984–1986
Acting Dean of the Faculty
    1986–1987

B.S., *United States Air Force Academy*
M.S., *North Carolina State University*
Ph.D., *North Carolina State University*

John May, the Academy's 36th Permanent Professor, was born in 1939 in Philadelphia, Pennsylvania. He graduated with the United States Air Force Academy's third class in 1961. He attended pilot training at Reese AFB, TX, earning his wings in 1962. He then began flying C-130s, an aircraft in which he eventually accumulated more than 5,000 hours, with three commands— Military Airlift Command, Air Force Aerospace Recovery and Rescue Service, and Air Force Systems Command. After pilot training, he served with the 41st Air Transport Squadron at Charleston AFB, SC, as a Pilot and Instructor Pilot. In 1967 he was assigned to the 39th Aerospace Recovery and Rescue Squadron at Tuy Hoa Air Base, Vietnam, where he was a Pilot and Instructor Pilot in the HC-130P, performing air-to-air refueling with HH-3 and HH-53 rescue helicopters, and coordinating rescue efforts for downed aircrew. After two years of graduate school at North Carolina State University, John earned his Master's degree in Physics in 1970 and was assigned to teach as a Physics Instructor at the Air Force Academy. He returned to North Carolina State in 1972, earned his PhD in Physics two years later, and then taught at the Academy as an Associate Professor of Physics. In 1976 he again resumed flying the C-130, this time with the 6594th Test Group at Hickam AFB, HI. He held the position of Chief of Standardization/Evaluation, and conducted flight testing of a heads-up display for aerial recovery of parachute suspended objects; he was the pilot on the first operational use of this system. After leaving Hawaii in 1979, he was assigned to the Air Force Office of Scientific Research in Washington, DC, where he was the manager for Air Force basic research in pulsed power, plasma physics, and particle beams. John once again was assigned to the Academy faculty with his appointment as Permanent Professor and Head of the Department of Physics, 1980–1984. During his tenure, he initiated several long-lasting innovations. He established a computer learning laboratory, where his faculty developed computer-delivered problems for review and testing, computer simulations for classroom use, and a computer-based gradebook. The latter was such a boon to record keeping that it was adopted faculty-wide. He formed a faculty laser group for theoretical and experimental research through joint efforts with the Frank J. Seiler Research Laboratory and the Air Force Weapons Laboratory. He modernized the Atmospheric Science Program to emphasize ionospheric research and solar-planetary interactions, and he introduced the Physics major's track in Space Physics. He also improved community outreach through the "Physics is Phun" program to encourage science curiosity in children through exciting demonstrations in local elementary schools. He served as Officer Representative for the men's basketball team. John was the Vice Dean of the Faculty, 1984–1986, and the Acting Dean for the academic year 1986–1987. In these roles he provided the justifying rationale for the use of networked computers in education, which helped bring about the Academy's first-in-the-world campus-wide networked computers in 1986. He retired in 1987.

From 1987 to 1988 John was a Visiting Professor of Physics at North Carolina State University, Raleigh. In 1988 he joined the Atlantic Community College in Mays Landing, NJ, serving as the Academic Dean, 1988–1993, and then became the college's President. Under his leadership, the college was expanded and renamed Atlantic Cape Community College; he retired as President of the college in 2005.

BRIGADIER GENERAL
ORWYN SAMPSON

Permanent Professor 1980–1992

B.S., *University of California,*
Los Angeles
M.S., *University of California,*
Los Angeles
Ph.D., *University of Oregon*

Orwyn "O" Sampson, the Academy's 37th Permanent Professor, was born in 1937 in Van Nuys and raised in Canoga Park, California. He graduated from UCLA in 1959 with a major in Physical Education (Kinesiology). At UCLA, O was a competitive gymnast and the Cadet Commander of the AFROTC detachment. Following his commissioning in 1959, O took an educational delay to pursue his Master's degree in Exercise Physiology, which he earned in 1960. He entered active duty as a Personnel Services Officer at Nellis AFB, NV. He came to the Air Force Academy as an Assistant Gymnastics Coach and Instructor of Physical Education, 1962–1964, during which time he taught skills classes, supervised cadet intramural athletics, and developed physical education standards. Selected for a PhD program, he attended the University of Oregon from 1964 to 1966; his degree was awarded in 1967. From 1966 to 1971, O again served in the Academy's Athletics Department as Gymnastics Coach and Assistant Professor. An expert in the areas of physical fitness and exercise science, he pioneered the development of the Human Performance Laboratory and the William S. Stone Cardiopulmonary Laboratory, and improved the Physical Aptitude Examination and the Cadet Physical Fitness Test. In 1971–1972 he was Chief, Special Services at Tan Son Nhut Air Base, Vietnam, where he was instrumental in greatly increasing the number and quality of facilities and programs for fitness, recreation, and morale. He returned to the Academy in

1972 and played a major role in the development of the academic discipline of physiology/biology. The subject was first in the Department of Life and Behavioral Sciences, then in Chemistry and Physiology, then in Chemistry and Biological Sciences. Finally, in 1980 the discipline was anchored in the stand-alone Department of Biology, with O Sampson as the Permanent Professor and Department Head. As Head, he was the driving force behind the expansion of the department into new teaching and laboratory facilities specifically designed for the discipline. He took sabbatical assignments at the School of Aerospace Medicine, Brooks AFB, TX, and the Cal Tech/Jet Propulsion Laboratory, Pasadena, CA. At Brooks, he became a certified Air Force Aerospace Physiologist and returned later as an instructor in that field. During his two-year sabbatical at JPL, 1984–1986, he studied and contributed to the understanding of the scientific assessment of body composition and how bone, muscle, and fat are affected by weightlessness. He was the Chair of the Basic Sciences Division from 1986 until his retirement in 1992. Throughout his 25 years of service at the Academy, O was a central figure in the Fellowship of Christian Athletes. He has always been out front and willing to share his thoughts and feelings about freedom, service to country, and the privilege of being an American. In retirement, he is using his life and professional education experience in a variety of areas to include teaching, research, and, most enthusiastically, in the creative area of inventing.

BRIGADIER GENERAL
HARVEY W. SCHILLER

Permanent Professor 1980–1986

B.S., *The Citadel*
M.S., *University of Michigan*
Ph.D., *University of Michigan*

Harvey Schiller, the Academy's 38th Permanent Professor, was born in New York City in 1939. He was an ROTC Distinguished Graduate from The Citadel in 1960. He entered an educational delay and accepted a graduate fellowship at the University of Michigan, where he earned his Master's degree in Chemistry in 1962. He began his active duty in pilot training at Moody AFB, AL—graduating first in his class—followed by operational flying assignments in the C-123 at Holloman AFB, NM, and Tan Son Nhut Air Base, Vietnam. He was assigned to the Academy as Instructor of Chemistry in 1967. In 1968 Harvey returned to the University of Michigan where he earned his PhD in Chemistry in 1970. He was next assigned as Pilot and Base Operations Officer at Robins AFB, GA. Returning to the Academy in 1972, he taught introductory and advanced inorganic chemistry and was a T-29 Instructor Pilot, Soaring Instructor, and Associate Air Officer Commanding for a cadet squadron. In 1975 he attended Armed Forces Staff College, Norfolk, VA, followed by a tour flying KC-135s at Grand Forks AFB, ND, 1976–1978. Returning to the Academy, he first taught chemistry and in 1979 was Director of Faculty Support in the Office of the Dean. He was appointed Permanent Professor and Head of the Department of Chemistry in 1980. During his tenure he served the Academy as its Faculty Representative to the National Collegiate Athletic Association. He was a consultant to the US Olympic Committee during the 1984 games in Los

Angeles, responsible for the boxing program. He retired in 1986 and was promoted to brigadier general in 2004.

Upon retirement from the Air Force, Harvey accepted the position of Commissioner of the Southeastern (Athletic) Conference (1986–1989). Under his guidance the SEC established itself as a leader in the areas of athletic scholarship and marketing. He was later Executive Director of the United States Olympic Committee (1989–1994); President of Turner Sports and President of the National Hockey League franchise the Atlanta Thrashers (1994–1999); and Chairman and CEO of YankeeNets, an integrated sports-based media company with ownership of the New York Yankees, New York Nets, and New Jersey Devils (2000–2002). Harvey served as Chairman of Assante U.S., a provider of financial and life management products and services (2002–2004). He was Chairman and Chief Executive Officer at Global Options Group, Inc. (2004–2013), and President of the International Baseball Federation (2007–2009). From 2014 to 2016 he was Commercial Commissioner of the America's Cup. He has been Managing Director of Diversifies Search since 2008, Chairman and CEO of Schiller Management Group since 2010, and was Chairman of "lettrs," a social autographs network, 2017. Harvey has received honorary doctorates from Northern Michigan University in 1994, the United States Sports Academy in 2011, and The Citadel in 2012.

BRIGADIER GENERAL
PHILIP D. CAINE

Permanent Professor 1981–1992

B.A., *University of Denver*
M.A., *Stanford University*
Ph.D., *Stanford University*

Phil Caine, the Academy's 39th Permanent Professor, was born in Chadron, Nebraska, in 1933. In 1955 he graduated from the University of Denver with a major in Social Sciences and a commission as a Distinguished Graduate from AFROTC. After graduating from pilot training at Vance AFB, OK, in 1957, he was assigned to fly the T-29 aircraft at Mather AFB, CA, where he became an Instructor Pilot and Flight Examiner. In 1961 he left active flying to be a full-time graduate student at Stanford, earning his Master's degree in History in 1963 prior to reporting to the Academy as an Instructor in the Department of History. A year later he returned to Stanford under Academy sponsorship. He completed his PhD degree in US Diplomatic History in 1966 and returned to the Department of History for a second tour, 1966–1969. During this assignment, he developed a new course on Unconventional Warfare and chaired the department's offering in American Diplomatic History. In 1969–1970 Phil spent a year in Headquarters, Seventh Air Force, Saigon, Vietnam, as Deputy Chief, then Chief, Project CHECO (Contemporary Historical Evaluation of Combat Operations). Returning once again to the Academy in 1970, Phil was subsequently appointed Tenure Associate Professor, then Tenure Professor, and in 1976 during Colonel Hurley's sabbatical, he served as Acting Head, Department of History. From 1977 to 1978 he was a Professor of International Studies at the National War College, Washington, DC. He began his fourth assignment to the Academy's History Department in 1978 as Deputy Department Head. However, in 1980, Phil was transferred from the faculty to the Commandant of Cadets as Deputy Commandant for Military Instruction and in 1981 was appointed Permanent Professor, the first such under the Commandant. In that position, he was responsible for Professional Military Studies (which subsequently became the Department of Military and Strategic Studies), Cadet Professional Development, cadet survival and small arms training, summer program scheduling, and the flying operations of the 50th Airmanship Training Squadron. During 1987 he took a one-year sabbatical to Washington, DC, first to serve on a select committee reviewing Professional Military Education in the Department of Defense and later for six months as a Senior Research Fellow, Institute for National Security Studies, National Defense University. A Command Pilot with more than 4,500 flying hours, Phil has an abiding interest in military aviation history. His book *Eagles of the RAF* (1991) tells the remarkable stories of American airmen who flew for the British prior to America's entry into World War II. Phil was promoted to brigadier general and retired in 1992.

In retirement, Phil has written three more books, including *The RAF Eagle Squadrons* (2009). He also edited the seven-volume compendium of interviews with members of the three Eagle Squadrons. He has been for many years the President of The Friends of the Air Force Academy Library, a non-profit group devoted to enhancing the quality of the McDermott Library as an educational, research, scientific, and cultural institution.

BRIGADIER GENERAL
DAVID O. SWINT SR.

Permanent Professor 1982–2000

B.S., University of Texas at Austin
M.S., California Institute of Technology
Ph.D., Michigan State University

Dave Swint, the Academy's 40th Permanent Professor, was born in 1936 in Oklahoma City, Oklahoma. He earned a Bachelor's degree in Mechanical Engineering from the University of Texas in 1960 and was commissioned a second lieutenant from AFROTC. He was first assigned in 1961 as a Mechanical Engineer for Base Civil Engineering at March AFB, CA. From 1964 to 1965 he completed a Master's degree in Mechanical Engineering prior to taking an assignment as Officer in Charge of Engineering and Construction at Cannon AFB, NM. At Forbes AFB, KS, in 1966, he was assigned to the 554th RED HORSE unit as part of the elite advanced cadre for training 400 personnel as replacements for duty in Southeast Asia. That same year Dave was assigned as Assistant Officer in Charge of Engineering and Construction with the 554th RED HORSE at Phan Rang Air Base, Vietnam. In 1967 Dave's first USAFA assignment was as an Instructor in the Department of Engineering Mechanics. After completing a PhD at Michigan State University in Structural Engineering, 1969–1972, he returned to USAFA in the Department of Civil Engineering, Engineering Mechanics and Materials. In 1974 he completed Armed Forces Staff College in Norfolk, VA, and returned to the Department of Civil Engineering and Mechanics. In 1977 Dave served as the 554th RED HORSE Detachment Commander at Kunsan Air Base, Republic of Korea. After completing Air War College at Maxwell AFB, AL, in 1980 he was assigned as Chief of Force

Development, HQ Strategic Air Command, Offutt AFB, NE. In 1982 Dave returned to the Academy when he was appointed Permanent Professor and Head, Department of Civil Engineering. In this role, he directed the development of a new core course on air base planning and operability. He also established the 50-acre Field Engineering and Readiness Laboratory, a nationally unique facility to demonstrate hands-on engineering principles to engineering majors. The lab's construction activities produce housing for Native Americans and integrate cadet education with readiness training and community service. Dave initiated an accredited Environmental Engineering major to meet the increasing demand for Air Force environmental expertise. He developed a US DoD-Russian Environmental Course to prepare senior Russian officers to manage complex environmental programs. Dave was promoted to brigadier general and retired from the USAF in 2000.

Dave became the broker/owner of Swint Realty Company, LLC, in 2001 and continues with his business in Colorado Springs today. He is a Registered Engineer in the State of Colorado. From 2010 to 2011 he served the USAFA Endowment as the Project Manager for the construction of the USAFA Holaday Athletic Center.

BRIGADIER GENERAL
CARL W. REDDEL

Permanent Professor 1982–1999

B.S., Drake University
M.A., Syracuse University
Ph.D., Indiana University

Carl Reddel, the Academy's 41ˢᵗ Permanent Professor, was born in 1937 in Gurley, Nebraska. He attended Drake University, Des Moines, IA, on a track scholarship and earned his Bachelor's degree in History and Education in 1959. He was awarded a Woodrow Wilson Fellowship to attend Syracuse University and a Ford Foundation Fellowship to complete his Master's degree in Russian Studies in 1961. He entered the Air Force as a Distinguished Graduate of Officer Training School, Lackland AFB, TX, in 1962. Carl's first assignment was to Toul-Rosières Air Base, France, where he was Chief of Administrative Services for a mobile communications group. In his off-time, he taught Russian and Soviet History for the University of Maryland and studied at the Université de Nancy. In 1967 he began the first of four assignments to the Academy's Department of History, 1967–1968, 1971–1976, 1977–1981, and finally, as Permanent Professor and Department Head, 1982–1999. During the first gap, he was in Vietnam (summer 1968) performing a study for Project CHECO (Contemporary Historical Evaluation of Combat Operations) and then attended graduate school at Indiana University, Bloomington (1968–1971); his PhD in Russian History and Soviet Studies was awarded in 1973. His widely traveled career included a tour as the first active duty officer on the official educational exchange with the Soviet Union at Moscow State University (1975); an assignment in Turkey as Executive Officer, Air Force Section, Joint US Mission for Military

Aid to Turkey (1976–1977); duty as the Air Force liaison officer to the Western world's leading Soviet military historian at the University of Edinburgh, Scotland (1981–1982); and a sabbatical research associateship at the National Air and Space Museum (1994). As a leader in global education and world history, he reestablished and chaired the Academy's Area Studies Program. Carl is a Russian and Soviet scholar and author of numerous publications and presentations, most recently, "Opening a New Era in Russian Historiography" in the Introduction to Vol. 1 (2014) of the multivolume *History of Russia* by Sergei M. Soloviev. From 1988 to 1991 he provided outstanding operational service to the nation as Team Chief for the On-Site Inspection Agency, leading missile destruction teams and performing inspections in the Soviet Union to ensure compliance with the Intermediate-Range Nuclear Forces (INF) Treaty. Carl was promoted to brigadier general and retired in 1999.

Following retirement, Carl became President and CEO of the Eisenhower World Affairs Institute, 1999–2000, and a Fellow in the Center for Public Service at Gettysburg College. Since 2001 he has been Executive Director of the Dwight D. Eisenhower Memorial Commission, charged by Congress with establishing a national, permanent memorial to the Supreme Commander of Allied Forces in World War II and the 34th US President. Construction of the Memorial, located at the base of Capitol Hill on the Mall in Washington, DC, has been underway since November 2017.

COLONEL
KENNETH H. FLEMING

Permanent Professor 1981–1988
Vice Dean of the Faculty 1986–1988

B.S., *United States Air Force Academy*
M.A., *University of California,*
   Los Angeles
Ph.D., *University of California,*
   San Diego

Ken Fleming, the Academy's 42nd Permanent Professor, was born in New York City in 1940. He graduated from the United States Air Force Academy in 1962 with a major in Economics. Ken earned his pilot's wings at Craig AFB, AL, a year later and embarked on a flying career that included some 3,000 hours flying in five major Air Force commands: Strategic Air Command, Military Airlift Command, Tactical Air Command, Pacific Air Forces, and US Air Forces in Europe! From 1963 to 1966 he flew the B-47 at Davis-Monthan AFB, AZ; Lincoln AFB, NE; and Pease AFB, NH. In 1966 he flew the C-141 at Travis AFB, CA. From 1966 to 1968 he flew the F-100 in Vietnam (he had 200 combat missions and earned a Silver Star). Following Vietnam, he was sent to UCLA in preparation for an Academy faculty assignment. He earned his Master's degree in Economics, with an emphasis on Price Theory and Industrial Organization, in 1969. Following UCLA, he was assigned for two years to the Academy's Department of Economics, Geography and Management. From 1971–1974 he was a doctoral student at UC San Diego; his PhD in Economics was awarded in 1978. Ken next flew the OV-10 at Osan Air Base, Korea, 1974–1975, before returning to teach at the Academy. He specialized in advanced economics and econometrics, the application of mathematical methods to analysis of economic issues. In 1978 he was reassigned to Sembach Air Base, Germany, as Operations Officer, later Commander of an OV-10

Tactical Air Support Squadron. He was appointed Permanent Professor in December 1981 and formally took over as Head of the Department of Economics and Geography in 1982. He served as Vice Dean of the Faculty from 1986 until his retirement in 1988.

Following his active service, Ken joined the faculty of Embry-Riddle Aeronautical University in Daytona Beach, FL, where he taught and conducted economics research on many areas of the airline industry. He was Chairman of the University's Aviation Business Administration Department, now expanded into the College of Business. Subsequently, he led an externally funded research initiative working on issues that were mainly concerned with the next-generation air traffic control procedures (which are now being implemented). During this period, he coauthored the influential textbook *Introduction to Air Transport Economics: From Theory to Applications* (2008), which merged the institutional and technical aspects of the aviation industry with their theoretical economic underpinnings. In 2008 he retired from Embry-Riddle to co-author a second text, *Foundations of Airline Finance: Methodology and Practice* (2010). In 2011 he returned to Embry-Riddle as an Adjunct Professor, teaching advanced economics courses, while completing 2nd and 3rd editions of both his textbooks.

BRIGADIER GENERAL
JAMES R. WOODY

Permanent Professor 1982–1997
Vice Commandant of Cadets
    1982–1984
Vice Dean of the Faculty 1988–1990

B.S., United States Air Force Academy
M.B.A., University of California,
    Los Angeles
D.B.A., University of Virginia

Jim Woody, the Academy's 43rd Permanent Professor, was born in Roanoke, Virginia, in 1944. He graduated from the United States Air Force Academy in 1966 with a Bachelor's degree in Engineering Management. He entered the Academy's graduate study "co-op" program and received a Master's degree in 1967 from the University of California, Los Angeles with a major in Finance. Jim then attended Undergraduate Pilot Training at Laredo AFB, TX. After Combat Crew Training at Castle AFB, CA, he was assigned to the 919th Air Refueling Squadron at McCoy AFB, FL, as a KC-135 Pilot and Instructor Pilot. Jim spent four years flying tankers and twice had six-month ARC LIGHT tours in Southeast Asia, where he flew more than 100 combat missions with 856 combat hours. He was assigned in 1972 to HQ Strategic Air Command, Offutt AFB, NE, where he served a career enrichment tour as Special Assistant to the Strategic Air Command's Chief of Staff. Jim returned to USAFA in 1973 as an Instructor of Economics in the Department of Economics, Geography and Management and taught economics while supporting cadet flying. In 1975 he was selected for doctoral study at the University of Virginia at Charlottesville. He returned to the Academy in 1978 and received his Doctorate in Business Administration in 1981 with a concentration in Finance. Jim served as Assistant Professor of Economics and Management, Deputy Department Head, and a T-39 Instructor Pilot until he became the Acting Head of the Department of Management in June 1981. He was appointed a Permanent Professor in March 1982. He next became the Vice Commandant of Cadets in December 1982. Jim conducted the investigation of the 1984 cadet honor scandal and co-authored the report to the Secretary of the Air Force. He returned to head the Department of Management in 1984. Jim became the Vice Dean of the Faculty in 1988 and served in that position until 1990 when he returned to his position as Head of the Department of Management. He also served in the cadet airmanship program as a T-41 and TG-7A Instructor Pilot. Jim Woody was promoted to brigadier general and retired from the USAF in 1997.

Upon retirement, Jim became the Business Administrator/Operations Pastor of the Pulpit Rock Church in Colorado Springs. In 2004 he returned to educational administration as the Chief Financial Officer of The Classical Academy in Colorado Springs, where he served until 2007. Jim was elected to The Classical Academy Board in 2009 and served as the Board Treasurer for five years and the Board Chairperson in 2015.

BRIGADIER GENERAL
ERLIND G. ROYER

Permanent Professor 1983–1991
Dean of the Faculty 1987–1991

B.S., *Montana State College*
M.S., *Stanford University*
Ph.D., *University of Illinois*

Lindy Royer, the Academy's 44ᵗʰ Permanent Professor, was born in 1939 in Missoula, Montana. In 1961 he earned a Bachelor's degree in Electrical Engineering from Montana State College, Bozeman, as a Distinguished Graduate of their AFROTC program. He accepted a scholarship for graduate study, entered active duty in October, and completed a Master's degree in Electrical Engineering from Stanford University in 1962. He then was assigned to the San Bernardino Air Materiel Area (AMA), Norton AFB, CA, as a Project Engineer for ballistic missile flight instrumentation and analysis. In 1965 Lindy transferred to the Sacramento AMA, McClellan AFB, CA, as a Project Engineer performing engineering analysis of Thor missile launches supporting a space program. He was a Distinguished Graduate of Squadron Officer School, Maxwell AFB, AL, in 1966. He entered the University of Illinois in 1967 and completed his PhD in Electrical Engineering in 1970. In 1969 Lindy was assigned to the Air Force Academy where, in addition to teaching, he was Director of the Radio Frequency Systems Laboratory in the Department of Electrical Engineering. He entered the Armed Forces Staff College in 1973. Upon completion six months later, he was assigned to the Deputy for Airborne Warning and Control Systems, Electronic Systems Division, Hanscom AFB, MA, as Navigation Guidance Functional Group Manager for the E-3A Sentry aircraft. He later also was responsible for developing a self-defense system and electromagnetic pulse protection for the aircraft. In 1975 Lindy transferred to the Over-the-Horizon Radar System Program Office as Chief, Engineering and Test Division. He next served as the program's System Program Director, 1977–1979, accomplishing a major restructuring of the project that reduced the cost by 30 percent. After graduation from the National War College, Washington, DC, in 1980, he was assigned to Supreme Headquarters Allied Powers Europe (SHAPE), Casteau, Belgium, as Chief of the Survivability Section, Command and Control Branch, Assistant Chief of Staff for Operations. In 1981 he became Deputy Chief of the Command and Control Branch. After SHAPE reorganized in early 1983, he served as Chief of the Command and Control Requirements Section. While at SHAPE, Lindy wrote and obtained approval of the first NATO policy for electromagnetic pulse protection of war headquarters (1981) and the first *NATO Command and Control Plan* (1983). He returned to the Academy in 1983 as Permanent Professor and Head, Department of Electrical Engineering. In 1984 he assumed additional duty as Director of the Microcomputers in the Dormitories Project. When completed in 1986 for one-third the estimated cost, this was the first academic local area network in the world with every student, faculty, and staff member connected to all academic computing facilities. Lindy became the Dean of the Faculty in 1987 and was promoted to brigadier general. As Dean he facilitated the transition to the daily use of networked microcomputers to increase cadet learning and ease Academy-wide administrative tasks. Lindy retired from the USAF in 1991.

After retiring, Lindy worked for several companies as a Vice President managing software development projects. In 1998 he returned to the Academy as a Distinguished Visiting Professor in Electrical Engineering for five years. After a year as a volunteer mentor to cadet design project teams, he occupied The Phillip J. Erdle Chair for Engineering Science, 2004–2006, and helped establish the Computer Engineering and System Engineering majors in addition to teaching. In 2006 Lindy became a part-time researcher and cadet mentor and helped establish the Academy Center for Unmanned Aerial Systems Research (ACUASR) in 2009. He then helped guide the integration of the remotely piloted aircraft program with the ACUASR in 2014, before retiring again in 2015. He currently serves as Vice President of the non-profit The Friends of the Air Force Academy Library. Lindy has been honored with the University of Illinois Distinguished Alumni Award and the Montana State University Alumni Achievement Award.

BRIGADIER GENERAL
DOUGLAS J. MURRAY

Permanent Professor 1984–2007
Vice Dean of the Faculty 1990–1991

B.S., *Georgetown University*
M.A., *University of Texas at Austin*
Ph.D., *University of Texas at Austin*

Doug Murray, the Academy's 45th Permanent Professor, was born in 1943 in Audubon, New Jersey. He entered the Air Force in 1965 as a Distinguished AFROTC Graduate with a Bachelor's degree in Foreign Service from George-town University School of Foreign Service, Washington, DC. He served as a Titan II Missile Combat Crew member in the Standardization/Evaluation Division at McConnell AFB, KS, 1965–1969. He entered graduate school in the Institute of Latin American Studies, University of Texas at Austin, in 1969 and earned a Master's degree in Latin American Studies in 1970. After six months as a student at the Armed Forces Air Intelligence Center, Lowry AFB, CO, Doug served as the Chief of the Operational Intelligence Branch, 432nd Tactical Reconnaissance Wing, Udorn, Thailand. In 1972 he became an Assistant Professor in the Department of Political Science at the USAF Academy. In 1974 he entered graduate school again at the University of Texas at Austin and earned his PhD in International Relations, Comparative Politics, and Defense Policy in 1979. Returning to the Academy in 1976 as an Associate Professor, he was named the Director of Comparative and Area Studies in the Department of Political Science. During this time he co-edited and wrote the first of three editions of *Defense Policy of Nations* published by Johns Hopkins. In 1980 he was assigned to the Pentagon as the Deputy Chief of the Secretary of the AF Staff Group. In 1983 he was selected to attend the National War College, Fort Lesley J. McNair,

Washington, DC. Upon graduation in 1984, he returned to the Academy, having been appointed the Permanent Professor and Head of the Department of Political Science. From July 1990 to December 1991 he served as Vice Dean of the Faculty. In 1994 during the Bosnian conflict he served as the Chief of the Staff Group Division, Plans and Policy Directorate, HQ US European Command, Stuttgart, Germany, where he led the effort to design and implement theater-wide planning, programming, and budgeting systems that later were approved by the Joint Chiefs of Staff for theater commands worldwide. Doug returned to the Academy in 1996 to again lead the Political Science Department and chair the Social Sciences Division. While serving in these positions, he chaired the Strategic Planning Staff of the Air Force Education and Training Review Council for HQ USAF that was responsible for drafting the first AF-wide education and training strategic plan. During this time he was selected for life membership in the Council on Foreign Relations. In collaboration with two others, he established the Dwight David Eisenhower Center for Space and Defense Studies at the Academy in 2005. For more than 11 years he chaired the faculty's Graduate Studies Committee. He was promoted to brigadier general and retired from the USAF in 2007.

Doug immediately assumed, and still holds, the position of Chief Academic Officer and Dean of Academics of the New Mexico Military Institute in Roswell, and he serves the State of New Mexico as its representative to the Alliance of the Western Interstate Commission for Higher Education.

BRIGADIER GENERAL
ROBERT B. GIFFEN

Permanent Professor 1984–1995

B.S., *United States Air Force Academy*
Ph.D., *University of Heidelberg*

Bob Giffen, the Academy's 46th Permanent Professor, was born in Princeton, New Jersey, in 1942. He earned a Bachelor's degree in Engineering Science from the United States Air Force Academy in 1965 as a Distinguished Graduate and the Outstanding Graduate in Astronautical Engineering. He completed pilot training at Randolph and Sheppard AFBs in Texas and received his pilot wings in 1966. He then went directly to Vietnam and flew over 200 combat missions in the HH-3 Jolly Green Giant helicopter with the 20th Special Operations Squadron in South Vietnam, Laos, and North Vietnam. From there he was stationed at Sembach Air Base and Ramstein AB, Federal Republic of Germany (FRG), where he flew the H-19 and the T-33. In 1969 Bob was selected as an Olmsted Scholar. After a quick upgrade in the T-38 at Randolph AFB, TX, he completed German language training at the Defense Language Institute in Monterey, CA. Bob then attended the University of Heidelberg in the FRG where he earned his PhD in Celestial Mechanics (*magna cum laude*) in 1972. From 1972 to 1974, after graduating from the US Navy Test Pilot School, Bob served as Engineering Test Pilot at the US Naval Test Center in Patuxent River, MD. Next, he flew as an Engineering Test Pilot for the Aerospace Rescue and Recovery Service at Hill AFB, UT. In 1975 he became Chief Engineering Test Pilot for the Aerospace Rescue and Recovery Service at Kirtland AFB, NM. In 1977 Bob returned to the AF Academy, where he served as

Associate Professor of Astronautics. In 1980 he transferred to the North American Aerospace Defense Command as Chief of the Space Analysis and Data Division, Cheyenne Mountain Complex, CO. While there, he became Deputy Director of the Space Operations Directorate. From 1981 to 1982 he attended the National War College in Washington, DC. Returning to the Academy in 1982, he was appointed the Head of the Department of Astronautics. In 1984 Bob was selected as Permanent Professor. While on sabbatical from the Academy from 1986 to 1987, he served as the Air Attaché to the FRG at the US embassy in Bonn. The President of Germany awarded Bob the Grand Service Cross, Germany's highest award, for his service as Air Attaché. During his tenure as a Permanent Professor, Bob served the Academy by chairing a Faculty Steering Committee that resulted in the Academy's athletic programs receiving national collegiate certification. He also served as the Chair of the First Class Committee and as the Academy's NCAA Faculty Representative. Bob Giffen was promoted to brigadier general and retired from the Air Force in 1995.

After his retirement, Bob started a small company, Teaching Science and Technology, Inc., that has grown into a respected name in space systems engineering. TSTI offers both on-site and online courses in space and systems engineering as well as providing project coaching and systems engineering consulting services, all in the pursuit of space workforce development. In 2005 Bob sold his interest in TSTI, but he continues with them to teach and consult for Air Force Space Command.

BRIGADIER GENERAL
RUBEN A. CUBERO

Permanent Professor 1984–1998
Dean of the Faculty 1991–1998

B.S., *United States Air Force Academy*
M.A., *University of New Mexico*
Ph.D., *University of Denver*

Randy Cubero, the Academy's 47th Permanent Professor, was born in the Bronx, New York, in 1939. He graduated from the United States Air Force Academy in 1961 with a Bachelor of Science degree. His first assignment was to undergraduate pilot training at Williams AFB, AZ, which he completed in late 1962. In early 1963 he finished transition training to the C-118 at Tinker AFB, OK, and moved to the 38th Air Transport Squadron, McGuire AFB, NJ. Early in 1966 he became a C-135 pilot at McGuire. Randy then piloted the C-141 in the 76th Military Airlift Squadron, Charleston AFB, SC, from 1966 to 1969. He completed 243 combat missions in the Republic of Vietnam from 1969 to 1970 as an OV-10 Pilot and Forward Air Controller at Tay Ninh West with the 25th Infantry Division, 19th Tactical Air Support Squadron. He also served as Pilot and Forward Air Controller Standardization and Evaluation with the 19th at Bien Hoa Air Base. Randy entered graduate school in 1970 and earned a Master's degree in Latin American Studies from the University of New Mexico, Albuquerque, in 1972. From 1972 to 1974 he served as Spanish Instructor and then Division Chief of Spanish in the Department of Foreign Languages at the USAF Academy. During 1975 Randy was a student in the School of the Americas, Fort Gulick, Panama Canal Zone. In late 1975 he became an Instructor and Director of Joint Operations at the school and was the Senior USAF Representative the year prior to his assignment in early 1978 to the Air University, Maxwell AFB, AL, as a Faculty Instructor. He returned to the Academy in mid-1978 as the Acting Department Head of the Department of Foreign Languages. From mid-1981 until late 1982, he was a doctoral student in higher education and administration at the University of Denver. He then returned to the Academy and served as Assistant to the Dean of the Faculty for eight months. He earned his PhD in Higher Education and Administration from the University of Denver in 1983 and became Professor and Head of the Department of Foreign Languages. In 1984 Randy was appointed a Permanent Professor. One of his lasting contributions was the development of a state-of-the-art computer-based education laboratory for interactive language instruction. He also facilitated the improvement of language training within the US government by serving as Executive Director of the Defense Exchange Committee on Language Efforts for five years. From 1985 to 1991, he was the Academy's Faculty Representative to the NCAA. During Academic Year 1990–1991, he took an "internal sabbatical" to develop, using authorization recently granted the Academy, a Cooperative Research and Development Agreement to jointly produce with a private enterprise a videodisc for foreign language learning. Under the agreement, the product was to be used at the Academy and sold commercially with the Academy sharing in the profits. He was an Instructor Pilot in the cadet flying program from 1984 until 1991. Randy was selected to be the Dean of the Faculty in 1991 and promoted to brigadier general. As Dean, Randy guided the formulation of the Academy's core values and Character Development Program. Randy retired from the USAF in 1998.

Upon retirement Randy became the Athletic Director at the University of Colorado at Colorado Springs. In October 2000 he was selected as the President of the Falcon Foundation, a non-profit organization that supports the Academy's admissions process by providing preparatory school scholarships to deserving young men and women seeking to gain admittance to the USAFA. Randy served the foundation for 10 years as President. From 2012 to 2014 Randy served as President/CEO of Parents Challenge Foundation, another non-profit that provides low-income families with funds so their children can attend a better performing K–12 school in the Colorado Springs area. He was selected for the USAFA Association of Graduates' Distinguished Graduate Award in 2011 and for the Colorado Springs (2001) and the USAFA's (2015) Sports Halls of Fame as a member of the 1958 Cotton Bowl Football Team. In May 2014 he was awarded the National Ellis Island Medal of Honor by the National Ethnic Coalition of Organizations that celebrated both his military career accomplishments and Puerto Rican heritage.

BRIGADIER GENERAL
MICHAEL L. SMITH

Permanent Professor 1985–2000

B.S., *University of Texas at Austin*
M.S., *University of Texas at Austin*
Ph.D., *University of Texas at Austin*

Mike Smith, the Academy's 48th Permanent Professor, was born in Austin, Texas, in 1943. He earned a Bachelor's degree in Aerospace Engineering from the University of Texas at Austin in 1966 and was a Distinguished Graduate from AFROTC. While on an educational delay, Mike completed a Master's degree in 1967, also in Aerospace Engineering. He then entered active duty with a first assignment as an Engineering Project Officer at the Space and Missile Systems Organization, Air Force Systems Command, Los Angeles Air Force Station, CA. In 1970 he returned to the University of Texas and was awarded the PhD degree in Aerospace Engineering in 1973. He then spent four years as an Assistant and then Associate Professor of Aeronautics in the Department of Aeronautics at the United States Air Force Academy. During that time Mike was recognized by the department as the Outstanding Instructor of Aeronautical Engineering. After a one-year assignment as a student at the Air Command and Staff College, Maxwell AFB, AL, 1977–1978, he became the Chief of the Performance Analysis Branch in the Propulsion Systems Program Office, Directorate of Engineering, Aeronautical Systems Division, Air Force Systems Command, Wright-Patterson AFB, OH. In 1980 Mike joined the faculty of the Department of Aeronautics and Astronautics at the Air Force Institute of Technology, also at WPAFB, as an Associate Professor and Deputy Head of the department. He served as the Executive Officer to the

Commandant of AFIT from 1984 to 1985. In 1985 he was selected Permanent Professor and Head of the Department of Aeronautics at USAFA. During his 15-year tenure in that position, in addition to cadet instruction and research, he was responsible for the Academy's Aeronautics Laboratory, which is a world-class facility consisting of hypersonic, supersonic, and subsonic wind tunnels, a water tunnel, a cascade tunnel, and three operating jet engines. Mike was promoted to brigadier general and retired from the Air Force in 2000.

Mike is the co-author with Dr. John J. Bertin of the textbook *Aerodynamics for Engineers*, first published in 1979 by Prentice Hall, 2nd edition in 1989, and 3rd edition in 1997. He is a registered Professional Engineer in the State of Colorado and continued to teach aeronautics at the Academy on a part-time, voluntary basis until 2015.

BRIGADIER GENERAL
DANIEL W LITWHILER

Permanent Professor 1986–2006
Vice Dean of the Faculty 1991–1994

B.S., Florida State University
M.S., Florida State University
Ph.D., University of Oklahoma

Danny Litwhiler, the Academy's 49th Permanent Professor, was born in Ringtown, Pennsylvania, in 1942 and grew up as a "baseball brat" (his father was a National League baseball player). Attending Florida State University, Tallahassee, he played baseball for a couple years until the coach, his father, subtly informed him he had a much better future in mathematics. He graduated in 1963 with a double major with Honors in Mathematics and Math Education, and in 1964 a commission as a Distinguished Graduate from the AFROTC. He stayed in school another year to earn his Master's degree in Mathematics, then entered active duty in 1965 at Keesler AFB, MS, for training as a Ground Electronics Officer (radars). Following another electronics school at Lowry AFB, CO, he was assigned to Chiang Mai, Thailand, directing operations at an Atomic Energy Detection System facility, 1967–1969. He then cross-trained into the management analyst field at Sheppard AFB, TX, before being assigned to Tinker AFB, OK, 1969–1970, as Management Analyst and Comptroller, Southern Communications Area, Air Force Communications Command. He next was assigned for two years to HQ Fifth Air Force, Tokyo, Japan, as the Programs Officer for all Air Force phase downs associated with the Okinawa Reversion. In 1972 he began his Academy service as an Instructor in the Department of Mathematical Sciences. After two years, Danny was sponsored for a PhD in Industrial Engineering/ Operations Research, which he earned at Oklahoma in 1976. Returning to the Academy for a four-year tour, 1977–1981, he was made a Tenure Associate Professor. In 1981–1982 he was sent for a career-broadening assignment to the Secretary of the Air Force's Staff Group, the Pentagon, Washington, DC, where he was an Issues and Policy Analyst and Speechwriter for Secretary Verne Orr. Back at the Academy he served as President of the faculty's Tenure Council. Among the many contributions of his team of tenured officers are the first manpower algorithm for the faculty, used successfully to justify manning in the face of threatened reductions, and a revision to the Dean's Grading Guidelines, a unique tool for assuring that grade inflation is kept to a minimum. He also served as Deputy Department Head until 1985 when he was sent to the Industrial College of the Armed Forces, Washington, DC. He was appointed as Permanent Professor and Head of the Department of Mathematical Sciences in 1986. In cooperation with three other departments, he created the interdisciplinary Operations Research major, one of the very first in the nation. He was Vice Dean of the Faculty, December 1991–June 1994. Spanning the years 1972 to 1998, he was also an Assistant Coach and Officer Representative for the Academy's intercollegiate baseball team, satisfying a life goal of teaching and coaching. From 2000 to 2002 he took a sabbatical assignment to US European Command, Stuttgart, Germany, as the Theater Basing Strategist, leading a joint service team identifying potential facilities that could be returned to host nations. He was promoted to brigadier general and retired in 2006.

BRIGADIER GENERAL
RICHARD L. HUGHES
_____

Permanent Professor 1987–1995

B.S., United States Air Force Academy
M.S., University of Texas at Austin
Ph.D., University of Wyoming

Rich Hughes, the Academy's 50th Permanent Professor, was born in Portland, Oregon, in 1946. He was the Outstanding Graduate in Psychology
and Leadership from the United States Air Force Academy in 1967. Upon
graduation, he accepted a graduate fellowship to the University of Texas at
Austin, where he earned his Master's degree in Psychology in 1969. He
then returned to the Academy faculty in the Department of Psychology and
Leadership. After one year as an Instructor, he served as the Director of
Administration in HQ 7/13 AF, Udorn Royal Thailand AFB. He returned
to the Academy faculty in 1971 to the reorganized Department of Life and
Behavioral Sciences. In 1972 Rich was sent to graduate school at the University of Wyoming, Laramie, where he earned his PhD in Clinical Psychology
in 1975. He next completed an internship in Clinical Psychology at Wil-
ford Hall Medical Center, Lackland AFB, TX. Returning to the Academy
in 1976 as an Assistant Professor in the again reorganized Department of
Behavioral Sciences and Leadership, he directed the individual behavior
track of the Behavioral Sciences major. In 1980 he was assigned to the Deputy for Military Instruction, Commandant of Cadets, where he assisted in
the development of several military training programs. In 1983 Rich was
assigned to the Executive Development Office, National Defense University
at Fort Lesley J. McNair, Washington, DC. He again returned to the Academy in 1984 where he served as Deputy Department Head of Behavioral

Sciences and Leadership. Following the retirement of Colonel Williams, Rich became the Department Head in November 1985. He was appointed a Permanent Professor in 1987. During his tenure he most notably served the Academy as the Chairperson of the Ad Hoc Committee on Respect and Dignity, which was established by the Superintendent in 1993. Perhaps the most significant of the committee's several recommendations that the Academy adopted was the establishment of an Office of Character Development. That office has evolved into the current Center for Character and Leadership Development. In 1993 Rich was the lead author on the textbook *Leadership: Enhancing the Lessons of Experience*, now in its 9th edition. He retired from active duty in 1995.

After retiring, Rich accepted a position in Colorado Springs with the Center for Creative Leadership where he taught, served in several senior leadership positions, and was senior author of the book *Becoming a Strategic Leader: Your Role in Your Organization's Enduring Success*, now in its 2nd edition. Rich returned once again to his alma mater from 2007 to 2012 as the USAFA Transformation Chair. In this position his duties were primarily to facilitate internal institutional transformation, which he did by leading the initial assessment of the USAFA Outcomes that formally state the expected results of the cadet experience, and the USAFA effort on Making Excellence Inclusive, reflecting the Academy's alignment with initiatives among colleges and universities across the nation. Rich was promoted to brigadier general in 2010.

BRIGADIER GENERAL
HANS J. MUEH

Permanent Professor 1987–2004
Vice Dean of the Faculty 2002–2004

B.S., *United States Air Force Academy*
M.S., *University of Wisconsin*
Ph.D., *University of Wisconsin*

Hans Mueh, the Academy's 51st Permanent Professor, was born in 1944, in Celle, Germany, and emigrated to the United States in 1951. He graduated with the Air Force Academy's eighth class, 1966, earning a Bachelor's degree in Chemistry and distinction as a record-holding soccer goalie. After completing training at Lowry AFB, CO, he served as an Intelligence Officer during three separate periods: at Headquarters Tactical Air Command, Langley AFB, VA, 1967–1969; in Saigon, Vietnam, and at Nakhon Phanom Royal Thai Air Base, Thailand, 1972–1973; and later as the Special Assistant for Technical Matters at the Defense Intelligence Agency, the Pentagon, Washington, DC, 1985–1986. Interspersed with these assignments was his graduate work in Chemistry at Wisconsin: 1969–1970 for his Master's degree, and 1973–1976 for his PhD. His Academy faculty duty began in 1970 with a two-year tour as an Instructor of Chemistry. Returning in 1977 Hans was soon selected as Tenure Associate Professor before leaving for his DIA assignment in 1985. He returned to the Academy in 1986 as Acting Department Head, and in 1987 was named Permanent Professor and Head of the Department of Chemistry. During his time on the faculty, Hans was also Vice Dean of the Faculty, 2002–2004. Ever the athlete, Hans competed in golf, racquetball, handball, and tennis, and promoted Air Force Academy intercollegiate sports throughout his tenure, beginning with work as chairman of the Hockey Eligibility Committee, golf team Officer

Representative, football team Officer Representative, and Faculty Athletics Representative to the NCAA. Hans was promoted to brigadier general and retired from active duty in 2004 in order to accept the position of Air Force Academy Athletic Director.

As the Director of Athletics, Hans led that department's team of 300 people, 27 Division I intercollegiate athletic programs, physical education, physical fitness testing, intramural competition, and the management of a huge complex of indoor and outdoor athletic venues. During his time as AD, Hans sat on the board of the Amateurism Cabinet of the NCAA for seven years after a two-year stint on the NCAA Golf Committee. He was also a member of the Joint Council of the Mountain West Conference. Hans retired as AD in 2015. Beyond his official duties, Hans is a strong leader in the local community. He has served on the Science Advisory Board of the University of Colorado at Colorado Springs, the Colorado Consortium for Earth and Space Science Education, and the Colorado Springs Sports Corporation; he is currently Board Member and Secretary of the Colorado Springs Cheyenne Mountain Zoo.

BRIGADIER GENERAL
JAMES H. HEAD
———————————————

Permanent Professor 1987–2006
Vice Dean of the Faculty 1994–1996
and 2004–2006

B.S., *University of Kansas*
Ph.D., *University of Kansas*

Jim Head, the Academy's 52nd Permanent Professor, was born in 1942 in Mason City, Iowa. He graduated from the University of Kansas, Lawrence, in 1964 with a Bachelor's degree in Engineering Physics and was named a Distinguished Graduate from AFROTC. He received a National Aeronautics and Space Administration fellowship and entered an educational delay at the University of Kansas, where he earned the PhD degree in Physics in 1968. His first assignment was as an Instructor of Physics at the Air Force Academy, later becoming Director of the Nuclear Radiation Laboratory and Director of the Advanced Physics Division. During 1974 he served a one-year tour on the Air Staff as a Special Projects Officer responsible for analysis and reporting of Western Europe politico-military affairs. From 1975 to 1978 he was assigned to the Defense Intelligence Agency, on exchange with the British Defence Intelligence Staff, Ministry of Defence, London, England, where he was an analyst for Soviet and Chinese fighter aircraft performance. In 1979 following graduation from Air Command and Staff College, Maxwell AFB, AL, Jim was assigned to the Air Force Foreign Technology Division, Wright-Patterson AFB, OH, as a Directed Energy Weapons Intelligence Analyst, where he won the Commander's Award for Merit in management in 1981. Subsequently, he was appointed Chief, Future Systems Division, responsible for specialized, long-range intelligence forecasts in support of weapon systems acquisition. He was next assigned to the Air Force Weapons Laboratory, Kirtland AFB, NM, as Program Manager and then Chief, Applied Technology Division, responsible for planning and directing Strategic Defense Initiative research on neutral particle beam weapons technologies. Appointed the Permanent Professor and Head, Department of Physics in 1987, Jim led the effort establishing nationally recognized research thrusts in lasers and optics, space physics, and physics education. The department's Laser and Optics Research Center and Space Physics and Atmospheric Research Center provided state-of-the-art research support to Air Force and Federal agencies, while engaging cadets in research with direct relevance to real Air Force missions. Additionally, he negotiated an agreement with Air Weather Service to provide manpower and laboratory equipment to stand-up the Academy's Meteorology minor (now major) jointly administered by the Departments of Physics and Economics and Geosciences. In 1992–1993 Jim spearheaded development of the Academy's civilian faculty program in response to a Congressional initiative. He was also the principal author of the popular book *Hiking the Air Force Academy*. He served as the Officer Representative for the men's basketball team, 1999–2005. From 1994–1996 and again 2004–2006, he served as the Vice Dean of the Faculty, the position from which he was promoted to brigadier general and retired in 2006.

In retirement, Jim was President of the booster group Friends of Air Force Basketball, 2006–2016. He serves on the Executive Committee of the non-profit The Friends of the Air Force Academy Library and enjoys researching and writing on family history.

BRIGADIER GENERAL
ALAN R. KLAYTON

Permanent Professor 1988–2008
Vice Dean of the Faculty 2000–2002

B.S., *Lowell Technological Institute*
M.S., *Pennsylvania State University*
Ph.D., *Lehigh University*

Alan Klayton, the Academy's 53rd Permanent Professor, was born in Brooklyn, New York, in 1944. He graduated from Lowell Technological Institute, Lowell, MA, in 1966 with High Honors and a Bachelor's degree in Electrical Engineering. He was a Distinguished Graduate from Lowell Tech's AFROTC program. He entered upon an educational delay and earned his Master's degree in Electrical Engineering from Pennsylvania State University, University Park, in 1968. He then earned a PhD in Electrical Engineering from Lehigh University, Bethlehem, PA, in 1971. Upon entry into the Air Force as a first lieutenant in 1971, he was assigned as a Project Engineer at the Rome Air Development Center, Griffiss AFB, NY. In August 1977 Al came to the Air Force Academy faculty as an Instructor in the Department of Electrical Engineering. In 1981 he was named the department's Outstanding Military Educator and earned the academic rank of Tenure Associate Professor in 1982. In 1984 he joined the System Integration Office (SIO), Air Force Space Command, Peterson AFB, CO, serving as a Project Engineer and as the Executive Officer for the Chief of SIO. Al returned to the Department of Electrical Engineering faculty in 1986. He was appointed a Permanent Professor in 1988 and assigned as the Department Head. He directed the efforts to establish the Computer Engineering major effective with the Class of 2001 and to change the department's name to the Department of Electrical and Computer

Engineering in 2006. During his tenure at the Academy, Al served as the Vice Dean of the Faculty from 2000 to 2002 before returning to again lead the Electrical Engineering Department. As an additional duty, he served as Engineering Division Chair, 2006–2008. He also served as an Accreditation Evaluator for the Accreditation Board for Engineering and Technology for eight years and as the Academy liaison to a local school district. Al was promoted to brigadier general and retired in 2008.

Al returned to the Academy in 2009 to serve for a year as the Philip J. Erdle Chair in Engineering Science for the Department of Electrical and Computer Engineering. Since 2010 he has continued to teach in the Department as needed to fill faculty vacancies. Al continued to serve higher education and the engineering profession as an ABET accreditation evaluator for four years after his retirement from the Air Force. He is currently a Board Member on the Academy School District 20 Educational Foundation. The department annually awards the Brigadier General Alan R. Klayton Design Excellence Award to the individual cadet or team that best exemplifies outstanding design techniques and execution as well as innovation and success in completing a complex electrical or computer system project.

BRIGADIER GENERAL
RICHARD R. LEE

Permanent Professor 1988–1997

B.S., *University of North Carolina*
J.D., *University of North Carolina*

Dick Lee, the Academy's 54th Permanent Professor, was born in Shelby, North Carolina, in 1933. In 1955 he received his Bachelor's degree in Business Administration from the University of North Carolina and then went on to attain his Juris Doctorate there in 1958. After law school, he received a direct appointment as a first lieutenant in the US Air Force and began his lengthy career as the Assistant Staff Judge Advocate, Davis-Monthan AFB, AZ. In 1960 he was sent to the 48th Tactical Fighter Wing, Royal Air Force Lakenheath, England, as Assistant Staff Judge Advocate. Dick came to the Air Force Academy in 1963, first to the Legal Office and then, in 1965, to the Department of Law, where over the next 14 years he was promoted through all the academic ranks from Instructor to Assistant Professor, to Associate Professor, to Tenure Associate Professor, and to Tenure Professor. He was instrumental in all aspects of the department's mission; he wrote portions of the texts *Introduction to Law* and *Law for Commanders*, and he was a legal advisor to the Cadet Honor and Ethics Committee as well as a member of the Academy Honor Review Committee. Dick returned to Europe in 1979 as Director of Civil Law, HQ US Air Forces in Europe, Ramstein Air Base, Germany. He was shortly made Deputy Staff Judge Advocate for USAFE, then in 1981 Staff Judge Advocate for 17th Air Force, Sembach Air Base, Germany. From 1982 to 1984 he was the Staff Judge Advocate for 9th Air Force, Shaw AFB, SC. In 1984 Dick returned to Ramstein as Command

Staff Judge Advocate for USAFE. During his four years in that position, he provided oversight for 39 separate legal offices in nine countries. Dick returned to the Academy in 1988 as Permanent Professor and Head, Department of Law. He is a member of the North Carolina Bar and is admitted to practice before the US Supreme Court, the US Court of Military Appeals, and the Supreme Court of North Carolina. Dick Lee has a special interest in personal estate planning, and his reputation as an expert is widespread. He taught that law course to cadets for over 13 years, and he lectured extensively on the subject throughout the Air Force, including to all the professional military schools, to the commanders and senior staffs of all the major commands, and at many Air Force and Army installations in both the US and Europe. Also legendary is his ability to conduct business on the golf course. Dick was promoted to brigadier general and retired in 1997 after 39 years of active service.

After retiring, Dick served as the volunteer Vice President and General Counsel, 2000–2009, of The Falcon Foundation, a non-profit organization that supports the Academy's admissions process by providing preparatory school scholarships to deserving young men and women seeking to gain admittance to the Academy. He continues to live in Colorado Springs.

COLONEL
WILLIAM E. RICHARDSON

Permanent Professor 1988–1994

B.S., *United States Air Force Academy*
M.S., *University of California,*
    Los Angeles
M.Sc., *Oxford University*
D.Phil., *Oxford University*

Bill Richardson, the Academy's 55th Permanent Professor, was born in 1948 in Tucson, Arizona. He attended Iowa State University, Ames, for one year before entering the United States Air Force Academy with the Class of 1971. He was named a Distinguished Graduate, earning majors in Computer Science, Astronautics, and Engineering Science. Following the Academy, Bill went directly to UCLA, where he earned his Master's degree in Computer Science in 1972. He was then assigned to McChord AFB, WA, as a Systems Analyst for the Semi-Automatic Ground Environment System. In 1975 he was transferred to Headquarters US Air Forces in Europe, Ramstein Air Base, Germany, where he served first as Systems Analyst for the World-Wide Military Command and Control System (WWMCCS), then as acting Executive Officer to the USAFE Vice Commander-in-Chief, and lastly as the Chief of the Computer Operations Division for the USAFE WWMCCS facility. In 1978 Bill returned to the Academy to teach in the Computer Science Department. Two years later he was sent to Oxford University, England, where he earned his Masters of Science and Doctor of Philosophy degrees in Computation in 1981 and 1983, respectively. Returning to the Department of Astronautics and Computer Science in 1983, Bill had a significant role in resolving technical and software issues in the Academy's Microcomputers in the Dormitories and Local Area Network projects. He was appointed Department Head in

December 1987 and confirmed as Permanent Professor the following fall. During his term as Permanent Professor he worked diligently to modernize and formalize the Computer Science discipline at the Academy and across the nation. He was ultimately named Chairman of the Computer Science Accreditation Board (CSAB), which oversees the disciplinary accreditation of Computer Science programs in the United States. Subsequently, he was designated a CSAB Fellow for his leadership in the early years of Computer Science growth into a technical academic discipline. In 1992 Bill took on the full-time duty of Associate Dean for Computing Resources, where he managed development of an upgrade to the USAFA FalconNet local area network. As President of the Academy's Association of Graduates, 1991–1993, Bill helped lead his fellow alumni in the development and dedication of Doolittle Hall. He retired from the Air Force in 1994.

Following his retirement from military service, Bill Richardson started private businesses in the retail, services, and technology sectors and served on several university and corporate boards. The success of these enterprises supported his selection as Senior Vice President and General Manager of the global Sun Educational Services, the customer training division of Sun Microsystems. After departing Sun in 2002, Bill focused his private consulting company on the application of computer technology to enhance productivity of small and not-for-profit companies and on the transition of technology from development to commercial viability. His enduring legacy of leadership, vision, and service is commemorated in The William T. Coleman III and Dr. William E. Richardson Endowed Chair in Computer Sciences.

BRIGADIER GENERAL
RAYMOND E. FRANCK JR.

Permanent Professor 1989–2000

B.S., *United States Air Force Academy*
A.M., *Harvard University*
Ph.D., *Harvard University*

Raymond "Chip" Franck, the Academy's 56th Permanent Professor, was born in Sac City, Iowa, in 1945. He was a 1967 Distinguished Graduate from the United States Air Force Academy with a major in International Affairs. Following graduation, he entered Harvard on a National Science Foundation Fellowship and earned his Master's degree in Economics in 1969. He later returned to Harvard and completed his PhD in Economics in 1983. Chip earned his pilot wings in 1970 at Columbus AFB, MS, and was assigned to fly the B-57 from several locations: Holloman AFB, NM; MacDill AFB, FL; Ubon Royal Thai Air Base, Thailand; Kadena Air Base, Japan; and Malmstrom AFB, MT. In 1975–1976 he was assigned to the Joint Operational Control Center at Keflavik Naval Station, Iceland, after which he returned to the Academy as Instructor of Economics in the Department of Economics, Geography and Management. Chip was next assigned to serve as a Staff Analyst for Bomber Programs, Office of the Secretary of Defense for Program Analysis and Evaluation, the Pentagon, Washington, DC, 1980–1982, where he was lead analyst for strategic bombers and related issues of aerial tankers and cruise missiles. In 1982 after B-52 training, he went to Barksdale AFB, LA, as Aircraft Commander and later served on the Wing Operations Staff. From 1985 to 1989, he was assigned to HQ Strategic Air Command, Offutt AFB, NE, as Deputy Chief, Program Evaluation Division and Special Assistant to the Commander. In this role, he helped frame modernization of nuclear forces within a national strategy for deterrence. In 1989 Chip was appointed Permanent Professor and Head, Department of Economics and Geography. Under his leadership, the department increased its research in defense-relevant economics and its outreach to other federal agencies. He brought in visiting professors from DIA, CIA, RAND Corp., and the Council of Economic Advisors. Working with Air Weather Service and the Air Staff, he helped established the Academy's interdisciplinary Meteorology major and the Harmon Meteorology Laboratory that supports it. From 1994 to 1996 he was on sabbatical assignment as Visiting Professor and Associate Dean of the School of Intelligence Studies at the Joint Military Intelligence College, Bolling AFB, Washington, DC. Chip was promoted to brigadier general and retired from active duty in 2000.

After retiring, Chip joined the faculty of the Systems Management Department, Naval Postgraduate School, Monterey, CA. In 2002 he was promoted to Chair of the newly formed Systems Engineering Department. An active scholar throughout his career, Chip authored or co-authored many publications related to analysis of defense strategy and policy. He retired from NPS in 2012.

BRIGADIER GENERAL
GUNTHER A. MUELLER

Permanent Professor 1991–2008
Vice Dean of the Faculty 1998–2000

B.A., *West Virginia University*
M.A., *West Virginia University*
Ph.D., *Ohio State University*

Gunther Mueller, the Academy's 57th Permanent Professor, was born in Frankenberg (Eder), Germany, in 1946 and immigrated into the United States in 1956, residing in New Jersey throughout high school. In 1969 he earned his Bachelor's degree in German from West Virginia University, Morgantown, and was named a Distinguished Graduate of AFROTC. He then took an educational delay to complete his Master's degree in German before entering active duty in 1970 to begin his career in Air Force Intelligence. Following intelligence officer training at Lowry AFB in Denver, CO, Gunther served for a year, 1970–1971, as an Intelligence Officer and briefer with the Strategic Air Division, Vandenberg AFB, CA. He was next assigned as Intelligence Branch Chief and Operations Plans Officer for the 95th Strategic Wing at Goose Air Base, Canada, 1971–1973. Following Squadron Officer School, Maxwell AFB, AL, he spent eight months at U-Tapao Air Base, Thailand, as a Combat Intelligence Briefer/Debriefer for the 307th Strategic Wing. Returning stateside in 1974, Gunther began his long association with the Air Force Academy as Instructor of German and Chair of the German Division, Department of Foreign Languages. In 1977 he entered the doctoral program in Foreign Language Education at Ohio State, and earned his PhD degree two years later in 1979. During the next four years he was a key figure in introducing computer-assisted learning into the Academy's foreign language curriculum. After a year as a student at Air Command and Staff

College, Maxwell AFB, AL, 1983–1984, he was assigned to Headquarters US European Command, Stuttgart, Germany, 1984–1987, where he served as Chief of the Indications and Warning Branch. Gunther returned to the Academy in 1987 as Deputy Head, Department of Foreign Languages. He was made Acting Department Head in 1990 and was appointed Permanent Professor and Head in 1991. From 1998 to 2000, he was the Vice Dean of the Faculty. During his tenure, he chaired the Academy's International Programs Council and oversaw the dramatic expansion of cadet international exchange opportunities. Moreover, he tirelessly advocated for foreign language skills for all military personnel and wrote extensively on the subject: "Global Skills: Vital Components of Global Engagement" (*Airpower Journal*, 1998) and "Beyond the Linguist, Global Engagement Skills" (*Applied Language Learning*, 2000). As Executive Director of the Defense Exchange Committee on Language Effects, he influenced language and foreign area studies programs and policies, and in cooperation with the Defense Language Institute he led efforts to assess and reward foreign language skills maintenance across the Department of Defense. He was promoted to brigadier general and retired in 2008.

Since 2009 Gunther has worked as a part-time consultant for the AF Culture and Language Center at Air University. His primary focus has been the highly successful Language Enabled Airman Program (which he helped create), providing foreign language sustainment and enhancement opportunities for airmen. He also serves on the Air Staff's Language, Regional Expertise, and Culture Action Panel, advising on all AF language and culture policies and programs.

BRIGADIER GENERAL
DAVID A. WAGIE

Permanent Professor 1992–2004
Vice Dean of the Faculty 1996–1998
Dean of the Faculty 1998–2004

B.S., *United States Air Force Academy*
M.S., *Stanford University*
M.S., *University of Southern California*
Ph.D., *Purdue University*

Dave Wagie, the Academy's 58th Permanent Professor, was born in White-water, Wisconsin, in 1949. He received a Bachelor's degree in Engineering Sciences as a Distinguished Graduate of the United States Air Force Academy in 1972. Entering graduate school, he received a Master's degree in Aeronautics and Astronautics from Stanford University in 1973. He completed pilot training at Williams AFB, AZ, in 1974 and flew KC-135s in the 310th Refueling Squadron at Plattsburgh AFB, NY, from 1974 until 1979. While at Plattsburg, Dave earned a Master's degree in Systems Management through the University of Southern California extension program and attended Squadron Officer School, graduating as a Distinguished Graduate. In 1979 he was assigned to the Air Force Academy to teach in the Department of Astronautics and Computer Science and serve as a T-41 Instructor Pilot. In 1981 Dave enrolled at Purdue University, Lafayette, IN, and received his PhD in Aeronautics and Astronautics in 1984. He then was assigned to the 4952nd Test Squadron, Wright-Patterson AFB, OH, where he served as an EC-135 Research Pilot, Director of Test Operations, and Deputy Division Chief, Aircraft and Avionics, until 1986. He then attended Air Command and Staff College where he was named a Distinguished Graduate in 1987. Dave returned to the Air Force Academy in 1987 to again teach in the Department of Astronautics and instruct in the T-41. He was appointed a Permanent Professor in 1992 and served as Head, Department of Military Arts and Science (also the Deputy Commandant for Military Instruction) until 1994. He was then chosen to be the Director of the Commandant of Cadets' Center for Character Development. He became the Vice Dean of the Faculty in 1996. Dave was selected as the Dean of the Faculty in 1998 and promoted to brigadier general effective July 1, 1998. Under his tenure, the Academy was 1 of 16 institutions nationally selected in 2000 as a prestigious "Leadership Institution" by the American Association of Colleges & Universities. Dave retired in 2004.

Upon his retirement, Dave served as an Educational Consultant to the United Arab Emirates Minister of Education for two years, responsible for upgrading the Khalifa Air College (the UAE's Air Force Academy). He also coordinated creation of a new campus of the Paris-Sorbonne University in Abu Dhabi. In this latter role, he directed the overall project, including marketing, advertising, enrollment, and a $9 million budget. In 2007 he became the 14th President of Saint Gregory's University, Shawnee, OK, and served in that position until 2009. From 2010 to 2014, he served as the Director of Aerospace and Defense Economic Development for the Oklahoma Department of Commerce, connecting universities, government, and industry to expand aerospace and defense businesses in Oklahoma. He makes his home in suburban Phoenix.

BRIGADIER GENERAL
RONALD D. REED

Permanent Professor 1995–2005

B.A., Oklahoma City University
Ph.D., University of California,
Berkeley

Ron Reed, the Academy's 59th Permanent Professor, was born in Caldwell, Kansas, in 1948, and was raised in Watonga, Oklahoma. He earned his Bachelor's degree in Chemistry and Biology in 1971 from Oklahoma City University, and immediately pursued his PhD at Cal–Berkeley. While a graduate student at Cal, Ron joined the Air Force Reserve Officer Training Corps program and received his commission in 1973. He then entered an educational delay to finish his PhD in Physiology, which was awarded in 1977. Based on his dissertation, he won the Outstanding Research Paper award from the Life Sciences and Biomedical Engineering Branch of the 80-nation Aerospace Medical Association (AsMA). More than two decades later as a Fellow of AsMA he would win the organization's 2002 Professional Excellence Award for enduring leadership in the aerospace life sciences. Ron's first Air Force assignment, 1977–1980, was as a scientist researching bioeffects of laser radiation at the School of Aerospace Medicine, Brooks AFB, TX—work that led to the development of Air Force safety standards. He came to the Air Force Academy's Department of Biology in 1980 and left in 1984 as Associate Professor and Director of Research, having received the department's Outstanding Military Educator Award. For the 1984–1985 academic year he was on a prestigious Air Staff Training Assignment in Legislative Affairs and Acquisitions at the Pentagon, Washington, DC. From 1985 to 1987 he was assigned to Headquarters, Air Force Systems

Command, Andrews AFB, MD, where he oversaw technology development for protection of aircrew and systems from laser devices. Following a year at Air Command and Staff College, Maxwell AFB, AL, where he was a Distinguished Graduate, Ron returned to the Academy from 1988 to 1992, before returning to Maxwell as a student at Air War College. He returned to the Academy in 1993 as Professor and Head, Department of Biology, and was subsequently appointed Permanent Professor in 1995. From 2000 to 2002 he took a sabbatical assignment to the Air Force's European Office of Aerospace Research and Development, London, England, where he oversaw Air Force interests in all life sciences and human factors research across Europe, Africa, the Middle East, and the former Soviet Union. Over his distinguished career Ron Reed led research and development in laser protection, human factors, advanced life support systems, manned spaceflight, cockpit automation, biomimetics, biowarfare defense, and environmental issues, and he brought cutting-edge realism to the Academy's curriculum. He retired in 2005 and died of cancer shortly thereafter. He is buried in the Air Force Academy Cemetery.

COLONEL
CHARLES R. MYERS

Permanent Professor 1995–2000

B.A., Tulane University
M.A., University of Texas at Austin
Ph.D., University of Texas at Austin
J.D., University of California, Berkeley

Charlie Myers, the Academy's 60th Permanent Professor, was born in Carlsbad, New Mexico, in 1945. He attended Florida State University for the 1963–1964 school year before transferring to Tulane University in New Orleans, LA. His time at Tulane included a term at the University of St. Andrews, Scotland. Charlie received his Bachelor's degree in Philosophy and History from Tulane in 1967, where he was a Distinguished Graduate of Air Force ROTC. Receiving Woodrow Wilson and National Defense Education Act Fellowships, he was granted an educational delay to attend the University of Texas at Austin, where he was awarded the Master's degree in Philosophy in 1969 and the PhD degree in Philosophy in 1975. Entering active duty in 1970, Charlie received intelligence officer training at Lowry AFB, CO, and then served as an Intelligence Officer at Da Nang Air Base, Vietnam, 1970–1971, and Bergstrom AFB, TX, 1971–1973. His next assignment was to the Academy's Department of Political Science and Philosophy. In 1975 Charlie entered law school at Cal–Berkeley under the Air Force's Funded Legal Education Program. Upon graduation with his Juris Doctor degree in 1978, Charlie was assigned as Deputy Staff Judge Advocate at Carswell AFB, TX. In 1980 he became the Staff Judge Advocate for the Air Force Satellite Control Facility at Sunnyvale Air Force Station, CA. From there followed a series of assignments of ever-increasing responsibility: 1983–1986, Chief of Acquisition Law and Director of General Law for HQ

Pacific Air Forces, Hickam AFB, HI; 1986–1989, Staff Judge Advocate for the training wing at MacDill AFB, FL; and 1989–1990, Deputy Director of the Air Force Judiciary, Bolling AFB, Washington, DC. Following graduation from the National War College in 1991, he was the Staff Judge Advocate for Seventh Air Force, Osan Air Base, Korea, and from 1993 to 1995 the Staff Judge Advocate for US Strategic Command, Offutt AFB, NE. Charlie was appointed a Permanent Professor on January 1, 1995, and he served as Head, Department of Philosophy, until his retirement in 2000. During this interesting period, the values of *Integrity, Service Before Self,* and *Excellence In All We Do* were developed at the Academy and adopted as the Air Force core values. Charlie wrote the seminal article "The Core Values: Framing and Resolving Ethical Issues for the Air Force" published in *Airpower Journal* in 1997, explaining the significance of these simple and forceful values based on the structure and purpose of morality.

Following his retirement, Charlie continued his teaching as a Professor at Northwest Florida State College, Niceville, until retiring from that position in 2016.

COLONEL
SAMUEL L. GRIER

Permanent Professor 1995–2001

B.S., *United States Air Force Academy*
M.S., *University of Colorado*
Ph.D., *University of Texas at Austin*

Sam Grier, the Academy's 61ˢᵗ Permanent Professor, was born in 1951 in Bethesda, Maryland, and spent his formative years in Hawaii and Fairfax County, Virginia. He graduated from the United States Air Force Academy in 1973 with a Bachelor's degree in Computer Science. He attended pilot training at Williams AFB, AZ, and began his career flying the KC-135 at Loring AFB, ME. In 1979 he received Academy sponsorship for a Master's degree in Computer Science and attended the University of Colorado, Boulder, earning his degree in 1980 and returning to the Academy to teach in his discipline. At the Academy, Sam ran the newly installed computer scoreboard at Falcon Stadium and maintained a database of graduates for the Association of Graduates, which was used to produce the annual *Register of Graduates*. In addition to teaching, Sam flew as a T-41 Instructor Pilot, giving many cadets their first Air Force flying experience. Following his faculty assignment, Sam was assigned to Fairchild AFB, WA, in 1983 where he upgraded to KC-135 Instructor Pilot and assumed responsibility as Chief of KC-135 Flight Standardization and Evaluation. He also flew in the Strategic Air Command's annual bombing and navigation competition, where his crew received the highest score ever recorded in the history of the competition and earned the honor of "Best KC-135 Crew in Strategic Air Command." In 1986 Sam entered the University of Texas at Austin, where he earned his PhD in Computer Science in 1989. He next was assigned to Strategic Air Command at Offutt AFB, NE, as Chief of Mission Planning Systems and then as Speechwriter for CINCSAC. He was appointed one of five Senior Controllers at SAC's worldwide command center during the period of the First Gulf War and when Strategic Air Command stood down its Alert Force. Graduating from the NATO Defense College, Rome, Italy, in 1992, Sam was posted to NATO HQ, Brussels, Belgium, as Chief of NATO's Situation Center shortly after the collapse of the Soviet Union and during the brutal conflict in the former Yugoslavia. From there, in 1995 he was selected as Permanent Professor and named Head of the Department of Computer Science. During his tenure, the department adopted the Ada computer language as the basis for its software curriculum, consistently scored in the top 3 percent of more than 200 universities in a national exam of senior students, and he established the Academy's computer laboratory and associated courses in cyber defense in cooperation with the Air Force Computer Warfare Center. In 1998 he took a sabbatical back to the NATO Defense College to establish the College's Academic Research Branch. He retired from the Air Force in 2001.

Following his active duty service, Sam joined the Institute for Defense Analyses, assigned to the Joint National Integration Center, Schriever AFB, CO, where he helped develop the initial technical and operational concepts for integrated, global ballistic missile defense. In 2004 Sam again returned to the NATO Defense College, serving as its Dean until 2007. Since 2007 he has been with the MITRE Corporation, working with the US Missile Defense Agency in Colorado and supporting the NATO Ballistic Missile Defense program for two years in the Netherlands.

BRIGADIER GENERAL
MICHAEL L. DELORENZO

Permanent Professor 1996–2005

B.S., *United States Air Force Academy*
M.S., *New Mexico State University*
Ph.D., *Purdue University*

Mike DeLorenzo, the Academy's 62nd Permanent Professor, was born in Knoxville, Tennessee, in 1952. He earned Bachelor's degrees in Astronautical Engineering and Engineering Science from the United States Air Force Academy in 1974 as a Distinguished Graduate. His first assignment was as a Gyroscope Test Engineer, Central Inertial Test Facility, 6585th Test Group, Holloman AFB, NM, from 1974 to 1978. In 1978 he earned a Master's degree in Electrical Engineering from New Mexico State University, Las Cruces. Mike then was assigned to the Academy's Department of Astronautics, leaving in 1980 to become a student at Purdue University, West Lafayette, IN. He earned a PhD in Control Systems in 1983. He returned to the Department of Astronautics as an Associate Professor and taught from 1983 to 1987. Then he attended Air Command and Staff College, Maxwell AFB, AL, where he was recognized as a Distinguished Graduate. In 1988 Mike was assigned as the Deputy Director of Flight Dynamics Test, Arnold Engineering and Development Center, Tullahoma, TN. Mike attended the Defense Systems Management College, Fort Belvoir, VA, during the last half of 1991. He then was assigned as Chief, Advanced Guidance Division and Acting Chief Scientist, Armament Division, Wright Laboratory Armament Directorate, Eglin AFB, FL. In 1995 he returned to the Academy to serve as Head of the Department of Astronautics and was appointed a Permanent Professor in January 1996.

In 2001 Mike took a sabbatical assignment as the Vice Commander, Air Force Research Laboratory, Wright-Patterson AFB, OH. He returned to his post as Head of the Department of Astronautics in 2003. As Department Head he was responsible for a dynamic research program funded by AF Space Command and other Department of Defense organizations. The program supported cadet construction, test, and operation of small satellites. He served as the Officer Representative for the men's basketball team, 1995–2000. Mike was promoted to brigadier general and retired in 2005.

After retiring Mike moved back to Tennessee and joined other former Astronautics Department alumni as a consultant with Teaching Science and Technology, Inc. TSTI presents online and on-site courses and workshops in space systems engineering and has grown into a respected name in space systems engineering and workforce development. Mike is also an Adjunct Professor at Stevens Institute of Technology, Hoboken, NJ.

COLONEL
DAVID B. PORTER

Permanent Professor 1996–2001

B.S., *United States Air Force Academy*
M.S., *University of California,*
    Los Angeles
D.Phil., *Oxford University*

Dave Porter, the Academy's 63rd Permanent Professor, was born in Berea, Kentucky, in 1949. He was a Distinguished Graduate of the United States Air Force Academy's Class of 1971 and was sponsored for graduate school at UCLA, where he earned his Master's degree in Industrial Relations in 1972. He underwent helicopter pilot training at Fort Walters, TX; Fort Rucker, AL; and Hill AFB, UT, before being assigned to fly the HH-53 "Super Jolly Green Giant" at Hickam AFB, HI, first with the 76th Air Rescue and Recovery Squadron and later with the 6594th Test Group. Dave also served as Chief Functional Check Flight Pilot, Chief of Quality Control, and Organizational Maintenance Officer for the 6594th, which was awarded the Daedalian Award for best aircraft maintenance in the Air Force in 1978. In 1979 he returned to the Academy to teach leadership and psychology in the Department of Behavioral Sciences and Leadership. He returned to operational flying with the 67th Air Rescue and Recovery Squadron, Royal Air Force Woodbridge, England, where he was also the squadron Executive Officer. His unit won the "Best in Rescue" unit distinction in 1982, and he was the Military Airlift Command's nominee for the Lance P. Sijan Leadership Award that year. In 1983 he entered Oxford University, earning his Doctor of Philosophy degree in Experimental Cognitive Psychology in 1986. Returning to the Academy from Oxford, he taught over a dozen different courses and published articles relating to psychology, leadership, education, assessment, and accreditation. He was made Department Head in 1995 and appointed a Permanent Professor in 1996. As Chair of the Faculty Educational Outcomes Assessment Working Group, Dave led initiatives that 20 years later have become the cornerstones of the Academy's educational assessment and accountability processes. Through the American Association of Higher Education and the North Central Association, he gave invited addresses and led workshops on classroom teaching, academic assessment, and total quality education, as well as serving as a Consultant Examiner and leading accreditation teams for large universities and small colleges. Active in many communities, Dave was President of a local Unitarian Church, a founding director of Citizens Project of Colorado Springs, a charter member of the Association of Psychological Sciences, and a council member for Western Governors University for over a decade. Dave retired from the Air Force in 2001.

Upon retirement, Dave became the Academic Vice President and Provost at Berea College, a position he held for four years. During this time, Dave also helped establish and conduct the Appalachian College Association's Annual Summer Teaching and Learning Institute. In 2005 he returned to teaching as a Professor of Psychology and General Studies at Berea. He has taught courses in General Psychology, Cultural Anthropology, Introduction to the Behavioral Sciences, Industrial/Organizational Psychology, Cognitive Psychology, Cross Cultural Psychology, and the Psychology Research Capstone course.

COLONEL
MICHAEL R. EMERSON

Permanent Professor 1997–2004

B.S., *University of Montana*
J.D., *University of Denver*

Mike Emerson, the Academy's 64th Permanent Professor, was born in 1944 to an Army family at Fort Benning, Georgia. After graduating from the University of Montana, Missoula, in 1966 with a major in Economics and a commission as an AFROTC Distinguished Graduate, he entered an educational delay while he earned a law degree from the DU Law School in 1969. Mike started active duty as an Assistant Staff Judge Advocate (SJA) with the 341st Combat Support Group, Malmstrom AFB, MT. From 1970 to 1971 he was an Assistant SJA at the 377th Combat Support Group, Tan Son Nhut Air Base, Vietnam. He was next assigned as Assistant SJA at the 32nd Tactical Fighter Squadron, Soesterberg Air Base, The Netherlands, 1972–1974, where he worked in international law, foreign criminal jurisdiction, and international claims. From 1974 to 1976 he was SJA at Tempelhof Central Airport, Berlin, Germany. From Berlin, he came to the Academy for his first assignment in the Department of Law, 1976–1980. Mike followed his faculty tour with an SJA assignment at Grand Forks AFB, ND, 1980–1983. From there he had a three-year assignment, 1983–1986, in the Office of the Secretary of the Air Force, Legislative Liaison (SAF/LL), the Pentagon. He was an action officer in the Legislation Division, which advocated the AF position to Congress on military personnel, military construction, nonappropriated funds, USAF Academy, and other issues and programs; then in the Long-Range Planning Division as Deputy Chief; and finally in the Weapons Systems Division. In this later position, he set up the first-ever SAF/LL intelligence desk and established enduring personal and institutional relationships with the nation's Intelligence and Reconnaissance components and with members and professional staffs on the House and Senate Select Intelligence Committees and Armed Services Committees. In 1986 he was assigned as Base SJA, Ramstein Air Base, Germany. He returned to the Air Staff in 1988 to lead the AF General Litigation Division and in 1991 moved back to Legislative Liaison as Chief, Legislation Division (later the Programs and Legislation Division). Mike returned to the Academy in 1993 as Senior Military Professor of Law, and he was appointed Permanent Professor in 1997. His tenure was marked by establishing a Legal Studies major capstone course, and by interdepartmental teaching in National Security Law and Policy, Space Law and Policy, and Negotiations. He regularly co-taught a classical music appreciation course, and he helped develop and teach a selective humanities history course for cadets preparing for national graduate scholarship competitions. He was the Officer Representative to the varsity tennis team. Mike was deployed twice, in 1996 and 1997, as SJA to the Commander, Operation SOUTHERN WATCH, in Saudi Arabia. In addition, Mike and his faculty regularly traveled to Central America, Africa, and the former Soviet bloc Eastern European countries as part of the Department of Defense International Military Education Program. In 2001 Mike returned to the Pentagon for an extended military sabbatical in the Academy Liaison Office, where his relationships and familiarity with both the Pentagon and Congressional processes paid huge dividends during periods of intense scrutiny of the service academies.

Mike retired in 2004 but was soon recruited to join the AF Judge Advocate General's elite Administrative Law Division, where from 2005 to 2010 he worked high-level military personnel and policy issues. He currently makes his home in Northern Virginia.

**BRIGADIER GENERAL
RITA A. JORDAN**

Permanent Professor 1998–2008

*B.A., Case Western Reserve University
M.A., Louisiana Tech University
Ph.D., University of Colorado*

Rita Jordan (née Brokans), the Academy's 65th Permanent Professor, was born in Stirling West, South Australia, in 1952. She graduated in 1974 from Case Western Reserve University, Cleveland, OH, where she majored in English and received her commission through the AFROTC program. She attended the Basic Munitions Maintenance Course, Lowry AFB, CO, in 1974. Upon graduation, she was assigned to the 449th Munitions Maintenance Squadron, Kincheloe AFB, MI, and served as Branch Chief for the Munitions and Short-Range Attack Missile Maintenance and Storage branches from 1975 to 1977. Transferring to Andersen AFB, Guam, in 1977, she served as Munitions Services Branch Chief and Munitions Maintenance Supervisor in the 43rd Munitions Maintenance Squadron. In 1978 she attended Squadron Officer School, Maxwell AFB, AL. In 1980 she became Chief, Munitions Services Division, HQ 8th Air Force, Barksdale AFB, LA. While at Barksdale, she earned a Master of Arts degree in Human Relations from Louisiana Tech University, Ruston, in 1981. Next, she served from 1982 to 1984 as Maintenance Supervisor, 380th Field Maintenance Squadron and 380th Avionics Maintenance Squadron, Plattsburgh AFB, NY. In 1984 she joined the USAF Academy Department of Management as an Assistant Professor with additional duty as Personnel Officer. From 1987 to 1990 she was a student in the doctoral program at the University of Colorado, Boulder. Returning to the Management Department, Rita completed her dissertation while teaching and was awarded a PhD in Business Administration from CU in 1993. In 1994 Rita became the Deputy Department Head as an Associate Professor, and in 1998 she was appointed Permanent Professor and Head, Department of Management. She led the effort that gained the initial accreditation for the Management major from the Association to Advance Collegiate Schools of Business (AACSB), the first service academy to gain this accreditation. She also chaired the Second Class Academic Review Committee, a USAFA Admissions Panel, and the NCAA Track and Field and Cross-Country Intercollegiate Eligibility Committee. In 2002 Rita served as the Associate Dean and Chair, Academic Review Board, of the Graduate School of Engineering and Management, Air Force Institute of Technology, Wright-Patterson AFB, OH, during a two-year sabbatical. Returning to Head the Department of Management in 2004, she also served as a member of the Board of Directors of AACSB International and from 2007 to 2008, as an additional duty, Chair of the faculty's Social Sciences Division. Rita was promoted to brigadier general and retired from the USAF in 2008.

From 2009 to 2011 Rita returned to the Management Department to teach Organization Behavior and Human Resources Management as well as help with the preparation for the Academy's AACSB Maintenance of Accreditation Peer Review Team visit. During this time, she also served AACSB as a volunteer Peer Review Team member for an initial and a maintenance visit; as Adjunct Faculty, Bachelor of Innovation Program, University of Colorado, Colorado Springs; and as a member of the Board of Trustees for the University of the Rockies, Denver. Rita also has taught in the School of Management, College of Professional Studies, Regis University in Denver. She continues teaching as Adjunct Faculty in the Bachelor of Innovation Program, University of Colorado, Colorado Springs.

COLONEL
THOMAS G. BOWIE JR.

Permanent Professor 1999–2004

B.S., *United States Air Force Academy*
M.A., *University of Denver*
Ph.D., *Brown University*

Tom Bowie, the Academy's 66th Permanent Professor, was born in 1954 in Seattle, Washington. He graduated from the United States Air Force Academy in the Class of 1976 with a Humanities major and was named the Outstanding Cadet Group Commander that year. He went on to undergraduate navigator training at Mather AFB, CA, where he was a Distinguished Graduate in 1977 and won the Husik Trophy for top flight performance. Tom then flew as a Navigator and Bombardier in Strategic Air Command, and also served in various staff positions at Fairchild AFB, WA, and K.I. Sawyer AFB, MI. In 1979 Tom was a member of the top bomber crew in the command, taking first place honors at the annual bombing and navigation competition. At K.I. Sawyer in the early 1990s, he directed the wing's flying training program and helped establish the Strategic Weapons School at Ellsworth AFB, SD. Tom left Fairchild AFB in 1982 to pursue his Master's degree in English at the University of Denver, which he earned in 1984. His thesis explored perceptions of history in Southern American literature, focusing on the legendary writer Robert Penn Warren. Tom then taught in the Academy's Department of English from 1984 to 1986. During his time at the Academy, Tom also taught basic navigation to cadets, flying as a Staff Instructor Navigator on the T-43 navigation training aircraft. He is a Master Navigator with over 2,500 flying hours in the B-52 and T-43 aircraft. He returned to school in 1986 and earned his PhD in English Literature from Brown University in 1989. Tom rejoined the faculty of the English and Fine Arts Department from 1992 to 1998, and then attended the Air War College at Maxwell AFB, AL. He was appointed a Permanent Professor and Head of the English and Fine Arts Department in 1999. Tom served during his final year as Permanent Professor at US Northern Command, Peterson AFB, CO, 2003–2004, as Chief of Homeland Defense Plans (a position established in the aftermath of the terrorist attacks on September 11, 2001) and Chief of Policy. Tom is an authority on the literature of war—his research and publications focus on the human dimension of conflict, on personal narratives that bear witness to modern war, and on the journey toward reconciliation that inevitably follows such conflicts. For over a decade he was editor of *War, Literature, and the Arts*, an international journal of the humanities. He retired in 2004.

Following retirement, Tom joined the faculty at Regis University in Denver as Director of their Honors Program, where he redesigned the curriculum around team-taught interdisciplinary classes. In 2011 he co-authored a highly successful grant for integrative faculty development, and then served for three years as Director of the Regis Integrative Teaching Institute. He became the Academic Dean of Regis College in 2014.

BRIGADIER GENERAL
THOMAS A. DROHAN

Permanent Professor 1999–2017

B.S., United States Air Force Academy
M.A., University of Hawaii
Ph.D., Princeton University

Tom Drohan, the Academy's 67th Permanent Professor, was born in Paris, France, in 1957. He graduated from the United States Air Force Academy in 1979 with a major in International Affairs/National Security Studies. Tom's first assignment was to the University of Hawaii as an East-West Center scholar, where he earned a Master's degree in Political Science in 1980. He then went to undergraduate pilot training at Reese AFB, TX, followed by a tour as an HC-130 Combat Rescue Pilot at Kadena Air Base, Japan, 1982–1985. He first came to the Academy faculty in the Department of Political Science, 1985–1988, during which time he also taught cadets to fly the T-41 aircraft. He next went to Princeton for three years, where he earned his PhD in Politics in 1991. Returning directly to the Academy, Tom was Chief, Comparative Politics & Area Studies Division, Department of Political Science, while continuing his work as a T-41 Instructor Pilot. From 1995 to 1998 he flew as a C-130 Tactical Airlift Pilot and Flight Commander, 23rd Operational Support Squadron, and then as Director of Staff and Director of Operations, 41st Airlift Squadron, Pope AFB, NC. During this time, he was deployed as Commander, 4410th Airlift Squadron, Prince Sultan Air Base, Saudi Arabia, and as Commander, 38th Airlift Squadron, Ramstein Air Base, Germany. In 1999 Tom spent a year as a Fellow of the Council on Foreign Relations at the Institute for International Policy Studies and at the National Institute for Defense Studies, Tokyo, Japan. He returned to the Academy in 1999 as the Permanent Professor of Military and Strategic Studies (and concurrently the Commander, 34th Education Group) under the Commandant of Cadets (the Commander, 34th Training Wing). Tom reorganized the Military Art and Science curriculum and established Military and Strategic Studies as a disciplinary academic major. From 2003 to 2004 he also served as Vice Commandant for Operations. Tom was on sabbatical from 2004 to 2005 in a dual role as Chief, Antiterrorism and Force Protection Division, United States Forces Korea, and Chief, Missile Defense Division, Combined Forces Command, Korea. In 2005 as he returned to the Academy, the Military and Strategic Studies program was transferred to the Dean of Faculty as the Department of Military and Strategic Studies. From 2006 to 2010, Tom deployed to the National Military Academy of Afghanistan each year as a curriculum advisor for military and airpower studies. He also had a sabbatical in 2012 as Visiting Scholar at the Reischauer Center for East Asian Studies at the Johns Hopkins School of Advanced International Studies, where he researched Asian security, strategy, and warfare. A prolific author, his publications include two books—*American–Japanese Security Agreements* (2007) and *A New Strategy for Complex Warfare* (2016)—and many articles on defense strategy, Asian security, and military education. He is a Command Pilot with more than 2,000 flying hours. He was promoted to brigadier general and retired in 2017 to become Dean of the National Defense College, United Arab Emirates.

BRIGADIER GENERAL
MARK K. WELLS

Permanent Professor 2000–2016

B.S., United States Air Force Academy
M.A., Texas Tech University
Ph.D., King's College, University of
   London

Mark Wells, the Academy's 68th Permanent Professor, was born in 1953 to an Air Force family at Reese AFB, Texas. He graduated from the Air Force Academy in 1975 with a major in History and went on to pilot training at Craig AFB, AL. After receiving his wings and attending KC-135 Combat Crew Training School, Castle AFB, CA, he was assigned to an Air Refueling Squadron at Fairchild AFB, WA, 1977–1979. From 1980 to 1983 he was a T-37 Instructor Pilot and Chief, Learning Center Branch at Reese AFB, during which tour he earned his Master's degree in History from Texas Tech, Lubbock. Mark returned to the Academy from 1983 to 1986 as Instructor of History and T-41 Instructor Pilot. After a year at Air Command and Staff College, he returned to Air Training Command as a Flight Commander at Randolph AFB, TX, 1987–1988. Next followed four years in Europe, where he was for one year a student at King's College, then two years as Military Assistant to the Commander, Supreme Headquarters Allied Powers, Europe, Casteau, Belgium, and finally another year at King's College, where his PhD in War Studies was awarded in 1992. His firsthand experiences with NATO's evolving strategy and changes in conventional force structure served him well during his year as a student at the Army War College, 1992–1993. Mark returned to the Academy and served as Associate Professor and Deputy Head, Department of History, from 1993 until his appointment as Department Head in 1999. In 2000 he was appointed a Permanent

Professor. Mark's deep personal interest in military history, airpower, and the personal dimension of combat drove him to write *Courage and Air Warfare: The Allied Aircrew Experience in the Second World War* (1995), which won the Society for Military History's 1997 Distinguished Book Award and was twice selected for the Air Force Chief of Staff's recommended reading list. He was editor of a second book, *Airpower: Promise and Reality* (2002), and author of numerous journal articles. From 2005 to 2007 he took a sabbatical assignment to Headquarters US European Command, Stuttgart, Germany, where he worked military/political policy and planning issues. In 2013 he was a Visiting Professor of Strategy for a semester at the Army War College. He is a Command Pilot with over 3,200 flying hours in the KC-135, T-37, T-41, T-3, T-52, and T-53 aircraft and for over two decades taught cadets to fly. Mark was Officer Representative for the Academy football team and the Faculty Athletics Representative to the National Collegiate Athletic Association. He was promoted to brigadier general and retired in 2016.

After retiring, Mark accepted a position with a subsidiary of a United Arab Emirates investment group to lead an American team evaluating the UAE's Air Force Academy and make recommendations for improvement. After returning home, Mark has been busy publishing articles, serving on the Heritage and Traditions Committee of the Association of Graduates, and being a docent at the National Museum of World War II Aviation in Colorado Springs.

BRIGADIER GENERAL
GREGORY E. SEELY

Permanent Professor 2000–2015

B.S., United States Air Force Academy
M.S., University of California, Berkeley
Ph.D., University of California,
*   Berkeley*

Greg Seely, the Academy's 69th Permanent Professor, was born in 1954 in Long Beach, California. He graduated from the United States Air Force Academy with a Bachelor's degree in Civil Engineering in 1976. His first assignment was as a Project Design Engineer, 44th Civil Engineering Squadron, Ellsworth AFB, SD. In 1978 he became the Section Commander within the squadron. From 1979 to 1981 he was an Environmental Engineering Officer, Deputy Chief of Staff for Engineering and Services, HQ Strategic Air Command, Offutt AFB, NE. He was a Distinguished Graduate from Squadron Officers School, Maxwell AFB, AL, in 1980. In 1982 Greg became the Chief of Bioenvironmental Engineering in the USAF Hospital, Beale AFB, CA. He entered graduate school in 1985 at the University of California, Berkeley, and received his Master's degree in Environmental Engineering in 1986. From 1986 to 1988 he returned to the Academy as an Instructor in the Department of Civil Engineering. Since 1988 Greg has been a Professional Engineer in the State of Colorado. He returned to Berkeley in 1988 and received his PhD in Environmental Engineering in 1991. Returning to the USAFA Department of Civil Engineering, he served as the Deputy for Environmental Engineering, progressed from Assistant to Associate Professor, was Deputy for Operations, and became the Deputy for Field Engineering and Readiness Laboratory before leaving in 1997. Greg then was assigned as the Chief, Consultant Operations Division, HQ Air Force Center for Environmental Excellence, Brooks AFB, TX, for a year before becoming the Director of the Environmental Quality Directorate at the Center. During this assignment, his teams won national awards for Texas pollution prevention. Returning to the Academy once again in 1999, he was the Senior Military Professor, Department of Civil and Environmental Engineering. In 2000 Greg was appointed Permanent Professor and Department Head. During his tenure at the Academy, Greg also served as an Officer Representative for the men's varsity football (2000–2004, 2006–2015) and basketball (1995–1997) teams and as Officer in Charge for the Fellowship of Christian Athletes (1992–1997, 1999–2002). He was the Chief, Readiness Plans in the AF Space Command Directorate of Installations and Mission Support, Peterson AFB, CO, during a sabbatical year, 2005–2006. He stood-up the Academy's Installations Directorate and served as its Director during an 18-month second sabbatical commencing in mid-2010. Greg was promoted to brigadier general and retired from the USAF in 2015.

Greg is enjoying retirement in Colorado Springs.

BRIGADIER GENERAL
DOUGLAS N. BARLOW

Permanent Professor 2000–2015
Vice Dean of the Faculty 2006–2008

B.S., *United States Air Force Academy*
M.S., *University of Washington*
Ph.D., *Arizona State University*

Neal Barlow, the Academy's 70th Permanent Professor, was born in Stillwater, Oklahoma, in 1956. He was a 1978 Distinguished Graduate from the United States Air Force Academy with a degree in Aeronautical Engineering. He entered undergraduate pilot training at Williams AFB, AZ, where he was a Distinguished Graduate. In 1980 he completed T-38 Instructor Pilot training as the Top Graduate at Randolph AFB, TX, and was assigned as a T-38 Instructor Pilot at Williams AFB from 1980 to 1983. He attended Squadron Officer School at Maxwell AFB, AL, in 1982, where he was recognized as an Outstanding Contributor and for Performance and Speaking Excellence. In 1983 Neal entered the University of Washington, Seattle, as an Order of Daedalian Fellow, and earned his Master's degree in Aeronautics and Astronautics in 1984. In 1985 he returned to the Academy as an Assistant Professor in the Department of Aeronautics. From 1988 to 1990 he served as an Instructional Program Developer in the 3305th School Squadron, HQ Air Training Command, Randolph AFB. Remaining at Randolph for an additional year, he served as a T-38 Command Flight Examiner. In 1991 he began PhD studies in Aerospace Engineering at Arizona State University, Tempe, which he completed in 1994. Returning to the Academy, he earned academic promotion to Associate Professor and served as Director of Research among other duties in the Department of Aeronautics. From 1997 to 1998 Neal was the Commander, 4417th Support Squadron and Site

Commander, Ali Al Salem Air Base, Kuwait. Again returning to USAFA in 1998, he served as the Commander, 94th Flying Training Squadron before becoming the Deputy Commander of USAFA's 34th Operations Group. In his 24 years of instructor experience he served at every level of undergraduate flight training. In 2000 Neal was appointed Permanent Professor and Head of the Department of Aeronautics. He served as the Officer Representative for the Academy's football team from 2009 until 2013. In 2004 he was deployed to Iraq and served as the "Mayor of the Green Zone" while assigned as the Multi-National Force's Commander, Joint Area Support Group, Baghdad. Returning in 2005 to again head the Aeronautics Department, Neal became the Vice Dean of the Faculty from 2006 until 2008, when he returned to his former position. He had the additional duty of Chair of the Engineering Division, 2008–2013. During 2013–2014, he served as the Interim Chief Scientist for AF Space and Cyber Command, Peterson AFB, CO. Returning to USAFA one final time, Neal served as the Associate Dean for the Core Curriculum until his promotion to brigadier general and retirement in 2015.

Upon his retirement, Neal became Professor of Engineering and the Dean, College of Applied Sciences, Arkansas Tech University in Russellville, AR, where he served until 2017. He was a Vice President and then Director-at-Large for The American Institute of Aeronautics and Astronautics, 2009–2016, and currently is an ABET Program Evaluator and Commissioner. Neal is a Fellow of the American Institute of Aeronautics and Astronautics.

BRIGADIER GENERAL
RICHARD L. FULLERTON

Permanent Professor 2002–2014
Vice Dean of the Faculty 2010–2012

B.S., *United States Air Force Academy*
M.S., *University of Texas at Austin*
Ph.D., *University of Texas at Austin*

Rich Fullerton, the Academy's 71ˢᵗ Permanent Professor, was born in 1961 in Moab, Utah, and raised in Norman, Oklahoma. He graduated first in his United States Air Force Academy Class of 1983 with majors in Economics and Operations Research. He went on to Sheppard AFB, TX, for Euro-NATO Joint Jet Pilot Training, then stayed there as a T-38 Instructor Pilot, 1984–1989. After transitioning to the F-15 at Luke AFB, AZ, Rich moved to the 525ᵗʰ Tactical Fighter Squadron, Bitburg Air Base, Germany, 1989–1992, and flew combat missions in Operations DESERT STORM and PROVIDE COMFORT. He was then selected for Academy faculty duty and sent to graduate school at UT–Austin, where in three years he completed both his Master's degree (1994) and PhD (1995) in Economics. He then joined the Academy's Department of Economics and Geography as an Assistant Professor of Economics. After two years he was tapped for assignment in the Office of the Secretary of the Air Force, the Pentagon, Washington, DC, where he made substantial contributions toward the development and acquisition of unmanned aerial vehicles in the Air Force. From 1999 to 2000 he was a National Defense Fellow at the Mershon Center for International Studies, Ohio State University, Columbus, following which he was the Executive Officer to the Deputy Chief of Staff, US Forces Korea, in Seoul. Rich returned to the Academy in 2001 as Head of the Department of Economics and Geography, where he finished out the last 13 years of his distinguished 31-year career. He was appointed Permanent Professor in 2002. During his tenure, he oversaw the major in Economics and the interdisciplinary majors in Meteorology and Operations Research. He modernized the geography curriculum, transforming the Geography major into Geospatial Sciences, and renaming the department to Economics and Geosciences. Rich was a prolific writer, with many published articles in top economics journals. He developed a deep interest in improving use of data for realistic assessment of college achievement and published in this area as well. He led the Academy's massive self-study in preparation for its academic reaccreditation in 2010. Moreover, he was the Vice Dean and also served the Academy as its Faculty Athletics Representative to the NCAA. Rich was promoted to brigadier general and retired in 2014.

Following retirement, Rich taught at Colorado College, and avidly pursued his love of all things outdoors, especially traveling with his family and climbing mountains. He died suddenly in 2016 and is buried in the Air Force Academy Cemetery.

BRIGADIER GENERAL
WILLIAM P. WALKER

Permanent Professor 2001–2013

B.S., *United States Air Force Academy*
M.A., *California State University,*
   San Bernardino
Ed.D., *University of Northern*
   Colorado

William "Billy" Walker, the Academy's 72nd Permanent Professor, was born in 1961 in Minneapolis, Minnesota, and raised in Hartland, Wisconsin. He graduated from the United States Air Force Academy in 1983 and was captain of the wrestling team that year. He attended undergraduate helicopter training at Fort Rucker, AL, and went on to fly the TH-1F *Iroquois* at George AFB, CA. During this tour, he earned his Master's degree in National Security Studies from Cal–State, San Bernardino (awarded in 1987). From 1987 to 1991 he was a Pilot in the 1st Helicopter Squadron, Andrews AFB, MD, providing priority airlift to the nation's highest-ranking officials. He returned to the Academy in 1991 as Instructor of Physical Education and Assistant Wrestling Coach, receiving his department's Outstanding Military Educator Award in 1993. From 1994 to 1996 he was a graduate student at the University of Northern Colorado, Greeley, where he earned his Doctor of Education degree in Physical Education, with an emphasis in Sports Administration and Law. In 1996 he was selected as the Operations Officer and later Commander of the 37th Rescue Flight, F.E. Warren AFB, WY, where his unit earned the distinction of "Best Helicopters" in Air Force Space Command and garnered 25 "Saves" and 25 "Assists" while flying 82 rescue missions. In 1998 he returned to Andrews AFB as Operations Officer, later Commander, of the 1st Helicopter Squadron, the largest helicopter squadron in the Air Force. While Commander, he instituted a new Head-of-State mission and began routinely transporting the Vice President of the United States for the first time in decades. Additionally, he saw his squadron surpass the rotary-wing record of 200,000 accident-free flying hours. He was subsequently named Deputy Commander of the 89th Operations Group, responsible for safe worldwide transport of the President of the United States and other dignitaries. He is a Command Pilot with over 3,000 hours of helicopter flight time. Billy was appointed the first Permanent Professor in the Athletic Department in 2001. As Head of the Department of Physical Education, he was responsible for a multifaceted program involving cadet fitness training and evaluation and an intramural program for 4,000 cadets. In addition, as Deputy Director of Athletics, he was responsible for 23 varsity Olympic sports competing in Division I of the National Collegiate Athletic Association. Billy was promoted to brigadier general and retired in 2013.

Upon retirement, Billy was selected as the Director of Athletics and Recreation at American University in Washington, DC. He was inducted into the National Wrestling Hall of Fame as an Outstanding American in 2016.

BRIGADIER GENERAL
DAVID S. GIBSON

Permanent Professor 2002–2017

B.S., *Duke University*
M.S., *Trinity University*
Ph.D., *Ohio State University*

David S. "Hoot" Gibson, the Academy's 73rd Permanent Professor, was born in Dayton, Ohio, in 1960. He is a 1983 Distinguished Graduate of the Duke University AFROTC program, where he served as Cadet Wing Commander his senior year and earned degrees in both Physics and Computer Science. After receiving his commission, he was assigned to the Air Force Electronic Warfare Center, Kelly AFB, TX, where he served as Chief, Software Development Section, Studies and Analysis Directorate. He earned his Master's degree in Computing and Information Science from Trinity University, San Antonio, TX, in 1986. From 1986 to 1990 Hoot served as a Secure Systems Analyst and then as Chief of the Computer Security Special Applications Branch at the National Security Agency, Fort Meade, MD. Upon reassignment to Detachment 4 of the Air Force Operational Test and Evaluation Center, Peterson AFB, CO, he served as the Chief of Information Systems and as Operational Test and Evaluation Test Director for the Cheyenne Mountain Space Defense Operations Center Upgrade. From 1992 to 1994 he taught in the Air Force Academy's Department of Computer Science. After earning his PhD in Computer and Information Science at the Ohio State University in 1997, he returned to the Academy and served as Deputy Head, Department of Computer Science, and later Department Head. In 2002 he was appointed Permanent Professor. During his tenure, the department continued to offer its major in Computer Science, added a new major in Computer and Network Security, and supported interdisciplinary programs in Operations Research, Computer Engineering, and Systems Engineering. His department also is home to the Academy Center for Cyberspace Research, which conducts research in cyber operations, information assurance, and cyberspace education. While deployed for six months in 2003–2004, he served as Chief of Information Operations and US Senior National Representative for HQ Kosovo Forces, Pristina, Kosovo. Returning again to head his department, from 2006 to 2008 Hoot served additional duty as Chairman of the Basic Sciences Division. During a sabbatical, Academic Year 2008–2009, he served as the Academy's Director of Communications and Information. From 2014 to 2015 he had another sabbatical assignment to the National Security Agency and the United States Cyber Command, Fort Meade, MD, where he served as Chief of the Weapons and Tactics Division in the Advanced Concepts and Technology Directorate. During most of his time at the Academy, Hoot was the institution's senior communications and information/cyber operations officer. He was promoted to brigadier general and retired in 2017, having been responsible for leading his department and the entire Academy into the cyber warfare age.

Hoot continues his support of cyber education by volunteering on several ABET projects and as a member of ABET's Computing Accreditation Commission Executive Committee. He also is helping the Association for Computing Machinery and other organizations develop cybersecurity curricula.

BRIGADIER GENERAL
DANA H. BORN

Permanent Professor 2002–2013
Dean of the Faculty 2004–2013

B.S., United States Air Force Academy
M.S., Trinity University
M.A., University of Melbourne
Ph.D., Pennsylvania State University

Dana Born (née Lindsley), the Academy's 74th Permanent Professor, was born in Lancaster, Pennsylvania, in 1960. She graduated from the United States Air Force Academy in 1983 with a Bachelor's degree in Behavioral Sciences. Her first assignment was as a Job Analyst, Occupational Measurement Center, Randolph AFB, TX. While at Randolph, she completed a Master's degree in Experimental Psychology at Trinity University, San Antonio, in 1985. She was the Executive Officer to the Center Commander in 1985 until she attended Squadron Officer School at Maxwell AFB, AL, and graduated in 1986. From 1986 to 1989 Dana was assigned as Personnel Measurement Psychologist, USAF Exchange and Liaison Office, Royal Australian Air Force HQ Support Command, Melbourne, Australia. While in Australia, she studied for a Master's degree in Research Psychology at the University of Melbourne, which was awarded in 1991. In 1989 Dana joined the USAFA faculty as an Assistant Professor in the Department of Behavioral Sciences and Leadership. She entered Pennsylvania State University, University Park, in 1991 and earned her PhD in Industrial and Organizational Psychology in 1994. From 1994 to 1997 Dana was the Assistant Director, Recruiting Research and Analysis, Accession Policy Directorate, Office of Assistant Secretary of Defense for Force Management Policy, Washington, DC. Remaining in the Pentagon, in 1997 she became a Speechwriter and Policy and Issues Analyst, Office of the Secretary of the Air Force and then

Aide to two consecutive Secretaries of the Air Force. From 1998 to 2000 Dana was Deputy Chief of the Personnel Issues Team, Office of the Deputy Chief of Staff for Personnel, HQ USAF. She served as the Commander of the 11ᵗʰ Mission Support Squadron, Bolling AFB, Washington, from 2000 to 2002 and led the squadron's efforts following the September 11, 2001, attack on the Pentagon. In 2002 Dana returned to the Academy as Professor and Head, Department of Behavioral Sciences and Leadership; later that year she was appointed a Permanent Professor. During her first year, she led the Academy's responses to Congressional, DoD, and Air Force panels investigating the widely publicized allegations of sexual assault/harassment. Subsequently, she was the Academy's chief architect for the groundbreaking Officer Development System, developed in 2003–2004. Dana was selected to be the Academy's 8ᵗʰ Permanent Professor Dean of the Faculty in 2004 and promoted to brigadier general. During her tenure as Dean, she bolstered the Academy's research programs, achieving a 15-fold increase in research funding, which earned the Academy a national reputation for having the largest research program of any wholly undergraduate institution. She led a revolutionary change in the Academy's educational paradigm by serving as chief architect and proponent of the shift to focus on cadet learning rather than teaching. Recognizing Air Force needs, she supported two new strategic cadet programs: Remotely Piloted Aircraft and Cyber Defense. From 2010 to 2011 she served on the Department of Defense Don't Ask, Don't Tell Comprehensive Review Working Group, Committee on Education and Training. She served in Afghanistan in support of Operation ENDURING FREEDOM assisting the National Military Academy in 2008 and 2010. Dana received the Air Force's Eugene M. Zuckert Management Award in 2009 and the Hoyt S. Vandenberg Award for Aerospace Education in 2011. Dana retired from the USAF in 2013.

Upon retirement Dana accepted a position as Lecturer in Public Policy at the Center for Public Leadership, Kennedy School of Government, Harvard University, Cambridge, MA. She also became the Faculty Chair of the Senior Executive Fellows Program in the Center in 2016 and Co-Director of the Center in 2017. She teaches and leads seminars at

Harvard and for many organizations and governments throughout the US, Europe, Asia, and the Middle East. She is the past President and a Fellow of the American Psychological Association (Society for Military Psychology). Dana has received the Kennedy School Dean's Teaching Award each of her first four years at Harvard and the Penn State University's Distinguished Alumni Fellow Award.

COLONEL
JAMES L. COOK

Permanent Professor 2002–Present

B.A., *Brandeis University*
B.A., *University of Colorado, Boulder*
M.A., *The Catholic University of*
America
Ph.D., *Universität Heidelberg*

Jim Cook, the Academy's 75th Permanent Professor, was born to an Air Force family in 1959 in Roswell, New Mexico, then home of Strategic Air Command's Walker AFB. He received a scholarship to Brandeis University and graduated with his Bachelor's degree in Philosophy in 1980, at age 20. While working at the National Oceanic and Atmospheric Administration in Boulder, Colorado, he decided to take a few courses and in 1983 ended up with a second Bachelor's degree, this time in Mathematics, from the University of Colorado. After graduating from the Officer Training School at Lackland AFB, TX, in 1985 he attended the Communications-Computer Officer Basic Course at Keesler AFB, MS, where he was a Distinguished Graduate. For his first assignment, 1986–1991, he was sent to the basement of the Pentagon as an Air Staff Project Officer and Command and Control Branch Chief to oversee communications-computer systems in the group that served Air Force and many Department of Defense command, control, communications, and intelligence services in the building. For the last two years of that tour, Jim was the Executive Officer for that 1,100-member organization. During that assignment, the Academy reached out to sponsor him for graduate work, and he attended The Catholic University of America, completing his Master's degree in Philosophy in 1992. He then came to the Academy and taught for four semesters in the Department of Philosophy and Fine Arts before being selected for sponsorship for his PhD. Jim chose to pursue his doctorate at the Ruprecht-Karls-Universität Heidelberg, Germany's oldest and top-ranked university, and the home of any number of philosophical luminaries (this despite his not ever having been to Germany and his only experience with the language was listening to his mother and grandmother talk). He completed his PhD in Philosophy and graduated *magna cum laude* in 1997. From 1997 to 1999 he was assigned to Ramstein Air Base, Germany, as the Chief, Communications-Information Systems, responsible for technical aspects of the first deployable NATO Combined Air Operations Center. During these two years at Ramstein he supported NATO's Partnership for Peace and other exercises, and he was certified as a Foreign Area Officer. In 1999 he returned to the Academy faculty and in 2002 was confirmed as Permanent Professor and Head, Department of Philosophy. During his tenure, the Department of Philosophy has continued its emphasis on military ethics while expanding its academic offerings. In addition to the traditional Philosophy minor, the Department began offering a Philosophy major (in 2012), and administers the multidisciplinary minor in Religion Studies (established in 2013). For eight months in 2009, Jim Cook was deployed as the Senior Advisor to the National Military Academy of Afghanistan. He took a sabbatical year in 2015–2016 as a Visiting Research Professor at Heidelberg, offering invited papers and teaching graduate lessons at the university as well as in Oslo, Prague, and Zürich. Jim serves on the Ethics Oversight Panel for the Defense Advanced Research Projects Agency.

BRIGADIER GENERAL
PAUL E. PIROG

Permanent Professor 2004–2014

B.S., United States Air Force Academy
J.D., University of Michigan

Paul Pirog, the Academy's 76th Permanent Professor, a native of Novi, Michigan, was born in 1955. He is a 1977 Distinguished Graduate of the United States Air Force Academy with a degree in Biological Sciences. He spent five years in flying operations, first at undergraduate navigator training and navigator-bombardier training at Mather AFB, CA, 1977–1978, graduating at the top of both classes, and then navigating B-52Ds at Carswell AFB, TX, 1978–1982. He accrued more than 1,500 flying hours and was the navigator of the 9th Bomb Squadron Crew of the Year (1980). He was selected for the Funded Legal Education Program and sent to the University of Michigan Law School, earning his Juris Doctorate in 1985. Paul then performed duties as Assistant Staff Judge Advocate, Ellsworth AFB, SD, 1985–1987; Senior Medical Law Consultant, Keesler AFB, MS, 1987–1990; Staff Judge Advocate, Onizuka AFB, CA, 1990–1992; Chief, National Security Law Branch, Office of the Air Force General Counsel, the Pentagon, Washington, DC, 1992–1995; Staff Judge Advocate, 16th Special Operations Wing, Hurlburt Field, FL, 1995–1997; Deputy Commandant, Air Force Judge Advocate General School, Maxwell AFB, AL, 1997–1998; Staff Judge Advocate, Wright-Patterson AFB, OH, 1998–2000; and Deputy Staff Judge Advocate, Air Mobility Command, Scott AFB, IL, 2000–2002. He returned to the Academy for his first faculty assignment in 2002, as Head, Department of Law. Two years later, he was appointed a Permanent Professor. During his tenure Paul revitalized the core course, Law for Air Force Officers, shifting its focus from a substantive knowledge of the law to a learning-centered approach concentrating on critical thinking and problem-solving skills, the ability to communicate, and knowledge of Air Force–oriented areas of the law. In addition, he created a new institutional post-graduate law school program for Academy graduates, performed duties as a judge at the International Institute of Humanitarian Law's Law of Armed Conflict Competition for Military Academies, and served as Chair of the Institutional Review Committee, responsible for approval and monitoring of all Academy research on human subjects. Active across all mission elements, Paul helped safeguard the fairness of the cadet honor system through oversight of all Honor Case and Board Legal Advisors, was Officer in Charge of the Catholic Cadet Choir, and was Officer Representative for the intercollegiate women's volleyball team. For six years, he chaired the Social Sciences Division, serving on the Academy Board and helping formulate the strategic direction of the Academy. He was a member of the Judge Advocate General School Advisory Group for many years, providing oversight and strategic direction for courses taught at the School. Paul took a sabbatical assignment as Staff Judge Advocate, 19th Air Force, Randolph AFB, TX, 2007–2008. He has published widely on legal issues, including the role of ethics in the fight against terrorism. Paul was promoted to brigadier general and retired from the Air Force in 2014.

Since retiring from active duty, Paul serves as a Trustee of the Judge Advocate General School Foundation and is active in his local community government.

COLONEL
KATHLEEN HARRINGTON

Permanent Professor 2004–Present
Vice Dean of the Faculty 2014–2016

B.S., *United States Air Force Academy*
M.S., *University of Southern California*
M.A., *University of Hawaii*
Ph.D., *University of Washington*

Kathleen Harrington, the Academy's 77th Permanent Professor, was born in Everett, Washington, in 1962. She graduated from the United States Air Force Academy in 1984 with a degree in Humanities. As a communications officer, Kathleen has served at the squadron, group, and headquarters levels in both US Air Forces Europe and in Pacific Air Forces. Her first assignment was as a student at the Basic Communication-Electronics Course, Keesler AFB, MS. From 1985 to 1987 she was a Systems Integration Analyst at Kapaun Barracks, Kaiserslautern, Germany. Then from 1987 to 1989 she was assigned as Chief of Operations, 2184th Communications Squadron, Hahn Air Base, Germany. While at Hahn, Kathleen earned a Master's degree in Systems Management from the University of Southern California in 1988. She was next transferred to the Pacific as Chief of Maintenance, 1957th Communications Group, Hickam AFB, HI, 1989–1992. While at Hickam, Kathleen was selected for an assignment to the Air Force Academy faculty and sent to the University of Hawaii, where she earned her Master's degree in English in 1994. During her first faculty tour as Instructor of English, 1994–1996, she was selected by the Department of English for PhD sponsorship. She performed her doctoral work at the University of Washington, Seattle, and graduated with her PhD in English in 1999. Her dissertation research centered on the literary foundation of leaders—what people read to develop themselves as leaders—a topic she would later apply directly to the Department of English curriculum. From 1999 to 2002 she was assigned to HQ US Air Forces, Europe, Ramstein Air Base, Germany, as the Commander's Speechwriter, where she prepared materials from informal talks to formal testimony before Congress. Subsequently she was selected to be the USAFE Commander's Executive Officer. Kathleen then went to Italy as Commander, 31st Communications Squadron and Deputy Commander, Mission Support Group, 31st Fighter Wing, Aviano Air Base, Italy, 2002–2004, providing direct support to ongoing air combat activity. Thus, her career in communications encompassed systems analysis, operations, maintenance, and command. In 2004 Kathleen was selected as a Permanent Professor and appointed Head, Department of English and Fine Arts. In this position, she applied her research to strengthen the cadet understanding of literature and leadership, and she developed a new approach to the literature of war, through interviews with women who write about war. She published articles on war literature and on academic freedom. In 2009 Kathleen received a prestigious fellowship from the American Council on Education (ACE) and spent the 2009–2010 academic year on sabbatical with the Office of the Chancellor, University of Colorado at Colorado Springs. As an ACE Fellow, Kathleen joined a select group of professionals studying strategic planning across a wide range of American institutions of higher education. From 2014 to 2016 Kathleen was the Vice Dean of the Faculty, where she took the lead to define, plan, and implement a new vision for the Academy McDermott Library as a center for cadet collaborative learning.

BRIGADIER GENERAL
MICHAEL E. VAN VALKENBURG

Permanent Professor 2005–2018

B.S., *Washington University, St. Louis*
M.S., *South Dakota School of Mines*
   & Technology
Ph.D., *University of Florida*

Mike Van Valkenburg, the Academy's 78th Permanent Professor, was born in West Point, New York, in 1963. He graduated from Washington University, St. Louis, MO, in 1985 with a Bachelor's degree in Chemical Engineering and a commission from Air Force ROTC. His first assignment was as Chief of Bioenvironmental Engineering Services, USAF Hospital, Williams AFB, AZ, 1985–1987, during which time he completed the Bioenvironmental Engineering Officer Course at the School of Aerospace Medicine, Brooks AFB, TX. Mike next went to the USAF Hospital at Ellsworth AFB, SD, as Deputy Chief of the large Bioenvironmental Engineering Services unit, 1987–1989. He then received sponsorship from the Academy and spent two years as a graduate student at the South Dakota School of Mines & Technology, Rapid City, where he earned his Master's degree in Civil Engineering (Environmental) in 1991. His first Academy tour, 1991–1994, was as Instructor and Assistant Professor, Department of Chemistry, followed by an assignment as Deputy Chief, Program Development Division, HQ Air Force Center for Environmental Excellence, Brooks AFB. In 1996 he entered the doctoral program at the University of Florida and earned his PhD in Environmental Engineering Sciences (minor in Chemistry) in 1999. Returning to the Department of Chemistry, 1999–2003, Mike taught General, Analytical, Organic, Physical, and Environmental Chemistry courses and rose through positions of responsibility to Deputy Department Head for Operations. He then returned to the USAF School of Aerospace Medicine, Bioenvironmental Health Division, as Associate Dean and Chief, Operational Health Division, 2003–2004, then Chief, Contingency Operations Division, 2004–2005. From that position, Mike was selected as a Permanent Professor and appointed Head, Department of Chemistry. In addition to providing all cadets with a fundamental education in chemistry, the department provides a comprehensive curriculum for cadets interested in chemistry, biochemistry, or materials chemistry. In 2007 he was deployed as a senior advisor to the National Military Academy of Afghanistan, Kabul. From 2010 to 2011 he had a sabbatical assignment as Director, Science and Engineering Workforce Strategy, Office of the Deputy Assistant Secretary of the Air Force for Science, Technology and Engineering, the Pentagon, Washington, DC, where his work encompassed science, technology, engineering, and mathematics (STEM) initiatives; strategic management of the scientist career field; and nuclear enterprise initiatives. Mike received a prestigious American Council on Education Fellowship and spent academic year 2015–2016 working in the Office of the Treasurer and Chief Financial Officer, Purdue University, gaining valuable insights for the Academy on a range of leading-edge initiatives in higher education. Throughout his faculty years, Mike was heavily involved in the Academy's men's ice hockey program, and for several years served as Officer Representative for the team. He also served as the Academy's Faculty Athletics Representative to the NCAA and Chair of the Basic Sciences Division. Mike was promoted to brigadier general and retired in 2018.

BRIGADIER GENERAL
JOHN M. ANDREW

Permanent Professor 2005–2016
Vice Dean of the Faculty 2008–2010

B.S., *United States Air Force Academy*
M.S., *Harvard University*
Ph.D., *Harvard University*

John Andrew, the Academy's 79th Permanent Professor, was born in 1954 at Clark Air Base, Philippines. He graduated from the Air Force Academy in 1976 as a Distinguished Graduate and the Outstanding Graduate in the Operations Research (OR) major. During his 40-year career, he held a variety of scientific analysis jobs. He began as an Operations Analyst, YC-14/15 Test Team, Edwards AFB, CA, 1976–1978. He was next assigned as Lead Analyst, Electronic Systems Division, Air Force Test and Evaluation Center, Kirtland AFB, NM, 1978–1981. He was then sent to Harvard University, where he earned his Master's (1982) and PhD (1985) degrees in Engineering. His first assignment to the Academy faculty was 1985–1988 as Assistant Professor, Department of Mathematical Sciences, followed by an assignment as a Research Fellow at the RAND Corporation, Santa Monica, CA, 1988–1989, where he conducted in-depth studies of manpower and personnel issues. From 1989 to 1993 John was Chief, Officer and Economic Analysis Branch, Deputy Chief of Staff/Personnel, HQ USAF, the Pentagon, Washington, DC, where he supervised five officers responsible for analyzing effects of new personnel policies. From 1993 to 1995 he was a Policy and Issues Analyst, Secretary's Staff Group, Office of the Secretary of the Air Force, the Pentagon, where he advised the Secretary on a diverse portfolio of issues. In 1995–1996 John was a student at the Air War College, Maxwell AFB, AL, during which he participated in the Chief of

Staff–directed study, *Air Force 2025*, and he also co-authored and published *Air Force 2025 Operational Analysis* (winner of the Koopman Prize for best military OR study of 1996). Next he was Deputy Commander, AF Agency for Modeling and Simulation, Orlando, FL, 1996–1999, where he helped stand-up and direct a 53-person field operating agency. From there John was selected as Head, Department of Operational Sciences, Graduate School of Engineering and Management, AF Institute of Technology, Wright-Patterson AFB, OH, 1999–2002. While there, he deployed for four months to HQ US European Command during Operation ALLIED FORCE (Kosovo air operations). He then returned to the Academy as Senior Military Professor, 2002–2004, before being deployed for six months as Chief, Assessment Division, Office of the Deputy Chief of Staff (Strategy, Plans, and Assessment), Multi-National Force-Iraq, Baghdad. He returned to the Academy in 2005 as Head, Department of Mathematical Sciences, and later that year, he was confirmed as Permanent Professor. During his tenure, he chaired Admissions Selection Panels and Academic Review Committees, as well as serving for 11 years as Officer Representative for the men's basketball team. John was also the longest-tenured member and chair of two AF-level senior policy-making committees: the Scientist Development Team (recommended assignments, education, and career development for 1,000 AF military scientists) and the AF Analytic Community Steering Group. He was also Vice Dean, 2008–2010, and Chair, Basic Sciences Division, 2010–2016. John was promoted to brigadier general and retired in 2016.

Upon retirement, the annual award to the outstanding graduate in OR was named in John's honor. He remains involved with the Academy as President of the Friends of Air Force Basketball booster group.

BRIGADIER GENERAL
MARTIN E.B. FRANCE

Permanent Professor 2005–2018

B.S., *United States Air Force Academy*
M.S., *Stanford University*
M.S., *National Defense University*
Ph.D., *Virginia Polytechnic Institute
and State University*

Marty France, the Academy's 80th Permanent Professor, was born in Bitburg, Germany, in 1959 and raised in Glendale, Arizona. He earned his Air Force commission from the United States Air Force Academy in 1981, graduating with Bachelor's degrees in Engineering Mechanics and Engineering Sciences. His first assignment was as a Laser Systems Structural Engineer at the Air Force Weapons Laboratory, Kirtland AFB, NM. In 1983 he became a graduate student at Stanford University, Stanford, CA, and earned a Master's degree in Aeronautics and Astronautics in 1984. He then joined the AF Academy faculty as an Instructor in the Department of Astronautics. In 1986 he entered graduate school at Virginia Polytechnic Institute and State University in Blacksburg and completed his PhD in 1989. He returned to the Academy as an Associate Professor in the Astronautics Department. After eight months at the Defense Language Institute, Presidio of Monterey, CA, Marty became an Exchange Engineer in the *Office Nationale d'Etudes et de Récherche Aérospatiale*, Toulouse, France, in 1992. In 1994 he entered the Air Command and Staff College, Maxwell AFB, AL, graduating in 1995. Marty was then assigned as Command Lead for Space Support Mission Area Plans, Directorate of Plans, HQ AF Space Command, Peterson AFB, CO, until 1997 when he became the Chief, Spacelift Requirements Branch, Directorate of Requirements. Marty moved to the Pentagon in 1998 and became the Chief of the Space Programs and Requirements Branch, HQ

USAF, Washington, DC. In 1999 he moved across the Potomac River to the National War College, National Defense University, Fort Lesley J. McNair, and graduated in 2000 as a Distinguished Graduate with a Master's degree in National Security Strategy. Marty returned to the Pentagon to serve as the Chief, C4ISR (Command, Control, Communications, Computers, Intelligence, Surveillance, and Reconnaissance) and Space Branch, Requirements and Acquisition Division, Joint Chiefs of Staff until 2002 when, for seven months, he became a Joint Concepts and Architecture Analyst, Joint Warfighting Capabilities and Analysis Directorate, JCS. In late 2002 he was assigned as a Program Manager with the Defense Advanced Research Projects Agency in Arlington, VA. In 2004 Marty became the Chief, Space Superiority Division and in mid-2005, Deputy Director of Requirements, HQ AF Space Command, Peterson AFB, CO. He was appointed Permanent Professor and Head, Department of Astronautics in 2005. From 2008 to 2009 Marty returned to Washington on a sabbatical and was Chief Scientist and Science Advisor to the Director, Joint Improvised Explosive Device Defeat Organization before returning to his Academy post. He was awarded a Fulbright Fellowship and spent the last five months of 2014 as a Visiting Scholar at Nanyang Technological University, Singapore, teaching undergraduate courses and conducting research in Nanyang's Satellite Research Centre. Following the Waldo Canyon fire just outside Colorado Springs, Marty was awarded the city's "Spirit of the Springs" Award for Public Service in 2012 for his efforts leading restoration work. He was the Officer Representative to the USAFA men's and women's cross country and track and field teams, 2006–2018. An avid photographer, his work has been featured in four separate exhibitions in the Permanent Professors Art Gallery in USAFA's Fairchild Hall. Marty was promoted to brigadier general and retired in 2018.

COLONEL
GARY A. PACKARD JR.

Permanent Professor 2005–Present
Vice Dean of the Faculty 2016–2018
Vice Dean for Curriculum and
    Strategy 2018–Present

B.S., *United States Air Force Academy*
M.A.S., *Embry Riddle Aeronautical*
    University
M.A., *Michigan State University*
Ph.D., *University of North Carolina*

Gary Packard, the Academy's 81st Permanent Professor, was born in 1960 in Ann Arbor, Michigan. He graduated in 1982 from the United States Air Force Academy with a Bachelor's degree in Behavioral Sciences. He immediately entered undergraduate pilot training, 71st Student Squadron, Vance AFB, OK, earning his wings in 1983. He was a Distinguished Graduate from pilot instructor training in the T-37 at Randolph AFB, TX, before returning to Vance as an Instructor Pilot, Class Commander, and Flight Examiner, 71st Flying Training Wing in 1984. In 1987 Gary was a Distinguished Graduate from Squadron Officer School at Maxwell AFB, AL. That same year he was assigned to the 68th Air Refueling Wing and later the 4th Wing, Seymour Johnson AFB, NC, as Co-Pilot in the KC-10. He progressed to Aircraft Commander, Instructor Pilot, and Executive Officer, and in 1991 earned a Masters of Aeronautical Science degree from Embry Riddle Aeronautical University while at Seymour Johnson. Gary entered Michigan State University, East Lansing, in 1992 and earned a Master's degree in Counseling in 1994. He then joined the AF Academy's Department of Behavioral Sciences and Leadership as an Instructor. In 1995 he became a Counselor in the Cadet Counseling Center and was appointed as the Chief of the Leadership Development Programs. Gary entered the University of North Carolina at Chapel

Hill in 1996, where he earned his PhD in Developmental Psychology in 1999. Next he was assigned again to Vance AFB from 1999 until 2003 as an Instructor Pilot, then Operations Officer, and finally Commander in the 32nd Flying Training Squadron. Returning to the Academy in the Department of Behavioral Sciences and Leadership, Gary served as Deputy Department Head and Director of the Air Officer Commanding Master's Program. In 2004 Gary became the Head of the Department of Behavioral Sciences. He was appointed a Permanent Professor in 2005. Gary was instrumental in the stand-up of USAFA's Character and Leadership Center and co-authored its original vision. He also stood-up his department's first research center bringing well more than $1 million of behavioral sciences research to the Academy. He served at the Pentagon as the Air Force writer on the Secretary of Defense's Comprehensive Review Working Group studying the repeal of Don't Ask, Don't Tell in 2010. In 2011 he deployed as the Director of Staff, 379th Air Expeditionary Wing, Southwest Asia, in support of Operations ENDURING FREEDOM, NEW DAWN, and COMBINED JOINT TASK FORCE—HORN OF AFRICA. In 2015 Gary assumed the Chair of the Core Curriculum Revision Committee. In the spring of 2016, he presented this major curriculum revision for approval. It passed, becoming effective with the Class of 2021. Gary was chosen to be Vice Dean of the Faculty in 2016 and served in that position until he assumed the newly created position of Vice Dean for Strategy and Curriculum in 2018.

COLONEL
REX R. KIZIAH

Permanent Professor 2006–Present

B.S., *United States Air Force Academy*
Ph.D., *University of Texas at Austin*

Rex Kiziah, the Academy's 82nd Permanent Professor, was born in 1959 in Granite Falls, North Carolina. He was a 1981 Distinguished Graduate of the United States Air Force Academy, where he was named the Outstanding Cadet in Physics. He immediately entered the University of Texas at Austin, earning a Physics PhD in 1984. From 1984 to 1988 Rex conducted neutral particle beam research for the Strategic Defense Initiative at the Air Force Weapons Laboratory, Kirtland AFB, NM. He returned to the Academy's Department of Physics, 1988–1993, teaching introductory courses and developing advanced classes in Computational Physics and Chaotic Dynamics, while directing the Academy's Nuclear Radiation Laboratory. He was named the department's Outstanding Military Educator in 1991. Following a year at Air Command and Staff College, Maxwell AFB, AL, 1993–1994, Rex was assigned to the Office of the Secretary of Defense (Nuclear, Chemical, and Biological Defense Programs), the Pentagon, Washington, DC, as Special Assistant for Research and Technology, 1994–1996, and Deputy Program Manager, Counterproliferation, 1996–1997. From 1997 to 1999 he served at the National Reconnaissance Office, Chantilly, VA, working national space requirements and technology issues, followed by a year as a student at Air War College, Maxwell AFB, AL. Then in 2000–2002 he received an assignment to the Air Staff Directorate of Global Power Programs, where he was Chief, Theater Air Defense Division, then Chief, Combat Support and Joint Counterair Division. Among his duties were directing, planning, and budgeting for Air Force air and missile defense programs, including Airborne Laser development. From 2002 to 2004 he was assigned to the Space and Missile Systems Center, AF Space Command, Los Angeles AFB, CA, where he directed the planning, development, testing, deployment, and sustainment of Presidential-priority space superiority systems. From 2004 to 2006 Rex was the Commander of the Phillips Research Site and Material Wing Director for the Air Force Research Laboratory's Space Vehicles Directorate, Kirtland AFB, NM. He was the senior leader responsible for research and development of advanced technologies in national security space and directed energy. Rex returned again to the Academy in 2006 as Permanent Professor and Head, Department of Physics. In 2011–2013 he took a sabbatical assignment as Deputy Chief Scientist, HQ AF Space Command, Peterson AFB, CO, where he crafted and executed the Command's first-ever Visionary Workshop, producing dozens of key recommendations and strategic insights for 20-year planning efforts. His Academy faculty team, in addition to teaching physics principals to all cadets, engages cadet Physics and Meteorology majors with relevant research through the Laser and Optics Research Center, Space Physics and Atmospheric Research Center, Center for Physics Education Research, Center for Space Situational Awareness Research, and the Academy's Observatory.

BRIGADIER GENERAL
THOMAS L. YODER

Permanent Professor 2006–2018
Vice Dean of the Faculty 2012–2014

B.S., *United States Air Force Academy*
M.S., *University of Washington*
M.S., *Army Command and General
    Staff College*
M.A., *Naval War College*
Ph.D., *University of Colorado*

Tom Yoder, the Academy's 83rd Permanent Professor, was born in 1960 and raised in Somerset County, Pennsylvania. In 1982 he received a Bachelor's degree in Astronautical Engineering as a Distinguished Graduate from the United States Air Force Academy and was commissioned a second lieutenant. He accepted a Boeing Fellowship for Engineering from the University of Washington, Seattle, and graduated with a Master's degree in Aeronautics and Astronautics in 1983. Tom entered pilot training in late 1983 at Reese AFB, TX, and earned his wings in 1984 as a Distinguished Graduate. He reported in 1985 to Randolph AFB, TX, for T-38 instructor training, earning his instructor rating as a Distinguished Graduate. Beginning his instructor duties in 1985 back at Reese AFB, he served as an Assistant Flight Commander, a Check Pilot, and as Wing Executive Officer to two consecutive training wing commanders. During this time, he also attended Squadron Officer School where he again earned Distinguished Graduate honors. In 1987 Tom reported to the 337th Bomb Squadron, Dyess AFB, TX, for training and upgrade in the B-1B bomber. During his time in the B-1B, he served as Aircraft Commander, Mission Commander, and Assistant Flight Commander. In 1992 Tom joined the faculty of the USAF Academy's Department of Astronautics as an Instructor. During the next three years, he assumed the additional duties of Instructor Pilot, Squadron

Training Officer, and Associate Air Officer Commanding for a cadet squadron. Tom earned the department's 1995 Outstanding Academy Educator award. He reported to the Army Command and General Staff College in Leavenworth, KS, in 1995 and expended the extra effort to graduate with a Master's degree in Military Arts and Sciences in 1996. He then entered graduate school at the University of Colorado, Boulder, and earned his PhD in Aerospace Engineering in 1999. Tom returned to the Department of Astronautics, 1999–2003, as an Assistant Professor. During this time he spent five months beginning in late 1999 as the Commander, 332nd Expeditionary Operations Support Squadron, Kuwait. In 2000 Tom became the Deputy Head of the Department of Astronautics as an Associate Professor. From 2003 to 2004 he attended the Naval War College, Newport, RI, graduating with distinction and a Master's degree in National Security and Strategic Studies. He then moved to HQ NORAD-US NORTHCOM, Peterson AFB, CO, and served as Chief, Capabilities Development and Integration Division of the Requirements, Analysis, and Resources Directorate. In 2006 Tom was appointed a Permanent Professor and Head of the Department of Engineering Mechanics, where he managed the Academy's largest research center, the Center for Aircraft Structural Life Extension, serving a number of organizations seeking aircraft structural integrity and life extension capabilities. During the first five years of his tenure, he piloted a cross-mission team that created the Academy's first institutional outcomes and chaired USAFA's 2009 NCAA certification efforts. He served as the Vice Dean of the Faculty, 2012–2014. Tom was promoted to brigadier general and retired in 2018.

BRIGADIER GENERAL
JOHN L. PUTNAM

Permanent Professor 2006–2016

B.S., *Michigan State University*
M.S., *University of Florida*
Ph.D., *University Maryland*

John Putnam, the Academy's 84th Permanent Professor, was born in Killeen, Texas, in 1956. The son of an Army officer, John spent his childhood years at many Army posts. In 1978 he graduated with Honors from Michigan State University, East Lansing, with a Bachelor's degree in Entomology. Upon graduation, he joined the US Peace Corps and worked in Thailand from 1978 to 1981, where he learned to speak Thai and worked as an Entomologist for the Thai Malaria Control Division. John then entered the University of Florida, Gainesville, and earned a Master's degree in Entomology in 1984. At Florida he studied the host-seeking behavior of the common malaria mosquito. In 1986, following a brief stint at a Florida mosquito control district, John was directly commissioned into the Air Force's Biomedical Sciences Corps as a Medical Entomologist. His first assignment, 1986–1989, was to the Aerial Spray Flight, 356th Tactical Airlift Squadron, Rickenbacker Air National Guard Base, Columbus, OH. The Spray Flight trained for and studied pesticide application with C-130 aircraft to control disease outbreaks. In 1989, through a Biomedical Sciences Corps scholarship, John began a doctoral program in Medical Entomology at the University of Maryland. For his dissertation he studied the feeding behavior of the yellow fever mosquito and was awarded his PhD in 1993. His follow-on assignment was to HQ Air Mobility Command, Scott AFB, IL, 1992–1995. As the Command Entomologist, John oversaw the Command's base-level pest management programs. In 1996 John joined the Air Force Academy's Department of Biology as an Instructor and later Associate Professor and Deputy for Academic Operations. For the year 2000, John completed a sabbatical as the Deputy Chief of Programming for the Academy's 10th Civil Engineering Group, where he started a biological control program for the base's noxious weeds. He then returned to the Biology Department as a Professor and the Deputy Department Head, 2001–2003. In 2003 John was assigned to the Air Force Institute for Operational Health at Brooks City-Base, TX. As Chief, Military-Civilian Partnerships, John first worked to unite Air Force and civilian preparatory efforts for terrorism. Then, as Chief, Medical Zoology, Epidemiological Services, John led the Air Force's medical zoology consultative and investigative service. While at Brooks, John deployed to Tallil Air Base, Iraq, as Chief of the *Leishmania* Surveillance and Investigation Team. His team monitored and studied sand fly–borne disease, leading to several noteworthy publications on the impact of sand flies on US military operations. In 2006 John was appointed Permanent Professor and Head of the Air Force Academy's Department of Biology. In 2012 he started a sabbatical year at the Department of Entomology, Walter Reed Army Institute of Research, Silver Spring, MD, to conduct a field trial in Thailand of control techniques for the yellow fever mosquito. During his tenure at the Academy, John sustained a community of biologists who engaged cadets through classroom experience, independent study, and summer internships in support of national security interests. John was promoted to brigadier general and retired in 2016.

John is enjoying his Colorado retirement by mountain biking and snowboarding.

COLONEL
CHERYL A. KEARNEY

Permanent Professor 2007–Present

B.A., *University of Pittsburgh*
M.A., *Naval Postgraduate School*
M.S., *National Defense University*
Ph.D., *Georgetown University*

Cheryl Kearney (née Lynd), the Academy's 85th Permanent Professor, was born in Pittsburgh, Pennsylvania, in 1961. She was an Honor Graduate from the University of Pittsburgh in 1983 with a Bachelor's degree in Legal Studies and received her commission through the AFROTC program. She entered the basic intelligence courses at Lowry AFB, CO, in 1984. Upon graduation later that year, she was assigned as the Chief of the Intelligence Branch, 44th Strategic Missile Wing, Ellsworth AFB, SD. In 1986 Cheryl was assigned to the Naval Postgraduate School and Defense Language Institute (Russian), Monterey, CA. She graduated in 1988 with a Master of Arts in National Security Affairs and was assigned to Scott AFB, IL, as Chief of the Russian and Warsaw Pact desks for Military Airlift Command. Cheryl was next assigned to NATO, Supreme HQ Allied Powers Europe, Casteau, Belgium, where she served as a Political/Military Strategic Analyst. In 1993 Cheryl joined the USAF Academy faculty in the Department of Political Science. She returned to school at Georgetown University in Washington, DC, and received a PhD in American Government in 1999. Assigned to the Office of the Secretary of Defense in the Pentagon, she served as the Executive Director, Defense Policy Board and Military Assistant to the Assistant Secretary of Defense for Strategy and Threat Reduction, Office of the Under Secretary of Defense for Policy. Cheryl moved within the Pentagon in 2001 to join the Executive Action Group supporting the Secretary and the Chief of Staff of the Air Force and served as Chief, Political and Legislative Affairs. In 2003 Cheryl became a student at the National War College, Ft. McNair, Washington, DC, and earned a Master's degree in National Security Strategy from National Defense University in 2004. She then moved to Misawa Air Base, Japan, where she served as the Deputy and Interim Group Commander of the 373rd Intelligence Group. Cheryl's next assignment in 2006 was as Deputy Director, National Security Agency/Central Security Service Colorado at Buckley AFB, CO. Cheryl was appointed Permanent Professor and Head of the Department of Political Science in 2007. From 2011 to 2012 she deployed to Forward Operating Base Union III, Bagdad, Iraq, as Deputy Director, Chief Initiative Group, Office of Security Cooperation, Iraq, and was one of fewer than 200 officers to remain in Iraq after the pullout in 2011. Returning to her position as Department Head, she had the additional duty of Social Sciences Division Chair from 2015 to 2016. In 2016 Cheryl began a sabbatical assignment as a Supreme Court Fellow, only the third military officer selected to be a Fellow since the program began in 1973, and was assigned to the Office of the Counselor to the Chief Justice, Supreme Court of the United States. Cheryl returned to her duties at the Academy in 2017. She leads a department that prepares cadets to comprehend the political events that will shape their careers. Cadets examine political theories and ideologies, international relations, the politics of American and foreign governments, international security, defense decision making, organizational behavior, and political economy.

BRIGADIER GENERAL
ANDREW P. ARMACOST

Permanent Professor 2008–Present
Dean of the Faculty 2013–Present

B.S., *Northwestern University*
M.S., *Massachusetts Institute of*
  Technology
Ph.D., *Massachusetts Institute of*
  Technology

Andy Armacost, the Academy's 86th Permanent Professor, was born in 1967 in Portland, Maine, the son of a Coast Guardsman. He graduated with Honors as an AFROTC Distinguished Graduate from Northwestern University, Evanston, IL, in 1989 with a Bachelor's degree in Industrial Engineering. That fall he was assigned as a Program Manager in the Integration Test Facility, Electronic Systems Center, Hanscom AFB, MA. In 1991 he joined the Electronic Systems Center Commander's Staff for a year and then became the Center's Program Manager to develop the Marine Corps Intelligence Center. In 1993 Andy entered the Massachusetts Institute of Technology, Cambridge, as a student and Draper Fellow. He earned a Master's degree in Operations Research in 1995. Andy then joined the Department of Management at the Academy as an Instructor. He graduated from Squadron Officer School, Maxwell AFB, AL, in 1996 as a Distinguished Graduate. In 1997 Andy became a student again at MIT and earned his PhD in Operations Research in 2000. He then returned to the Academy as a professor in the Department of Management. His dissertation was selected for the George B. Dantzig Dissertation Award by the Institute for Operations Research and the Management Sciences (INFORMS) in 2001. In 2002–2003 he attended the Air Command and Staff College, Maxwell AFB, AL. Also in 2003, INFORMS named him a Franz Edelman Laureate as a member of the United Parcel Service Team recognized for their significant contribution to work selected as representative of the best applications of analytical decision making in the world. From 2007 to 2008, Andy spent a sabbatical year as Chief Analyst and Division Chief, Analysis and Assessments, AF Space Command, Peterson AFB, CO. In 2008 Andy was appointed Permanent Professor and Head of the Department of Management. Among his key accomplishments in that role were revising the department's core course, growing capstone opportunities for cadets, increasing cross-departmental work on innovative technology, and redesigning the Systems Engineering program. In 2013 he was the 9th Permanent Professor selected to become the Dean of the Faculty, a position he presently holds. As the Dean, he has led the organization during tumultuous times following Congressional budget sequester and significant staffing reductions. At the same time, Andy oversaw efforts to revise the institution's approach to outcomes assessment, to review and significantly revise the core curriculum, to promote greater opportunities for technology transfer, and to enhance the Academy's efforts to educate cadets in areas related to air, space, and cyberspace. He led the successful planning and budgeting efforts to secure construction, personnel, and operations funding for Air Force CyberWorx (a new AF public-private design center focused on cyber capability), located at the Academy.

BRIGADIER GENERAL
JEFFREY T. BUTLER

Permanent Professor 2008–2018

B.S., *United States Air Force Academy*
M.S., *Florida State University*
M.A., *Air Command and Staff*
  College
Ph.D., *Air Force Institute of Technology*

Jeff Butler, the Academy's 87th Permanent Professor, was born in Fort Campbell, Kentucky, in 1966. He graduated from the United States Air Force Academy in 1988 as a Distinguished Graduate with a Bachelor's degree with Honors in Mathematics and Electrical Engineering. His first assignment was as Lead F-16 Radar Engineer in the 84th Test Squadron, USAF Air Warfare Center, Tyndall AFB, FL. While assigned to Tyndall, he earned a Master's degree in Electrical Engineering from Florida State University in 1991. He was a Distinguished Graduate of Squadron Officer School, Maxwell AFB, AL, in 1993. He then was assigned to the F-22 System Program Office, Aeronautical Systems Center, Wright-Patterson AFB, OH, as an Armament Integration Program Manager and Support Systems Engineer. In 1995 Jeff entered the Air Force Institute of Technology at Wright-Patterson and earned a PhD in Computer Engineering in 1998. Remaining at Wright-Patterson, he next served as an Adjunct Professor at AFIT as well as Deputy Chief, Radio Frequency Sensors Division, Sensors Directorate, Air Force Research Laboratory. In 2000 Jeff became a student again at the Air Command and Staff College, Maxwell AFB, leaving as a Distinguished Graduate with a Master's degree in Military Studies in 2001. He next joined the Secretary of the Air Force Office of Research, Washington, DC, as the Chief of the Joint Programs Division. In 2003 he became Chief of the Advanced Spacecraft Division, National Reconnaissance Office, Chantilly, VA. Jeff became a National Defense Fellow for Russia and Eurasian Security Issues at the Institute for the Study of Conflict, Ideology, and Policy at Boston University, MA, in 2005. He returned to Washington in 2006 to become Deputy Director for Systems Engineering of the Missile Defense Agency. In 2008 Jeff was appointed Permanent Professor and Head, Department of Electrical and Computer Engineering. He directed an active faculty and cadet research program and in 2009 established the Academy Center for Unmanned Aerial Systems Research. His department provided all cadets with an introduction to the principles of Air Force electronic and cyber systems through analysis and evaluation of analog, digital, and radio-frequency systems, and it offered Electrical Engineering majors four different areas of study: electronics, communications, computer systems, and controls. From 2013 to 2014 he was on sabbatical assignment as Senior Technical Advisor and Cyber Domain Chief at HQ NORAD, USNORTHCOM, Peterson AFB, CO. Jeff served as the Officer in Charge of the Cadet Sabre Drill Team, 2009–2013; was the Engineering Division Chair, 2015–2018; and chaired the Class of 2018 Academic Review Committee. Jeff was promoted to brigadier general and retired in 2018.

COLONEL
DANIEL URIBE

Permanent Professor 2008–Present

B.S., *United States Air Force Academy*
M.S., *Air Force Institute of Technology*
Ph.D., *Arizona State University*

Dan Uribe, the Academy's 88th Permanent Professor, was born in Juarez, Mexico, in 1964. He immigrated to the United States in 1978 and became a US Citizen in 1984 while a student at the Air Force Academy Preparatory School. He graduated from the Academy in 1988 with a Bachelor's degree in Astronautical Engineering and a minor in Spanish. His first assignment was as a Strategic Missile Guidance Systems Engineer, Test and Evaluation Group, Vandenberg AFB, CA, where he was lead Guidance and Control Engineer for two ICBM programs. In 1991 Dan was assigned to the Air Force Institute of Technology, Wright-Patterson AFB, OH, earning his Master's degree in Astronautical Engineering in 1992. His thesis involved GPS Navigation on reentry vehicles. He next went to the 46th Test Group, Holloman AFB, NM, 1993–1995, first as Chief, Global Positioning System Integration Element; then Chief, Navigation Systems Element; and finally Chief, Group Financial Management Branch. Dan led efforts to integrate GPS into every AF weapon system. In 1995 he was assigned to the Academy's Department of Foreign Languages as an Instructor of Spanish, but he was also an Instructor of Astronautics and even taught the core Astronautics course in Spanish. He left the Academy in 1999 to serve as Chief, Advanced Development and Program Manager, Joint Precision Approach and Landing Systems Program, Electronic Systems Center, Hanscom AFB, MA. In that position, he led a joint program to develop the next-generation precision landing system for the Air Force, Army, and Navy, and opened technical discussions to adopt the system as the NATO standard. In 2000 Dan entered a doctoral program at Arizona State University, Tempe, earning his PhD degree in Educational Technology in 2002. His research focused on using a computer-mediated environment for language production while working collaboratively to solve complex problems. This work led directly to acquisition of the language laboratory system still in use at the Academy today. Returning to the Academy, he served the Department of Foreign Languages as Operations Officer, Deputy Department Head, and in 2006, Department Head. During 2007, he was deployed for a year to the NATO Air Component Command HQ, Izmir, Turkey, as the Lessons Learned Branch Chief and Executive Officer to the Commander. During this time, he led NATO inspection teams to assess the readiness of Ukraine to join the Alliance. Dan was appointed Permanent Professor and Head, Department of Foreign Languages, in 2008. In this role, he led the largest expansion in personnel and programs in the department's history with the addition of Portuguese and the establishment of cadet study abroad programs in foreign universities. Dan served on the Air Force Language Action Panel, the Air Force Language and Culture Executive Steering Committee, and the Air Force Security Cooperation Working Group. He also led efforts to align the curriculum with new World Readiness Standards for foreign language education. During 2014–2015 he was on sabbatical assignment as Executive Officer, Senior Military Advisor, and Defense Policy Advisor to the Ambassador, US Mission to NATO, Brussels, Belgium. During this time, Dan represented the United States in the Political Security and Cooperation Committee and provided advice on defense matters. Returning in 2015, Dan also has served as Chair of the Humanities Division.

COLONEL
JOSEPH E. SANDERS III

Permanent Professor 2010–2015

B.S., *Central Washington University*
M.S., *Lesley College*
Ph.D., *Colorado State University*

Joe Sanders, the Academy's 89th Permanent Professor, was born in Alexandria, Louisiana, in 1969. In 1991 he earned his Bachelor's degree in Industrial Electronics Technology from Central Washington University, Ellensburg, and received his commission through AFROTC. His first assignment was to a Peacekeeper ICBM crew at F.E. Warren AFB, WY, 1992–1996, where he progressed to Missile Combat Crew Commander and Assistant Division Chief. In 1995 he received his Master's degree in Management from Lesley College, Cambridge, MA. Joe came to the Air Force Academy's Department of Behavioral Sciences and Leadership, 1996–2000, as Instructor, then Assistant Professor and Chief Leadership Consultant. Selected for a doctorate, he attended Colorado State University, Fort Collins, where he earned his PhD in Education and Human Resource Development in 2003. From 2003 to 2005 he was Chief, Diversity Policy and Strategic Leadership, Assistant Secretary of the Air Force, Manpower and Reserve Affairs, the Pentagon, Washington, DC, where he developed and reviewed human capital policies and strategic plans for the Secretary of the Air Force. Joe was Commander of the 320th Training Squadron, Lackland AFB, TX, from 2005 to 2007, transforming recruits into highly motivated airmen. During this time, he was deployed for five months to Saudi Arabia as Commander, 64th Expeditionary Support Squadron. He returned to the Academy's Department of Behavioral Sciences and Leadership in 2007 as Deputy Department Head for Leadership, responsible for designing and assessing leadership education programs for cadets and faculty. In 2008 he moved to the Academy's Center for Character and Leadership Development as Assistant Director for Scholarship. In 2010 Joe was appointed Permanent Professor and Director of the Center. He was the first to occupy this newly established position under the Commandant of Cadets. The Center provides leadership, honor, and character education for the Cadet Wing; oversees administration of the Cadet Honor Code; hosts several large fora including the annual National Character and Leadership Symposium; and conducts research, instruction, and assessment for advancing the 21st century profession of arms. During his tenure, Joe was instrumental in publishing the Journal of Character and Leadership Integration, the Academy's first peer-reviewed forum in this field of study. He guided the creation of a nationally award-winning character coaching program and initiated character development camps for local high school students. In addition to laying the foundation for expanded research, integration, and outreach, he also provided expert insight on the design, functionality, and architecture of the Academy's showpiece Center for Character and Leadership Development building, Polaris Hall, completed in 2016. He retired in 2015.

After retirement, Joe founded the Touchstone Leadership Academy; as its President, he leads a team of professionals committed to improving community through character and leadership transformation. He is also the Director of Leadership Development for All American Leadership, LLC, which works with businesses to improve leadership and corporate culture. Additionally, Joe is an Adjunct Professor at the University of Colorado, Colorado Springs.

COLONEL
TROY R. HARTING

Permanent Professor 2014–Present
Vice Dean of the Faculty
  2018–Present

B.S., *United States Air Force Academy*
M.B.A., *University of Pittsburgh*
Ph.D., *University of Virginia*

Troy Harting, the Academy's 90th Permanent Professor, was born in Fallston, Maryland, in 1971. He graduated from the United States Air Force Academy in 1993 with a Bachelor's degree in Management. He accepted a USAFA Graduate Studies Program scholarship from the Management Department, studying at the University of Pittsburgh, where he earned his Master's degree in Business Administration in 1994. He then was assigned as a Program Manager in the Spaced-Based Infrared Systems Program Office, Space and Missile Systems Center, Los Angeles AFB, CA. In 1997 Troy became a Program Manager, Information Warfare Programs, Intelligence, Surveillance, and Reconnaissance Program Office, Electronic Systems Center, Hanscom AFB, MA. Next he was assigned in 2000 as an Instructor of Management and Advisor in Charge in the Department of Management, USAF Academy. In 2002 Troy entered the doctoral program at the University of Virginia, Charlottesville, where he earned his PhD in Business Administration in 2005. He was then assigned as Program Manager in the Acquisition Chief Process Office, a branch of the Acquisition Integration Leadership Directorate, Office of the Assistant Secretary of the Air Force for Acquisition, the Pentagon, Washington, DC. He was charged with executing a variety of acquisition reform initiatives. Troy became the Military Assistant to the Deputy Assistant Secretary for Acquisition Integration in 2007. Moving to Europe in 2008, Troy was assigned as a Project Director and Panel Executive, NATO System Analysis and Studies Panel, NATO Research and Technology Organization (RTO) in Neuilly-sur-Seine, France. In this role he supervised, advised, and assisted in the execution of over 20 research activities aimed at furthering basic technology research on behalf of NATO. Returning to the Academy in 2011, he taught as an Assistant Professor and was Director of Operations in the Department of Management. After a short deployment to Creech AFB, NV, to lead the construction of various upgrades for the remotely piloted aircraft of the 432nd Air Expeditionary Wing, he was selected to be the Director of the Commander's Action Group for the Dean of the Faculty in 2013. Troy was appointed Permanent Professor and Head of the Department of Management in 2014 to lead a unit that aims to produce critical thinkers who can adapt quickly in today's dynamic, technologically complex, global environment. The department is heavily engaged in the Systems Engineering and Operations Research majors, disciplines that address the development and modeling of large, complex systems. In 2016 the Department of Management's flagship Management major was reaccredited by the Association to Advance Collegiate Schools of Business, a designation earned by only 5 percent of business and management programs worldwide. From 2016 to 2018 Troy was Chair of the Social Sciences Division. He was chosen to be Vice Dean of the Faculty in 2018 and is currently serving in that position.

COLONEL
JENNIFER C. ALEXANDER

Permanent Professor 2014–Present

B.S., *University of Arizona*
M.S., *Texas A&M University*
Ph.D., *University of Utah*

Jen Alexander, the Academy's 91st Permanent Professor, was born in Augsburg, West Germany, in 1970. She attended the University of Arizona on a four-year AFROTC scholarship, graduating in 1992 with a Bachelor's degree in Atmospheric Science and an Air Force commission. Her first assignment was as a Wing Weather Officer, 410th Bomb Wing, K.I. Sawyer AFB, MI, 1992–1994. She was next sent to Texas A&M, where she was awarded her Master's degree in Meteorology in 1996. Following school, Jen was assigned to the Air Force Weather Agency, Offutt AFB, NE, as Programmer and Lead Analyst, Numerical Weather Models Team, where she was part of a team that increased the resolution of the Air Force's operational weather model 100-fold. From 1998 to 2001 she was the Weather Flight Commander, 21st Air Support Operations Squadron, providing weather support for US Army aviation operations at Fort Polk, LA. She spent the subsequent three years at the University of Utah, receiving her PhD in Meteorology in 2004. Jen then returned to Offutt for a series of assignments at the Air Force Weather Agency. As Chief, Warfighter Support Development Team, she improved operational forecasting of turbulence and icing. As Chief, Training Requirements Branch, and then Chief, Training Division, she was responsible for all non-resident training requirements for Air Force weather officers and enlisted personnel. As Director of Operations, 2nd Weather Squadron, 2007–2008, she oversaw weather operations supporting space, satellite support, Special

Operations Forces, and National Intelligence Community operators. Her next assignment was to Patrick AFB, FL, as Director of Operations, 45th Weather Squadron, where she led forecast support to the Space Shuttle and Atlas and Delta rockets. From 2009 to 2011 she was the Commander, 368th Recruiting Squadron at Hill AFB, UT, a 500,000-square-mile zone with 100 recruiters. In 2011 she brought her expertise to the Academy faculty as Assistant Professor and Director of Meteorology, Department of Economics and Geosciences. In 2012 Jen was selected as Director, Commander's Action Group, Dean of the Faculty, where she served for a year before taking a deployment to Kabul, Afghanistan, as Joint Command Chief Meteorological Officer with the International Security Assistance Force. Returning to the Academy at the end of 2013, she was the Dean of the Faculty's Director of Staff for over 700 faculty members. In 2014 she was selected as the Academy's 91st Permanent Professor and Head, Department of Economics and Geosciences, the first meteorologist to be selected for this position. Jen is a strong supporter of the American Meteorological Society, having served on its Council and Executive Committee, and five sub-committees. Her department's Economics major is the scientific study of decision-making, analyzing tradeoffs to recommend optimal decisions, and making predictions about behavior. It allows cadets to focus on business, finance, international economics, public policy, or quantitative economics. The Meteorology major uniquely focuses on the impact of weather on military operations. The Geospatial Science major provides excellent international insight and cultural understanding of the battle space.

COLONEL
LINELL A. LETENDRE

Permanent Professor 2015–Present

B.S., *United States Air Force Academy*
J.D., *University of Washington*

Linell Letendre (née Bartholic), the Academy's 92nd Permanent Professor, was born in Jackson, Michigan, in 1974. She graduated from the United States Air Force Academy in 1996 as a Distinguished Graduate with a Bachelor's degree in Astronautical Engineering. She served as the Spring Cadet Wing Commander her first class year. After graduation, she served for two years as an Acquisitions Officer for the Air Force/Navy Joint Air to Surface Standoff Missile Program Office, Eglin AFB, FL. From 1998 to 2001 she was a student in the Funded Legal Education Program at the University of Washington Law School, earning her Juris Doctorate with High Honors. She entered the judge advocate field in 2001 as Chief of Environmental Law and General Law, 375th Airlift Wing, Scott AFB, IL, and later she served as Area Defense Counsel at Scott, 2003–2004. In 2004 Linell came back to the Academy for a three-year tour as Assistant Professor of Law. During this period, she published on salient policy/legal issues, including "Religion in the Military: Navigating the Channel Between the Religion Clauses" (2007). Following her faculty tour, she was assigned as Chief of Strategic Communication Branch, Office of the Judge Advocate General, Pentagon, Washington, DC, 2007–2008. She next served as Deputy Chief, Military Personnel Branch, General Litigation Division, Air Force Legal Operations Agency, Arlington, Virginia, 2008–2009, and as Executive Officer, Civil Law and Litigation Directorate, 2009–2010. Moving back to the Pentagon, she served as Legal Advisor, Department of Defense Comprehensive Review Working Group, 2010, and as Air Staff Counsel, Administrative Law Division, Office of the Judge Advocate General, 2011. Returning to the Air Force Legal Operations Agency, now at Joint Base Andrews, MD, she served as Deputy Chief, Trial and Appellate Government Counsel Division, 2011–2012, before becoming the Staff Judge Advocate, 375th Air Mobility Wing, Scott AFB, 2012–2014. Through these assignments, she defended Airmen in courts-martial, represented the Air Force in appellate reviews, defended the Air Force in a range of federal civil litigation, and advised on important legal and policy issues, including those surrounding repeal of Don't Ask, Don't Tell. She also co-authored "Military Lawyering and Professional Independence in the War on Terror" (2008), which was published in the *Stanford Law Review*. In 2014–2015 she was a Distinguished Graduate from the Eisenhower School, National Defense University, Washington, DC, where three of her autonomous systems papers won writing awards and were later published, including "Women Warriors: Why the Robotics Revolution Changes the Combat Equation" (*Prism*, 2016). Linell was appointed Permanent Professor and Head, Department of Law in 2015. Early in her tenure as the Law Permanent Professor, she established two major initiatives, the Leadership and Alternative Disputes Resolution Program and the Law, Technology, and Warfare Research Cell.

COLONEL
JOHN A. CHRIST

Permanent Professor 2015–2018

B.S., *United States Air Force Academy*
M.S., *Air Force Institute of Technology*
Ph.D., *University of Michigan*

John Christ, the Academy's 93rd Permanent Professor, was born in Downey, California, in 1973. He graduated from the United States Air Force Academy in 1996 with a double major in Civil Engineering and Environmental Engineering. He immediately entered the Air Force Institute of Technology, won the Commandant's Award for best thesis, and earned a Master's degree in Engineering and Environmental Management in 1998. He was then assigned as an Environmental Engineer, Environmental Flight, Civil Engineering Squadron, Minot AFB, ND. In 1999 he became the Chief of the Environmental Engineering Flight, Civil Engineering Squadron, Prince Sultan Air Base, Saudi Arabia, for five months. Returning to Minot in mid-1999, he was a Design Engineer and Chief of Construction Management in the Engineering Flight. In 2000 John was assigned as Chief, Plans and Programs, Engineering Flight, Civil Engineering Squadron, Osan Air Base, South Korea. He returned to the States in 2001 for five weeks to complete Squadron Officer School, Maxwell AFB, AL. In 2002 he entered graduate school at the University of Michigan, Ann Arbor, was awarded their Distinguished Achievement Award, and earned his PhD in Environmental Engineering in 2005. John joined the AF Academy faculty in 2005 as an Assistant Professor and became Associate Professor, Deputy Department Head for Curriculum, and Faculty Development and Environmental Engineering Division Chief in the Department of Civil and Environmental

Engineering. He spent two months in 2007 as Faculty Advisor, National Military Academy of Afghanistan, Kabul. He won the Frank J. Seiler Award for research excellence in 2007 and in 2008 was the department's Outstanding Academy Educator. In 2008–2009 John again was assigned overseas for six months to Al Udeid Air Base, Qatar, as Construction Management Officer-Gulf Region, AF Forces/A7, Combined Air and Space Operations Center. He next moved to Poggio Renatico, Italy, for five months as Chief of Information Operations for the Combined Forces Air Component Command that executed Operation UNIFIED PROTECTOR. The next seven months he spent as Branch Chief, Joint Military Air Cooperation, NATO Air Component Command, Izmir, Turkey. Returning to the Academy in 2012, John was promoted to Professor in 2014 and was Environmental Engineering Division Chief in the Department of Civil and Environmental Engineering. He was the USAFA Nominee for the US Professor of the Year Award in 2013. In 2014 he became the Director, Commander's Action Group for the Academy Superintendent. John became Permanent Professor and Head, Department of Civil and Environmental Engineering in 2015, engaging cadets in challenging courses that are complemented by hands-on experiences in surveying as well as construction methods and materials at the 50-acre Field Engineering and Readiness Laboratory. He is a registered Professional Engineer in Colorado. John retired in 2018.

COLONEL
MARGARET C. MARTIN

Permanent Professor 2016–Present

B.S., *United States Air Force Academy*
M.A., *College of William and Mary*
M.S., *Air Force Institute of Technology*
M.A.A.S., *School of Advanced Air*
 and Space Studies
Ph.D., *University of North Carolina*

Meg Martin, the Academy's 94th Permanent Professor, was born in Chicago, Illinois, in 1974. She graduated from the United States Air Force Academy in 1996 with a degree in History. Through the graduate studies program, she was sent immediately to the College of William and Mary, Williamsburg, VA, where she earned her Master's degree in History in 1997. Her first flying assignment was to specialized undergraduate pilot training at Laughlin AFB, TX, earning her wings in 1998. From 1998 to 2000 she was assigned as a Strategic Airlift Pilot flying the C-141B from Charleston AFB, SC. In 2000 she transitioned to the C-17A where she was selected for the Special Operations Low Level (SOLL) II mission. She flew numerous combat missions including the airdrop of the 27th Combat Engineering Battalion into Afghanistan and the airlift of Abrams main battle tanks to Balad Air Base, Iraq. As an Instructor and Evaluator Aircraft Commander, she was responsible for the upgrade and evaluation of pilots within the SOLL II program and helped implement night vision goggle assault landing training for the entire C-17A community. She returned to the Academy, 2005–2008, as Instructor and then Assistant Professor of History, winning the 2008 Shiner Award for excellence in teaching military history. Meg left the Academy in 2008 to become a student for three successive school assignments. First, from 2008 to 2009, she attended the Advanced Study of Air Mobility, USAF Expeditionary Center, Fort Dix, NJ, for which the Air Force Institute of Technology awarded her a Master of Science degree in Logistics. Next, from 2009 to 2010, she was a student at the School of Advanced Air and Space Studies (SAASS), Maxwell AFB, AL, the Air Force's graduate school for strategists. SAASS selected her to enter its faculty pipeline program and, after earning Air University's Master of Airpower Art and Science degree, she became a doctoral student in History at the University of North Carolina. Her PhD was awarded in 2014. Following her time as a doctoral student, Meg returned to the Academy in 2013 as Director of Operations, 306th Operations Support Squadron, underpinning the Academy's cadet airmanship programs. There, she also flew as an Instructor Pilot with the 557th Flying Training Squadron, supporting the Academy's powered flight program. In 2014 Air Mobility Command selected her to command the 571st Mobility Support Advisory Squadron, Travis AFB, CA, one of only two general purpose forces squadrons in the Air Force supporting the Building Partner Capacity mission. As the Commander, she led a team of 77 officers and enlisted members drawn from 30 different AF specialties. The squadron deployed in Mobile Training Teams across the US Southern Command area to provide instruction to partner-nation air forces in areas as diverse as airfield security, supply, aircraft maintenance, airdrop procedures, and crew resource management to improve interoperability. Meg is a Command Pilot with more than 3,100 flight hours in the C-17A, C-141B, T-53A, and TG-10B, including 320 combat hours in the C-17A. She was appointed Permanent Professor and Head, Department of History, in 2016. The department teaches history for the profession of arms as an essential foundation for effectively confronting complex and ambiguous situations.

COLONEL
JOHN D. CINNAMON

Permanent Professor 2016–2018

B.S., *United States Air Force Academy*
M.S., *University of Texas at Austin*
M.S., *National Defense University*
Ph.D., *Air Force Institute of Technology*

John Cinnamon, the Academy's 95th Permanent Professor, was born in 1969 in Seattle, Washington. He graduated with Academic Distinction from the United States Air Force Academy with a Bachelor's degree in Engineering Sciences in 1991. He immediately became a graduate student at the University of Texas at Austin, graduating with a Master's degree in Aerospace Engineering in 1992. John then reported to undergraduate pilot training at Laughlin AFB, TX. After receiving his wings in 1993, he became a C-5 Pilot, advanced to Aircraft Commander, and served as Chief of Squadron Safety at Dover AFB, DE. In late 1996 John was a Distinguished Graduate from Squadron Officer School at Maxwell AFB, AL. Reporting for the spring semester of 1997 to the USAFA Department of Aeronautics, John became an Instructor, both of Aeronautics and in the T-3 aircraft. In 1999 he moved to Beale AFB, CA, as a T-38 Instructor/Evaluator Pilot and Life Support Officer for the U-2 Program, 1st Reconnaissance Squadron. In 2001 he moved to the 9th Operations Support Squadron at Beale and served as Assistant Director of Operations and then Director of Operations Support while continuing his duties in the T-38. In 2003 John became a student again, this time at the Air Force Institute of Technology, Wright-Patterson AFB, OH. He received his PhD in Aeronautical Engineering in 2006 and was awarded the Ivan B. Thompson Leadership Award. From 2006 to 2011 he served as T-1 Instructor and Evaluator Pilot, Operations Officer, and then Commander in the 86th Flying Training Squadron back at Laughlin AFB. In mid-2011 John became a student at the Joint Advanced Warfighting School, Joint Forces Staff College (National Defense University), Norfolk, VA, graduating in 2012 as a Distinguished Graduate with a Master's degree in Joint Campaign Planning and Strategy. He next served as the Director of Plans, US Strategic Command Center for Combating Weapons of Mass Destruction/Defense Threat Reduction Agency, Fort Belvoir, VA. In 2013 he became the Lead Planner for the Secretary of Defense Syria Integration Group, the Pentagon, Washington, DC. He next was assigned in 2014 as the Commander and T-1 Instructor/Evaluator Pilot, 71st Operations Group, Vance AFB, OK. John returned to head the Department of Aeronautics at the Academy in 2016 and was appointed Permanent Professor. He led a department that provided every cadet an introduction to aircraft design, fluid mechanics, airfoil and wing aerodynamics, aircraft performance, and stability and control, and he oversaw the Aeronautics Research Center conducting research in aerodynamics, flight mechanics, propulsion, aircraft structures, and experimental methods. John retired in 2018.

COLONEL
SCOTT E. WILLIAMS

Permanent Professor 2016–Present

B.S., *Massachusetts Institute of*
  Technology
M.S., *North Carolina State University*
M.A., *Naval War College*
Ph.D., *North Carolina State University*

Scott Williams, the Academy's 96th Permanent Professor, was born in St. Paul, Minnesota, in 1969. He was commissioned in 1991 as an AFROTC graduate of the Massachusetts Institute of Technology with a Bachelor's degree in Mathematics. After a brief course in Acquisition Fundamentals at Lowry AFB, CO, Scott was assigned to Los Angeles AFB, CA, 1992–1996. While there, he spent two years as a Mission Algorithm Branch Chief in the Follow-On Early Warning Systems Program Office, a year as an Education with Aerospace Corporation Exchange Officer, and a final year as the Orbital Operations Manager in the Military Satellite Communications Joint Program Office where he directed the launch and deployment of defense communication satellites. Scott was then selected for an Academy faculty position and sent to North Carolina State University, Raleigh, where he earned his Master's degree in Applied Mathematics. He came to the Academy in December 1997 as an Instructor in the Department of Mathematical Sciences, but was soon selected for an Academy-sponsored doctoral program and sent in July 1999 back to North Carolina State. His PhD in Applied Mathematics was awarded in 2003. Following his studies, Scott went in January 2003 to Ramstein Air Base, Germany, to serve an intervening tour before returning to the Academy. While in Germany, he served as an Operations Analysis Branch Chief at the Warrior Preparation Center, where he stood-up the Air Force's first "A9" (Operations Analysis Directorate) as part of the operational staff supporting Operation IRAQI FREEDOM. In 2004 Scott was tasked with formalizing the A9 role on the emergent standing operational staff (then AFEUR, now 13th Air Force) as the Deputy Director and acting Director of the Air Forces Europe A9 before being selected later in 2004 to serve as Chief Analyst in the US Air Forces Europe Commander's Action Group. In 2006 he returned to the Academy as an Assistant Professor in the Department of Mathematical Sciences, where he remained until 2010, serving as the Calculus Division Chief and, later, the Deputy Head for Academics. His primary emphasis was on pedagogical initiatives aimed at improving the learning focus, quality, and relevance of the mathematics curriculum. He also deployed in 2008 as Military Advisor to the fledgling National Military Academy of Afghanistan, Kabul. From 2010 to 2012 Scott was assigned as Deputy Commander of the 35th Mission Support Group, Misawa Air Base, Japan. While there, he led the base's disaster response, recovery, and evacuation efforts during Operations Tomodachi and Pacific Passage following the earthquake, tsunami, and nuclear reactor incident in northern Japan. He next went as a student to the US Naval War College, Newport, RI, where he graduated in 2013 with Highest Distinction and yet another degree: Master of Arts in National Security and Strategic Studies. He was then assigned as Chief Analyst and Director of Analyses, Assessments, and Development in the AF Studies, Analyses, and Assessments Directorate, the Pentagon, Washington, DC. In this dual-hatted role, he managed the 1,100-member Operations Research Analyst career field and led strategic assessments directly informing corporate Air Force strategic planning choices. In 2016 Scott was named a Permanent Professor and appointed Head of the Department of Mathematical Sciences.

COLONEL
STEVEN C.M. HASSTEDT

Permanent Professor 2016–Present

B.S., *United States Air Force Academy*
M.S., *Southern Illinois University*
M.S., *Air Force Institute of Technology*
Ph.D., *Colorado State University*

Steve Hasstedt, the Academy's 97th Permanent Professor, was born in Denver, Colorado, in 1970, a third-generation Colorado native. He received his Bachelor's degree from the United States Air Force Academy with the Class of 1992. In his career he has served in numerous operational logistics assignments, beginning as Commander of Vehicle Operations and then the Combat Readiness and Resources Flight responsible for wing deployments at Luke AFB, AZ. In 1995 Steve was assigned to Charleston AFB, SC, where he held Flight Commander positions in the 437th Aerial Port Squadron, refining deployment, cargo, and aerial delivery operations with the C-17 initial cadre before being selected as the 437th Operations Group Executive Officer. From 1998 to 2000 he was Chief of the Cargo Operations Section, Directorate of Operations, Air Mobility Command, Scott AFB, IL, and in 2000 was recognized as the joint National Defense Transportation Association Junior Executive of the Year. He next attended Southern Illinois University, Edwardsville, in preparation for a faculty assignment, and earned his Master's degree in Environmental Sciences at the end of 2001. He joined the Academy's Department of Biology for the Spring 2002 semester, and over the next five semesters taught a variety of courses and served as the Academic Advisor in Charge for cadets in the Biology major. From 2004 to 2005 he was a student in the Advanced Study of Air Mobility program at the Air Mobility Warfare Center, Fort

Dix, NJ. This in-residence program culminated in a second Master of Science degree in Air Mobility/Logistics from the School of Engineering and Management, Air Force Institute of Technology. He was the first non-rated Commander of Detachment 1,715[th] Air Mobility Operations Group, Diego Garcia, British Indian Ocean Territory, 2005–2006, where he served as the primary advisor to the US Navy and British commanders on mobility operations. Steve then served at US Joint Forces Command, Joint Concept Development and Experimentation, Suffolk, VA, from 2006 to 2009. He led a multinational logistics working group consisting of personnel from NATO, the US Joint Staff, US Transportation Command, and 13 other nations focused on improving coalition logistics and developing a multinational guide to humanitarian assistance and disaster relief operations. This was followed by his second command, at Lajes Air Base, Azores, Portugal, 2009–2010, where he led the 729th Air Mobility Squadron to honors as Air Mobility Command's Small Air Terminal Unit of the Year for 2009. Steve returned stateside in 2010 to pursue his doctorate at Colorado State University, Fort Collins. He earned his PhD in Ecology from CSU in 2013 and returned to the Department of Biology as Assistant Professor and Director of Curriculum Integration. In 2014 he was assigned as the Dean's Director of Staff and was serving in that position when selected in 2016 as Permanent Professor and Head, Department of Biology. Steve's goal is to sustain the elite faculty community of Air Force professionals and biologists developing the ability to apply critical thinking and scientific reasoning/problem-solving skills in graduates who serve in the medical and health professions, as rated officers, and in many other Air Force careers.

COLONEL
MARK C. ANARUMO

Permanent Professor 2016–Present

B.S., *Rutgers University*
M.A., *Rutgers University*
Ph.D., *Rutgers University*

Mark Anarumo, the Academy's 98th Permanent Professor, was born in Middletown, New Jersey, in 1970. He joined the US Army in 1988 and served as an M-1 Abrams tank crewman at Ft. Hood, TX, and as a tank commander at Grafenwoehr, Germany, before his honorable discharge in 1990 to attend Air Force ROTC. In 1994 he was awarded a Bachelor's degree in Administration of Justice from Rutgers University, New Brunswick, NJ, and a commission as a Distinguished Graduate from AFROTC. A 1994 Honor Graduate of the Security Police Academy, he began his Air Force career with the 96th Security Police Squadron, Eglin AFB, FL. After a three-year assignment there, he was sent to graduate school and earned his Master's degree from the Rutgers School of Criminal Justice in 1999. His next assignment was to HQ Air Combat Command, Langley AFB, VA, 1999–2001, where he was Deputy Chief of Force Development and later Executive Officer to the Director of Security Forces. Then followed a deployment, 2001–2002, as Operations Officer, 363rd Expeditionary Security Forces Squadron, Prince Sultan Air Base, Al-Kharj, Saudi Arabia, and a tour as Operations Officer, 305th Security Forces Squadron, McGuire AFB, NJ, 2002–2003, after which Mark was sent back to Rutgers to pursue his doctorate. In 2005 he was awarded his PhD in Criminal Justice, completing his dissertation on terrorist threat forecasting. He was then assigned as Commander, 43rd Security Forces Squadron, Pope AFB, NC, 2005–2007, during which time he was deployed for six months as Commander, 376th Expeditionary Security Forces Squadron, Manas Air Base, Kyrgyzstan. From 2007 to 2010 Mark was the Chair of Homeland Security and Terrorism Studies at The Richard Stockton College of New Jersey, Pomona, NJ, providing graduate-level education for military and civilian personnel from the Department of Defense and other government agencies. In 2010–2011 he was Commander, Eighth Security Forces Squadron, Kunsan Air Base, Korea. He was then sent to Harvard University, 2011–2012, as a National Security Fellow at the John F. Kennedy School of Government. Next he became Chief, Programming Branch, Headquarters US Air Force, Washington, DC, 2012–2014. His final assignment before the Academy, 2014–2016, was as Vice Commander, 39th Air Base Wing, Incirlik AB, Turkey. He was responsible for the combat readiness of American units at Incirlik and four other geographically separated units in Turkey during periods of mission expansion, base attacks, dependent evacuations, and the establishment of Incirlik as the premier power projection platform for combat operations in Iraq and Syria. He is also a graduate of the Federal Bureau of Investigations National Academy, US Army Pathfinder School, US Army Air Assault School, and several courses at the US Air Force Special Operations School. Mark was appointed the Permanent Professor and Director of the Center for Character and Leadership Development in 2016. The Center's goal is to advance understanding and implementation of effective character and leadership development practices across military, academic, and athletic settings—for cadets, faculty, and staff. Mark responded to a short notice tasking and deployed to Korea from February to June 2018 in support of the United Nations PRESSURE CAMPAIGN against North Korea, directly contributing to North Korea's participation in multinational peace talks throughout 2018. He returned to the Center in summer 2018 and resumed the position of Director, reporting directly to the Academy Superintendent.

COLONEL
MAIYA D. ANDERSON

Permanent Professor 2017–Present

B.S., *United States Air Force Academy*
M.S., *Oregon State University*
M.Ed., *University of Washington*
Ph.D., *Ohio State University*

Maiya Anderson, the Academy's 99th Permanent Professor, was born in Seattle, Washington, in 1975. She graduated from the United States Air Force Academy in 1997 with a degree in Environmental Engineering. As a cadet, she led the Academy's women's swimming team to NCAA Division II national titles in 1995 and 1996, was a 12-time All-American as well as 2-time national champion, and was named the Academy's Most Valuable Female Athlete in 1997. Awarded an NCAA post-graduate scholarship, Maiya attended Oregon State University, Corvallis, earning her Master's degree in Bioresource Engineering in 1998. From 1998 to 2003, she was assigned to the Bioenvironmental Engineering Flight, Langley AFB, VA, rising to Deputy Flight Commander. During this tour, she deployed for four months to Prince Sultan Air Base, Saudi Arabia, as Bioenvironmental Engineering Flight Commander. Maiya was assigned to Hill AFB, UT, from 2003 to 2005, serving various roles including the Executive Officer for the 75th Medical Group. Her next assignment was to the Academy's Department of Athletics, 2005–2009, as Instructor, Course Director, Assistant Coach, Intercollegiate Program Manager, Chief of Scheduling, Executive Officer to the Deputy Director of Athletics, and Chief of the Physical Education Division, winning the department's Outstanding Academy Educator Award in 2007. During this time, Maiya began a Master's degree program in Intercollegiate Athletic Leadership through the University of

Washington, Seattle, receiving her degree in 2010. In 2009 Maiya pursued doctoral studies at Ohio State, Columbus, where she earned her PhD degree in Sport Management in 2012. She then returned to Hill AFB, 2012–2015, as Bioenvironmental Engineering Flight Commander and Deputy Squadron Commander, 75th Aerospace Medicine Squadron, earning Air Force Material Command's Biomedical Science Corps Team of the Year Award in 2015. From 2015 to 2017 she was assigned as Commander, 30th Medical Operations Squadron, Vandenberg AFB, CA. Her unit drove patient satisfaction, access to care, and provider productivity to number one in AF Space Command and won "Best Clinic of the Year" Award two years in a row. She returned to the Academy in July 2017 as Permanent Professor and Head, Department of Physical Education. In this capacity, she leads her team administering the Academy's curriculum of required and elective physical education courses as well as programs in cadet fitness and testing, reconditioning, and intramural sports. Over the years, she has been active in international competitions, helping the Armed Forces women's team to the military pentathlon championship in 2002 and 2004. Maiya also competed at the Ironman World Championships in 2001 and 2006 and is a six-time International Military Sports Council (CISM) world championship athlete in triathlon and orienteering. She was inducted into the Air Force Academy Athletic Hall of Fame in 2015 as an individual, and again honored in 2017 when the 1995 and 1996 swimming teams were inducted.

COLONEL
DAVID J. CASWELL

Permanent Professor 2018–Present

B.S., *United States Air Force Academy*
M.S., *Air Force Institute of Technology*
Ph.D., *Stanford University*

David Caswell, the Academy's 100th Permanent Professor, was born in 1979 in Alexandria, Virginia. He graduated from the United States Air Force Academy in 2001 with majors in Computer Science and Operations Research. David's first assignment was as a graduate student at the Air Force Institute of Technology, Wright-Patterson AFB, OH, where he earned his Master's degree in Computer Science in 2002. In his subsequent assignments, he applied his education in areas that included software design and engineering, artificial intelligence and automation development, intelligence analysis, decision and risk analysis, and information operations. From 2003 to 2005 he was assigned to the Air University's College of Aerospace Doctrine, Research, and Education, Maxwell AFB, AL, first as Chief, Joint Wargaming Development Section and later as Chief, Joint Warfare Simulation Integration Section. In the years 2005–2007 he was the Flight Commander, 29th Intelligence Squadron and Senior Military Analyst at NSA/CSS, Fort Meade, MD. The National Security Agency/Central Security Service (NSA/CSS) is the lead Department of Defense organization in cryptology, encompassing both Signals Intelligence and Information Assurance as well as cyberspace operations. From 2007 to 2010 David was a doctoral student at Stanford University. His dissertation research used artificial intelligence techniques to analyze national strategies for combating nuclear weapons proliferation. During this period, he completed the Program for Emerging Leaders at the

Center for the Study of Weapons of Mass Destruction, National Defense University, Fort McNair, Washington, DC. His PhD degree in Decision and Risk Analysis was awarded in 2010. Following Stanford, he was assigned, 2010–2012, as Chief, Analysis and Lessons Learned, 7th Air Force, Osan Air Base, Korea. In this position, he led the Commander's top issue resolution process as well as orchestrating several South Korea–wide command post and field training exercises for Air Force units. David came to the Academy in 2012 for a three-year tour as Assistant Professor of Computer Science. During this time he helped design the Academy's major in Computer and Network Security and directed several courses focused on cyber operations. He also designed and led planning for the Air Force Cyber Innovation Center (CyberWorx), which applies design thinking principles to solve Air Force cyber requirements. From 2015 to 2017 he was Commander of the 690th Network Support Squadron, Lackland AFB, TX, providing global tactical control of Air Force Information Network Operations through synchronization of activities across the Cyberspace Security and Control Weapon System, the Air Force Intranet Control Weapon System, the Air National Guard Network Operations Squadron, and base communication squadrons. David returned to the Academy in 2017 as a Permanent Professor nominee and Head of the newly named Department of Computer and Cyber Sciences. He was appointed a Permanent Professor in early 2018. He leads a faculty that helps cadets develop computer-based skills that can be applied in all Air Force career fields. Their Center for Cyberspace Research focuses on cyber warfare, information assurance, unmanned aerial systems, and cyberspace education.

THE PERMANENT PROFESSOR BADGE
by Mark K. Wells, Brigadier General, USAF (Ret)

The unique badge worn by Permanent Professors at the United States Air Force Academy was developed in 1966 by Brigadier General Robert F. McDermott, the Academy's first permanent Dean of the Faculty and its first Permanent Professor. The badge, which has remained unchanged for 50 years, is shown at the right. The major design elements include an outer ring 2½ inches in diameter, consisting of indented tetrahedrals—meant to symbolize the spires of the Academy's Cadet Chapel. There are 13 stars between. The center of the device, consisting of a gold eagle sitting on a wreath in front of a white cloud, is enameled and has a plated satin finish. It is further surrounded by a field of ultramarine blue. The divided shield underneath depicts the Earth's atmosphere in light blue and outer space in black. Both are crossed by an ascending five-pointed star with three rays passing through an orbit, over a burning lamp. The motto, black lettering on the gold scroll, reads "Potestas Doctrinae Vitam Sustinet," which corresponds roughly to the inscription on the Academy's Eagle and Fledgling statue, "Man's Flight Through Life Is Sustained by the Power of His Knowledge."

ORIGIN AND DEVELOPMENT

Permanent Professors have existed at the Air Force Academy since 1957, with the appointment of the first, Colonel Robert F. McDermott.

McDermott was Dean of the Faculty at the time and was subsequently promoted to Brigadier General in 1959. He served as Dean until his retirement
in 1968. Sometime in 1964, inspired perhaps by his memories of West Point's
senior faculty and simultaneously working issues related to the rank and status
of the 20-plus USAFA Permanent Professors, General McDermott decided
to create a distinctive identification badge. He believed it would recognize
their special position and improve their morale. Academy legend holds that
General McDermott sketched out his rough design ideas on notebook paper.
That may be true, but he was also assisted by Colonel Malham M. Wakin,
Permanent Professor of the Department of Philosophy and Fine Arts. In July
1965 McDermott made a formal recommendation for the badge to Lieutenant
General Thomas S. Moorman, the Superintendent. Interestingly, McDermott's original idea included three distinct variations or "degrees" of the badge,
to distinguish between Permanent Professors, Tenure Associate Professors,
and Instructors. The Superintendent referred the issue to the Academy Board.
Not surprisingly, some of the Permanent Professors and other members of the
faculty were less than universal in their support, with several of them expressing opinions quite pointed in opposition. Nevertheless, by all accounts General
McDermott could be very persuasive, and he convinced the Superintendent
and the Academy Board to approve the concept early in 1966.

Energized by his success, McDermott immediately began working
with the US Army's Institute of Heraldry (IOH) in Alexandria, Virginia.
It was a lengthy and detailed process. McDermott's first design (below) was
completely circular in form, 2 inches in diameter, and featured three con-
centric rings alongside the elements of stars and tetrahedral forms. The
badge's original motto was "Homo Sapiens
Astra Spectat," taken to mean "The Wise
Man Looks to the Stars." Although the basic
design was sound, for various reasons the
IOH found the draft unworkable and made
recommendations for modifications. These
suggestions included changes in color and
materials, largely designed to bring the badge

into compliance with traditional heraldic principles and rules. Interestingly, General McDermott insisted that the main element of the badge be made of sterling silver, doubtless to enhance its value and prestige as an insignia. Of more significance, the IOH noted that McDermott's initial design inadvertently divided the shield "per bend sinister," carrying a dishonorable connotation in heraldry. If a shield is to be divided by a diagonal line into two parts, it should be "per bend dexter." Thus—to be correct and honorable— the diagonal line was corrected to run from the upper right (the viewer's left) to lower left (the viewer's right).

After much correspondence and a face-to-face meeting at the IOH in mid-July 1966, General McDermott accepted a final design and gave his approval for development and manufacture. By that time he had been persuaded that offering the badge in three degrees with varying design—for potentially 400 people—was not going to win support, so he settled for a single version, designated only for the 23 Permanent Professors. The Air Force, through the Air Force Uniform Board and Aeronautical Systems Division, had earlier provided $5,000 for developmental purposes. A couple of significant further changes occurred by late summer. The outer edges of the badge, now enlarged to 2½ inches, were indented to correspond to the tetrahedrals. As before, there were 13 stars between. The badge would be constructed of two parts soldered together, the outer base and the center device. The center device, consisting of a gold eagle sitting on a wreath in front of a white cloud, was enameled and had a plated satin finish and surrounded by a field of ultramarine blue. The divided shield underneath depicted the Earth's atmosphere in light blue and outer space in black. Both were crossed by the "astronaut device," an ascending five-pointed star with three rays passing through an orbit, over a burning lamp. The motto, black lettering on the gold scroll, was changed to "Potestas Doctrinae Vitam Sustinet." The literal translation of this Latin inscription is "The Power of Knowledge Sustains Life," but corresponded nicely to the inscription on the Academy's Eagle and Fledgling statue, "Man's Flight Through Life Is Sustained by the Power of His Knowledge." It's not entirely clear when the badge's Latin motto was changed, but it is known that Colonel Wakin and Lieutenant Colonel Joseph Berthelot from the Department of English worked together to make recommendations after examining and translating several alternatives. They and General McDermott doubtless saw the elegance of linking the badge to the Academy's motto.

The Wilbur C. Kiff Company of Attleboro, Massachusetts, was selected in late fall 1966 to manufacture the new badge. It would take a further four to five months to produce the dies, manufacture the first metal prototypes, and ship them to General McDermott for his final approval and distribution. Apparently, he preferred not to wait because he issued special versions of the badge sometime before the process for the metal version could be completed.

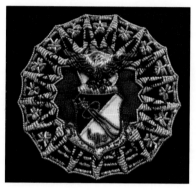

Thus, the earliest known examples of the Permanent Professor badge are not official nor metal at all, but rather made of black felt and feature embroidered silver bullion thread on a circular, indented pattern. No recoverable record exists of when or where they were manufactured. There is oral evidence, however, that General McDermott arranged for their production and paid for them personally. They generally conformed to the design details settled on by McDermott and the IOH. But, interestingly enough, these embroidered badges depict shields that are divided into the "per bend sinister" position. Apparently, nobody noticed. General McDermott reputedly handed out these badges with little ceremony in his office. Images of Permanent Professors wearing this early badge can be found in photos in the faculty section of Academy yearbooks from 1966. Many wore it on Mess Dress uniforms, because it fit nicely with the embroidered insignia of the period. Very few examples of the badge still exist and are doubtless preciously guarded. General McDermott's own—perhaps rightfully considered Permanent Professor Badge #1—currently resides in a display case in Fairchild Hall's Faculty Heritage Room.

The Kiff Company, through the IOH, delivered the first shipment of 30 official Permanent Professor Badges to General McDermott in May

1967. Each sterling silver badge cost $29.80 at the time. There's little record of how General McDermott distributed them to their earliest recipients, but it's clear that they were worn with considerable pride. It wasn't long before Permanent Professor investiture ceremonies and the awarding of the badge became significant events for the faculty and those selected for the position. They remain so today.

Sometime in the 1970s the original producer, the Kiff Company, was bought by Balfour Military Supply Service. Subsequently, the responsibility went to N.S. Meyer of New York. Eventually, production of the Permanent Professor badge fell to the Vanguard Military Insignia Company, Norfolk, Virginia. By the year 2000, given their uniqueness and metal content, the badges cost more than $200 each.

NEW VERSIONS

The original badge was designated to be worn on the left pocket of the service dress, but the weight of it made it less comfortable on regular uniform shirts when the faculty moved away from teaching class in the service dress uniform. Accordingly, in the mid-1980s, the Dean, Brigadier General Ervin J. Rokke,

asked the Academy's Training Device Branch to create a lighter-weight version. Technicians there responded with a near-perfect resin copy, which was painted by a craftsman, Mr. Bob Jensen. It closely approximated the original and was very popular among the Permanent Professors. These badges saw widespread use until about the year 2000, when the skilled Mr. Jensen retired. Training Devices was subsequently unable to find someone capable of duplicating the quality of his work; the few badges that were produced in the attempt were not suitable and were not issued.

At that point, however, Colonel Thomas A. Drohan, Permanent Professor of Military and Strategic Studies, who had served in Korea, was able to find a vendor there willing to produce relatively inexpensive copies of the badge. This vendor was Song's Coin and Plaque in Osan. In addition to producing a full-size badge, Song's could scale the badge to any desired size. It was decided to produce a badge at approximately 60 percent of full size to match the size of the smaller Air Force insignia then in use on regular uniform shirts. Otherwise it appears exactly the same as its full-size service dress counterpart. This version also worked nicely with the newer Mess

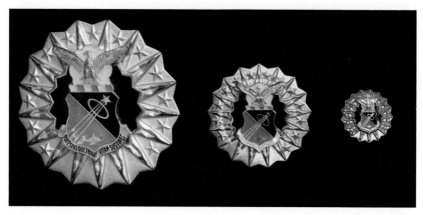

Dress uniforms, when metal insignia were required to be worn. Further, since Deans at the time found themselves unable to justify the increasing cost of purchase of the original badges, they began to use the vender in Korea to produce full-size versions that were virtually indistinguishable from the original badges, without the expense of sterling. The vendor also produced an exquisitely detailed, miniature badge, at 30 percent (just ¾-inch in diameter). Generally issued by the Dean to the Permanent Professor after appointment and to retired Permanent Professors, the miniature is designed for civilian wear. With a single-pin back, it's typically affixed on the left lapel of a man's jacket or a suitable location on women's clothing.

Eventually, Vanguard Industries also agreed to produce a badge without the expensive sterling. Thus, today, Vanguard remains the principal supplier of the full-size badge, at a current cost of $29. It is interesting to note that some Permanent Professor badges—with or without sterling silver content—have found their way to online military auctions and can garner prices above $300. Given its rarity, this should come as no surprise. In its more than 50-year history, the number of full-size badges produced probably does not exceed 120. Vanguard will still produce sterling silver badges as a special order for Permanent Professors who desire to purchase one. Song's is the only supplier of the two smaller badges.

None of the badges described above are suitable for wear on Air Force flight suits or utility uniforms. That deficiency was corrected in 2016, when Colonel John D. Cinnamon, Permanent Professor of the Department of Aeronautics, arranged for a private vendor, Aviator Gear, Inc., to produce a 4-inch cloth patch version of the badge. It attaches to the flight suit with Velcro mounting.

There are two further examples of the Permanent Professor badge. The first is a large-scale wall plaque badge, made from ceramic material mounted on blue velvet in a black frame measuring 17 x 21 inches. Produced locally by the Academy's Training Devices team, for many years it was given to each new Permanent Professor at the investiture ceremony. Many of the Permanent Professors subsequently mounted the plaques on the wall of their department offices. Production of these plaques (left) ceased around 2012, but another version, 16 x 16 inches, has begun to be produced.

Then, there is a line-drawing replica of the badge design. Some Permanent Professors use this element as a logo on personal stationery, business cards, and the like.

SYMBOLISM

The understanding of the symbolism associated with the Permanent Professor badge has varied and expanded over time, partly as a result of different interpretations of its original heraldic design features and partly as a result of individual explanations of those who have spoken about it. There is, however, universal consensus that the badge itself beautifully manifests the nature of the responsibilities associated with the office of the Permanent Professor. These responsibilities can be considered to reside in the following principal areas:

- Responsibility to the nation
- Responsibility to the mission of the Air Force to defend the nation
- Responsibility to the mission of the Academy to prepare young men and women to that end
- Responsibility to the role of the Permanent Professor to lead that effort

The symbolism of the badge is thus reflected in these four distinct parts.

First, on the outer edges of the badge, the 13 stars symbolize the United States and are a reminder that America's strength and greatness rest upon the original 13 colonies that came together to form one nation, guided by a Constitution and the rule of law. According to General McDermott's original notes, the 17 alternating chapel spires represent the beauty and inspirational physical environment of the Academy itself. Doubtless their use was also a signal of the importance of the moral, spiritual, and ethical development of all cadets. The color of the burnished and bright silver disc was deliberately selected by General McDermott to reflect a mixture of shiny and oxidized silver ... the very color of contemporary US Air Force aircraft and the wings insignia of an Air Force aviator.

Next, the centerpiece shield and its colors were intentionally designed to remind the badge's wearers of the mission of the Air Force. The shield stands on a field of ultramarine blue, the color of the Air Force and its uniforms. The gold American bald eagle atop the shield represents both the United States and its airpower. The cloud formation behind the eagle depicts the creation of a new firmament—the Department of the Air Force. It also symbolizes the vision to achieve the Air Force's global responsibilities, while earning the nation's trust ... the public trust in the men and women who defend the country. The light blue of the divided shield below shows the aviator's traditional domain of the sky, while the black depicts the domain of Air Force space operations. The Air Force's fundamental mission at the time of the badge's creation was to defend the nation with air and space power. That mission now includes cyberspace power.

Third, on the part of the shield that experts in heraldry call the "middle base" stands a lamp. It's the lamp of knowledge, representing human wisdom, learning, and its components of education, training, and experience. These words summarize the academic mission of the Academy. It's noteworthy that there are not three lamps, or even two, but only one. This reminds us that at the Air Force Academy the three mission elements are integrated into one. At USAFA, unlike in ancient Greece, Athens and Sparta come together. In the words of President John F. Kennedy, "Leadership and learning are indispensable to one another." The lamp also is a reminder of the words of Plutarch, the first-century scholar, who said, "The mind is not a vessel to be filled but a fire to be kindled." Permanent Professors like to think they hold the match.

Finally, the polar star in the upper right cuts across the entire shield at the center of the badge, as if holding it together. The star Polaris is the traditional guide for navigation. It symbolizes the role of the Permanent Professor, to lead and guide the mission to educate and train cadets to be tomorrow's leaders. The star is clearly ascending ... climbing at a high rate of speed up to the right. The climb passes through a satellite orbit and symbolizes a constant striving for improvement ... a commitment to excellence. Once again, the high-right position on the shield as the viewer examines it is considered the place of honor ... clearly linked to integrity. Thus, in just these first few parts of the badge, it's possible to see—almost incredibly because the badge was designed in the 1960s—a very discernible and real connection to the Air Force Academy's current core values of:

- Integrity First
- Service Before Self
- Excellence in All We Do

Once again, the scroll beneath the shield is gold and carries the inscription "Potestas, Doctrinea, Vitam, Sustinet" in black letters. As indicated in the previous summary of the development of the badge, these words are Latin for "Power, Knowledge, Life, Sustain." This phrase elegantly summarizes the entire symbolism of the badge and is a remarkable translation of the Air Force Academy's motto: "Man's Flight Through Life Is Sustained by the Power of His Knowledge."

Finally, it's worth considering the shape of the badge. Note that it is not square, triangular, or oval. It is generally round … an indented circle … comparable to the circle of life. It reminds us of time, not simply in terms of the tenure of a Permanent Professor, but more of his or her long-standing impact on the institution and its cadets over their professional career and lifetime. In a word, "timeless."

SOURCES

Correspondence, documents, and notes from the Institute of Heraldry, Brigadier General Robert F. McDermott, and various officers assigned to the Dean of the Faculty (1965–1985).

Interviews with retired Brigadier General Malham M. Wakin, US Air Force (various dates 2000–2017).

Ringenbach, Paul T. *Battling Tradition: Robert F. McDermott and Shaping the U.S. Air Force Academy.* Chicago: Imprint Publications, 2006.

"Symbology of the Permanent Professor Badge," oral and written presentations at Permanent Professor investiture ceremonies by Colonels Douglas J. Murray and Cary A. Fisher (various dates 2000–2005).

CHAPTER 7 PERMANENT PROFESSOR TRADITIONS

The Permanent Professors embrace a few unique traditions that have arisen over the years. These begin with the investiture and continue through the retirement and beyond.

INVESTITURE CEREMONY

An *investiture* ceremony is the formal occasion for conferring the authority and symbol of a high office. For the office of Permanent Professor, the ceremony consists of the reading of the appointment order, often including a promotion to the grade of Colonel, the oath of office, and the presentation of the Permanent Professor badge.

In the photo on the left from 1967, the 21ˢᵗ Permanent Professor, Colonel Mark Kinevan, is presented his badge by Brigadier General McDermott. The photo at right shows new Permanent Professors Orwyn Sampson

(right, the 37ᵗʰ) and Harvey Schiller (the 38ᵗʰ) receiving congratulations from Brigadier General Orth, at their investiture ceremony in 1980. It is interesting to see that the newbies had not yet pinned on the eagles of their new rank but were already wearing their new badges.

At the Air Force Academy this is a very public ceremony, involving the participation of the Superintendent, the Dean of the Faculty, the Commandant of Cadets, and the Director of Athletics. The ceremony is much unchanged from the onset.

The most recent investiture ceremony was held on April 4, 2018 in honor of Permanent Professors no. 99 (Maiya Anderson) and no. 100 (Dave Caswell). The ceremony was presided over by the Superintendent, Lt Gen Jay Silveria, shown at left presenting Colonel Caswell with the traditional wall-size replica of the Permanent Professor badge. At right is Colonel Anderson during her remarks to the audience. Both the Dean of the Faculty and Director of Athletics also spoke at this ceremony, which was held in the Press Box of Falcon Stadium to recognize Maiya's appointment as Permanent Professor and Head of the Department of Physical Education. Dave is the new Permanent Professor for the Department of Computer and Cyber Sciences.

The appointment to the office of Permanent Professor is finalized with the oath of office. It is the standard oath officers take when commissioned and for every promotion. Some years ago, Colonel Orwyn Sampson wrote a commentary to help explain the meaning of the oath and the commitment to duty it underscores. His reflections are both profound and moving.

The Military Oath of Office
A Personal Reflection

by Colonel Orwyn Sampson
Published in the *J. Prof. Mil. Ethics*, Sept., 1981.

I (FULLNAME)

All that signifies my individuality. A personal reference to no one else which implies that I accept full responsibility for my actions.

HAVING BEEN APPOINTED

An historical event signifying the accomplishment of some requisite evaluation and/or training. An act conferred by a ruling authority.

A CADET (2ND LT, REGULAR OFFICER, PERMANENT PROFESSOR)

A position of esteem, respect, privilege, and reward that carries with it professional responsibility.

IN THE UNITED STATES AIR FORCE,

A branch of our nation's military that has a unique role to play in military operations and defense of American values and interests.

DO SOLEMNLY SWEAR

An oath to be taken seriously. One to which I offer my full allegiance.

THAT I WILL

An active call. One that demands my energy, my time, and if necessary, my life.

SUPPORT AND DEFEND

A directed call. My activity is to be both offensive and defensive.

THE CONSTITUTION

Not the parchment, but the principles—the ideal of liberty for all men and women.

OF THE UNITED STATES

It isn't just anybody's idea. It is ours! Tried by fire and found to be genuine, lasting, and valuable.

AGAINST ALL ENEMIES

There is inherent risk in my work. It is a call to arms and a call to sacrifice. The stakes are high. It is life we are supporting and defending and it is life that it may cost—whether supremely or on a moment-by-moment basis.

FOREIGN AND DOMESTIC

No matter the foe we are ready, even if he arises among us.

THAT I WILL BEAR TRUE FAITH AND ALLEGIENCE TO THE SAME

My complete loyalty—my heart—is tied up in this commitment.

THAT I TAKE THIS OBLIGATION FREELY

An active decision on my part, delegated to no other, mine alone to make. Weighing the costs, in liberty I choose.

WITHOUT ANY MENTAL RESERVATION OR PURPOSE OF EVASION

My pledge is not ill-advised, half-hearted, or deceptive.

AND THAT I WILL WELL AND FAITHFULLY DISCHARGE

A commitment to excellence.

THE DUTIES OF THE OFFICE UPON WHICH I AM ABOUT TO ENTER

All the duties, not just the pleasant or rewarding ones, remembering that the value of true service comes not in the job you get but the job you do.

SO HELP ME GOD

My allegiance can go no higher.

HERITAGE ROOM

The Heritage Room is a small multipurpose room located on the sixth floor of Fairchild Hall, part of the Dean's office complex. Its walls are decorated with large paintings depicting early aviation history, and there are two display cases of early Academy memorabilia. The cases feature uniforms of the Academy's first Superintendent, Lieutenant General Harmon, and the first permanent Dean, Brigadier General McDermott. Fittingly, the Heritage Room overlooks the terrazzo with a fine view of the Cadet Chapel, the new Polaris Hall, and the mountains beyond.

For many years The Heritage Room also served the Permanent Professors as a private luncheon facility. It was managed from the Dean's office as a non-appropriated fund activity, with a single employee, the cook. Professors paid a flat monthly fee sufficient for the cook to provide a simple cooked meal, served on a come-as-one-can basis five days a week for the Professors, senior faculty and staff, and their guests. Unfortunately, the economics of the small operation eventually didn't work out. Perhaps it was the emphasis on physical fitness that pulled the members away from a sit-down lunch, but by the early 1990s, the number of regular participants declined to a level that didn't support the operation. The Heritage Room closed as an organized lunch facility, but it does continue as a rather special venue for meetings or ceremonies.

It was actually an amazing concept, that Professors from vastly different departments should eat together. To paraphrase a colleague, "It helped build a cohesiveness that colleagues across the country envy. I mean, it's unheard of for a Head of an English Department at Princeton to have lunch regularly with the Professor of Engineering Mechanics or the Professor of Physics. They just don't have anything in common to talk about often unless they're very exceptional and very fortunate people. Here, it was quite common … and it affected the way the institution functioned in a positive way."

(Brigadier General Jack Shuttleworth, Oral History interview, 2000)

THE PERMANENT PROFESSORS ART GALLERY

The Permanent Professors Art Gallery was opened in 1983 to display both aviation art and contemporary art forms for the benefit of Academy cadets and staff. The Dean of the Faculty, Brigadier General Orth, initiated the formal design of the Gallery in 1980 following a suggestion by Lieutenant Colonel Carlin Kielcheski, a Tenured Professor of Art. Funds for the Gallery were donated by Mr. Jasper Ackerman to honor the Permanent Professors, past, present, and future. The Gallery was constructed on Fairchild Hall's third floor, near the south elevators, and was dedicated in September 1983, shortly after General Orth's retirement. The wording on the plaque at the entrance of the Gallery was as follows:

> This Gallery stands as a tribute to the Permanent Professors of the United States Air Force Academy, through the generosity of Mr. J.D. Ackerman, Chairman of the Board, Air Academy National Bank.

The Gallery was updated in 2009 as a prominent feature of the Hall of Exemplars. For more than 35 years the Gallery has offered a wide variety of exhibits to broaden cadets' appreciation for heritage, cultural traditions, and the arts as an enduring part of the values of our country.

RETIREMENT CEREMONY

The retirement ceremony for a Permanent Professor is more or less the same as the ceremony for any other senior officer, with one possible significant exception, namely, the ceremony often includes the retiree's promotion to the rank of brigadier general. In those instances, the promotion portion of the ceremony comes first, then the retirement. The other traditional elements are always there, including the presentation of a decoration, the career recap by the general officer who is the retirement official, remarks by the retiree, and a reception. With the promotion and retirement elements combined into a single ceremony, the event really can be a grand occasion.

One other presentation is often made: the designation of the retiree as a Professor Emeritus. Emeritus is an adjective to describe a person of distinction in a profession who retires or hands over the position to a successor. At the Air Force Academy, the Professor Emeritus designation is not automatic, but may be awarded by the Dean to any retiring full professor with ten years or more in office or to a retiring Dean regardless of time in office. It comes with small but tangible benefits: a designated common office space in the McDermott Library and a lifetime faculty library card.

RETIREMENT DINNER

It is a custom for the Permanent Professors, both active and retired, to fete the retiring Professor and spouse to a dinner at the Academy Club or another good restaurant. This is an occasion for the active Professors to present several traditional gifts. These include:

SCROLL—a framed document extending the sincere good wishes of the Permanent Professors to the retiree and recapping his or her contributions to the Academy over the years since first assigned. The scroll is signed by each of the active Permanent Professors.

CHAIR WITH ENGRAVED PERMANENT PROFESSOR BADGE—When Mark Kinevan retired in 1988, he was given an elegant handcrafted wooden chair as a retirement gift. It is now presented either as the captain's arm chair shown here or as a rocker, the retiree's choice. Black with cherry stain arms and top panel, it is engraved with the Permanent Professor badge, name, and dates of service. The chair soon replaced the hinged plaque as the traditional retirement gift.

HINGED PLAQUE—When Jim Wilson retired in 1965 (he was the first Permanent Professor to retire) the Dean presented him with a hinged plaque (right). The plaque was a hollow walnut box which opened to reveal two engraved metal plaques. On one side was a presentation-style commemoration of the event and on the other a few memorable photo-  graphs. This plaque was a traditional retirement gift for nearly four decades. It was phased out after 2000 as the engraved chairs became the norm.

GOLD PROP AND WINGS—a traditional retirement gift to the retiree's spouse. It is given as a necklace to women and a lapel pin to men. The prop and wings is the iconic symbol of the Air Force Academy. The  prop and wings insignia originated with the Army Air Service in the 1920s, but now is most closely associated with the Air Force Academy. The pin is traditionally awarded to Academy cadets at the end of their fourth class training, signifying their "recognition."

CHERRIES JUBILEE. For many years, the featured dessert at the dinners for retiring Permanent Professors was Cherries Jubilee, a dish with sweet cherries and liqueur (typically Kirschwasser or sometimes rum), which is subsequently flambéed, and served as a sauce over vanilla ice cream. How- ever, most restaurants no longer serve this kind of flaming dish due to the fear of fire. Sadly, we almost never see Cherries Jubilee anymore.

JESSE GATLIN'S DOGGERELS

Retirement dinners from the 1980s for 30 years or so were marked by Jesse Gatlin's poems. Jesse had the most amazing ability to sit during the dinner and jot notes, then stand up at the end and read a poem he had scratched on the back of an envelope. These are doggerels, which dictionaries define as a kind of poetry that is irregular in rhythm and in rhyme, often deliberately for burlesque or comic effect. Here are two short examples:

Written at the
Retirement Dinner
for Danny Litwhiler
and Jim Head
Sunday Night,
March 12, 2006

I suppose the Academy
will still try to go on,
Now that both Danny
and Jim Head have gone.
But it won't be the same,
it never could be,
When two PPs at once
leave the menagerie.
I'm sure it will flourish
as it has year by year
(It has done so for decades
without some of us here.)
So long as we cherish
what all of us love,
Our history, traditions,
and far, far above.
All else, our loyalty
and friendship, we'll be,
Rewarded forever
to have been a PP.

Written at the Retirement Dinner for
Rita Jordan, Alan Klayton, and Gunther Mueller
Sunday Night, September 21, 2008

Tonight the occasion's both happy and sad
To lose one Professor is always too bad
To lose two Professors just deepens the feeling
Of losses that leave the whole faculty reeling
But to lose three just makes the reeling spin faster
And creates a state not too far from disaster.

With Rita and Gunther and Alan retired
How can electric connectors be wired?
Or all the potential problems be managed?
Or students learn French, Chinese, German, or Spanish?
But all of us know from experience we've seen
Our successors all will be equally keen.

A few may even stand out well above us
But at least we can hope they'll continue to love us
So tonight as we honor these illustrious three
We can all be most grateful to be a PP
And can tell them they've done a great deal to admire
And wish them great happiness as they retire.

PAST PERMANENT PROFESSORS EVENTS

In 2007 the Dean of the Faculty, Brigadier General Born, organized a conference of retired Permanent Professors, dubbed "Heritage to Horizons."
Brigadier General Phil Erdle generously sponsored it with funds from the
Academy Research and Development Institute. The purpose was to inform
the retirees of current Academy initiatives and provide a forum for feedback
based on the experience of the retired Permanent Professors. The two-day
schedule also encouraged the retirees to visit their former departments for
the same purpose. Based on the attendance and enthusiasm for the first Heritage to Horizons, the event has been repeated every couple of years, most
recently in April 2018.

The retired Permanent Professors in the Colorado Springs area gather
for a dinner two to three times a year. The gatherings are always at a restaurant; the two wives that suggested this tradition in the early 1990s, Doris
Caine and Jan Royer, insisted on dinners out "because wives never get to
retire." These are good opportunities to catch up on old friendships, learn
what's new at the Academy, and swap memories. Jesse Gatlin's last doggerel
was written for one such occasion in 2016. This poem is different from the
others, as it reflects on the entire Permanent Professor experience. Jesse's last
doggerel is included as the Afterword on the next page of this volume.

Afterword

Jesse Gatlin's Last Doggerel

Written for the Past Permanent Professors' Dinner
February 2016

When I first joined the faculty
Back in '57
It seemed to me that I had found
A kind of earthly heaven.

Although the buildings which we used
Were built for WWII
We christened them with Air Force names
which all historians knew

Were men who'd made the Air Force be
Not just an Army Corps
But a new force now equal with
The two that came before.

We also knew that south of us
Near Colorado Springs
A great new home was being built
Like a palace made for kings.

We knew our future years would be
A time of resolution
Which would evolve the question of
What kind of institution

The Air Academy would become
In future years. We knew
The precedents we set would be
A contribution to

What would become a vital role
In forming the conditions
Which would in future years help shape
Academy traditions.

Those were exciting times for me
who had no idea then
That we would stay around to see
A time in future when

We would be ancient artifacts
But still alive to be
Included in this gathering
As a retired PP.

And so tonight I'm happy to
Still be here with you all.
I'll stand in line and drink and dine
Until the day I fall.

Until that day I'll always say
How glad I am to be
Among professors who have been
Around so Permanently.

Appendix A

Air Force Academy Senior Leaders
Lists of Superintendents, Commandants, Deans, and
Athletic Directors

Air Force Academy Superintendents

#	Start	End	Name	School	Class Year
1	1954	1956	Lt Gen Hubert R. Harmon	USMA	1915
2	1956	1959	Maj Gen James E. Briggs	USMA	1928
3	1959	1962	Maj Gen William S. Stone	USMA	1934
4	1962	1965	Maj Gen Robert H. Warren	USMA	1940
5	1965	1970	Lt Gen Thomas S. Moorman	USMA	1933
6	1970	1974	Lt Gen Albert P. Clark	USMA	1936
7	1974	1977	Lt Gen James R. Allen	USMA	1948
8	1977	1981	Lt Gen Kenneth L. Tallman	USMA	1946
9	1981	1983	Maj Gen Robert E. Kelley	Rutgers	1956
10	1983	1987	Lt Gen Winfield W. Scott Jr.	USMA	1950
11	1987	1991	Lt Gen Charles R. Hamm	USMA	1956
12	1991	1994	Lt Gen Bradley C. Hosmer	USAFA	1959
13	1994	1997	Lt Gen Paul E. Stein	USAFA	1966
14	1997	2000	Lt Gen Tad J. Oelstrom	USAFA	1965
15	2000	2003	Lt Gen John R. Dallager	USAFA	1969
16	2003	2005	Lt Gen John W. Rosa	Citadel	1973
17	2005	2009	Lt Gen John F. Regni	USAFA	1973
18	2009	2013	Lt Gen Michael C. Gould	USAFA	1976
19	2013	2017	Lt Gen Michelle D. Johnson	USAFA	1981
20	2017	Present	Lt Gen Jay B. Silveria	USAFA	1985

COMMANDANTS OF CADETS

#	Start	End	Name	School	Class Year
1	1954	1958	Brig Gen Robert M. Stillman	USMA	1935
2	1958	1961	Brig Gen Henry R. Sullivan Jr.	USMA	1939
3	1961	1963	Brig Gen William T. Seawell	USMA	1941
4	1963	1965	Brig Gen Robert W. Strong Jr.	USMA	1940
5	1965	1967	Brig Gen Louis T. Seith	USMA	1943
6	1967	1971	Brig Gen Robin Olds	USMA	1943
7	1971	1973	Brig Gen Walter T. Galligan	USMA	1945
8	1973	1975	Brig Gen Hoyt S. Vandenberg Jr.	USMA	1951
9	1975	1978	Brig Gen Stanley C. Beck	USMA	1954
10	1978	1981	Brig Gen Thomas C. Richards	VA Tech	1956
11	1981	1982	Brig Gen Robert D. Beckel	USAFA	1959
12	1982	1984	Brig Gen Anthony J. Burshnick	USAFA	1960
13	1984	1986	Brig Gen Marcus A. Anderson	USAFA	1961
14	1986	1989	Brig Gen Sam W. Westbrook III	USAFA	1963
15	1989	1992	Brig Gen Joseph J. Redden	USAFA	1964
16	1992	1993	Brig Gen Richard C. Bethurem	USAFA	1966
17	1993	1994	Brig Gen Patrick K. Gamble	TX A&M	1967
18	1994	1996	Brig Gen John D. Hopper Jr.	USAFA	1969
19	1996	1999	Brig Gen Stephen R. Lorenz	USAFA	1973
20	1999	2001	Brig Gen Mark A. Welsh III	USAFA	1976
21	2001	2003	Brig Gen S. Taco Gilbert III	USAFA	1978
22	2003	2005	Brig Gen Johnny A. Weida	USAFA	1978
23	2005	2008	Brig Gen Susan Y. Desjardins	USAFA	1980
24	2008	2010	Brig Gen Samuel D. Cox	USAFA	1984
25	2010	2012	Brig Gen Richard M. Clark	USAFA	1986
26	2012	2014	Brig Gen Gregory J. Lengyel	TX A&M	1985
27	2014	2017	Brig Gen Stephen C. Williams	USAFA	1989
28	2017	Present	Brig Gen Kristin E. Goodwin	USAFA	1993

DEANS OF THE FACULTY

(the number sequence is for Permanent Deans)

#	Start	End	Name	School	Class Year
	1954	1957	Brig Gen Don Z. Zimmerman	USMA	1929
1	1957	1968	Brig Gen Robert F. McDermott	USMA	1943
	1964	1965	Col James V.G. Wilson (Acting)	USMA	1935
2	1968	1978	Brig Gen William T. Woodyard	Missouri	1950
3	1978	1983	Brig Gen William A. Orth	USMA	1954
4	1983	1986	Brig Gen Ervin J. Rokke	USAFA	1962
	1986	1987	Col John T. May (Acting)	USAFA	1961
5	1987	1991	Brig Gen Erlind G. Royer	MT St.	1961
6	1991	1998	Brig Gen Ruben A. Cubero	USAFA	1961
7	1998	2004	Brig Gen David A. Wagie	USAFA	1972
8	2004	2013	Brig Gen Dana H. Born	USAFA	1983
9	2013	Present	Brig Gen Andrew P. Armacost	NW'ern	1989

DIRECTORS OF ATHLETICS

#	Start	End	Name	School	Class Year
1	1954	1957	Col Robert V. Whitlow	USMA	1943
2	1957	1960	Col George B. Simler	Maryland	1948
3	1960	1963	Col Maurice L. Martin	USMA	1943
4	1963	1967	Col Edmund A. Rafalko	USMA	1945
5	1967	1975	Col Francis E. Merritt	USMA	1944
6	1975	1991	Col John J. Clune	USNA	1954
7	1991	1996	Col Kenneth L. Schweitzer	MT St.	1966
8	1996	2003	Col Randal W. Spetman	USAFA	1976
9	2003	2004	Mr Bradley J. DeAustin (Acting)	USAFA	1969
10	2004	2015	Dr Hans J. Mueh*	USAFA	1966
11	2015	2018	Mr James A. Knowlton	USMA	1982
12	2018	Present	Col Jennifer A. Block (Interim)	USAFA	1992

*Permanent Professor, Brig Gen (Ret)

APPENDIX B

SOME DETAILS ON FACULTY ORGANIZATION

DIVISION CHAIRS AND DEPARTMENT HEADS

The 1956 structure that established the four Academic Divisions is shown below, along with the names of the Division Chairs and Department Heads appointed at that time. (The current divisional alignment is shown in a chart in Chapter 4.)

Humanities Division—Chair: Colonel Peter R. Moody

English	Colonel Moody
Foreign Languages	Colonel Moody (additional duty)
Law	Colonel Allen W. Rigsby

Social Sciences Division—Chair: Colonel John L. Frisbee

History	Colonel Frisbee
Economics	Colonel Robert F. McDermott (additional duty)
Political Science	Colonel Frisbee (additional duty)
Military History	Colonel Josephus A. Bowman
Psychology	Lt Col Fred E. Holdrege Jr.

Basic Sciences Division—Chair: Colonel Edwin W. Brown

Mathematics	Colonel Archie Higdon (additional duty)
Graphics	Colonel James S. Barko
Chemistry	Lt Col William T. Woodyard
Physics	Colonel Brown

Applied Sciences Division—Chair: Colonel Archie Higdon

Mechanics	Colonel Higdon
Electrical Engineering	Colonel James V.G. Wilson
Thermodynamics	Colonel Paul H. Dane
Aerodynamics	Lt Col Gerhardt C. Clementson

The roles and responsibilities of the Department Head and Division Chair were much different. A detailed list of duties of each position was first published in a 1956 Academy Regulation. These duties were refined somewhat over time, but really changed very little. For instance, the oversight of majors and minors was not added until majors and minors became part of the curriculum. The following lists are from 1967 (USAFAR 20-1, October 4, 1967).

THE DEPARTMENT HEAD:

1. Exercises supervisory authority over the department and is responsible to the Dean for the performance of the department
2. By precept and example promotes scholarship, research, and good teaching in the department
3. Implements policies legislated by the Academy Board and the Faculty Council or prescribed by the Superintendent or the Dean
4. Within policies prescribed by higher authority, establishes policies for the department
5. Supervises the courses of instruction offered by the department
6. Provides guidance in the development or modification of the department's academic majors or minors programs
7. Represents the department at meetings of the Faculty Council, Curriculum Committee, and the academic division to which the department is assigned
8. As a member of the Faculty Council and of committees to which assigned, assists in the formulation of academic and faculty policies
9. Coordinates with other departments to assure both vertical and horizontal integration of courses
10. Presides at department meetings
11. Teaches courses offered by the department
12. Monitors classroom activities of the department to evaluate the effectiveness of instruction
13. Recommends to the Dean the assignment, relief, graduate training, and academic promotion of instructor personnel in the department

14. Approves leaves of absence and temporary duty of instructor personnel in the department

15. Maintains contacts with other educational institutions (civilian and military) and with professional societies and promotes the educational advancement of instructors through in-service training programs

16. Submits a report of departmental activities to the Dean at the end of each academic year

17. Performs other duties as directed by the Dean.

The Department Head plays multiple roles in intrafaculty relationships. Within the department the Head has the dual roles of military command and academic leadership. Within the division and in relationships with other departments, the Department Head coordinates and cooperates in carrying out the academic program.

THE DIVISION CHAIR:

1. Assists the Dean in the development of academic and faculty policies

2. Exercises academic leadership in the integration of courses and the improvement of instruction within the division

3. Provides guidance in the development and modification of the division's academic majors or minors programs

4. Represents the division in matters that are of concern to all departments and courses within the division

5. Coordinates the work of the division with the work of other divisions

6. Presides at divisional meetings

7. Coordinates the preparation of catalog material for the division

8. Performs other duties as directed by the Dean.

The relationship between the Division Chair and the Department Heads is clear. The Chair is a coordinator, not a director. The sole role is one of leadership in academic matters; the Chair has no supervisory or administrative role or responsibilities over other departments or courses.

And what is the nature of these other duties as directed assigned to Permanent Professors in both roles? The list includes recurring tasks such as leading the Academy through its periodic accreditation events; chairing standing committees of the Academy Board, such as the Class Committees (now called Academic Review Committees); serving as officer representatives to various athletic teams; and leading committees to investigate significant issues such as allocation of cadet time or the operation of the honor code system. Some committees have been convened to address persistent issues, others to investigate and make recommendations for new initiatives. These activities are often cited in the individual biographies of Chapter 5.

VICE DEANS OF THE FACULTY

As detailed in Chapter 3, the Vice Dean plays an essential role in executing the Academy's programs. To give proper credit, here is a complete list of the Permanent Professors who served as Vice Deans of the Faculty:

1954–1956	Colonel Robert F. McDermott
1966–1967	Colonel Peter R. Moody
1967–1968	Colonel William T. Woodyard
1968–1970	Colonel Wayne A. Yeoman
1970–1973	Colonel Roger R. Bate
1973–1978	Colonel Philip J. Erdle
1978–1984	Colonel John P. Wittry
1984–1986	Colonel John T. May
1986–1988	Colonel Kenneth H. Fleming
1988–1990	Colonel James R. Woody
1990–1991	Colonel Douglas J. Murray
1991–1994	Colonel Daniel W Litwhiler
1994–1996	Colonel James H. Head
1996–1998	Colonel David A. Wagie
1998–2000	Colonel Gunther A. Mueller

2000–2002 ....Colonel Alan R. Klayton
2002–2004 ....Colonel Hans J. Mueh
2004–2006 ....Colonel James H. Head
2006–2008 ....Colonel Douglas N. Barlow
2008–2010 ....Colonel John M. Andrew
2010–2012 ....Colonel Richard L. Fullerton
2012–2014 ....Colonel Thomas L. Yoder
2014–2016 ....Colonel Kathleen Harrington
2016–2018 ....Colonel Gary A. Packard
2018–Present ....Colonel Troy R. Harting

THE DEAN'S STAFF AGENCIES

The Dean's staff provides assistance to the Dean in faculty administration in the areas of military and civilian personnel, fiscal planning and execution, and also broad support to the departments in their individual missions. Some functions of the faculty are best organized centrally under the Dean rather than distributed to the individual departments. Two obvious examples are course scheduling and the library, but also audiovisual services, training devices, supplies, and budget. When General McDermott became Dean in 1957, he opted for a very small staff, a move which was appreciated by the Permanent Professors. At the time of General McDermott's retirement in 1968, the staff included a small Faculty Executive and the following major elements:

- Faculty Research
- Counseling and Scheduling
- Instructional Technology
- Cadet Library

These essential central functions, by one name or another, have carried forward to the present day, with the notable addition of the category of International Programs:

+ Office of Research
+ Student Academic Affairs and Academy Registrar
+ Center for Educational Innovation
+ Cadet Library (the McDermott Library)
+ International Programs Office

The first four of those listed are headed by Associate Deans who report to the Vice Dean of the Faculty. In addition to the four Associate Deans who are directors of the major support agencies, there is a **Senior Associate Dean** (discussed below) who, like the Permanent Professors, reports directly to the Dean.

In 2005 the Dean, General Born, established the new position of **Associate Dean for Curriculum and Strategy**. The position was designed to be occupied by a civilian professor, brought out of one of the academic departments for a period of three to four years for the primary purpose of assisting in the coordination and integration of the core curriculum, especially as regards the USAFA Outcomes. Additionally, appointing the individual from the ranks of the civilian full professors provided opportunities for individual professional growth as well as providing the Dean with a senior civilian faculty advisor. The first incumbent in the position was Dr. Evelyn T. Patterson (Department of Physics), who served from 2005 to 2009. Next were Dr. Aaron R. Byerley (Aeronautics), 2009–2013, and Dr. David A. Westmoreland (Biology), 2013–2016. In 2016 General Armacost renamed the position as **Senior Associate Dean** and appointed Dr. Steven K. Jones (Behavioral Sciences and Leadership) to the position, which he presently holds.

OFFICE OF RESEARCH. General McDermott established a research office in 1962 and appointed Colonel Richard C. Gibson as Assistant Dean for Research. The Research program is now overseen by an **Associate Dean of Research**, currently Lieutenant Colonel Donald W. Rhymer. The Office of Research serves as the support hub for the research and development programs at the Academy. The Academy is now home to 19 Research Centers and two Institutes. These Centers are listed in Appendix F and their activities are described in the Academy's annual research report. Those research efforts associated with an academic department are also highlighted in Chapter 4.

STUDENT ACADEMIC AFFAIRS AND THE ACADEMY REGISTRAR. The current **Associate Dean for Student Academic Affairs** is Dr. Thomas R. Mabry, who was appointed to the position in 2014. The office is responsible for all academic record keeping, producing the academic schedule and assigning cadets to classes and sections each semester, maintaining a cadet's status with regard to meeting graduation requirements, identifying cadets deficient in academics, supporting cadets' selection of academic majors and their counseling by their academic advisors, determining graduation order of merit and graduation lists, and procuring diplomas to be awarded at graduation. The bulk of the detailed work for the graduation ceremony is handled by the Registrar's office. The organization includes the Academic Success Center, encompassing the Academy's Strategies for Academic Success Program, a Writing Center, a Reading Enhancement Program, the Quantitative Reasoning Center, and the Graduate Studies Office.

The registrar function, the keeping of student records including transcripts, was initially established under the Superintendent as part of the office that managed cadet admissions. The first Registrar was Colonel Boudreau, who had been reassigned from the Dean's staff to the registrar position. The scheduling of classes and academic counseling of cadets, both critical to the success of the institution, had always been a function of the Dean's staff. However, a reorganization in 1985 separated the functions of the Director of Admissions, who still reported to the Superintendent, and the Registrar, who was relocated under the Dean of the Faculty. Lieutenant Colonel Dean H. Wilson become the Director of Curriculum and Scheduling in 1984. In 1985 he became the Academy Registrar as well, and in 1987 he was named the Registrar and Director of Academic Affairs. In 2006 the Director's title changed to Associate Dean for Student Academic Affairs and Academy Registrar. Dr. Dean Wilson retired from the Air Force in 1993 and returned to the position as a civilian. In 1994 he stood-up the Center for Student Academic Services, now expanded into the Academic Success Center. Dean Wilson served with distinction in the post of Academy Registrar for nearly 30 years, until he passed away from cancer in 2013. He had earned the trust and respect of every Permanent Professor.

CENTER FOR EDUCATIONAL INNOVATION. From the earliest days, the Dean's office had managed support functions such as audiovisual services, the TV studio, and graphics. As technology advanced, operation of the USAFA local area computer network and a help-desk to resolve cadet computer issues were added. Lieutenant Colonels Bruce Doyle and Larry Bryant, respectively, were instrumental in providing outstanding AV and computer support.

In 1992 the Dean, General Randy Cubero, took the big step to establish a Directorate of Education to enhance the quality of teaching and learning at the Academy and to coordinate and facilitate educational innovation and research. The Directorate included the Center for Educational Excellence as the primary academic support agency for faculty development and academic assessment (including institutional and programmatic accreditation), and also the Technical Assistance Center, which promoted educational technology integration and provided audiovisual, video teleconferencing, and computer hardware and software support for all faculty and cadets. In 2000 the Multimedia Laboratory was opened in the McDermott Library to provide cadets with access to a wide range of office productivity resources and on-site training on their use whenever the library was open. The Directorate also housed the Office of Faculty and Cadet Research, the Air Force Institute for National Security Studies, and the Air Force Institute for Information Technology Applications (see Appendix F).

The individuals responsible for the growth and development of the Directorate of Education were Colonels Joe Burke and Randy Stiles (the first two directors) and Colonel Rolf Enger, who was Director for 16 years. Colonel Enger joined the Directorate of Education at the beginning as its Director of Faculty Development, 1992–1994, and returned as the Center's

Director in 1999–2002. In 2002 Rolf retired from active duty and served in the post for another 13 years as a civilian. Upon his second retirement in 2015, the Directorate of Education was broken into two parts: a new Office of Research and the Center for Educational Innovation. Absent in the reorganization was direct support for the information technology infrastructure and cadet and faculty computers, part of which had been taken up by the Air Base Wing's 10th Communications Squadron and part by a contractor directed from the Dean's office.

CENTER FOR EDUCATIONAL INNOVATION, currently directed by **Associate Dean for Educational Innovation** Dr. Rob Flaherty, is the Dean's central focus for supporting departments in their pursuit of providing the highest quality education for cadets. The key goal is to stimulate evidenced-based improvement in academic programs and learning experiences. To that end, the Center's interconnected programs are Academic Assessment (to develop and sustain a culture of accountability and commitment to improving cadet learning), Instructional Design (to promote innovative and effective course design to support cadet learning), Faculty Development (to engage faculty in continuous development and the use of effective, evidence-based practices in curriculum delivery), Scholarship of Teaching and Learning (SoTL) (to guide and encourage peer-reviewed scholarship that enhances understanding of effective teaching and learning practices), and Educational Technology (to support access to proven technologies that enhance cadet learning). In addition, the Center oversees the Academy Scholars Program (discussed in Chapter 3). The SoTL is considered one of the Academy's research centers.

CADET LIBRARY. The early directors of the library were introduced in Chapter 1. Lieutenant Colonels Arthur Larsen and George Fagan did a truly superb job establishing the library in a very short time. The 1959 accreditation report, based on a February 1959 evaluation visit, had the following to say:

+ "The library, like the other parts of the Academy, is magnificently housed and has all the most modern equipment."

- "Its books, periodicals, and other holdings … give clear evidence of being selected to support the Academy's curriculum."
- "…a weapon of great force and range in the Academy's arsenal and gives promise of further improvement."

The report went on to say the authors felt there was not another college of the Academy's size that had a library as good. The library continued to improve under Colonel Fagan's leadership for the next 10 years. His talents were recognized when he was appointed a Permanent Professor in 1962. Among his innovations was creation of the Special Collections Branch, housing the archival documents and photographs of the Academy's development. He played a key role in the Academy's acquisition of the Richard Gimbel Aeronautical History Collection, one of the most comprehensive early aviation archives in the world. Following George Fagan, there was a series of officers who served admirably as Library Director, and the library continued to grow under their leadership. Perhaps most notable among them was Lieutenant Colonel Reiner "Swiss" Schaeffer, Library Director from 1982 to 1992. In 1981 the library space was expanded by about 40,000 square feet by covering a space on the third floor that had previously been an open-air garden. The result was a grand entrance directly from the terrazzo and more floor space for cadet study, reference librarians, and the periodicals collection. In 1995, taking advantage of the new civilian faculty program, the Academy hired its first professional librarian, Dr. Edward A. Scott, who served as McDermott Library Director until his retirement in 2017. During his 22-year tenure, Ed Scott laid the foundation for moving the library into the modern age.

Modern technology and student desires for a better study environment have been changing library requirements all across the country for at least the past decade. Libraries are no longer just book depositories. Now they serve as hubs of learning and collaboration that extend through the campus and into the community. In response, the Dean of the Faculty established a "Library of the Future" Committee to develop plans to modernize the McDermott Library. The effort was chaired by Dr. Aaron Byerley,

Associate Dean for Curriculum and Strategy. A preliminary "Library of the Future" plan, completed in early 2016, calls for a substantial reduction in book holdings (removal to an external storage and retrieval facility), features a collaboration hub on the third floor, and relocates the Academics Success Center and tutoring program to the library, among other changes. The plan does not increase the amount of space assigned to the library, but significantly redesigns and reassigns the available space.

Although the tentative target for the project is 2020, the first phase was completed in 2017. This was the renovation of the third floor of the McDermott Library to remove periodical stacks and install individual and group-study carrels. Half of the funding for the project came from USAFA Endowment gift funds, while the remainder came from appropriated monies. This kind of private-public partnership is expected to be necessary to complete the project. When the Library of the Future is fully operational, the collaboration hub on the third floor is expected to be available to cadets 24/7.

OFFICE OF INTERNATIONAL PROGRAMS. Located within the Department of Foreign Languages, and currently led by Lieutenant Colonel Daniel E. Szarke, this office is described briefly in that department's section of Chapter 4. The office administers the various international programs for both USAFA and international cadets, as well as the International Officer Program. It is also the point of contact for all official foreign visitors to USAFA. Historically, the office grew out of the Foreign Area Studies Program Council, the group that coordinated the Foreign Area Studies major, namely the Permanent Professors/Department Heads of Foreign Languages, History, Political Science, Economics, and Military and Strategic Studies. The Chair of the Council was rotated among departments, until it settled in Foreign Languages in 2007. At about that time the Office of the Secretary of Defense urged the academies to significantly increase opportunities for foreign exposure for cadets and midshipmen and provided the funds and manpower to enable the effort. The result is the dramatic expansion of foreign exchanges, foreign visits, and study abroad programs for cadets as described in Chapter 3. The international emphasis also included USAFA hosting "International Week," attended by 60 cadets and 13 officers from 26 foreign countries in Academic Year 2017–2018. Several of these countries reciprocated by hosting 42 cadets and 13 officers at their academies, either during spring break or during the summer. Moreover, 13 international cadets graduated with the Academy Class of 2018 after completing the four-year International Cadet Program. What began in the 1960s as a bold initiative to create a cadet exchange with the French has blossomed into a multifaceted program enriching the education and life experiences of hundreds of cadets each year.

Appendix C

Civilian Faculty and Endowed Chairs

A Brief History of the Military/Civilian Mix

As noted in Chapter 3, discussions of the faculty composition took place from the beginning of planning for the Academy. After considering the arguments for a mixture of civilians and military officers, General Harmon decided to follow an all-military model.

In the summer of 1957 Headquarters USAF raised the issue again and requested the Academy consider adding civilians to the faculty. The principal consideration was cost. A survey done at the Academy showed the salary of military officers, including flight pay, was generally well above civilian educators of comparable seniority. As described in Chapter 3, the Superintendent and Dean decided to maintain the all-military position, which effectively settled the question in favor of preserving the all-military faculty, for almost 20 years.

The debate over adding civilians to the Academy faculty arose again in 1975–1976. The two major contributors to the argument were an economic analysis by the General Accounting Office and a study on educational excellence by the Department of Defense. The DoD study was the "Department of Defense Committee on Excellence in Education." Often referred to as the Clements Committee, it was chaired by Deputy Secretary of Defense William P. Clements. The Clements Committee conducted a comprehensive examination of officer schooling throughout the DoD. The committee spent considerable time on the subject of faculty composition at the academies.

The two studies, both published in 1975, reached nearly opposite conclusions regarding civilian/military faculty mix. The GAO study concluded that the Naval Academy, with its 45 percent civilian faculty, was less expensive to operate than West Point or the Air Force Academy. The Clements Committee concluded that service academies are best served by the utilization of highly qualified young officers with recent field or fleet experience as instructors. However, the Committee noted that civilian faculty members also play a valuable role "to the extent that they provide levels of academic achievement, expertise, and national recognition beyond that which can be expected from line military officers." The Committee did suggest that West Point and the Air Force Academy analyze the availability and educational advantages of adding civilian instructors to the faculty at a very modest level of between 5 and 10 percent.

Congressional hearings on the perceived conflict between the GAO and Clements Committee recommendations were held in 1976. Even Secretary Clements himself reportedly stated at a hearing: "If forced to make a comparison, the Naval Academy faculty would rank third in terms of academic excellence." However, in May 1976 Senator John Glenn introduced an amendment to the Military Appropriations Bill to direct the DoD to study greater use of civilian faculty. It included the directive that "professional military instructors shall be retained for solely military and naval subjects," although this specific language was stricken in the conference with the House. The final form of the so-called Glenn Amendment called for the Secretary of Defense to conduct a study to determine whether greater utilization of civilian faculty may be desirable at the service academies (Public Law 94-361 Sec. 809, July 14, 1976).

The Academy responded promptly. First it was noted that it had already instituted a Distinguished Visiting Professor Program (just begun in the 1975–1976 academic year; see Chapter 3). Next, a faculty-mix cost comparison study was completed with the conclusion that the all-military faculty was more cost effective than any of various military/civilian mixes. The Superintendent, Lieutenant General Allen, stated his belief that a predominantly military faculty was in the best interests of the nation, and especially objected to civilian faculty in excess of 5 percent. The DoD responded to Congress by establishing a working group under the Assistant Secretary of

Defense, Manpower and Reserve Affairs, which concluded that the Academy should consider increasing its civilian faculty membership to 5 percent using a mixture of visiting professors and longer-term civilian faculty.

Meanwhile, the House Appropriations Committee picked up the issue and in 1978 directed the DoD to provide a plan to increase use of permanent civilian faculties. Members of the Academy's Board of Visitors weighed in with letters of support for the Academy's position, including one advising that there was no need to prepare plans to accomplish this undesirable goal.

The issue was effectively set aside for a decade or more, although the tensions between advantages of civilians (reducing cost) and importance of military (imparting culture) were essentially unresolved. The Academy was content to ignore this standoff. However, a third dimension lurked in the background, seldom mentioned. Some lawmakers wondered whether civilian faculty might provide cadets with a deeper respect for civilian authority. The issue erupted again in 1992.

The 1992 Defense Authorization Bill, signed in December 1991, authorized the Secretary of the Air Force to employ civilian faculty members at the Academy and required a plan, by April 1, 1993, for the increase of civilian faculty members and the decrease of permanent military faculty. This time the issue was not debatable. The action originated in the Senate Armed Services Committee at the behest of Senator Sam Nunn. The Secretary of the Air Force responded to Senator Nunn by letter on September 18, 1992, confirming that the Academy would move toward a goal of 50 percent civilian faculty as quickly as possible. This initiative was one of five actions proposed by Senator Nunn changing the character of the Air Force Academy: to civilianize the faculty, to convert the Dean of the Faculty position to a civilian, to reassign the Academy's T-41 flight screening program to Air Training Command, to reassign the Academy Band to Air Force Space Command, and to award reserve commissions (rather than regular commissions) to Academy graduates. This last measure was a provision requiring all officers commissioned after September 30, 1996, to enter the service with a reserve commission. Since the first class graduated in 1959, Academy graduates had earned regular commissions. By comparison, AFROTC graduates were given reserve commissions and only offered a regular status after some time on active duty. The effect of the legislation was to place all newly commissioned officers on an equal footing at a time when there were vastly constricted opportunities for pilot training. The immediate reaction by the Academy was very negative, but the change to reserve commissions was effective with the Academy Class of 1997.

The Dean formed a working group to develop a program to implement the civilianization effort. Led by Colonel Jim Head, Permanent Professor of Physics, a plan was developed, briefed, and coordinated with Academy leadership, as well as appropriate Air Staff and DoD offices, including Personnel, Manpower, Finance, General Counsel, Legislative Liaison, DoD Military Manpower, and DoD Personnel Policy. The implementation schedule was aggressive. By December 1992 the policies and procedures had been established to permit hiring and paying civilian faculty members under an excepted civil service authority similar to that at Air University and the Air Force Institute of Technology. The Superintendent responded to the AF Chief of Staff in December 1992 with the Academy's plan: "A Blend of Excellence—Composition of the USAF Academy Faculty." This plan was accepted by the Chief and Secretary and, when merged with a similar one from West Point, was submitted by OSD to Congress in March 1993.

The Civilian Faculty Plan included the following key implementation milestones:

+ Begin immediately with 14 positions advertised for Academic Year 1993–1994
+ Expand across all academic departments by the fall of 1994
+ Build steadily to about 25 percent civilian by 2000; pause there for assessment
+ Grow toward 50 percent if warranted by experience and program needs
+ Program numbers include visiting faculty, normally about 5 percent of total

Key features of the personnel policies affecting the civilian faculty:

+ Faculty are provided five-year appointments, renewable, without tenure
+ First year probation
+ Salary established administratively, based on regional civilian faculty rates by academic discipline and academic rank, separate from the civil service salary scales
+ Most initial hires are assistant professors with doctoral degrees
+ Academic promotion through full professor based on performance
+ 12-month contracts, supporting faculty research in summer
+ Sabbaticals, full year at half pay or half year at full pay

One of the issues that arose as the program was developed was hiring of retired officers, especially those who had served on the Academy faculty. Colonel Head and his team foresaw that some retired military faculty might find the civilian positions attractive and many would be very well qualified. However, it was understood that the clear intent of Congress was to add *bona fide* civilians to the faculty, individuals from civilian academia with no or little military background. In briefings to the Air Staff, the issue was resolved in the following manner. Retired military would be considered along with other applicants, and if best qualified they would be hired. However, it was believed the issue would not be of concern if the Academy advertised widely and set most new positions at the assistant professor level. The figure of 30 percent retired military was informally agreed upon as an acceptable level.

ENDOWED CHAIRS

The endowed chair is a special symbol of excellence in education. For decades, endowed chairs have enhanced the faculty at many of America's outstanding academic institutions. The Air Force Academy joins them by means of two endowment programs, both of which have involved Permanent Professors.

THE ACADEMY RESEARCH AND DEVELOPMENT INSTITUTE (ARDI). ARDI was co-founded in 1984 by Brigadier General Philip J. Erdle, USAF (Ret) (Permanent Professor Emeritus) and Major General William Lyon, USAF (Ret), in consultation with the Honorable Verne Orr, Secretary of the Air Force. ARDI enhances academic excellence at the Academy by establishing and managing endowed chairs. Its goal is to establish an endowed chair in each USAFA academic department. As each endowed chair approaches full funding, it is the subject of an ARDI offer of gift to the Secretary of the Air Force. The Dean of the Faculty nominates distinguished individuals to occupy the endowed chairs each academic year. To date, ARDI has raised more than $20 million, endowing chairs and supporting other academic programs benefiting cadets and enriching the faculty. ARDI fully endows eight chairs, three of which honor Permanent Professors:

- THE WILLIAM A. ANDERS ENDOWED CHAIR IN THE ECONOMICS OF THE DEFENSE INDUSTRIAL BASE. Endowed by a principal gift from the General Dynamics Corporation, the Anders Chair provides a distinguished visiting professorship in the Department of Economics and Geosciences.

- THE WILLIAM T. COLEMAN III AND DR. WILLIAM E. RICHARDSON ENDOWED CHAIR IN COMPUTER SCIENCES. Endowed by principal gifts from Mr. Coleman and retired Permanent Professor Colonel Bill Richardson, members of the USAFA Class of 1971. This chair provides a distinguished visiting professorship in the Department of Computer and Cyber Sciences.

- THE HOLLAND H. COORS ENDOWED CHAIR IN EDUCATION TECHNOLOGY. Endowed by principal gifts of several foundations of the Coors family of Golden, Colorado, the Coors Chair provides a distinguished visiting professorship in a Dean of Faculty department selected by the Dean of the Faculty each year. During the 2017–2018 academic year, the Coors Chair professorship was in the Department of Aeronautics.

- THE ARDI ENDOWED CHAIR IN ARABIC STUDIES. Endowed by a principal gift from the International Education Foundation, this endowed chair provides a distinguished visiting professorship in the Department of Foreign Languages.

- THE PHILIP J. ERDLE ENDOWED CHAIR IN ENGINEERING SCIENCE. Endowed by principal gifts from Mrs. Carolyn Knies Erdle and the International Education Foundation to honor ARDI's co-founder, the Erdle Chair provides a distinguished visiting professorship in any one of the several departments of the Engineering Division.

- THE WILLIAM LYON ENDOWED CHAIR IN PROFESSIONAL ETHICS. Endowed by a principal gift from the William Lyon Foundation to honor Major General William Lyon, USAF (Ret), a co-founder and honorary Chairman of ARDI and former chairman of the Falcon Foundation, the Lyon Chair provides a distinguished visiting professorship in the Department of Philosophy. The Lyon Chair also supports the annual Alice McDermott Lecture in Applied Ethics.

- THE ROBERT F. MCDERMOTT ENDOWED CHAIR IN ACADEMIC EXCELLENCE (THE "DEAN'S CHAIR"). Endowed by a principal gift from the United Services Automobile Association, USAA. Brigadier General McDermott was USAFA's first Permanent Professor and its first permanent Dean of the Faculty. Upon retirement he served as Chief Executive Officer and Chairman of USAA for 25 years. The McDermott Chair helps meet faculty needs as determined by the Dean.

- THE BERNARD A. SCHRIEVER CHAIR IN SPACE SYSTEMS ENGINEERING. Endowed by a principal gift from the Emerson Electric Company in honor of General Bernard A. Schriever, USAF (Ret), "architect of the Air Force's ballistic missile and military space program." This endowed chair provides a distinguished visiting professorship in the Department of Astronautics.

THE UNITED STATES AIR FORCE ACADEMY ENDOWMENT (UE). The UE was founded in 2007 with the intent of becoming the major fund-raiser for the Academy. The UE first sponsored the "Superintendent's Chair for Character and Leadership Development," which for 2007–2009 was retired Permanent Professor Lieutenant General Erv Rokke. The UE currently endows three chairs located in the Center for Character and Leadership Development:

- ♦ **THE HELEN AND ARTHUR JOHNSON CHAIR FOR THE STUDY OF THE PROFESSION OF ARMS.** Endowed by a gift from the Helen K. and Arthur E. Johnson Foundation.
- ♦ **THE RISNER-PEROT MILITARY SCHOLAR CHAIR.** Endowed by a gift from the Perot Foundation in honor of Brigadier General James Robinson "Robbie" Risner, USAF (Ret).
- ♦ **THE FOX-ROKKE CHAIR IN THE PROFESSION OF ARMS.** Endowed by a gift from John and Marci Fox in honor of retired Permanent Professor Lieutenant General Ervin J. Rokke.

It is appropriate to mention that there was another chair at the Academy. The Department of Defense sponsored a "Transformation Chair" at each of the academies to help stimulate adoption of best business practices. The USAFA Transformation Chair for 2007–2012 was retired Permanent Professor Rich Hughes.

APPENDIX D

ACCREDITATION

INSTITUTIONAL

The story of the first institutional accreditation efforts was told in Chapters 1 and 3. Colonel Dick Rosser, Permanent Professor and Head, Department of Political Science, chaired the Academy's second Accreditation Steering Committee to prepare for the 1969 accreditation by the North Central Association of Colleges and Secondary Schools (NCA). The self-study defended the all-military faculty, recognized the need for tenured faculty sabbaticals, and expressed concerns about meeting the goal of 50 percent rated officer staffing. In 1977 Colonel Bill Orth, Permanent Professor and Head, Department of Physics, chaired the Accreditation Steering Committee for the Academy to prepare for the 1979 accreditation evaluation. This time, among other things, the NCA report recommended increasing internal Permanent Professor sabbaticals devoted to research with no administrative duties. The evaluators thought these sabbaticals should re-address the state of the art in the member's academic discipline and result in scholarly publications. The report also suggested the Academy find a way to include additional full professors who were not Department Heads. The table below shows the Permanent Professor chairs of the Accreditation Steering Committees for 1969 and subsequent accreditations and the salient findings by the NCA. All concerns listed were found to be resolved by the following evaluation..

    The NCA findings have often supported significant changes to Academy programs. For example, the 1979 report recommended reducing the distinction between military and academic instruction. Subsequently, a Permanent Professor position was established as the Deputy Commandant of Cadets for

Steering Committee Chair	Salient NCA Findings
1969 Col Rosser, Political Science	• Commend effort to increase faculty research • Consider decreasing core to provide more major's electives • Too little travel money for faculty attendance at professional society meetings • "USAFA appears to have attained a truly remarkable and unique record of achievement."
1979 Col Orth, Physics	• Provide more electives in the core curriculum • Increase cadet remedial and academic support • Provide non-administrative positions for Permanent Professors • Reduce distinction between military and academic studies • Find ways to better support the few female cadets
1989 Col Fisher, Engineering Mechanics	• Move graduate assessment from Admissions and improve it • Adverse impact of relative lack of faculty PhDs • Commitment to equal opportunity should be more visible • Academic facilities are stretched to the limit • Formalize a long-term planning process
1999 Col Reed, Biology	• Address diversity across faculty, staff, and cadets • Library needs attention • Very supportive environment for cadet success • Technology infrastructure is out-of-date • Finish current cadet workload study, reexamine core, provide time for more cadet creativity and intellectual development • Rapid curriculum changes need assessment, stabilize and assess
2009 Col Fullerton, Economics and Geosciences	• "USAFA is a learning-focused institution of higher learning which promotes academic rigor, enrichment, and educational excellence for cadets and faculty." • Clear improvement in IT resources; but should investigate if support of the .edu domain would improve if under the Dean of Faculty • Carefully consider what assessment data is meaningful and try to automate collection and analysis to avoid assessment fatigue and ensure the continuous improvement loop is closed • Support of the Center for Educational Excellence is key to continue ensuring a quality faculty in the USAFA environment

Military Instruction. Colonel Phil Caine, who had extensive experience in the History Department, was appointed Permanent Professor to fill the position. He led a thorough review of military studies and training that resulted in a new model of the entire leadership development program, increased cadet motivation, and reduced attrition. The frequently expressed concerns about cadet workload have kept persistent pressure on the Academy to reexamine the entire program for relevance and degree of applicability to the needs of the Air Force. The next accreditation visit will be in 2019 and Colonel Dan Uribe, Permanent Professor and Head, Department of Foreign Languages, has already started preparation of the self-study. The accreditation will be done by the Higher Learning Commission, which is now the organization responsible for accreditation actions in the central United States.

ENGINEERING

Early engineering accreditations were summarized in Chapter 3. For accreditations after the year 2000, ABET significantly revised their accreditation criteria, becoming a higher education pioneer in focusing on learning outcomes-based education (what is learned rather than what is taught) with a renewed emphasis on gathering graduate performance data. To receive the benefits of feedback from the Air Force engineering community, the Engineering Division formed an Engineering Program Advisory Council that meets periodically to review the Academy's engineering programs in the context of USAF needs and provide feedback on Academy engineering graduates' performance. All engineering programs have been accredited for the maximum term, many retroactively. When the evaluators listed observations or concerns, these were always addressed in the following self-study report and found to be resolved in the accompanying evaluation visit. The evaluators typically raised concerns about faculty development through research or graduate study, support of laboratories and computing infrastructure, and cadet workload. They praised laboratory facilities and equipment, training and supervision of faculty, the high level of team integration in senior capstone design courses, and the large amount of interaction between faculty and cadets. Recommendations on specific department curricula led to careful consideration by the faculty for changes to the curriculum or cadet schedule. Those recommendations concerning faculty were addressed by changes in policy, procedures, schedules, or allocation of funds when appropriate.

The evaluation visit occurs in the fall of the academic year prior to the end of the accreditation, and the self-study report is submitted well in advance of the visit. The self-studies typically are prepared by a committee comprising senior military or civilian tenured professors representing each program and chaired by one of the members. Guidance and oversight is provided by a steering committee chaired by the Chairman of the Engineering Division and includes the other Engineering Division Department Heads. Each Permanent Professor carefully reviews the self-study for his or her department to ensure successful accreditation. Academy staff functions furnish other necessary data.

COMPUTER SCIENCE

The Permanent Professor and Head of the Department of Computer Science has led each accreditation effort beginning with Joe Monroe in 1985, continuing with Bill Richardson in 1989 and 1995, and Hoot Gibson leading for 2001, 2006, 2009, 2015, and 2017. The concerns and praise listed by the evaluators were very similar to those of the engineering programs, with one, not surprising for the computer science discipline, additional concern about support for the information technology infrastructure. All concerns were found to be resolved by the following evaluation. Although cadets graduated with Computer Science degrees starting in 1969, no accrediting agency existed until 1985 when the Academy's program was the first one evaluated. The Computer Science major was accredited effective with the Class of 1986. Reaccreditation was granted in 1989, 1995, 2001, 2006 (to align with the Academy's engineering programs), 2009, and 2015. The Computer and Network Security major was accredited in 2018, retroactive effective back to the Class of 2016, the program's first graduates.

Appendix E

Curriculum

Major Changes

This appendix provides some additional detail on the changes to the curriculum and majors through the years. It is not our intent to provide a complete history of the Academy curriculum. The Permanent Professors have invested many hours of study and discussion as they have carefully evolved the curriculum to ensure it provides the best-educated graduates for service in our Air Force. For a more detailed study of the curriculum, a complete collection of the Air Force Academy Annual Historical Reports, the Academy Catalogs, and the records of the Curriculum Committee are archived in the McDermott Library Special Collections.

The Air Force Academy curriculum has changed significantly since the first curriculum was developed and published by the Air Academy Planning Group in 1949. The Sterns-Eisenhower Commission approved the Planning Board's work later that year. That curriculum was refined by General Harmon's Air Academy staff in the Pentagon, 1949–1954, and published on September 1, 1954, to guide the new Academy faculty. This curriculum had about 138 semester hours in 46 courses that all cadets would take. Humanities/social sciences subjects were 46 percent and basic science/engineering were 54 percent. This planning curriculum did need revision, as the planners, when unable to choose between two alternatives, often had included both for decision by the faculty then charged with implementing the curriculum. The newly formed faculty worked earnestly to abide by the principles established by the Planning Group and validated by the Sterns-Eisenhower study. One founding principle that rose to prominence was that there should be a balance between humanities/social sciences studies and basic science/engineering. As can be seen in Table E-1, the prescribed curriculum approved by General Harmon on April 29, 1955, had a difference of only $1/3$ of a semester hour. It is interesting that the 1955 curriculum lists credits in fractional semester hours down to $1/18$. Later practice allowed no smaller units than $1/2$ semester hour. By choice of the senior year elective a cadet could achieve greater emphasis in the technical or non-technical. Every cadet took navigation training because flight training had not been authorized yet.

Table E-1. USAFA Curriculum Academic Year 1955–1956			
Freshman Year	**Semester Hours**	**Sophomore Year**	**Semester Hours**
Mathematics	$3^1/_2$	Mathematics	$3^1/_2$
Chemistry	3	Physics	$3^1/_2$
English	3	English	$2^1/_2$
History	$2^1/_2$	History	$2^1/_2$
Philosophy/Geography	$2^1/_2$	Psychology/Law	5
Graphics	$1^1/_3$		
Total Academics	$15^5/_6$		17
Military Training/Navigation	$^5/_6$	Military Training/Navigation	$^5/_6$
Physical Education	$^3/_4$	Physical Education	$^5/_{18}$
Semester Total	$17^5/_{12}$		$18^1/_9$
Year Total	$34^5/_6$	Year Total	$36^2/_9$
Junior Year	**Semester Hours**	**Senior Year**	**Semester Hours**
Mechanics-Materials	$3^1/_2$	Thermodynamics	3
Electrical Engineering	$3^1/_2$	Aerodynamics	3
Economics	3	International Relations	3
Government	$2^1/_2$	Military History	$2^1/_2$
English	$2^1/_2$	Engineering/Materials Elective	2
History	$2^1/_2$	Elective	4
Total Academic	$17^1/_2$		$17^1/_2$
Military Training/ Navigation	$^5/_6$	Military Training/ Navigation	$^5/_6$
Physical Education	$^5/_{18}$	Physical Education	$^5/_{18}$
Semester Total	$18^{11}/_{18}$		$18^{11}/_{18}$
Year Total	$37^2/_9$	Year Total	$37^2/_9$

Total Semester Hours for Graduation = $145^1/_2$
Basic Science/Engineering = $67^2/_3$
Humanities/Social Sciences = 68
Military Training/Navigation = $6^2/_3$
Physical Education = $3^1/_6$

As the enrichment program matured, elective majors became available, and then majors were required, the principle of a balanced core remained. There continued to be considerable effort by the faculty to ensure a core curriculum that best served the Air Force while developing academic majors to both challenge the cadets' interests and meet the Air Force's changing needs. In the early 1960s the semester hours earned for military training and physical education were revised upward to better match the hours devoted to these subjects. Thus, for Academic Year 1961–1962 the academic core was 136 semester hours of prescribed courses, evenly divided between humanities/social sciences and basic science/engineering, with an additional 7½ semester hours, two courses, chosen by the cadet among pilot screening, navigation indoctrination, or enrichment courses. The military training/airmanship program was 25½ semester hours and the athletic program was 12½ hours for a graduation requirement of 185 semester hours. Another innovation tried in the physics core courses this academic year was non-homogeneous sectioning. Prior to this experiment the cadets had been assigned to a section based on their potential performance in the course. For physics, homogeneous sectioning meant that cadets with high grades in previous math and chemistry courses were grouped together for the first physics course, and remaining sections were formed down the line until the cadets who had done the poorest in prior courses also were together. Similar procedures were followed by the other departments for the other courses. The operating principle was that the section instructor could better address the needs of the students when they were of similar ability. This method of sectioning was used at West Point. Non-homogeneous sectioning, with the advantage that each section had a natural mixture of stronger and weaker students, was eventually adopted by the Academy. However, several departments partially retained the principle by offering honors sections for the better students even when there was no formal "honors" program.

With the introduction of the "majors for all" program for the Class of 1966, the core became 54 semester hours of humanities/social sciences and 49 hours of basic science/engineering. Cadets earned a major by taking

16 additional courses (43 semester hours.) Leadership and military training was 27½ semester hours and physical education was 14½ hours for a total core curriculum of 145 semester hours and a graduation requirement of 188 semester hours. Six years later for the Class of 1973, these requirements had changed very little: the academic core was now 99 hours, leadership and military training had decreased ½ semester hour, PE did not change, and the majors' requirements increased by 3½ semester hours, leaving the graduation requirement 1 semester hour lower.

Table E-2 on the opposite page (from Dr. Dean Wilson/USAFA/ DFR/Talking Papers/May 12, 2005, and April 11, 2011) shows representative changes to the curriculum through the years. Changes to the curriculum made in an academic year usually became graduation requirements for a class graduating two to three years later. The years in Table E-2 refer to the effective class year. The major curriculum change for the Class of 2021 is not included because it was covered in Chapter 3.

MAJORS

Table E-3 on page 414 shows the majors that cadets earned arranged by the year that cadets first graduated with the major. The major usually was approved two to three years prior to the first graduates. Often there were more majors available to the cadets, but no one chose that field of study. For example, when majors were first required of all graduates in the Class of 1966, there were 17 majors available, but cadets chose only 13 of them for their studies.

In most years there have been roughly equal numbers of graduates in non-technical majors (humanities, social sciences, or interdisciplinary) as there have been in technical majors (basic sciences, engineering, or interdisciplinary), although the ranges have varied about 20 percentage points: from 31–57 percent of majors and 43–69 percent, respectively.

Table E-2. Representative Curriculum History (Semester Hours)									
	1975	1980	1985	1990	1995	2000	2005	2009	2011
Academic Core	99	111	109.5	90.5	100.5	96	91.5	85	96
Basic Science/Engineering	49.5	58.5	58.5	47	51	49.5	49.5	48	45
Humanities/Social Sciences	49.5	52.5	51	43.5	49.5	46.5	52	37	45
Military Studies/Airmanship	6.5	10	13	10	8	10	9	6	6
Physical Education*	4.5	4	4	12	12	6	6	5	5
First Year Experience									1
Electives (majors courses)	47	27–33	27–33	39–57	42–57	33–49	36–52	45–52	24–46
Total for Bachelor of Science Degree	158	152–158	153.5–159.5	151.5–169.5	162.5–177.5	145–161	142.5–158.5	141–148	132–148
Summer Mil Training**	20.5	17.5–18.5	17	19–21					
Phys Ed-Intramurals***	10	10	10	2					
Other (Typing class, study skills)	0	1	1	0					
Total Semester Hours	188.5	180.5–187.5	181.5–187.5	172.5–192.5	162.5–177.5	145–161	142.5–158.5	141–148	132–148

Notes

*The physical education requirement was essentially the same for the Class of 1980 through the Class of 2005, but the credit awarded varied. All cadets took 12 PE courses (3 each year) until 2009. In 1980 and 1985, 1 semester hour graded credit was given each year (4 total). In 1990 and 1995 each of the 12 PE courses was given 1 semester hour credit (12 total). In 2000 and 2005 each of the 12 courses was given 0.5 semester hour credit (6 total). In 2009 and subsequent years the PE requirement was 10 PE courses, each for 0.5 semester hour credit.

**In the early years, the Academy used semester hours to help track cadet time. Semester hour credit was given to military training activities beyond those required for the Bachelor of Science degree. For example, Basic Cadet Training (BCT) was awarded 7 semester hours of credit (5 semester hours for Military Training and 2 semester hours for PE) for the Classes of 1975 through 1990. Since that time, BCT remains a military requirement, but receives no semester hour credit. Other Summer Military Training and specific Character and Leadership Training requirements remain graduation requirements but are no longer awarded semester hour credit.

***The Classes of 1975, 1980, and 1985 received 2 semester hours credit for BCT Physical Education and 8 semester hours credit for intramural participation (1 each semester). The Class of 1990 received credit for the BCT Physical Education, but intramural semester hour credit was not awarded. Intramurals are still a required activity but receive no semester hour credit.

| Table E-3. Academic Majors ||
First Grad	Major (year of last graduate, if major discontinued)
1959	Basic Science, Engineering Sciences (2002), English, Public Affairs (1963)
1960	Aeronautical Engineering, Humanities (2016)
1963	International Affairs (1991), Military Arts & Sciences (1973)
1965	Astronautical Engineering, History, Management, Mathematics
1966	Chemistry, Civil Engineering, Electrical Engineering, Physics
1967	Engineering/General Engineering (2016), Behavioral Sci/Psychology, Economics, General Studies (1978), Engineering Mechanics (2012)
1968	American Studies (1973), Geography/Geospatial Science, Political Science (1973)
1969	Biology/Life Science, Computer Science, Far East Studies (1973), Latin American Studies (1973), Soviet Studies (1973), Western European Studies (1973)
1978	Operations Research, Social Science (2016)
1979	Aviation Science/Av Space Science (1985)
1986	Space Operations
1990	Legal Studies, Political Science
1993	Biochemistry, Materials Science/Chemistry
1994	Mechanical Engineering
1998	Environmental Engineering (2016), Foreign Area Studies, Meteorology
2000	Military Strategic Studies
2001	Computer Engineering
2006	Systems Engineering, Systems Engineering Management
2012	Philosophy
2016	Computer and Network Security
2018	General Studies (with 4 divisional areas of emphasis)

Appendix F

Research Centers and Institutes

At the time of this writing (2018), the Office of Research identified 19 Research Centers and 2 Institutes at the Academy. Here is a list of the Centers, along with a brief description of each center's core competencies.

- **Academy Center for Cyberspace Research** (Department of Computer and Cyber Sciences)
    Cybersecurity education
    Malware analysis
    Provably secure internet software
- **Aeronautics Research Center** (Department of Aeronautics)
    Aerodynamic flow control
    Subsonic wind tunnel testing in five different facilities
    Supersonic/hypersonic experiment and computation
    Gas turbine and internal combustion research
    Small air vehicle design/build/fly
    Parachute canopy development/computation
- **Astronomical Research Group and Observatory** (Department of Physics)
    Space object tracking, identification, photometry, and spectroscopy
    Astronomical photometry and spectroscopy
- **Center for Aircraft Structural Life Extension** (Department of Engineering Mechanics)
    Structural testing and analysis (full scale, component level, and coupon)
    Material degradation (corrosion, cracking, etc.)
    Material processing, testing, and development

Structural teardown analysis and root-cause analysis

Service loads and environment measurement and structural impact analysis

+ **CENTER FOR AIRPOWER STUDIES** (Department of Military and Strategic Studies)

Joint air, space, and cyberspace power

Cadet-centered, faculty-assisted research

Multi-domain, operational military expertise

Multidisciplinary research methods

Modeling and simulation

+ **CENTER FOR PHYSICS EDUCATION RESEARCH** (Department of Physics)

Developing research-based educational resources

Assessing effectiveness of educational approaches

Providing resources and support for the Just-in-Time Teaching pedagogy

+ **CENTER FOR SPACE SITUATIONAL AWARENESS RESEARCH** (Department of Physics)

Small aperture optical telescopes for satellite characterization

Non-imaging photometric, spectral, and polarimetric techniques for characterization of unresolved space objects

Data fusion and modeling

+ **CENTER FOR UNMANNED AIRCRAFT SYSTEMS RESEARCH** (Department of Electrical and Computer Engineering)

Simulating and test flying autonomous algorithms for multiple unmanned aerial vehicles

Sensor fusion (electro-optical, infrared, radio frequency)

Global positioning system-denied navigation

Sense and avoid path planning

Counter-unmanned aerial systems methods

+ **CENTER OF INNOVATION** (part of Air Force CyberWorx)

Design Thinking

Public-Private partnerships

Basic and applied research with market-shaping companies

- CHEMISTRY RESEARCH CENTER (Department of Chemistry)

  Advanced materials and composites processing and fabrication

  Robust small molecule, biomolecular and macromolecular synthesis and characterization

  Molecular computational modeling and simulation

- EISENHOWER CENTER FOR SPACE AND DEFENSE STUDIES (Department of Political Science)

  National security policy, with an emphasis on deterrence theory, particularly in the space and cyber domains

  Research and scholarship related to challenges to US security

  Collaboration with the Office of the Secretary of Defense, US Strategic Command, US Northern Command, and AF Space Command

- HIGH PERFORMANCE COMPUTING RESEARCH CENTER (Department of Aeronautics)

  Access to DoD supercomputing resources

  High-speed network access and local storage systems

  Partnerships with local universities for high-performance computing research

  Expertise in computational fluid dynamics

- HUMAN PERFORMANCE LAB (Department of Athletics)

  Various exercises for cadet athletes to train and enhance vision for sports performance

  Hyperoxic tent to simulate sea level

  Dual Energy X-ray Absorptiometry scans for body composition

  Resting Metabolic Rate

  Maximum oxygen volume testing

  Anaerobic Endurance, Anaerobic Power, and Anaerobic Threshold

- LASER AND OPTICS RESEARCH CENTER (Department of Physics)

  Pulsed tunable lasers

  Laser and optical test equipment

  Laser and optical modeling

  Design and fabrication of unique laboratory apparatus

High power continuous wave lasers

+ LIFE SCIENCES RESEARCH CENTER (Department of Biology)

Screening methods for detecting bacterial agents and interrogating select cell lines

Cultivating/isolating select extremophile organisms as a source of alternative energy production for biosensing capabilities

Cellular lipid and protein analysis

+ SCHOLARSHIP OF TEACHING AND LEARNING (Center for Educational Innovation)

Educational resources for evidence-based teaching approaches

Research method design and ethics approval for educational research

+ SPACE PHYSICS AND ATMOSPHERIC RESEARCH CENTER (Department of Physics)

Miniaturized payloads

Space physics

Applied physics

+ SPACE SYSTEMS RESEARCH CENTER (Department of Astronautics)

Designing, building, testing, and flying small spacecraft

Space systems engineering

Avionics testing/simulation

+ WARFIGHTER EFFECTIVENESS RESEARCH CENTER (Department of Behavioral Sciences and Leadership)

Sociocultural, psychological, organizational, and clinical perspectives toward enhancing respect for human dignity

Evidence-based research methods in leadership development

Transdisciplinary approach to the research and design of more effective human-machine teams

Human subjects research

The two institutes are the USAF Institute for National Security Studies and the Institute for Information Technology Applications; both are located at USAFA.

From its inception in 1992, the Institute for National Security Studies (INSS) has focused on strategic security, arms control, and strategic stability studies, advising the Air Force strategic policy and arms control communities on current and emerging issues of interest. The mission of INSS is to promote national security policy research for the Department of Defense within the military academic community, to foster the development of strategic perspective within the United States Armed Forces, and to support national security discourse through outreach and education. Sponsorship of INSS comes from the HQ USAF/Deputy Chief of Staff for Strategic Deterrence and Nuclear Integration. In 2016 INSS assumed management of the Defense Threat Reduction Agency's Project on Advanced Systems and Concepts for Countering Weapons of Mass Destruction.

The Institute for Information Technology Applications (IITA) is funded by the Air Force Research Laboratory Sensors Directorate, and directed by General James P. McCarthy, USAF (Ret). The Institute engages in multidisciplinary research and development of products with information technology that would benefit education and operations within the Academy, the Air Force, and the Department of Defense. Key projects involve unmanned aerial vehicles command and control and mission planning. The Remotely Piloted Aircraft (RPA) Program teaches cadets tactical airmanship concepts via the RQ-11 Raven unmanned aircraft and operational airpower employment via an air operations center simulator. A state-of-the-art RPA Operations Center provides command and control for all unmanned aircraft operations at USAFA. IITA supports the Department of Military and Strategic Studies to purchase and install experimental simulators for integration into the Air Warfare Laboratory, works with the Department of Electrical and Computer Engineering in developing a power grid system test bed for detection and mitigation of cyber anomalies and information vulnerabilities, and collaborates with the Department of Civil and Environmental Engineering to use RPA technology to assess pavement conditions and determine required maintenance for flexible and rigid pavements.

APPENDIX G

ORAL HISTORIES OF PERMANENT PROFESSORS

The following oral histories are archived in the McDermott Library (Special Collections Branch).

These are based on interviews conducted by the USAFA Department of History, the USAFA Center for Oral History, and The Friends of the Air Force Academy Library.

Interviewee	Date	Interviewee	Date
Andrew P. Armacost	2013	Anthony J. Mione	1999
Roger R. Bate	2006	Joseph Monroe	2010
Jeffrey T. Butler	2012	Peter R. Moody	1982
Philip D. Caine	1999, 2002	Christopher H. Munch	2000
Ruben A. Cubero	2000, 2003	Douglas J. Murray	2012
Philip J. Erdle	2000	Carl W. Reddel	2010
George V. Fagan	1979, 2000, 2002	William E. Richardson	2000
Wallace E. Fluhr	2000	Ervin J. Rokke	1986
Jesse C. Gatlin Jr.	2000	Erlind G. Royer	2000, 2002
Robert B. Giffen	2012	Wilbert H. Ruenheck	2000
Archie Higdon	1979, 2000*	Orwyn Sampson	2000
Richard L. Hughes	2000	Jack M. Shuttleworth	2000
Alfred F. Hurley	1999	Michael L. Smith	2012
Marcos E. Kinevan	2000	David A. Wagie	2002
Richard R. Lee	2000	Malham M. Wakin	2000, 2003
Daniel W Litwhiler	2012	John W. Williams Jr.	2010
Robert F. McDermott	1971, 1980, 1981, 2001, 2002	James R. Woody	2000
		William T. Woodyard	2001
Alfonse R. Miele	1979, 2000*		
* A joint interview with Generals Higdon and Miele			

INDEX

Note: The names of Academy leaders listed in Appendix A are not indexed.